THE ROAD OF EXCESS

THE ROAD OF EXCESS

A History of
Writers on Drugs

MARCUS BOON

HARVARD UNIVERSITY PRESS
Cambridge, Massachusetts
London, England

2002

Library of Congress Cataloging-in-Publication Data

Boon, Marcus.
The road of excess : a history of writers on drugs / Marcus Boon.
p.   cm.
Includes bibliographical references and index.
ISBN 0-674-00914-2 (hardcover : alk. paper)
1. Narcotics in literature.   2. Authors—Drug use.
3. Literature, Modern—History and criticism.   I. Title.
PN56.N18 B66 2002
809'.93356—dc21
2002068522

To the memory of Jon Ende and Eric Mottram

CONTENTS

Prologue   1

1. Addicted to Nothingness:
   Narcotics and Literature   17

2. The Voice of the Blood:
   Anesthetics and Literature   87

3. The Time of the Assassins:
   Cannabis and Literature   123

4. Induced Life:
   Stimulants and Literature   170

5. The Imaginal Realms:
   Psychedelics and Literature   218

Epilogue   276

Bibliography   279
Notes   303
Acknowledgments   329
Illustration Credits   331
Index   333

ILLUSTRATIONS

1. An opium den in London's East End, 1872.   54

2. "Through the mouth of his wound," a drawing by Jean Cocteau, 1928, from *Opium.*   72

3. *Junkie* by William Lee (William Burroughs), 1953.   76

4. *Narcotic Agent,* by Maurice Helbrant, 1953.   77

5. A group of poets carousing and composing verse under the influence of nitrous oxide, 1829.   93

6. René Daumal conducting an experiment with "paroptic vision."   114

7. Self-portrait painted by Charles Baudelaire when he was under the influence of hashish, 1844.   141

8. Cannabis book images: the 1903 edition of *The Hasheesh Eater,* by Fitzhugh Ludlow; *Assassin of Youth! Marihuana,* by Robert James Devine, 1943; *Pot and Pleasure,* by James Simpson, 1972; and *A Hundred Camels in the Courtyard,* by Paul Bowles, 1962.   155

9. Stimulant book images: *Cocaina* by Pitigrilli, 1923; *Dealer: Portrait of a Cocaine Merchant,* by Richard Woodley, 1970; *Speed,* by William Burroughs Jr., 1971; and *A Scanner Darkly,* by Philip K. Dick, 1977.   210

10. Embryo text/drawing made by Walter Benjamin while he was under the influence of mescaline, 1934.   239

11. "Portrait of Nena Stachurska," drawn by Stanislaw Ignacy Witkiewicz when he was under the influence of peyote, 1929.   241

12. "Mescaline Drawing," by Henri Michaux, ca. 1956.   247

The palace of excess leads to the palace of excess.

MARK E. SMITH, 1993

PROLOGUE

For the protection of the reader, we have inserted parenthetical notes to indicate where the author clearly departs from accepted medical fact or makes other unsubstantiated statements in an effort to justify his actions.

PUBLISHER'S NOTE at the front of *Junkie,* by
William Lee (William Burroughs), 1953

It is customary to begin a book about drugs by issuing a warning or a disclaimer—not all books on drugs of course, since for most, the conventions of genre, of fiction or scientific research, are enough to offer the author and publisher adequate protection. But the books I will be most concerned about here precisely lack this kind of protection. So Thomas De Quincey begins his *Confessions of an English Opium Eater* by apologizing "for breaking through that delicate and honorable reserve, which for the most part, restrains us from the public exposure of our own errors and infirmities."[1] Ernst Jünger warns that "literary reading invokes a set of criteria which cannot be maintained in real life; the field of play is too largely circumscribed"; and asks what his responsibility in writing about drugs is.[2] Other examples could be mentioned. The original edition of William Burroughs' *Naked Lunch* is a notable exception. Burroughs throws us directly into a first-person account of spoons, droppers, and cops, with only a ghost-like trace of fifties Mickey Spillane pulp noir to shield himself from the "nakedness" of his "lunch." But observe how quickly later editions of the book add prefaces, warnings, transcripts from legal hearings, papers submitted to scientific journals: "a word to the wise guy."

Although books about drugs have only very rarely been prosecuted under obscenity laws, the discourse of the obscene lingers around drug books: a discourse of voyeurism, of a pleasure taken in other people's experiences, leading to inevitable moral corruption; of exhibitionism, of narcissistic displays of transgression, flaunted before the general public, so as to exploit its cravings for sensation. Maybe this is in fact what drug literature is about; but in order to determine whether or not it is so, it would be necessary to actually read some of these books, and think about what they mean. Surprisingly, this has rarely been done.

Should I also begin this book by issuing a disclaimer of my own? Having taught a class on drugs and literature for a number of years at several universities, I have reflected on my own responsibility in these matters. I was once called to a meeting, before being hired to teach, by a college dean who asked me what I would do if one of my students overdosed in my classroom. I replied that I would refer the student to a college substance-abuse counselor. But I was left wondering: Is it possible to overdose on books? In the process of writing this book I have been asked numerous times how much "research" I have done. To read a book about drugs, to write about books about drugs, is evidently a sign that one has been exposed to something, and possibly contaminated by it. I don't deny that this may be the case. But—exposed to what?

I first became aware of the existence of what I call drug literature as a teenager growing up in London in the late 1970s. Drugs have always been a part of the music scene, and coming of age at the tail end of the punk era, I discovered them in the lyrics of the Velvet Underground, in rumors and gossip about major figures like Sid Vicious and Ian Curtis, in photographs of John Lydon smoking spliffs with Big Youth in Jamaica, and in the intoxicated staggering of band members and fans at shows that I went to. In the music press, names of writers like Burroughs and Jean Cocteau and books with titles like *The Electric Kool-Aid Acid Test* were bandied about by journalists and musicians, and dog-eared copies of the books in question were obtained and passed around by my friends and me, to be read during the interminable wait for night buses or last tube trains home from shows. Although quite well known, these books and writers constituted a secret literary history that offered information otherwise unattainable and spoke of states of consciousness that offered the promise of escape from the tedium of urban or suburban life. Such books came as close to the joyful sensory bombardment of the music that was so important to us then—and that has retained its importance to this day.

These books were not always easy to find. Where libraries or bookstores carried them at all, they were often stolen. To this day, many bookstores keep them behind the counter in a special secure area, and my own library research has been made considerably more challenging by the crooked bibliophiles who have already cruised the stacks of New York University and Columbia—and stolen the most interesting or obscure titles. In college, most of the books I discuss in this book were studiously ignored by professors, and to this day are rarely regarded as being worthy of the name of literature. Meanwhile, in the underground, the unavailability or unacceptability of these books fed the transgressive allure that surrounded them—which created its own set of distortions, both around the meaning of drug literature and around the lives of its authors. I fully acknowledge that by writing this book, this transgressive allure may be damaged—if so, so much the better. What is valuable in these books will not disappear easily.

I have consciously tried to keep music out of this book. But I realize that I am writing from within a cultural space in which it is music, and not literature, that is the center of activity, in a way that very few people besides Antonin Artaud would have claimed sixty years ago. I am not saying this in order to use the new to terrorize the old, but because I feel in my heart that it's true, when I examine what has been most valuable, most powerful to me. I say this as a writer who wants to know what it means to write now. Frank Zappa said in the 1960s that jazz hadn't died, it just smelled funny. It's the same with literature now. No attempts to fill the room with cheap nostalgic or fancy new avant-garde air fresheners will change this. We either open the windows, get used to the smell, or get out.

What kind of history is the history of the association of writers and drugs? An interdisciplinary one, no doubt; the history of an idea perhaps, but an idea whose location (or even existence), as Avital Ronell has shown, is far from clear.[3] And I hesitate to call it an idea because the notion of a writer taking drugs is already more or less than an idea—it is linked to material traces, to chemicals, to plants, to economics, all fields of activity that go beyond the history of ideas.

There have been several books that have presented historical material about drug use by writers. Two seminal works on nineteenth-century literature, Alathea Hayter's *Opium and the Romantic Imagination* (1968), and Arnould de Liedekerke's *La belle époque d'opium* (1984) both begin with reviews of contemporary scientific belief about drugs and then present literary history in its light.[4] Although this is a reasonable approach, it underplays the extent to which drug experiences are determined by what Timothy Leary and others have called set and setting (meaning mental state and environment) as much as by biochemistry. Outside of such broad categories as "stimulants" and "psychedelics," I have therefore avoided a precise clinical description of the effects of each drug, preferring to allow the dynamic historical properties of the drugs discussed to appear alongside the more repeated properties that allow us to draw up a clinical profile of the effects of specific substances.[5]

Other more general histories of drug use, such as Jean-Louis Brau's *Histoire de la drogue* (1968) and Alexander Kupfer's *Göttliche Gifte* (1996) use literary material as though the literary history of drug use were the entire history of drug use, except for primitive culture beforehand and rock music after. It cannot be assumed that literary history represents or summarizes this broader history. Extensive evidence has been collected by other authors that opium use was widespread in nineteenth-century European and American societies—and by no means confined to literary milieus.[6] The most thorough works on the history of drugs to date, Antonio Escohotado's three-volume *Historia de las drogas* (1995), and recent works by Virginia Berridge and Jean-Jacques Yvorel, are very careful to historically situate literary drug use within a very broad spectrum of human relationships to drugs; they also take a dynamic approach to pharmacological developments, at least leaving open the question as to how scientific knowledge about substances is produced within a historical context.[7] None of these books, however, addresses the question of why literature and drugs came to be associated.

Recent works by David Lenson and Sadie Plant talk of literary experimentation with drugs in the belief that writers act as scientists when they describe their use of drugs, or that writers have an expertise in aesthetics or in representation that allows them a kind of scientific objectivity when describing their experiences.[8] This may indeed be so in some cases, but it is not my intention to aestheticize drug use or celebrate writers' aestheticization of drugs. Nor am I celebrating (or condemning) some act of transgression associated with writing about drugs, particularly in the "counterculture." I ask instead how it came to be that aesthetics and transgression, and the literary genres associated with them, came to be associated with drug use.

I have written this book not from the point of view of literature, or from the point of view of science, but the way an ethnographer would, studying how a society came to believe certain things. Literature and drugs are two dynamically developing domains of human activity that have coevolved alongside and interpenetrated with many other such domains, human or not. As such, this is a history of books that were written and published, but equally of the lives of those who wrote them, the substances they took, how those substances became available, what those substances were. The histories of religion, literature, and science all intersect in the production of the artifact known as the writer on drugs.

Although my book is without question a contribution to literary studies, a certain vision of literature is called into question by my analysis—the Romantic one that posits experience and experimentation as its arena and "drugs" as its mascot. I believe that this Romantic vision of drugs as an aesthetic experience is precisely what needs to be called into question, since it fuels much of the contemporary excitement about drugs, especially within the youth culture. But I also question that more classical tradition which sees literature as "drug free," and writing as a kind of pure activity of consciousness or tradition. Both of these literary positions rely on the same set of conceptual choices and structures that are also used when we try to define what "drugs" are—ideas of experience, experimentation, the pure activity of consciousness, tradition, and so on—and these are eminently historical in nature, not "facts." Instead of making literature, deconstructed or not, into a means of justifying drug use, of redeeming it, I propose an open field of interdependent cultural activity, which would include both drugs and literature, one in which science, biography, literary analysis, and ethnography are used as necessary. It is my belief that this is inevitably the direction that literary studies as a whole must head toward: a cultural study of literature, as one out of many forms of human activity.

◇

The aim of this book is to describe, for the first time, the history of the connection between writers and drugs. My first concern has been to establish a corpus of primary materials and present them within a historical context. In an area where amnesia is the rule, and the newspapers are forever rediscovering the new menace of drugs that is invading their supposedly drug-free territory, it is important to document the fact that there is a long and varied history of drug use by writers. My goal has been to present this history in a clear, readable way so that it is impossible to ignore any longer.

The volume and diversity of the works covered plays an essential role in my argument. A study that limited itself in a more traditional academic way to chapter-length analyses of the more famous writers in this field, notably De Quincey and Samuel Taylor Coleridge, Charles Baudelaire, Henri Michaux, and the Beats, would only reify the notions that are already prevalent regarding literature and drugs, in particular the notion that drug use was always associated with the Romantic movement in the nineteenth century and the politically charged world of 1960s youth culture.

Drugs have traditionally been associated with Romanticism and the various aesthetic movements that developed out of it. In this book I show that the notion of a specifically Romantic or aesthetic attitude toward drugs masks a profound interdependence with the scientific practices and the marketplace of the day, as well as the fate of religion in the West. I argue that at the moment that literature staked out a position for itself at the end of the eighteenth century, it was inevitable that it would discover "drugs" as a hidden, but always present, prop to its newfound independence. More generally, the peculiar structure of transcendental subjectivity, which literature has invoked repeatedly, necessitated material agents that were able to evoke or provoke the subject into some form of manifestation, whether drugged or drug free. What is called the Romantic attitude to drugs (usually personified by De Quincey) is in fact a much more complicated matrix of historical, cultural, and scientific developments.

This does not mean though that there was no connection between drugs and literature before Romanticism. The ubiquity of psychoactive substances in human culture means that wherever Western culture made contact with these plants, they appear in some form or other in literature. Before Romanticism, there were allegorical, mythological herbs and plants that often performed literary functions similar to those performed by their more infamous descendants. With Romanticism (or more precisely, modernity), we see a vigorous reconfiguration of human relationships to these plants—new in one sense, to be sure, but also one in a series of such reconfigurations that have periodically occurred—such as the rise to power of Christianity in Europe and the accompanying destruction of the pagan world. Ultimately, one must conclude that there is no literary movement that has not materially or discursively incorporated drugs into its practices.

What is a drug? I define the word in a twofold manner: first, as the current group of proscribed substances; second, as any agent of allegedly material origin, whether mythical or not, capable of exerting psychoactive effects.[9] The first definition is a legal one. What makes marijuana a drug and coffee a beverage has little to do with the pharmacological effects of each substance. It is the result of laws applied during the twentieth century to the sale and consumption of these substances outside of highly specific, medico-legally defined circumstances. Much of the drama that surrounds drugs, even when it seems far removed from the legal sphere, involves a dialectic of law and transgression that did not exist before World War I.

The second definition is more complicated. I was tempted to use the word "intoxicating," rather than "psychoactive," but a whole range of substances, from tea and coffee to Prozac, which are entirely relevant to any discussion of drugs, can hardly be considered intoxicants. Nor, for that matter, is the word "intoxicating" adequate to describe the radical alterity induced by smoking DMT (dimethyltryptamine). Louis Lewin, generally considered the foremost scientific authority on the topic, used the word "phantastica," which he defined as "the agents capable of effecting a modification of the cerebral functions, and used to obtain at will agreeable sensations of excitement or peace of mind"—reflecting the somaticist biases of a turn-of-the-century toxicologist and a founder of psychopharmacology.[10] Contemporary psychedelic theorists prefer the term "psychedelic," meaning "mind-manifesting," or "entheogenic," meaning "realizing the divine within," because of their resonances of non-Western religions as opposed to the clinical Western scientific implications of "psychoactivity."[11] It is not any particular definition of *psyche* that interests me, but the diaspora of ways of thinking about mind.

I use the words "allegedly material" and "whether mythical or not" because I believe that much of the history of these substances has been written by people who never took them, or by people who embellished their accounts of their experiences for various reasons—in other words, by producers of literature. I do not mean this critically, nor do I think that such embellishment was always avoidable. Furthermore, the reception that these substances were given when they became of importance in Europe and America was very much conditioned by preexisting tales of substances that were believed to be in use in other cultures. It is not possible to separate completely the mythical and the "real" components of any drug, since the historical meanings that are attached to any substance become part of the user's experience of the substance.

Which brings me to the question: what is drug literature? When looking through recent collections of drug literature, I was struck by the coexistence of texts from radically different fields of human endeavor, such as a retelling of legends of the Fang tribe of northwest Africa, a medical paper by Sigmund Freud, pulp fiction from Arthur Conan Doyle and the high modernist antics of Stanislaw Ignacy Witkiewicz.[12] All of these are forms of literature. But how is it possible to write about them all in a single book like this, without the subject becoming hopelessly amorphous? To the postmodern reader whose reply to this question is, "Well, it *is* amorphous!" my response is sure, but we want some kind of reliable information about the subject.

Although all scientific texts about drugs, from the most abstruse dissertation on the role of methyl groups in amphetamine pharmacology onward, are "literary" to some degree, I have focused on the way both scientific and literary texts address the problem of writing on drugs, and how the mythical figure of the "writer on drugs" evolved in both scientific and literary texts. I have mixed "high" and "low" cultural texts as I see fit. Iceberg Slim, Colette, and Martin Heidegger all confront being through their writings in their own ways, and I for one would have to think very carefully before I chose which one of them I would like to be my guide to its mysteries.

I do not argue that the relationship between drugs and literature is more essential than those involving other expressive media. The history of human drug use involves many cultural practices, even in the West, that have linguistic elements but that are not primarily textual: highly localized traditions of drinking songs, tales, rituals, and so on that do not primarily result in texts. Film, music, comic books have all developed their own relationships to psychoactive substances, as Western culture evolves, in Marshall McLuhan's terminology, from the linear structures of the world of print that have dominated since the time of Gutenberg, to the electroacoustic spaces of our current world. I have confined myself to written texts and, for the most part, works believed by those who read them to have a marked aesthetic value, rather than works belonging to a particular technical domain.

I have avoided writing a single chronological history of drugs in which individual substances presented nothing more than minor variations on a single theme—though there is some truth to this notion, at least after World War I when the medico-legal notion of drugs became almost inescapable, for writers and others. The major events in this history are quite well known by now. What interested me was to reveal more subtle, micropolitical *histories* of everyday interactions between human beings and particular psychoactive substances and to find out whether these histories had left their traces in literature. Pharmacologically, different drugs have different effects and are, or should be, treated accordingly. The notion that all drugs are the same (except those, like alcohol and coffee, that are not drugs at all!) continues to fuel the fantasies about drugs that dominate contemporary society's treatment of drug users and drugs themselves.

Rather than continuing to perpetuate these fantasies, or to crudely debunk them in the name of some higher truth, whether scientific, literary, religious, or political, I have tracked down whatever traces I could that went into the composition of the story of a particular substance and its relationship to literature. A plurality of myths or stories clustered around specific substances might serve to liberate us from the monolithic totem of drugs. At the very least I hope that my work contributes to a real attempt to discriminate or discern between different stories, different substances.

I have written this history without relying on a particular conceptual framework beyond that of a set of names of substances around which stories, texts, practices have clustered, and that of chronology, which I have used for convenience. My approach has been to study the way the idea of a particular drug,

and the association of writers with drugs, have emerged from a mass of tiny
lived or inscribed connections between humans and the substances. I share
with the neuroscientist Francisco Varela the conviction that

> the proper units of knowledge are primarily concrete, embodied,
> incorporated, lived; that knowledge is about situatedness; and that
> the uniqueness of knowledge, its historicity and context, is not a
> "noise" concealing an abstract configuration in its true essence. The
> concrete is not a step toward something else: it is both where we are
> and how we get to where we will be.[13]

Drugs have no meaning outside of the set of moments and situations in which
they are used or referred to by particular groups of beings. I have cataloged
these situations as best as I am able, and tried to articulate the way in which
the more general beliefs that people have about drugs emerge from these tiny
but concrete moments of experience and expressivity.

I have located an interdisciplinary consistency in the information I found
about each drug: not exclusively medical, literary, or historical, but an assem-
blage in the Deleuzian sense, composed of a variety of relations, associations,
and connections. The drugs I describe are to be understood culturally and historically as well as pharmacologically, and the texts that I analyze are the products of chemistry and botany as much as of the new historicism or semiology.
I hope that this study will prove informative to medical and social scientists,
not because I have summarized a set of "case histories" in which literary texts
are mistaken for sets of facts, but because the problems raised by the act of
writing about drug experiences are themselves very revealing about drugs and
the people that use them. I also hope that my study will introduce to literary
scholars the possibility that a part of what we call literature is chemically con-
figured in quite specific ways—and that this notion is quite compatible with
more traditional ways of understanding a text.

Methodologically, my approach to writing and research has been profoundly
influenced by the work of Bruno Latour. Latour trained originally as an anthropologist, but after several years working in Africa in the 1970s in the
French equivalent of the Peace Corps, he began an ethnographic study of

Jonas Salk's genetics laboratory in California, which was published in 1981 as *Laboratory Life*. Since then, Latour has pursued a number of trajectories in the history and philosophy of science, culminating in his essay *We Have Never Been Modern* (1993), in which he offers a broad critique of the foundational myths of modernity, those of science and culture as autonomous spheres of investigation and engagement, focused respectively on nature and man. According to this myth, premodern man erroneously and superstitiously confounded man and nature and accounted for the existence of both in ways that we would call religious, by introducing god or gods into the picture. Modern man believes that he has separated himself from such superstitions, and that he has successfully separated a domain of culture from one of nature, while dispensing with the religious dimension altogether. Latour observes, however, that modern society is permeated by the very hybrids of nature-culture-transcendence that it officially claims it has eradicated. Such hybrids play fundamental roles in our society, yet their identity and value is either ignored or misplaced on one side or other of the nature/culture divide (which is a divide constructed so as to exclude the transcendental).

Drugs are hybrid in precisely the way Latour defines the word: material and at the same time constructed. The evolution of interest in the entity known as drugs, as well as the angry denial, from groups like the Partnership for a Drug-Free America, that drugs are even a part of human culture, is characteristic of the fate of hybrid objects in modernity. Although I do not dwell on the word "hybrid," my concern in writing these histories has been to pay particular attention to the way in which drug literature is composed of nature-culture hybrid tropes and to map the moments where connections of particular significance between science and literature, nature and culture, chemical substance and discursive practice occur, and to show their reliance on each other.

I insist, however, on the importance of the third aspect of all hybrids, the transcendental one. By "transcendental," I mean that which goes beyond materiality, and materialist explanations—that which has traditionally, but by no means exclusively, been the concern of religions and spirituality. This transcendental impulse or meaning is to be found everywhere in drug literature, and nowhere more so than in its negation or absence. In fact, the notion of a nature-culture hybrid without this transcendental impulse is merely another part of the modernist materialist mythology, which places a boundary around nature and culture, and then situates the transcendental outside it, as though that would be the end of it. If that really were the end of it, there would be no feeling of being trapped, no feeling of emptiness, no craving for an outside. Yet these are precisely the sentiments that appear over and over again in modern, materialist literature. For all purposes, they constitute what we call modernity, despite occasional displays of bravado from existentialists. This notion, as it applies to drugs, was defined in its most reductively modern form by Roger Gilbert-Lecomte in the 1930s as the desire to take narcotics "simply [for] a change of state, a new climate where their consciousness will be less painful."[14] What is it that Gilbert-Lecomte wants? He will not admit that he wants anything at all, except for a "change of state." But where would such a change of state come from if not from the outside of a world that has been defined in advance as consisting of nothing but nature and culture? And that outside, for moderns like Gilbert-Lecomte, is the space of the transcendental—a space that, for reasons I shall explore, he believes he can reach through using drugs and writing books.

I have no particular version of the transcendental to push, and I certainly do not wish to return to a traditional transcendental discourse that would see drugs and literature as symptoms of a fallen world of sinners. What interests me is to affirm an inclusive, polyvalent movement around the boundaries that modernity has built for itself that would integrate transcendental experience within the realm of the possible. I chose the title *The Road of Excess* because William Blake, who was not to my knowledge a drug user, was the last writer in the West who was able to see the universe as a manifestation of the open, unbounded excess of the imagination. By an act of will, he saw Newton, Jerusalem, and the dark Satanic mills of the Industrial Revolution in the same space. Those that followed him, even the "early Romantics" of Germany, already believed in the separation of mind and matter, the death of God. And it was to them, in the West at least, that drugs first appeared—not the substances themselves necessarily, but socially, naturally, or spiritually potentiated substances that contain in them the promise of the reunion of mind and matter, the transcendental and material realms. It was to them, also, that "literature" first appeared as a way of living, a way of thinking about the world that was separate from all other ways.

Blake's road of excess, he claimed, led to the palace of wisdom. But the roads of excess taken by later generations, in particular those involving psychoactive drug use and modern literature, open up only under conditions that block access to precisely the destinations that these roads were supposedly leading to.[15] Where, in fact, do these roads lead to? As Bataille has shown in *The Accursed Share,* boundaries exist in an ambiguous and often parasitical relationship to the excess that they "prevent." Often they give rise to particularly violent new forms of excess. This, as Thomas Szasz notes, is certainly the case with drugs.[16] I believe, as Burroughs and others did, that the most promising solution to the "drug problem" is neither negating or affirming drugs, but learning to discriminate between different drugs through unbiased studies of how human beings interact with them, and, at a deeper level, opening up new realms of excess so that drugs no longer carry the whole weight of our legitimate desire to be high.

Since De Quincey's *Confessions of an English Opium Eater,* published in 1821, is indisputably the first literary text devoted to drug use, I originally intended this book to cover the period from the Romantics to the present day. However, I became fascinated by the question of why no writer appeared to have talked about drugs before De Quincey. To a large degree the answer to this question is a matter of definition. If alcohol, tobacco, and coffee are considered to be drugs, then there is certainly a pre-Romantic history of literary drug use, even though its forms are quite different from the modern ones. Leaving aside alcohol, it also became clear to me that, in Latourian terms, a whole range of hybrid substances that have a meaning similar to that of what we now call drugs can be found in premodern literature. The existence of such substances (for example mandrake, moly, belladonna, the waters of Lethe, ambrosia) is much more difficult to accept, either because, in the case of mandrake for example, we no longer believe the plant to be psychoactive or because, in the case of moly or ambrosia, we think these substances are entirely mythical. Documentation of the usage and effects of premodern psychoactive plants is also a problem, since the most objective manuals available, namely the herbals, are themselves a hybrid mixture of folklore, botany, and classical literature.[17] When one reads the literature on witchcraft in medieval Europe, it is striking that the question of whether actual plants could have triggered phenomena associated with witchcraft was hardly even considered until about a decade ago.[18] It is also only quite recently that basic issues regarding the dietary habits of ordinary people in premodern Europe have begun to be studied by scholars like Piero Camporesi.

There is no epistemological break in which drugs suddenly appeared or were discovered by the West. I have integrated premodern literature about drugs when I have found it, so that the continuum of human relationships with plant substances appears alongside the evolution and changes in such relations. Much of what has been written concerning the history of drugs reinforces the notion that drug use is a strictly modern "problem," through its focus on post-1800 developments, whether in discussing literature or broader social relations to drugs.[19] In broad outline, it is clear that something changed or appeared with De Quincey, but if this change is not seen in the context of the pre-1800 period, we risk taking the modern myth of the origins of drug use and drug literature at face value. Many of the problems that our society has with drugs are held securely in place by allegiance to this myth of origins in which De Quincey is implicated, which posits a pre-1800 utopia in which either there were no drugs, or drugs were found only in primitive societies, or drugs were simply "no problem."

It is clear, however, that there has been a quite rapid evolution in Euro-American society's relationship to the substances that become known as drugs in the modern period, an evolution so rapid at certain points in history that it does approximate what Gaston Bachelard meant by a "break." The hybrid artifacts that we call drugs now appear because of the evolution of highly complex systems of economic, scientific, religious, and aesthetic production at the end of the eighteenth century. It may well be that one day drugs will become irrelevant because of further evolution in these fields; as I shall show, I believe that the association of drugs with literature may already now be a thing of the past.

Those who read this book hoping for a neatly packaged answer to "the drug problem," or a clever all-encompassing theory about the relationship between drugs and literature, will be disappointed. The whole weight of my argument consists in separating drugs from each other, showing how each has quite specific historically emergent discourses attached to it, and avoiding theoretical generalizations on the subject that reify precisely what they claim to dissipate through the supposed illumination of conceptualization.

I have not avoided drawing moral or ethical conclusions when they were necessary. Although I am not writing for or against "drugs," I make no claims to neutrality. To describe repeated acts of human self-destruction, such as can be found in the history of morphine and heroin, without commenting on them would be dishonest—a form of intellectual posturing. Similarly, I have not censored my belief in the positive value of some of the psychedelics, for what they can teach us about the human mind. My main goal, however, has been to open up a field in such a way that it can be discussed with clarity and precision.

I

ADDICTED TO NOTHINGNESS

Narcotics and Literature

I can do nothing with opium, which is the most abominable illusion, the most formidable invention of nothingness that has ever fertilized human sensibilities. But I can do nothing unless I take into myself at moments this culture of nothingness.

ANTONIN ARTAUD, "Appeal to Youth:
Intoxication—Disintoxication," 1934

On May 15, 1778, Voltaire, then seventy-three and suffering from acute pain in his bladder and kidneys, probably due to advanced prostate cancer, lay in bed at the home of his host the Marquis de Villette. The marquis refused to send for a physician, but instead called the local apothecary, who offered a potion of his own invention that Voltaire refused to take. Madame de Saint-Julien, who tasted the potion, noted that it burned her tongue so badly that she was unable to eat any supper.

In the evening, Voltaire received a visit from his childhood friend the Duc de Richelieu, who suggested an opium potion, which he himself was using as a painkiller. In one account, Voltaire is said to have drunk an entire vial of the potion.[1] In others, it is said that his physician prescribed him a moderate, regular dose of laudanum, but that in the night he sent a domestic out three times for further doses.[2]

Voltaire reacted badly to the laudanum. "His body seemed to be set aflame from his throat to his bowels, and for two days he was wildly delirious. He thought Richelieu, his childhood friend, had poisoned him, and would refer to him only as 'Brother Cain.'"[3] His stomach became paralyzed. He alternated between sleep and fits of derangement, in which clerical pundits claimed that he saw the devil at the side of his bed, come to claim him, while others said that he had become unintelligible.[4] He was neglected by his servants, who roamed the room drunk. Finally, after reaching a state of calm induced by exhaustion, he died on the night of May 30, 1778.

Few people consider the tale of Voltaire's death noteworthy. Some of Voltaire's biographers have reacted to the story with embarrassment or muted outrage, as if it revealed a disagreeable secret about the hero of the siècle des lumières. The *Encyclopedia Britannica* says that "he suffered much pain on his deathbed, about which absurd legends were quickly fabricated . . . he died, peacefully it seems."[5] Others ignored the details surrounding Voltaire's death entirely.

Although it would be excessive to suggest that Voltaire died because of opium—he was old and sick when he died—it seems that at his death, the man of the Enlightenment tasted the narcotic poison of modernism and was visited by its dark, demonic forces—forces that grew out of the "health" of the Enlightenment itself. How would such an incident have been treated had it occurred a mere forty years later in the England of De Quincey and Coleridge? It is evident that many scholars of literary history prefer to think that the association of narcotics and writers goes back no farther than De Quincey. For them, the heroes of the Enlightenment and earlier ages exist in a drug-free zone of literature and culture that was corrupted by the arrival of the Romantics, with their morbid preoccupations. What was it exactly that Voltaire was visited by on his deathbed? And how did it happen that opium, a painkiller in wide use in the eighteenth century, came to be associated with literature? And what about that darkness which accompanies opium—was it always there, as it was in the tale of Voltaire's death, and as it is now in the endless succession of addiction narratives that are published each year? How did that darkness come to be embodied in an extract from a common plant?

In fact, writers discussed narcotics in the eighteenth century and before—because opium was a drug that was in wide use in European society from the time of the Renaissance, if not earlier. In the very beginnings of the Western literary tradition in Homer's *Odyssey*, narcotics were described: nepenthes, a pain-relieving drink that Helen gives to Telemachus, and the lotus, an oblivion-inducing plant that seduces some of Odysseus' sailors. In "The Knight's Tale" (circa 1390), Chaucer described the powers of the juice of the poppy in familiar terms:

> For he had yeve his gayler drynke so
> Of a claree maad of a certeyn wyn
> of nercotikes, and opie of Thebes fyn
> That al that nyght though men wolde hym shake,
> The gayler sleep, he myghte nat awake.[6]

Spenser and others used nepenthes as the image of the good, healing drug that would counteract the alien, Circean poisons lurking in the gardens of Renaissance epic, while in *Othello*, Shakespeare warns that

> Not poppy nor mandragora,
> Nor all the drowsy syrups of the world,
> Shall ever medicine thee to that sweet sleep
> Which thou owed'st yesterday.[7]

References to opium in belles lettres after the Renaissance reflect the ubiquity of opium use in Europe at that time. Since just about anyone might have had recourse to opium for pain relief or to procure rest or sleep, it is not surprising to find mentions in texts of its use for these purposes. It was the relationship of drugs to literature that was different. For example, the seventeenth-century English dramatist Thomas Shadwell was publicly recognized as an opium addict.[8] Dryden, in *The Second Part of Absalom and Achitophel* (1681–82) wrote about him:

> Thou art of lasting Make, like thoughtless men,
> A strong Nativity—but for the Pen
> Eat Opium, mingle Arsenick in thy Drink
> Still thou mayst live, avoiding Pen and Ink.[9]

And on the occasion of Shadwell's dying in 1692, in his sleep, owing to an overdose of opium, Tom Brown wrote the following epitaph:

> *Tom* writ, his Readers still slept o'er his Book;
> For *Tom took Opium,* and they Opiates took.[10]

In other words, Shadwell was a bore whose work induced a sleep as deep as any laudanum could offer. Nobody suggested that opium could enhance creative powers. Shadwell himself had nothing to say about opium, although it is notable that he did not refute Dryden's claims regarding his opium use.

Dr. Johnson, better known as a tea drinker, was, like many doctors throughout history, a habitual opium user. In his dictionary he noted that if used in moderation, opium "removes melancholy, excites boldness and dissipates dread of danger"; and also said that those who "accustomed themselves to an immoderate use . . . are apt to be faint, idle and thoughtless."[11] According to his biographer Sir John Hawkins, Johnson took opium for "rheumatism of the loins . . . as a means of positive pleasure whenever any depression of spirits made it necessary."[12] In a letter to a friend, Johnson wrote, "You are, as I perceive afraid of the opium. I had the same terror, and admitted its assistance only under the pressure of insupportable distress, as of an auxiliary too powerful and too dangerous."[13] Johnson was inconsistent, in a way not untypical of opium users, on the subject. In Boswell's *Life of Johnson,* for example, he is quoted as saying, "I am sometimes gloomy and depressed; this too I resist as I can, and find opium, I think, useful, but I seldom take more than one grain."[14] But there are no reports of opium-triggered visions, ecstasies, pains, or pleasures in Johnson's work. In fact there is no indication that Johnson saw anything of any literary interest in the effects of the drug on his body and mind.

At the same time, reference to recreational use of opium, and to it's aesthetic qualities, can be found in eighteenth-century poetry—and in travel literature of the same period.[15] Thomas Warton, Jr., in "The Pleasures of Melancholy" (1747) writes:

> No being wakes but me! 'till stealing sleep
> My drooping temples bathes in opiate dews.
> Nor then let dreams, of wanton folly born,
> My sense lead thro' flow'ry paths of joy;
> But let the sacred Genius of the night
> Such mystic visions send, as Spenser saw or Milton knew.
> When in abstracted thought he first conceiv'd
> All heav'n in tumult, and the Seraphim
> Come tow'ring, arm'd in adamant and gold.[16]

What separates such a poem from the work of Coleridge, or one of the other Romantics? Very little, in terms of the actual imagery—these "dreams of wanton Folly born" that "lead thro' flowery paths of joy." But "opiate dews" are used in the poem as a generic motif—in the same way that "ambrosia" or "poison" is used further on in the poem. The motif of opium is entangled in a dense web of neoclassical allegorical conventions, so that it would be impossible to draw conclusions as to whether the author is writing about an actual opium experience, as Coleridge for example indicates in his preface to "Kubla Khan," or just following the tradition.

Unambiguous descriptions of recreational use of opium can be found in seventeenth- and eighteenth-century European literature, but only when the subject is Asia. A steady stream of travelers to Turkey, Persia, and the Middle East wrote popular accounts of the use of opium in these societies, which featured descriptions of "the Turk" or Persians.[17] The seventeenth-century French traveler the Chevalier de Chardin said of the recreational use of opium among the Persians that "it entertains their fancies with pleasant Visions, and a kind of Rapture . . . they grow Merry, then Swoon away with Laughing, and say, and do afterwards a thousand Extravagant Things."[18]

The *Mémoires du Baron de Tott, sur les Turcs et les Tartares* (1784), by the eighteenth-century traveler Baron de Tott, contains a description of the Teriaky Tcharchiffy, an area of Constantinople where opium users gathered, along with descriptions of the physical deformities and other effects that opium caused in recreational users.

> These Automatons . . . throw themselves into a thousand different Postures, but always extravagant, and always merry . . . each returns home in a state of total Irrationality, but likewise in the entire and full enjoyment of Happiness not to be procured by Reason. Disregarding the Ridicule of those they meet, who divert themselves by making them talk absurdly, each imagines, and looks and feels himself possessed of whatever he wishes. The Reality of enjoyment often gives less Satisfaction.[19]

Besides the use of opium by those who visit the market, Tott noted its use in private houses, where "it principally infects the Professors of the Law; and all the Dervishes."[20] Opium was also used as an adjunct to sexual pleasure and to give courage to soldiers.

The Orientalist vision of irrationality, luxury, sensuality, and degeneration, which would feature so prominently in nineteenth-century European discourse about opium use, was already fully developed in the popular travel books of the Abbé Raynal (1776):

> The Javanese chews betel, smokes opium, lives with his concubines, fights or rests. One finds in this people great spirit, but there remain few traces of moral principles. They seem less a primitive people, than a degenerated nation . . . They spend their lives smoking, taking coffee, opium or sorbet. These pleasures are preceded or followed by exquisite perfumes which are burnt before them and whose smoke by this means enters their clothing, which is lightly covered with a sprinkling of rose water.[21]

The link between opium and crime, a major feature of twentieth-century narcotic literature, was also already present. Captain Cook, in the journal of his first voyage around the world, notes of the phenomenon of amok among the Malays of Batavia that "to run a muck in the original sense of the word, is to get intoxicated with opium, and then rush into the street with a drawn weapon, and kill whoever comes in the way, till the party is himself either killed or taken prisoner."[22]

The situation of opium and other drugs in the eighteenth century is captured in the *Encyclopédie* (1751–1772) of Denis Diderot and Jean D'Alembert. The *Encyclopédie* separated the pleasurable and aesthetic qualities of opium from its medical qualities by situating the former entirely abroad, while speaking of the latter as located within a familiar European discourse of science and medicine. Opium, according to the entry in the *Encyclopédie*, came from "Anatolia, Egypt, and the Indies." It was also used in Persia, "because these people regard opium as the remedy praised by the Poets, which brings tranquility, joy and serenity." The article, based on a dissertation by Engelbert Kaempfer on opium in Persia, focused almost exclusively on the Middle Eastern use of opium, and concluded: "it is said that it stimulates an amazing joy in the spirit of he who takes it, and that it charms the brain with enchanted ideas and pleasures."[23] No mention was made of European use; for that one had to turn to the entry for "narcotique"—which spoke exclusively of the medical uses of opiates, except for a brief mention of the intoxicated Turks. Although recreational use of opiates has continued to be associated with Asia until today, it was in part through literature that the idea of the opium use as an aesthetic pleasure would, in Eve Sedgwick's words, be "brought home" to Europe in the nineteenth century.[24]

The road to a specifically literary use of opium begins with two now seldom read physicians, Erasmus Darwin (1731–1802) and John Brown (1735–1788), who were both taken very seriously in a variety of circles at the end of the eighteenth century.

Darwin, a member of the Lunar Society and an early speculator on evolution, as well as being the grandfather of Charles, had a reputation of being the finest physician of his day (not necessarily a compliment in eighteenth-century England).[25] Perhaps not coincidentally, Darwin was a very liberal dispenser of opium. His medical textbook *Zoonomia* prescribed opium as the remedy for hundreds of ailments. Besides having the dubious claim of introducing Coleridge's friend Thomas Wedgwood (and possibly therefore Coleridge himself) to opium, Darwin was also a poet and one who played a crucial role in linking the scientific or medical study of opium to the neoclassical poetic discourse that I identified above—thus making possible the strange hybrid form that we now know as "drugs."

When it was first published, Darwin's *Loves of the Plants* (1789), an attempt to put the new Linnaean taxonomy of plants into verse form, was very popular. Darwin was perhaps the last poet to write allegorically (in the neoclassical sense) about plants, yet he was also one of the first to place the allegorical form of the plant side by side with a realistic prose description of the plant. Thus every plant in *Loves of the Plants* receives a dual description. He says of the poppy:

> Sopha'd on silk, amid her charm-built towers,
> Her meads of asphodel, and amaranth bowers,
> Where Sleep and Silence guard the soft abodes,
> In sullen apathy PAPAVER nods.
> Faint o'er her couch in scintillating streams
> Pass the thin forms of Fancy and of Dreams;
> Froze by inchantment on the velvet ground

Fair youths and beauteous ladies glitter round;
On crystal pedestals they seem to sigh,
Bend the meek knee, and lift the imploring eye.
. . . . .

So with her waving pencil C R E W E commands
The realms of Taste, and Fancy's fairy lands;
Calls up with magic voice the shapes, that sleep
In earth's dark bosom, or unfathom'd deep;
That shrined in air on viewless wings aspire,
Or blazing bathe in elemental fire.
As with nice touch her plaistic hand she moves,
Rise the fine forms of Beauties, Graces, Loves;
Kneel to the fair Inchantress, smile or sigh,
And fade or flourish, as she turns her eye.[26]

Underneath this passage, in prose, we find:

Papaver. l.270. Poppy. Many males, many females. The plants of this class are almost all of them poisonous; the finest opium is procured by wounding the heads of the large poppies with a three-edged knife, and tying muscle-shells to them to catch the drops. In small quantities it exhilarates the mind, raises the passions, and invigorates the body: in large ones it is succeeded by intoxication, languor, stupor and death. It is customary in India for a messenger to travel above a hundred miles without rest or food, except an appropriated bit of opium for himself, and a larger one for his horse at certain stages. The emaciated and decrepid appearance, with the ridiculous and idiotic gestures of the opium-eaters in Constantinople is well described in the Memoirs of Baron de Tott.[27]

The allegorical powers of the plant, the pleasurable qualities of the drug (still broadly located in Asia), and its medical uses (to be found in his *Zoonomia*) remain separate in *Loves of the Plants*—but a connection is established between them. As with Goethe's excursions into poetic botany, there is considerable charm in the poem, with its attempt to describe the human meaning of each plant, and in the case of the poppy, it's *pharmakon*-like indeterminacy, as an agent of pleasure, love, or death. In general, Darwin does not dwell on the psychoactive plants, though in the third canto of *Loves of the Plants*, devoted mainly to poisons, he does discuss nightshade's use in witchcraft and the use of infusions of laurel leaves by the Pythian Oracle, who speaks "with words unwill'd, and wisdom not her own."[28]

Darwin's reputation as a poet and a scientist has suffered considerably. His scientific ideas played a role in Germany in the development of Naturphilosophie, but when Romantic science was abandoned, his name was consigned to a footnote appended to the biography of his grandson. The British Romantics had a love-hate relationship with him.[29] Coleridge, for example, observed that Darwin was "the first *literary* character in Europe and the most original-minded Man"[30] but also said, "I absolutely nauseate Darwin's Poem."[31] The preface to the *Lyrical Ballads,* with its praise for simplicity, was in part a response to Darwin's poetry. Although some of the criticism of Darwin is based on his clumsy neoclassical rhyme and rhythm, much of it must be attributed to a change in aesthetic taste that occurred at almost the exact moment that Darwin was writing. Darwin was perhaps the last great European didactic poet, the last to bring together aesthetics and science, or, as he himself put it, "sense" and "description." The Romantics considered this pompous, or, in Coleridge's words, "not poetry," because for them, poetry should be something separate from science, competitive with it even to the point of being a different kind of science.

The Edinburgh physician John Brown made no claims to poetry, but his medical writings were read throughout Europe as philosophical texts of considerable importance. Brown had suffered a severe attack of gout at the age of thirty-six, which he treated on the advice of his mentor, William Cullen, by abstaining from meat and alcohol for a year. When this treatment failed, the enraged Brown abandoned Cullen's approach, and returned to meat and drink—whereupon he grew healthier. But the gout returned again, and this time Brown treated it with opium, increasing the dose until he became addicted. This experience, along with the theories of the German physician Albrecht von Haller, provided the basis for Brown's theory of medicine.[32]

In his *Elementa Medicinae,* Brown wrote that living beings are defined by their ability to respond to external and sometimes internal stimuli. Thus pathology is the result of overstimulation ("sthenic disease") or understimulation ("asthenic disease") and therapy consists in regulating the level of stimulation to normal levels. Brown described the symptoms of asthenia thus:

"Before the disturbance, which only supervenes in a violent degree of morbid state, all the senses are dull; the motions, both voluntary and involuntary, are slow; the acuteness of genius is impaired; the sensibility and passions become languid . . . the intellectual faculties and the passions are impaired."[33]

Brown believed that most illness was caused by lack of stimulation, for which wine or opium was the cure. As to why opium was a stimulant: "Has it not the same effect upon the Turks, that wine has upon us? Or, are we to suppose that the troops of that people, on their march to battle, chew opium to check their natural alacrity and to depress their courage?"[34]

Liberal application of these principles, notably in military medicine,[35] has been said to have killed more people than all the Napoleonic wars,[36] although compared to standard eighteenth-century therapeutics, which included blistering, purging, cupping, and bleeding, Brunonian methods (those based on Brown's ideas) might also be considered relatively benign.[37]

Brown's work was well known in various parts of the world at the turn of the eighteenth century. It was especially popular in Germany, where it attracted the interest of a number of writers and philosophers.

The flourishing of German Romanticism in Jena during the last decade of the nineteenth century is chiefly associated these days with the development of what Philippe Lacoue-Labarthe and Jean-Luc Nancy in *L'absolu littéraire* call the first literary avant-garde among the writers of the *Athenaeum* review, principally the brothers August Wilhelm and Friedrich von Schlegel and Novalis. But these were also the golden years of Romantic biology, when under Goethe's influence, natural history collections and scientific societies were set up both at Weimar and at Jena, and when Friedrich von Schelling lectured on Naturphilosophie, his attempt to reunify mind and nature in the face of Kantian idealism. The Romantic writers at Jena had a strong interest in science—so strong that some, like Schelling, tried to "do" science.[38]

Under the name of "der Brownismus," Brunonian ideas played a crucial role in the development of Romantic science in Germany.[39] Schelling integrated Brunonian views on excitability into his *First Outline of a System of a Philosophy of Nature* (that is, Naturphilosophie) of 1799 after becoming friends with the German physician and university professor Andreas Röschlaub, the first major proponent and major reviser of Brunonianism in Germany. Schelling wrote of Brown that he "had elaborated the only true principles for the whole organic *Naturlehre* because he was the first to understand that life is neither absolutely passive nor absolutely active."[40]

Brown's appeal to the German Romantics lay in his development of a simple (and abstract) principle that could be applied to the whole of creation, without recourse to empiricism. Using Brunonian theory, one could view all organisms as a combination of "excitability" (internal) and "stimulus" (external). This was important because it allowed the Romantics to achieve a compromise between the Newtonian mechanism they detested and a vitalism that was otherwise easily dismissed as superstitious or unscientific. Although it is doubtful that Brown saw things thus, in the view of the Germans he had developed a dialectical explanation of the relationship between organism and environment. Roschlaub, responding to the search of German physicians at that time for a Kantian medicine based on a priori concepts, even suggested that Brown's excitability was such an a priori—since all states of health or disease could in theory be reduced to a point on a scale of excitability, which would be quantifiable and therefore mathematical.

Such theories inevitably led to actual medical experiments. Indeed, if, as Lacoue-Labarthe and Nancy say, the Romantic writers in Jena inaugurated literature as a way of living, this is another way of saying that they were eager to put their ideas into practice. Whether the results of the experiments they conducted had anything to do with the theories that inspired them is an open question, but it was certainly possible to *try* to put theory into practice—and this was something new, at least as far as literature was concerned. Literature had certainly been used to express medical or scientific ideas, and scientists certainly cited literature at times as evidence. But the German Romantics came up with their own form of medicine, developed out of their own philosophical and literary beliefs—and opium played a major role in it.

As Rita Wöbkemeier observes, it is difficult to find details of how Romantic medicine translated into medical practice.[41] Some of Caroline Schlegel's biographers believe that Schelling played a role in the death of her daughter, Auguste Böhmer, in 1800 when he administered an excessively large dose of opium to her during a bout of sickness.[42] This did not stop Landshut University from giving him an honorary doctor of medicine degree in 1802. Letters from Friedrich von Schlegel's wife, Dorothea, reveal that Caroline Schlegel herself was treated by Schelling for "nervous fever" with "volatile stimulants and a continual infusion of tonics from China, Hungarian wine, nourishing creams and strong bouillon," with miraculous results. Opium and musk were also used.[43] Goethe also had an unpleasant experience with Brunonian opium therapy that resulted in Brown's being added to a list of Goethe's enemies.[44]

Novalis is also known to have used opium in the period before his death, at the age of twenty-nine, from tuberculosis in 1801.

Novalis was familiar with Brown's ideas on medicine. Although known mainly as a poet, he studied science and technology for two years at the School of Mining Technology at Freiberg and filled copious notebooks with speculation on science and medicine, in which he applied Brunonian categories to everything from epic poetry to the Zeitgeist (both asthenic). He was probably introduced to Brown through the work of Röschlaub, and spoke of wishing to treat himself using opium, in the Brunonian fashion.[45]

Even before his final sickness, Novalis was convinced that he suffered from "excess sensibility," which he equated with Brunonian asthenia, for which opium or wine would have been the cure. At the same time, in direct contradiction to Brunonian theory, he cautioned, "all people of excess sensibility should be given few, and then very diluted—mental (narcotic) remedies—they already have too much of them."[46] Novalis had a highly ambiguous theory of sickness, which he developed far beyond anything Brown had written—as did many of the contributors to the Naturphilosophie or "speculative medicine" of the time.

> Intoxication from weakness, intoxication from strength. Narcotic poisons such as wine, etc., are intoxicating due to the weakness they produce—they draw something out of the mind.—They incapacitate it for its usual stimuli/passions; fixed ideas are more likely to stem from intoxication due to strength—these induce local inflammations. Sensuality (lust) is intoxicating as well, just like wine. Intoxication due to weakness produces far more vivid, permeating sensations in the person.[47]

Intoxication through strength or weakness led to different modes of thought. Use of "narcotic poisons" led to an intoxication through weakness that enhanced or stimulated sensation, producing a different kind of health, an aesthetic health or richness. Along with a number of other sick writers who used narcotics (Coleridge, Nietzsche, Artaud, and Burroughs, for example), Novalis wrote about the development of a new body that would overcome the "sicknesses" of this one. Although such talk is usually labeled "science fiction" in the absence of any serious proposals for how to construct a new body, the use of drugs can be seen precisely as achieving this transformation through chemical means. Narcotics, viewed this way, belong to what Michel Foucault calls the technologies of the self.

Novalis said some extraordinary words on this topic. Playing with Schelling's *Naturphilosophie*, he observed that "with sensibility and its organs, the nerves brought sickness into nature. And with it freedom and arbitrariness were brought into nature; and with them, sin, a violation of the will of nature, the cause of all evil."[48] He continues: "all sicknesses resemble sin in that they are transcendences. Our sicknesses are all phenomena of a higher sensibility, which wishes to be transformed into higher powers. When man wanted to become God, he sinned. The sicknesses of plants are animalizations . . . the sickness of stones—vegetation."[49] Thus sickness, meaning deviation from nature, became for Novalis a principle of evolution, a way of rebelling against the laws of nature and introducing new forms into the world. It is this idea that would become the cornerstone for what Nietzsche calls "the great health," the health of the Superman who transcends the mere animal body—and it is probably what led Goethe to proclaim "the Romantic is the sick, the classical is the healthy." Already, the battle lines were being drawn.

Novalis speaks of opium a number of times in his *Hymns to the Night*. Opium is clearly aligned with the night, with dreams, with darkness, with that whole realm of negative aesthetic experience that Nietzsche says was opened up in Shakespeare's *Hamlet*. "Costly balm," Novalis writes,

> Drips from your hand,
> From a bundle of poppies.
> In sweet drunkenness
> You unfold the heavy wings of the soul,
> and give us joys
> Dark and unspeakable,
> Secretly, as you are yourself,
> Joys which let us
> Sense a heaven.[50]

Such lines must be read in the context of Novalis' speculations on medicine—and, indeed, in the context of what we know of his actual use of opium. We can no longer say that the poppies in the poem are just a convention—they are linked to an articulated philosophy, whose goal is a new way of life, albeit one whose roots lie in *literature*. In a prose passage from *Hymns*, Novalis elaborates on the dark pleasures of opium: "Holy sleep—don't make Night's elect too rarely happy in this earthly day-labor. Only fools misrecognize you and know no sleep but the shadow which, in that twilight before the true Night, you, pitying, throw over us. They don't feel you in the grapes' golden flood—in almond trees' wonder oil—in poppies' brown juice."[51]

When the gods of light are forced to retreat by enlightenment, they hide themselves in darkness, night. "Night became the mighty womb of revelations—the gods drew back into it—and fell asleep, only to go out in new and more splendid forms over the changed world."[52] Thus night becomes the gathering places for all authentic spiritual forces, be they old (the Orient) or new (opium). Interestingly, while wine and opium are usually contrasted as social versus antisocial substances, Novalis considered them both forces of the night, in accordance with Brunonian theory.

Novalis speculated on the existence of a series of inner senses, turned away from external experience, that could open out onto the imagination, or "our inner world." As John Neubauer suggests, opium, along with the golden grape, is a potentiator of this inner world of "night," a world that, as Novalis acknowledged, could be torn free from nature. Wine and opium may come from nature ("day"), but they contain within them, hidden, the night. Although "night" is often interpreted as referring simply to death (and thus a mystical, impossible Ideal), Novalis believed in the possibility of exploring the negative realm that he described, and of bringing back data from that realm. In fact, this negative realm was now the realm of art itself, that aspect of human life and experience supposedly banished by Newtonian mechanism and scientific rationality. And intoxication ("Rausch") would become a method of entry to this realm.

Novalis can thus be seen as one of the originators of a modern gnostic approach to drugs, in which nature is abandoned for negative, transcendental space. Gnosticism is a vast and diffuse subject, but I will use the word "gnostic" in this chapter to describe a worldview that sees the material world and nature, as a fallen, corrupt, inauthentic place, and man as an alien, trapped within it.[53] To escape, man seeks the flash of gnosis, or knowledge, in the form of a transmission from another cosmos or transcendental dimension in which the truth resides, and which is in fact man's real home. This transmission can take various forms, but drugs, as Novalis uses them, are certainly one of them: opium may come from nature but its essence belongs to the transcendental night, and by taking the drug, the user is able to negate his or her own body and environment, temporarily.

When nature and the human body are abandoned, a new, gnostic theory of health becomes necessary, since "natural health" is precisely what is to be abandoned. This new notion of health would consist precisely in an organism's ability to sustain an abandonment or overcoming of the body. But the body does not naturally sustain such a state of "health"; in fact, the word we use to describe this state is "sickness." Drugs appear in Romanticism as one of the more obvious ways of producing, or sustaining, this unnatural state of health—of revolt against the limits of the animal body. To quote Wöbkemeier, the Romantics initiate "sickness as critique."[54]

Many of the British Romantics took opium—but as I have already noted, so did many people in England in the late eighteenth century and early nineteenth—as a "medicine," but one whose nonmedical effects might also be enjoyed. Keats, Byron, and Shelley all used laudanum at various points in their lives, both as a means of easing physical pain and as a mood stabilizer, but their writing does not indicate any particular interest in the drug—all spoke much more lyrically about a variety of alcoholic beverages. As the British historian of medicine Virginia Berridge notes, it is merely the fact that these writers' lives were documented in detail that makes their use of opium stand out.[55]

In the early nineteenth century, opium was given to women for the same reason that Valium and other tranquilizers have been in more recent years, as a "calmative." Surveys of opium use in the nineteenth century indicate that 60–70 percent of narcotic users were women.[56] There are a striking number of women who wrote poems about opium during this period.[57] One of the earliest of these was Mary "Perdita" Robinson, an actress who turned to opium in middle age owing to rheumatism. Robinson dictated her poem "The Maniac" (1791) to her daughter one night in 1791, after taking a dose of laudanum, "her eyes closed, apparently in the stupor which opium frequently produces, repeating like a person talking in her sleep." She knew both Coleridge and De Quincey, and it is possible, given Coleridge's reputation for plagiarism, that the description of the composition of "Kubla Khan" that accompanied the poem in 1816 was derived from her.

Coleridge and De Quincey are of course the most famous quaffers of the Romantic narcotic syrups. Although they both adhered to the Brunonian view that opium was a stimulant, Brown was much less important to them than the German philosophers were. And yet, although both Coleridge and De Quincey saw themselves as philosophers, they used their philosophical interests to create a *literary* context for opium use. The evolution of opium in nineteenth-century European culture follows a series of displacements: from medicine to philosophy, philosophy to literature, literature to social mythology, and mythology on to politics, where it rejoins a radically transformed medicine at the end of the century in the Decadent movement and the theory of degeneration.

Both Coleridge and De Quincey gave medical reasons for their first use of opium. De Quincey first took opium in London in the fall of 1804, during an attack of neuralgia (one of those poorly defined illnesses that plagued both him and Coleridge and many others to follow). The "immortal druggist" who sold De Quincey the opium was doing nothing unusual. Opium use was extremely common in England at the beginning of the nineteenth century, whether the opium came in pills, children's syrups, or in De Quincey's favored form, the ruby solution of opium in alcohol and water known as laudanum.[58] Although it is clear that he began using opium at some point in the 1790s,[59] Coleridge claimed that he began using it in 1800 during a rheumatic attack, while in Keswick in the Lake District:

> I may say that I was seduced into the ACCURSED Habit ignorantly.—I had been almost bed-ridden for many months with swellings in my knees—in a medical Journal I unhappily met with an account of a cure performed in a similar case (or what to me appeared so) by rubbing in of Laudanum, at the same time taking a given dose internally—It acted like a charm, like a miracle!—I recovered the use of my Limbs, of my appetite, of my spirits—& this continued for near a fortnight—At length, the unusual Stimulus subsided—the complaint returned . . . suffice to say, that effects were produced which acted on me by Terror & Cowardice of PAIN & sudden Death, not (so help me God!) by any temptation of Pleasure, or expectation or desire of exciting pleasurable Sensations.[60]

At this time, Coleridge used a locally produced laudanum-like preparation known as Kendal Black Drop that was two or three times the strength of regular laudanum and therefore potentially more addictive—which may account for the fact that De Quincey also first became addicted to opium when he moved to the Lake District.[61]

After 1800, Coleridge took opium until his death in 1834. For a number of years, he was convinced that opium acted medicinally on him, despite protestations from his wife and friends. Wordsworth, who had apparently made no comment beforehand, confronted Coleridge on the grim trip to Scotland that they made together in 1804, to no avail. The same year, Coleridge traveled to the Mediterranean, at least in part in a failed attempt to break free of his opium habit.

At times during the following decades Coleridge's intake of laudanum was as high as two pints a day, according to Robert Southey. Coleridge became clearer about opium's possible contribution to his various symptoms, although this did not help him break his habit. He struggled to keep his laudanum use under control, even employing a man to physically block his entry into any chemist's shop that he might attempt to visit.[62] In 1816, he moved into a house in Highgate, London, with his future biographer Dr. James Gillman, who became responsible for regulating Coleridge's dosage. In the 1820s, however, he also purchased additional quantities of laudanum from a chemist, to supplement his regimen.

There was a period, in the second half of the 1790s, when Coleridge was discreetly enthusiastic about opium. In a letter written in 1798, he declared: "Laudanum gave me repose, not sleep: but YOU, I believe, know how divine that respose [sic] is—what a spot of inchantment, a green spot of fountains, & flowers & trees, in the very heart of a waste of sands!"[63] And, in another letter written the year before, he said:

> My mind feels as if it ached to behold and know something great— something one and indivisible, and it is only in the faith of this that rocks or waterfalls, mountains or caverns give me the sense of sublimity or majesty! But in this faith all things counterfeit infinity! . . . It is but seldom that I raise and spiritualize my intellect to this height—and at other times I adopt the Brahman Creed, and say— It is better to sit than to stand, it is better to lie than to sit, it is better to sleep than to wake—but Death is the best of all!—I should much wish, like the Indian Vishna, to float along an infinite ocean cradled in the flower of the Lotus, and wake once in a million years

for a few minutes—just to know that I was going to sleep a million years more.[64]

Both of these passages were written in 1797–98, when Coleridge was living in Nether Stowey, Somerset, reading Spinoza and drinking laudanum. The imagery in both cases is strongly reminiscent of that of "Kubla Khan," in its topography and Oriental references. The stretching out and carving up of enormous periods of time into blocks that end only to begin again can be related to the anticipation with which the opium user (or for that matter, the drinker) looks forward to the next dose. Coleridge had plans to write a Spinozist poem, a "Great Work":

> thus it should begin/
> I would make a pilgrimage to the burning sands of Arabia, or &c
> &c to find the Man who could explain to me there can be oneness,
> there being infinite Perceptions—yet there must be a oneness, not
> an intense Union but an Absolute Unity, for &c[65]

Molly Lefebure writes that Coleridge, like many of the Romantics, went through a period of enthusiasm for Spinoza, seeing in him a way of modeling the unity of mind and cosmos.[66] With Coleridge, this enthusiasm was tempered by his interest in Kant, who made an absolute separation between mind and phenomena. Opium, embodying Oriental wisdom (as did the figure of Kubla Khan), offered hope to Coleridge of experiencing, perhaps only surreptitiously, the absolute union of mind and world.[67] However, the difficulty of achieving such a union is apparent even in Coleridge's ecstatic experience described above, where the Spinoza-like perception of the infinite in the cosmos turns into a "Brahmanic" withdrawal from phenomena into eternal sleep and silence—in other words, a transcendental position. De Quincey, who also proposed to write a major Spinoza-like treatise, was much more explicit about the transcendental nature of opium eating. In his vision of ideal happiness, it is a book of German metaphysics that sits next to his bottle of laudanum, in his Lake District cottage.

Pain relief is a kind of transcendence of the body. And Coleridge, like Sir Humphry Davy's mentor Thomas Beddoes, was concerned, both personally and politically, with the idea of pain relief.[68] He wrote to Davy in 1800, asking whether the surgeon Sir Anthony Carlisle did "ever communicate to you, or has he in any way published, his facts concerning Pain, which he mentioned when we were with him? . . . I want to read something by somebody expressly on Pain, if only to give an arrangement to my own thoughts—For the last month I have been tumbling on through sands and swamps of Evil, and bodily grievance."[69] Interest in pain relief was a consequence of the Romantic interest in exploring subjectivity and, in the midst of the turmoil of the Industrial Revolution, a developing concern with the idea of public health.[70] Where before pain was to be endured as a sign of Divine Providence, for a writer like Shelley in *Prometheus Unbound*, pain was to be overthrown as one of the shackles of tyranny.

Coleridge's "Kubla Khan" gave first expression to one of the fundamental tropes of literary drug use, that of dictation: the sense that words or thoughts are being dictated to the writer by some unknown agency, without conscious effort on his or her part. In his introduction to the poem, Coleridge described how he fell into a drug-induced sleep while reading *Purchas's Pilgrimage*, "during which time he has the most vivid confidence, that he could not have composed less than from two to three hundred lines; if that indeed can be called composition in which all the images rose up before him as things." When he awoke, Coleridge began to write down what he remembered, only to be interrupted by the famous Man from Porlock.

The scenario is not uncommon with opiate-using writers. Walter Scott, another great narcotic user of the Romantic era, took opium to fend off abdominal complaints that would leave him roaring like a bull, according to the assistant to whom he dictated his works. When he read the proofs of his novel *The Bride of Lammermoor* (1819), he claimed that he did not recognize a single character, incident, or conversation found in the book. More recently, Burroughs noted in his introduction to his own book that he had "no precise memory of writing the notes which have now been published under the title *Naked Lunch*." Burroughs wears his aphasia like a badge of pride, an antidote to pedantic aestheticism. But for the Romantics, this experience was bewildering. At the very moment that the Romantics began to focus on the self as creative source, they experienced, whether through narcotics or other means, their own alienation from the texts they wrote. Opium provided a new myth of poetic inspiration, but a disturbing one, one that revealed a curious impotence or aphasia in the writers' own psyches.

In later years, Coleridge was ashamed of his opium use. There are a number of passages in his letters and notebooks where Coleridge speaks of opium in negative terms. For example, in 1814, he wrote to John Morgan:

> What crime is there scarcely which has not been included in or fol-
> lowed from the one guilt of taking opium? Not to speak of ingrati-
> tude to my maker for the wasted Talents; of ingratitude to so many
> friends who have loved me I know not why; of barbarous neglect of
> my family . . . I have in this one dirty business of Laudanum an
> hundred times deceived, tricked, nay, actually & consciously
> LIED.—And yet all these vices are so opposite to my nature, that
> but for this free-agency–annihilating Poison, I verily believe that I
> should have suffered myself to be cut in pieces rather than have
> committed any one of them.[71]

That opium was a "free-agency–annihilating Poison" was news. The most
striking aspect of Coleridge's explicit writings about opium, principally in his
notebooks and letters, is the sense that he was discovering, through the struggle in and with his own body, the phenomenon we now familiarly term "addiction." The concept did not exist in the early nineteenth century (or before)
and so the formulas that Coleridge developed to explain his struggles were his
own. "Is not Habit the Desire of a Desire?" he asks in one of his notebooks.[72]
The sense of pleasure that Coleridge experienced in the early days, when
opium induced a world of dreamlike reverie that appeared to be controlled by
the dreamer, turned to horror when this process of "desiring" became autonomous and the dreamer became the servant of the dream. Desire itself became unreliable: "the still rising Desire still baffling the bitter Experience, the
bitter Experience still following the gratified Desire."[73] Subject and object became confused—"I could not know / whether I suffered, or I did," he writes in
"The Pains of Sleep."

Opium laid ruin to Coleridge's hopes for unifying the Self and the World.
Even the most intimate structures of self—such as "Imagination" and "Fancy,"
which Coleridge and some of the other Romantics had worked so hard to protect from the world of Newtonian mechanism—could become alienated or
mechanical in a way that divided the self against itself. It was De Quincey's lot
to articulate this more fully.

De Quincey lacked Coleridge's philosophical sophistication, but was similarly at a loss to explain why he could not stop taking opium: "at the time I began to take opium daily, I could not have done otherwise" was all he could say
in the *Confessions*.[74] De Quincey used opium regularly (once every three

weeks) for a number of years without becoming habituated. As with Coleridge, it was only when he moved to the Lake District that he became addicted to opium (possibly because of the potency of the Black Drop preparation made there). And as with Coleridge, it was a similar combination of emotional stress (caused by the death of Kate Wordsworth) and physical pain (gastric problems) that led him to increase his use. Despite his claim at the end of the *Confessions* that he had freed himself from opium, he took opium on a daily basis from 1812 to his death. During certain periods (1813–1815, 1817, 1828, 1844), his dosage rose as high as 12,000 drops of laudanum a day with accompanying derangement of his sleep and waking hours. At other times he was apparently able to reduce his dose to a maintenance level (50–1,000 drops a day) at which he could function reasonably well.

De Quincey invented the concept of recreational drug use: in the *Confessions,* which was published anonymously in the *London Magazine* in two parts in 1821, he makes it quite clear that opium's value is more than medicinal—or for that matter, spiritual. Although De Quincey did not claim that he was the first to use opium for pleasure—he noted that it was used as a cheap substitute for alcohol by workers in the north of England—he was the first person to write about it in this way. In the "Pleasures of Opium," De Quincey described his favored activities after taking opium. These were going to the opera—in general, De Quincey, like E. T. A. Hoffmann, found a profound connection between states of intoxication and the pleasures of music—and wandering through the poorer neighborhoods of London, talking to people. Coleridge was for the most part unable to acknowledge such pleasures, and it is striking that opium seems to have offered him little conscious insight into his own mind or thought processes.

De Quincey constructed a myth around his use of opium where Coleridge tried to hide it. *Confessions of an English Opium Eater* collects a peculiar set of energies and obsessions of the nineteenth century and packages them into a character, an image. As with all myths, the ultimate truth of the tale is beside the point. What matters is that the myth capture something that is important to people, that they want or need to believe—which is not to say that a myth is untrue. Opium for De Quincey, and for those who read him, offered dreams that money can buy, a fabled, mythical substance from the East that could be purchased from any pharmacist in England and would allow transport to the realms of imagination. When De Quincey first buys opium on a Sunday afternoon in central London for a toothache, the drug is a "dread agent of unimaginable pleasure and pain! I had heard of it as I had of manna or ambrosia, but no further."[75] The pharmacist who sells the opium to De Quincey is an "unconscious minister of celestial pleasures . . . the beatific vision of an immortal druggist, sent down to earth on a special mission to myself."[76] Everywhere, opium opens doorways from nineteenth-century England into strange mythical territories, whether it be the "sphinx's riddles of streets"[77] of London at night, or the Orientalized Lake District in which the mysterious opium-gobbling Malay appears, or the prehistoric times and spaces that manifest when De Quincey begins to dream. From the Roman invasion of England, back to China and India and to "Nilotic mud," De Quincey undertakes an Odyssean voyage without leaving his bed, a reverse *Odyssey*, in which his mind and body are invaded by the world of myth lying outside European history, transported by the foreign contagion of the poppy.

In the middle of the eighteenth century, Edmund Burke had described a kind of pleasure taken in painful, overwhelming, or intense situations experienced at a distance. He called this the sublime. The inventory of effects and attributes that De Quincey gives opium reflects the fascination of the Romantics—but also nineteenth-century culture in general—with the sublime: a pleasure taken in abysses, murky darkness, the vast architectural fantasias of Giovanni Battista Piranesi and John Martin. When De Quincey first takes opium he says: "Oh! Heavens! What a revulsion! What an upheaving from its lowest depths, of the inner spirit! What an apocalypse of the world within me! That my pains had vanished, was now a trifle in my eyes:—this negative effect was swallowed up in the immensity of those positive effects which had opened before me—in the abyss of divine enjoyment thus suddenly revealed."[78] The *Confessions* constantly echoes the great poet of the sublime, John Milton.

Today, the sublime plays a major role in a large portion of our cultural and recreational industries—from Hollywood thrillers to bungee jumping to adventure holidays—an easy formula that caters to and trains us to crave sensation. Recreational drug use remains a part of the culture of the sublime. De Quincey surrounded opium use with a veil of darkness and fear that he knew (or hoped) would be avidly consumed by his readers. The ironies in this particular constellation mount quickly. Opium, in its ability to transform a sensation of pain into a sensation of pleasure, by creating a distance, a numbness that removes the user from unpleasant sensation, echoes the formula of the sublime itself. The antinarcotic campaigns, with their endless evocation of darkness and ruin, also recreate the atmosphere of the sublime, with all its mystique and excitement, in every ad campaign, every hyperbolic speech. The antinarcotic laws, and the organizations that act as advocates on their behalf, thus directly promote an atmosphere that makes drugs attractive to people.

The sublime can be linked to economics. It is well known that, despite his claims to being a philosopher, De Quincey wrote his *Confessions* because he needed the money. In general, De Quincey has a surprising interest in economy, echoing Burroughs' observation that "opium is profane and quantitative like money."[79] This manifests itself as a concern with dosages—which the narcotics literature displays to a degree not found with any other drug—with De Quincey's tens of thousands of drops of laudanum, Jean Cocteau's pipes of opium, and, more recently, Ann Marlowe's $10 bags of heroin. But there is also in the *Confessions*—as there will be in Edgar Allan Poe's, in William Burroughs', and in Alexander Trocchi's writing—an obsession with finding shelter (I am thinking of Trocchi's scow, tied up on a wharf in Manhattan; of the importance of the house in "The Fall of The House of Usher"; of the endless descriptions of the rooms, apartments, hotels, and houses in which junkies get high), with nutrition and starvation (opium's famous ability to slow all digestive activity to zero). And there is an obsession with economic theory: De Quincey's philosophic master is not, as one might imagine, Kant or one of the other German Idealists, but the economist David Ricardo.[80] In his intoxicated state, De Quincey dreams of writing *A Prologomena to All Future Economic Systems*—like many such *grands projets* of narcotic users, it was never actually written. Burroughs of course also gives us a general economic theory based on narcotic addiction—"the algebra of need." So does Artaud with his notion of the body without organs—a body undivided, sufficient unto itself, one that does not need to enter into exchange with the outside.

Economy is another way of saying "mechanism." Despite all that is said about the Romantic flight from reason, De Quincey and Coleridge were very much concerned with cause and effect. Coleridge would have preferred not to believe in cause and effect; in his early years, he wanted to be a magician; only later, when he was forced to acknowledge the problems caused by opium, did he write the introduction to "Kubla Khan," where he links the work of the imagination to the "anodyne" that he had been prescribed; for the most part he raged mutely at the "injustice" of what had happened (economy has a legal aspect, as we shall see). De Quincey sought to explain his extraordinary dream life through the combination of opium and his childhood, which makes him a predecessor of that other great economist of dreams, Freud. But De Quincey was also clearly uncomfortable with the idea that his dreams were the product of opium consumption:

> If a man "whose talk is of oxen," should become an opium-eater, the probability is, that (if he is not too dull to dream at all)—he will dream about oxen: whereas, in the case before him, the reader will find that the opium-eater boasteth himself to be a philosopher; and accordingly, that the phantasmagoria of his dreams . . . is suitable to one who in that character
>
> Humani nihil a se alienum putat.[81]

A crucial element in the association of narcotics and literature is that most authors deny the creative value of the substance that they are talking about. Opium became the connecting factor between many realms, but at the same time, to use Latour's phrase, opium, as a mediator of realms, was "crossed out." This ensured the mythical status of the drug, which was never fully allowed to emerge into the "real world"—except in the work of a man like Cocteau, who transformed his own life into myth to such a degree that opium was merely one of the props he used in the staging of his own identity.

De Quincey most eloquently formulated the mechanism of opium's effect on dreams in the unfinished *Suspiria de Profundis* (1845), part of what was to be a follow-up to the *Confessions*. Opium has a power "not merely for exalting the colours of dream-scenery, but for deepening its shadows; and, above all, for strengthening the sense of its fearful *realities*."[82] Opium allows the transfer of material from the real world to the dream world—and back again. The analogy for this transfer is that of writing, as De Quincey notes in the *Confessions:*

> a sympathy seemed to arise between the waking and the dreaming states of the brain in one point . . . whatsoever things capable of being visually represented I did but think of in the darkness, immediately shaped themselves into phantoms of the eye; and, by a process apparently no less inevitable, when thus once traced in faint and visionary colours, like writings in sympathetic ink, they were drawn

out by the fierce chemistry of my dreams, into insufferable splendour that fretted my heart.[83]

In *Suspiria de Profundis*, De Quincey discusses the palimpsest, an ancient piece of parchment on which successive generations have erased others' ideas and added their own. "Chemistry, a witch as potent as the Erictho of Lucan . . ., has extorted by her torments, from the dust and ashes of forgotten centuries, the secrets of a life extinct for the general eye, but still glowing in the embers."[84] The human brain is also a palimpsest on which countless layers of impressions and feelings are written and overwritten. Death, fever, and "the searchings of opium" can "resurrect" these impressions, transforming them into symbol patterns.[85] These patterns would later contribute to Symbolist aesthetics, through their influence on Baudelaire.

Response to De Quincey's *Confessions* was mostly favorable—fifteen reviews appeared in the first two years after it was published. In 1823, a young man died in London of an opium overdose, and at the inquest, a doctor suggested that an increase in such deaths could be connected to the appearance of De Quincey's book. Similar claims would continue to be made until the present day, although, as Grevel Lindop observes, the effect of the book was unpredictable. Thomas Carlyle, for example, decided firmly not to try to laudanum after reading De Quincey.[86]

Imitations and parodies of De Quincey proliferated. Charles Kingsley's *Alton Locke* (1850) for example, contains a chapter called "Dreamland" where the narrator finds himself in "Hindoo temples," is chased by an angry Siva and Kali, flees across vast deserts, and experiences his own devolution into a polyp, crab, ostrich, mylodon, ape, and so on.[87] In America, an English immigrant named William Blair published "An Opium Eater in America" in the July 1842 issue of *The Knickerbocker*. In France, a translation of De Quincey's *Confessions* appeared in 1827 by an A.D.M., who turned out to be the young Romantic poet Alfred de Musset. The translation, which transformed De Quincey's text into a Romantic potboiler, was quickly passed around, and opium began to appear in other works, such as *L'opium* by Le Comte Alex de B., a pseudonym for Balzac, and an early story with the same title by Théophile Gautier, and others.

But De Quincey was hardly the only reason for taking opium in the nineteenth century. Medical and neomedical use of a variety of preparations of opium and morphine proliferated in Europe and the United States, and writers, along with many others, became users.[88] The writer most associated with opium in the mid-century was the mystery novelist Wilkie Collins. Collins had taken laudanum for at least the last twenty years of his life and referred to opium in *No Name* (1862), *Armadale* (1866), and *The Moonstone* (1868); his inferior output during the last years of his life has been attributed to his use of laudanum, although Collins felt that the drug had a stimulating effect on him that helped him work. When only nine years old, Collins had overheard a conversation between Coleridge and his parents, who were friends. Coleridge was bemoaning the tortures of his opium habit and Collins' mother said to the poet, "Mr. Coleridge, do not cry; if the opium really does you any good, and you must have it, why do you not go and get it?" Coleridge, immediately consoled, turned to Collins' father and said, "Collins, your wife is an exceedingly sensible woman!"[89] The novelist-to-be took note.

Collins, who was of course familiar with De Quincey's and Walter Scott's opium use, struggled with his inability to stop; he also bragged on occasion about his tolerance for large doses, noting that the wine glass of laudanum he was in the habit of taking had killed one of his servants who had foolishly tried to imitate him. He spoke of seeing ghosts, and of a second Wilkie Collins, who would appear before him when he wrote at night.[90] Significantly, after singing the praises of laudanum to his friend Hall Caine, his friend asked him whether he should begin taking laudanum for his own exhaustion. Collins paused and quietly replied, "No."

More than actual discussion of opium, what developed in nineteenth-century literature was an opiated atmosphere or mood. Opium became the scent, the material trace of the century's transcendentalist obsessions, shorthand for an entire mental state, easily exploited to gain a certain effect—and easily condemned for the same reason. The principle source for this atmosphere was the German short story writer E. T. A. Hoffmann, the originator of the fantastic tale. Hoffmann, who was writing at the very beginning of the century, made no reference to opium, preferring instead to make use of alcohol or a series of nameless elixirs and potions to act as the material agents of his characters' entry into the worlds of fantasy.[91] But Hoffmann's chief disciples—Gautier in France and Poe in America—were ready to make use of De Quincey's mythopoetic transformation of opium.

Although Poe's alcohol consumption is amply attested to, there is very little evidence that he himself used opium more than occasionally. As Alathea Hayter says, his link to opium is based on two factors, his repeated references to opium in his fictional writings and the cult of Poe that developed in France—partly through the influence of Baudelaire.[92]

In his stories, Poe associated opium with hyperaesthesia, "a morbid acuteness of the senses," a condition he says characterizes Roderick Usher. Another of his heroes, Augustus Bedloe in "A Tale of the Ragged Mountains," is a morphine user (he takes it orally) who likes to wander the hills of Virginia near his home:

> The morphine had its customary effect—that of enduing all the external world with an intensity of interest. In the quivering of a leaf—in the hue of a blade of grass—in the shape of a trefoil—in the humming of a bee—in the gleaming of a dew-drop—in the breathing of the wind—in the faint odours that came from the forest—there came a whole universe of suggestion—a gay and motley train of rhapsodies and immethodical thought.[93]

On one such stroll, the intoxicated Bedloe has a vision (Poe quotes Novalis on the distinction between a vision and a dream) of an Oriental city, which turns out to be Benares in 1780. Just as De Quincey's English dreams are haunted by an opium-eating Malay, Bedloe's American dreams are haunted by the East. Once again, opium is the substance through which the colonies come to manifest themselves in the consciousness of the West.

Gautier, who was no stranger to Orientalism, used opium to tell a much more gothic tale in his "La pipe d'opium" (1838).[94] The pipe, which would have been a highly unusual method of absorbing opium at that time in France, probably reflects Gautier's passion for Hoffmann and his magical tobacco blends. One of De Quincey's first dreams took him back to the time of the English Revolution; Gautier is taken back to revolutionary France, and a mysterious town in which he meets a woman who has been sentenced to death. The internal, physiological revolution of opium is matched by these visions of

a history that consists of layers of social insurrection, each of which is represented as a death that can be reversed in dreams through the power of the
poppy. The opium user feels a sentimental attachment to those classes overthrown during these revolutions, feels the pathos of their disappearance before
the mob or the army.

The last word of Gautier's tale is "hallucination"—and as with his hashish
tales, Gautier writes a kind of phenomenology of perception, showing how
the senses are opened up into strange Kantian realms by the drug. With splendid irony, one of the hallucinations takes the form of Alphonse Esquiros, one
of the first French psychologists to study hallucinations.

Aside from De Quincey, the connection between opium and dreams that
writers such as Poe and Gautier contributed to was further popularized by
writers like Henry Murger, whose *Scenes from Bohemian Life* (1851) featured the
laudanum-smoking sculptor Jacques (he soaks it into his tobacco).[95] But it was
Baudelaire, translator of Poe and admirer of Gautier, who was first profoundly
associated with opium in the French public's mind—and Baudelaire who was
to provide the same mythical example for French writers that De Quincey did
in the Anglo-Saxon world. Reviewing *Les fleurs du mal* (*The Flowers of Evil*)
in 1862, the critic Charles Sainte-Beuve summarized this myth:

> Mr. Baudelaire has found the way to build for himself, at the very
> limit of earthly language, in a place believed inhabitable and be-
> yond the borders of Romanticism as it is known, a bizarre kiosk,
> highly ornamented, highly tormented, but charming and mysteri-
> ous, where one reads Edgar Poe, recites exquisite sonnets, where
> one becomes intoxicated with hashish in order to reason after-
> wards, where one takes opium and a thousand abominable drugs in
> tea cups made of perfect porcelain.[96]

Baudelaire's letters indicate that he began taking opium as early as 1842 and
continued, on and off, for the rest of his life. The reasons given vary: depression, various pains, syphilis, pleasure. Once again, it is worth emphasizing that
none of this was in itself unusual in the nineteenth century. But in the context
of Baudelaire's poetry and the myth of the poet that Sainte-Beuve's review indicates, it becomes significant. If challenged to find a text of Baudelaire's devoted to opium, most people would draw a blank. Baudelaire was curiously
reticent about his opium use. While willing to describe his own experiences

with hashish in *Les paradis artificiels,* when it came to opium he chose to re-translate sections of De Quincey's *Confessions* (adding sections of *Suspiria de Profundis*), claiming that De Quincey had already said everything that needed to be said on the subject.[97] Explicit mentions of opium in *The Flowers of Evil* are few. But a case can be and has been made for the influence of narcotics in many of the poems.[98]

As with Poe, the absence of explicit mention of opium in itself contributes to a certain literary myth regarding narcotics. At a time when the older classical discourses that structured poetry were dead or dying (and Baudelaire would have been the first to give the corpse a hearty kick), opium provided a new mythology on which to base aesthetic practice. Since this aesthetic practice, best encapsulated in the phrase "art for art's sake," was concerned with the autonomy of the writer, his independence from material conditions, it could not be linked too directly to drugs. Thus when we read the beautiful poem "Corréspon-dences," a cornerstone of Symbolist aesthetics, we find no mention of hashish in the poem. But when we read the hashish chapter of *Les paradis artificiels,* we find passages identical in imagery and meaning to parts of this poem that are pre-sented explicitly as being the products of hashish intoxication. The work of imagination and the discussion of the real remain separated. Anyone having read both texts would connect them immediately, but they are separated by a di-vide, which can only be bridged mythically, in secret. This may also be one of the secrets of Baudelaire's prose poems, those headless, tailless pieces (that is, hy-brids) like "La chambre double" in which he again describes the "silent lan-guage" of flowers; "the furniture seems to be dreaming; one might say that, like the vegetable and the mineral, it is endowed with the life of a sleepwalker." At the end of the poem, as the vision of peace (so often a *room* in the narcotic lit-erature), dissolves back into the misery of bohemian poverty, "a single known object smiles at me; the flask of laudanum: an old and terrible friend."[99]

Perhaps in order to maintain the mythical status of drugs, Baudelaire's take on drug use was typically caustic:

> That is why, thinking no further than immediate gratification, he has, without worrying about violating the laws of his constitution, sought in the physical sciences, in pharmaceuticals, in the most crude liquors, in the most subtle perfumes, in all climates and at all times, the means to flee, even if only for a few hours . . . Alas! Man's

vices, however horrifying they seem, contain proof (if only in their infinite varieties) of his taste for the infinite; only, it's a taste which often goes astray.[100]

Drug use for Baudelaire was evil—but with the irony of a devout gnostic, he chose to celebrate and even market moral failure, as the title of his book of poetry, *The Flowers of Evil,* indicates. For Baudelaire, narcotics were one more snare by which nineteenth-century culture sought to trap—and succeeded in trapping—the human spirit in the world of matter. The search for pleasure, attempts at flight from intolerable surroundings, even craving for beauty, led man further astray into Satan's territory. Gnostic flight from this world into the infinite was as desirable as it was impossible and led only to further entanglement in the snares of false infinities that drugs, with their ineradicably material basis, offered.

Whether Baudelaire merely reflected changing attitudes in European society, or whether he himself was able to package Romantic darkness through his own idiosyncratic genius in such a way that the scent of "evil" would forever be attached to a certain literary attitude toward drugs, *The Flowers of Evil* marked a decisive shift in the culture of narcotics. De Quincey and Coleridge did not consciously aestheticize self-destruction; they were genuinely bewildered by what happened to them under the influence of opium. Baudelaire lacked even the pretense of innocence. With him, for the first time, drugs became a "guilty pleasure."

Morphine, named after Morpheus, the god of sleep, had been available for over half a century before a significant literary culture became associated with it. The discovery of morphine is a complicated tale. In 1803–04 a Parisian pharmacist named Louis Derosne isolated a salt from opium, a mixture of morphine and narcotine—but did not publish his results. A year later, Armand Seguin presented a description of an experiment extracting colorless crystals from opium to the French Academy of Sciences. But he was soon after thrown in prison for ten years for embezzling money from Napoleon's army and never got to publish his discovery.[101] It was, therefore, a young German pharmacist, Friedrich Sertürner, who in 1805 published the first description of morphine, after testing the substance orally on himself and his friends.

Morphine was the first alkaloid ever to be discovered. This is significant for a number of reasons. It indicates the intense interest in the properties of opium during this period. It marks the shift in pharmacology from a knowledge of plants and their properties (herbology) to a knowledge of refined, potent substances with precisely defined physiological effects. This shift opened the door to the large-scale industrial production and distribution of drugs by pharmaceutical companies, which flooded the world marketplace at the end of the nineteenth century and which were to some degree responsible for the subsequent regulation of drugs.

For the first half of the nineteenth century morphine was taken orally— Elizabeth Barrett Browning was quite fond of it, for example. The widespread dissemination of morphine awaited the discovery of the hypodermic syringe by Charles-Gabriel Pravaz in 1850 and, a few years later, the use of the syringe to inject morphine by Alexander Wood, an Edinburgh doctor. According to contemporary French accounts, Wood (whose wife, significantly, became the first injected morphine addict) was considered the uncontested father of morphine addicts.[102]

It was in the 1870s, following the American Civil War, the Crimean War, and the Franco-Prussian War, with their many casualties, that injected morphine use became popular. The drug initiated a series of fadlike enthusiasms among the medical profession for the panacea-like qualities of morphine, cocaine, heroin, chloral hydrate, and other drugs—all followed, predictably, by backlashes against the drugs' side effects. Injected morphine avoided the side effects of orally ingested morphine, such as gastric distress. It was more potent, more of a euphoriant, and worked faster. Morphine had none of the Oriental mystique of opium—even the name was derived from the Latin. Morphine was profane, modern, part of the culture of speed, intensification, and molecularization that developed in the second half of the nineteenth century—the time of the invention of the automobile, the cinema, and the germ theory of disease.

This was also the period when the medicalization (and pathologization) of narcotic use, along with many other areas of human life (work, recreation, sexuality), expanded rapidly. The medical concept of addiction was developed by German psychologists in the 1870s, and was taken up quickly in France. The drug user became a specific type of personality, a "toxicomane" or drug addict. To this, criminologists such as Cesare Lombroso added the notion of degeneration, a hereditary biological predisposition toward weakness, crime, and decadence, which was also linked to drug use. Versions of this theory, such as neurasthenia in America, which Thomas Crothers, in his *Morphinism and Narcomanias from Other Drugs* (1902) used to explain how morphine created a "pathologic impression" on a person that could then be transmitted through heredity, were important in marking the growing hostility of Western culture to narcotic use.

Although morphine use was prevalent throughout Europe and the Americas, it was in France that it became a part of a major literary culture—and, thanks to Arnould de Liedekerke, we have a good deal of information about this era.[103] A number of novels purporting to describe morphine use appeared in France, beginning in the 1880s. The focus was often on society women who became addicted to morphine injections at "morphine institutes," which occupied a place between salons and shooting galleries. Novels such as Jules Clarétie's *Noris: moeurs du jour* (*Noris : The Morals of the Day*, 1883) and Marcel Mallat's *La comtesse morphine* (*Countess Morphine*, 1885) appeared; in the latter, the countess becomes a morphine addict, and is destroyed by the aphrodisiac effects of the drug, taking lover upon lover (of both sexes) and hallucinating herself on the cross with Christ. Drugs themselves were pictured as seductresses like Salome or the Odyssean Circe in this literature. Heroin was "the white fairy," morphine "the gray fairy," opium "the black idol," and absinthe "the green fairy." "She" (the drug) seduced with her beauty and the pleasure she offered, and then led you to ruin. The popularity of morphine among women was seen as a sign of the decadence of modern culture—and of what happened when women gave up their traditional roles. Women "who call with exultation for their rights, are in the process of obtaining a new one . . . the right to morphine," noted Jules Clarétie, caustically.[104]

But in fact, men too, and not merely poets but alpha males such as Prince Otto von Bismarck, General Georges Boulanger, and the neurologist Jean-Martin Charcot, became addicted to morphine.[105] Edouard Levinstein, one of the first addiction experts, remarked in 1877 on the existence of

> a set of people who are morphine addicts in the highest degree, and who are not only in plain possession of their mental health, but who

have shined and continue to shine like splendid stars on the scientific horizon. Men of state, men of war, artists, doctors, surgeons, people of great fame are slaves to this passion, and their activity is not in the least hindered.[106]

Morphine use was beyond the means of most people in French society. It was a status symbol. Users carried boxes with elegant handmade syringes: "the use of morphine," claimed one writer, "does not imply any notion of vulgarity whatsoever, but rather that of an elegant refinement, a luxurious, sensual pleasure."[107]

Dubut de Laforest's *Morphine* (1891) is a catalog of the folklore surrounding morphine at the fin de siècle. When he turned his pen to "the gray fairy," De Laforest was already a noted exploitation author, probably one of the first writers to use Emile Zola's naturalism as a rhetorical tool with which to provide "scientific documentation" of whatever prurient subject matter he could lay his hands on.

The book's hero is a soldier called Raymond de Pontaillac, "that magnificent male," who is introduced to morphine following a duel.[108] At first, "he used morphine against all abnormal sensations."[109] But after he had been taking morphine for fifteen months, "his thoughts blended dream and reality."[110] He becomes an addict about town, corrupting women, hallucinating, until he finally metamorphosizes into a poet: "He admired the Symbolist's school, the music and color of words, translating 'A' into black, etc. . . . he knew that black is the organ; white, the harp, etc. . . . and rather than being content with normal language, he sought a general orchestration of the harp which is serenity."[111] As his hallucinations continue, he increases his dose, adds cocaine to his shots, and, in a delirium, tries to shoot down his own shadow. He dies in the countryside after one last injection, crying, "Forward! Long live France!"

De Laforest dwells at length on the susceptibility of women to morphine. Pontaillac introduces a friend's wife, Blanche de Montreu, to morphine for the treatment of neuralgia, and she soon becomes addicted. She slips out of a dinner party to take a hit in the winter garden, and Pontaillac follows her. "The sparkle of her eyes met the fire of the man's glance and revealed in her two creatures: the chaste wife, the immaculate mother, and the other, the new one, a morphine addict whose body trembled with love."[112] Like *Dr. Jekyll and Mr. Hyde,* and so many other fin-de-siècle works, *Morphine* returns obsessively to the double body of the drug user, a moral monster waiting to be released from the confines of bourgeois life by modern chemistry.

One of the principal differences in the effect of morphine intoxication on the two sexes is that "while men sometimes suffered from a state of depression of the generative life, in women . . . it resulted in a high level of nymphomania."[113] Blanche, when she takes morphine, dreams of becoming a second woman, "the stranger," who gives herself to Raymond. "'Madame Pravaz' is the Circe of our decadence,"[114] the narrator observes. Meanwhile, Raymond has delusions of grandeur and declares himself Adam, creator of a race of beings in whom "the sexes were confused."[115] Morphine is a "contagion,"[116] spreading to almost all the women that Pontaillac encounters.

The novel moves smoothly between the sensationalism of pulp fiction and medical jargon, which offers an *ER*-like frisson of fin-de-siècle infotainment. At one point, the narrator sagely observes that "Marquise Blanche's entire nervous system, cerebro-spinal and ganglionnary, was profoundly shaken by the disappearance of the morphine from her organism."[117] Pontaillac writes a disintoxication diary,[118] in which he describes performing experiments on a pigeon, on his dog, Myrrha, and on a rabbit—all of whom die of morphine poisoning. He contemplates experimenting on his horses but can't bring himself to. So he writes a letter to be opened on his death, in which he offers his own body as autopsy material in the study of morphine addiction.

Morphine was dedicated to the Italian criminologist and theoretician of degeneration Cesare Lombroso, "who has given me the greatest fortune which a writer could wish for, by commenting on my books in his admirable lessons on criminal anthropology."[119] The book was part of a vogue for books examining "degeneration," the medical version of decadence, which reached its full development in Max Nordau's 1895 book *Entartung (Degeneration)*.[120] Theorists of degeneration decried the hereditary progressive deviation and decline of Western civilization, attributing it to a number of biological factors, which, in a peculiarly Lamarckian twist, included drugs like coffee, tobacco, narcotics, and absinthe.

Writers were often seen as being as degenerate as criminals, prostitutes, and anarchists. According to Nordau, "the physician . . . recognises at a glance, in the fin-de-siècle disposition, in the tendencies of contemporary art and poetry, in the life and conduct of the men who write mystic, symbolic and 'decadent' works . . . the confluence of two well-defined conditions of disease, with which he is quite familiar, viz. degeneration (degeneracy) and hysteria."[121] Writing was a vector by which disease could be transmitted—including the newly discovered disease of morphine addiction. The Parisian "alienist" Henri Guimbail, in *Les morphinomanes* (*Morphine Addicts*, 1891) commented that "I know pages written by our masters of the novel that have done more for the development of morphine addiction than all of the other causes put together."[122] Paul Rodet spoke of "contagion by the book . . . all these works are in the hands of inactive, idle people, neurotic women who take delight in reading novels describing sensations which are new to them. Curiosity is quickly aroused in all of these poorly balanced beings, and they waste no time in transforming the descriptions of morphinic sensations into lived ones."[123]

Although most of the narcotic literature of the time was profoundly anti-drug, there were a number of writers who publically embraced this image of degeneration, or, as they termed it, decadence. The Decadents offered celebrations of the pleasures of artificial paradises, derivative of Baudelaire for the most part, but replacing his irony with a hysterical fatalism. Where Baudelaire's revolt, for all its connections with Parisian bohemia, was highly individual, the Decadents were a type: pale, cadaverously thin young men with nihilistic preoccupations (Arthur Schopenhauer was a favorite). Precursors of punk, they achieved the same dubious distinction of being naive ironists, striking postures, acting out roles whose meaning and consequences they understood only in the vaguest way.

The most famous of these figures was the Decadent poster boy Stanislas de Guaita (1861–1897), morphine addict, hashish and cocaine user, and occultist, who was satirized in the press as "Lugubric de Pravas," author of a book of poems entitled *Seringa Mystica (The Mystical Syringe)*. Guaita had started using morphine in solidarity with Baudelairean aesthetics, and as a remedy for attacks of migraine that he claimed made it impossible for him to write, but found it difficult to stop after the attacks ended. Laurent Tailhade recalled that "in his happy days of morphine addiction, [Guaita] bought the alkaloid by the kilo."[124] In 1885, Guaita started using cocaine, probably as an attempted cure for morphine addiction in the manner suggested by Freud, but remained a narcotics user until his death at the age of thirty-five. His collections of poetry, such as *Rosa Mystica,* in which he celebrated the fatal joys of drugs, are superficial, crudely written broadsides that function more as signs of a way of life, anthems for the initiated, than literature as it is usually conceived. Their "vacancy" is an indication of an intense activity that is taking place, for better or for worse, away from the written page.

Guaita was accused of seducing many others, including Edouard Dubus and Alphonse Retté, into morphine or hashish use, by drugging their drinks. Morphine, like many drugs since, was considered contagious, like a virus, and the circle of pharmacological promiscuities expanded. Retté accused Guaita of having corrupted Dubus; but Retté himself was accused by Gabriel de Lautrec of having used "auto-suggestion" to initiate him into use of dawamesk (hashish). Dubus copied Guaita in a variety of ways: he was an occultist, a Satanist, and a morphine addict. He was found in the toilets at the Place Maubert, unconscious, at the age of thirty, on June, 10, 1895, with a syringe in his pocket, and died two days later at the Pitié Salpetrière.

Another notable morphine-addicted writer was Laurent Tailhade, who took to morphine when he was wounded in an anarchist bombing of a restaurant where he was dining on April 4, 1894, a few months after he had declared, "What do the victims matter, if the act is beautiful!"[125] Tailhade devoted two books to the subject of drugs. In *Omar Khayyam et les poisons de l'intelligence* (*Omar Khayyam and the Poisons of the Intelligence*, 1905), Omar is compared to François Rabelais, Voltaire, and Schopenhauer as a man bringing a civilization out of the dark ages of asceticism and superstition. In *La noire idole* (*The Black Idol*, 1907), Tailhade alternates between analyzing the "types" most susceptible to morphine addiction (doctors, apothecaries, prostitutes, nightbirds, "les unsexeds," and "gynecological patients")[126] with rapturous De Quincey–like descriptions of the drug's creativity-enhancing powers.

The Decadent writers saw sickness as a fundamental fact of human culture, which could only be transcended through an act of will in which it was embraced. Decadence, according to Barbara Spackman, denied "the existence of an isle of health and of the clear-eyed ones who claim to reside there. There is only decadence, only sickness, and only those who welcome it can represent 'progress.'"[127] But the aesthetic autonomy of the Decadents relied on the very concepts of the normal and pathological that it claimed to cross out in the name of Universal Sickness. The false pathological dimensions decried by the psychologists of *dégenerescence* and the *décadent* reality beyond bourgeois health that the poets sought were symbiotic with each other.

Morphine, which was a product of the advances in medical science in the nineteenth century, allowed precisely the kind of moral reversal that the Decadents loved. It was a profane, scientific substance whose effects provided an escape from bourgeois life into a world of aesthetic autonomy. Where the psychiatrists saw morphine as producing undesirable side effects, the Decadents saw it as yielding progress, experimental states of being, and a more authentic relationship with death—just as Novalis had suggested at the beginning of the century. But the materialist transcendental experience that drugs like morphine and cocaine offered was paradoxical, because the body was transcended only to be replaced by another kind of body, that of a morphine addict, which, far from being freed from the repugnant qualities of the material world, was ever more reliant on precisely the set of forces that it sought to escape.

Morphine, abused or not, always retained some degree of medical respectability. This cannot be said for opium smoking, which became a vogue in Europe and America toward the end of the nineteenth century. This drug use was overtly recreational and aesthetic. Mostly the spread of opium smoking was due to the expansion of trade and colonialism in East Asia—the English colonies in China, the French in Indochina—and to the immigration, forced or not, of Chinese laborers to America and the establishment of Chinese settlements and communities in England, France, and America.

There were quite neutral accounts of Chinese opium smoking in London in the 1860s.[128] Charles Dickens' *Mystery of Edwin Drood* (1870) was one of the first books to describe the practice in terms of mystery and moral decay. Dickens visited an opium-smoking place in East London in the 1860s (and also medicated himself with opium in later years). John Jasper, the book's protagonist, is the choirmaster of Cloisterham Cathedral; he also frequents opium dens, and in his intoxicated state his cathedral becomes part of an Oriental fantasia, ruled by "cruel" sultans. These themes of invasion by the East and the double character of the drug user would dominate medical, journalistic, religious, and fictional discussion of opium at the end of the nineteenth century. The last theme is taken up in Oscar Wilde's *The Picture of Dorian Gray* (1891), where Gray, after killing his portrait painter, Basil Hallward, flees to an opium den "where one could buy oblivion, dens of horror where the memory of old sins could be destroyed by the madness of sins that were new."[129] Something similar occurs in Arthur Conan Doyle's Sherlock Holmes tale "The Man

Figure 1. An opium den in London's East End. Note the book on the bed next to the pipe. Engraving by A. Doms after Gustave Doré, 1872.

With the Twisted Lip" (1892) and in the most famous Victorian doppelgänger tale, Robert Louis Stevenson's *Dr. Jekyll and Mr. Hyde* (1886).

In America, opium smoking appeared among the first generations of Chinese indentured laborers who arrived in California and the far West after the gold rush of 1848, to meet the demand for cheap labor to work the mines.

Opium use in "Chinatowns" developed along with gambling and prostitution, as a "safety valve" for the harshness of mine life and, as with the other two vices, as an escape through which the laborer incurred further debt to his employer or to the Tongs that controlled the opium traffic.[130] Opium quickly became the focus of American fears of foreigners and the subject of books such as Allen S. Williams' *The Demon of the Orient and His Satellite Fiends of the Joints: Our Opium Smokers as they are in Tartar Hells and American Paradises* (1883). Lurid accounts of the degenerate activities in opium dens proliferated in newspapers, but made little impression on the literature of the time.[131]

Meanwhile, writers who had spent time in the Asian colonies, as sailors, navy officers, or travelers, such as Rudyard Kipling, B. L. Putnam Weale, Lafcadio Hearn, Victor Segalen, Claude Farrère, and Pierre Loti wrote accounts of expatriate and native opium use in India and China.[132]

It is in France though that a fashion for smoking opium developed. Opium smoking in "fumeries" (opium dens) began around 1850 in large ports like Le Havre, Brest, and Marseilles, but did not spread to other places until the end of the century, after the French campaigns in Indochina. Toulon had two hundred fumeries in 1905 and opium use in the French navy became notorious. In 1907, a scandal hit the headlines about a notorious opium addict and naval officer named Ulmo who was arrested as he prepared to sell military documents concerning the secret code of the French marines to Germany (à la Alfred Dreyfus). In 1908, a decree was passed regulating the sale and use of opium (but not morphine).[133]

Much of the opium literature from this period was written by former navy and army people who were first exposed to the drug during the campaigns in Indochina, and often retained their habits when they returned to France.

Paul Bonnetain's *L'opium* (1886) was the first book dedicated to the topic. Bonnetain had traveled to Saigon as a war correspondent for *Le Figaro*, and gave a clinical description of colonial opium addiction in the style of his hero, Zola (Bonnetain had previously used the lens of naturalism to write a novel about masturbation, *Charlot s'amuse* [*Charlot Enjoys Herself*, 1884]). A steady stream of similar novels followed.[134] The fears which were inspired by opium use in the navy are captured in an amusing way in Jules Boissière's *Fumeurs d'opium* (*Opium Smokers*, 1896), in which Guy-Emmanuel de Césade, an ambitious young marine, arrives in Tonkin hoping to become an officer. But he is introduced to opium by an Annamite soldier and ends up smoking away his

salary, at a rate of sixty pipes a day. He's put in jail, escapes, and joins the Annamite pirates and plans all-out war on France and its colonial empire, only to
be captured by his old comrades and sentenced to be shot.

One of the most prolific authors on opium was Albert de Pouvoirville, a sinologist of some repute, who published a series of books about opium.[135] He
had participated in the pacification of Tonkin as a cavalry officer and claimed
that his pseudonym Matgioi ("the day's eye") had been given to him as part of
an initiation into Taoism by a village chief, Tong-Song-Luat, in Indochina.
Matgioi's characters view opium smoking as part of an initiation into Chinese
manners. Baly, one of the characters in *The Master of Sentences* (1899), has converted a pagoda into his colonial residence, which contains a room with an
opium bed "where the master of the house . . . dreamed that he was some high
Mandarin, disdainful of deed and action."[136] The book dwells obsessively on
the details of Chinese décor and on the paraphernalia of opium smoking,
and celebrates the quietist wisdom of the Taoists—a curious philosophy for a
group of officers engaged in a military campaign to adopt, and one that was
rationalized in part by drawing a line in the sand between the refined manners
of the opium-smoking Chinese and the barbarity of the Annamites and the
Tonkinese.

Pouvoirville and other writers contrasted the smoking of opium with the
use of morphine, and indeed alcohol and all other drugs. Outright advocacy of
drug use in literature is rather rare, but opium smoking was enthusiastically
embraced by a number of writers. In *L'opium* (1908), Pouvoirville claimed of
the Chinese that opium "exacerbates their intelligence . . . the fumerie is a
means of political investigation, just as much as it is an intellectual distraction
or simply sensual."[137] There follows a list of the symbols of Chinese culture to
which opium smoking is linked, as well as the virtues of skepticism, subtlety,
contemplativeness, and "forgetfulness of the past, disdain for the present, and
indifference to the future."[138] Pouvoirville argued that opium and fumeries
should not be banned in Indochina as they had been, that France had no right
to destroy the culture of nations "whose charge we have assumed,"[139] and that
use of "a natural product is never a vice, because vice consists solely in abuse,
and in those terms, opium is very similar to wine, alcohol, and absinthe."[140]

These arguments were also employed by the most popular writer about
opium during this period, the former naval officer Claude Farrère. Farrère's
Fumée d'opium (*Opium Smoke*, 1906) was published at the height of the opium

vogue and enjoyed great popularity. The "F" and "o" in the title refer to the letters by which the French navy noted in his records that a marine was a known
opium smoker. The book is a strange mixture of Chinese legends (along with
the tale of Faust), essays on opium pipes and other paraphernalia, meditations
on the ghosts that appear during a smoke, well-observed portraits of colonial
opium smokers in Shanghai and Parisian dives, and homages to the drug,
which Farrère believed exalted the intelligence and initiated the user into the
mysteries of religion so that very soon he would be "the absolute equal of
God,—pure spirit"[141]—the embodiment of everything Baudelaire warned
about in the "l'homme-Dieu" passage in Les paradis artificiels. Farrère achieved
the curious feat of being ironic and sentimental at the same time: probably he
did not know which attitude was more true. This sense of superiority, arrogance if you take it seriously, has been a part of opiate culture from the distinguished Greek scholar De Quincey to the self-identified Harvard graduate
Ann Marlowe—and takes the form of class snobbery, inverted snobbery, na-
tionalism, or aesthetic hauteur, depending on the individual.

Farrère made the case for opium smokers being a kind of nation in the
monologue of a French colonial in Shanghai:

> Opium, in reality, is a fatherland, a religion, a strong and jealous tie
> between men. And I can better feel a brother to the Asiatics smok-
> ing in Foochow Road than I can to certain inferior Frenchmen now
> vegetating at Paris, where I was born . . . Opium is a magician
> which transforms, and works a metamorphosis. The European, the
> Asiatic are equal,—reduced to a level,—in the presence of its all-
> powerful spell. Races, physiologies, psychologies,—all are effaced;
> and other strange new beings are born into the world—the Smok-
> ers, who, properly speaking, have ceased to be men.[142]

Of course, Farrère admitted, in the morning, the colonial returns to his own
identity. Descriptions of opium use in the colonies continued into the twentieth century; André Malraux, who apparently was addicted to smoking opium,
described the dens in La condition humaine (1933), as did Graham Greene in
the 1950s in The Quiet American (1955).[143] Farrère himself is said to have continued smoking until his death in 1957.

Farrère was one of the first writers to introduce elements from physics into
his descriptions of drug use. A smoker was "no longer an individual but an

unlimited particle of matter";[144] "in the opium-saturated den, filled with odor-ous atoms, peaceful and triumphant, other atoms now burst tumultuously."[145] The opium user was a kind of machine: "I have thought since that his body was like a constant current storage battery, a storage battery for opium, where energy is accumulated. So long as there is a particle of this energy left, the en-gine appears to be fully charged and runs at a uniform speed. But when the last atom has been consumed, it stops abruptly."[146]

A number of narcotics users have embraced science in this way. Pseudo-scientific speculation, such as Burroughs' descriptions of cellular cravings or Cocteau's anatomical pipe drawings, provides a convenient way of describing the distance between the narcotized transcendental consciousness (which is also to say, the literary consciousness) and the material, hungry, ugly flesh. Narcotic use led to a reorganization of the body, its organs, and their func-tions: I am thinking of the pipe orifices that proliferate in Cocteau's drawings (see Figure 2), and the talking asshole in *Naked Lunch* that demands equal rights for itself. Under the influence of opiates, the flesh itself, as opposed to the mind, begins to speak.

Parisian culture of the first decade of the twentieth century emerged out of a haze of opium smoke: Pablo Picasso's rose and blue period paintings with their amorphous hermaphroditic figures; Claude Debussy's and Erik Satie's repetitive, minimalist music in which time stretches, reverberates; Guillaume Apollinaire's calligram of an opium pipe. Alfred Jarry, Blaise Cendrars, Octave Mirbeau, Max Jacob, Salvador Dali, Francis Picabia, Picasso, André Salmon, Colette: there were few artistic figures in Paris at that time who did not smoke opium.[147]

The culture of morphine was dark, grim, obsessed with poisoning and decay, leaving behind it a number of young, dead poets, but the culture of opium smok-ing was one of pleasure. Most of the authors who smoked opium either did so transiently, without developing addictions, or lived reasonably long and produc-tive lives if they did continue to smoke. We could draw from this the simple conclusion that refined, intravenously administered drugs are more dangerous than smoked, unrefined ones. But the cultural contexts, too, were very different. Many of the morphine users took the drug, from what we know of their writ-ings, with a fatalistic attitude, with a veiled or explicit goal of destroying them-selves, although, as I have noted, there were other figures, such as Bismarck, for whom this was not true (perhaps they were content to destroy others).

The opium smokers of Paris benefited from the hyperaestheticized Orientalism with which they surrounded the drug. The image of the Chinese opium smoker provided a model of passivity, control, measure, even equilibrium, which was opposed to the more modern culture of intensification, speed, and death that surrounded morphine. But the two cultures were not completely separate. Opium smoking was a kind of Indian Summer of nineteenth-century drug use, a last moment of pleasure before the clampdown—or conversely, a painkiller taken during the initial period of the decay of the great Western empires. Something for bored soldiers to do with their long nights after the natives had been subdued. Or something to ward off the fear of impending collapse, deterioration.

This sense of foreboding was particularly evident among writers in the Austro-Hungarian empire. I will discuss Georg Trakl, who was a narcotics user, and his brief life elsewhere. Here I will talk about the Hungarian short story writer Géza Csáth. He had a life similar in brevity to Trakl's, and like Trakl, a career in medicine. Csáth became addicted to opiates during his medical training in Budapest and subsequently while working at a neurology clinic there. He began smoking opium in 1909, but quickly moved to injecting morphine. During this period he also contributed to literary journals and worked as a music critic.

In 1913, he moved to the country, to work as a doctor and, apparently, to be able to to pursue his addiction to narcotics with more discretion. His journal entries from this period drip with self-loathing. Like Trakl, Csáth served in World War I, and developed increasing signs of madness during that conflict. When he returned from the war he became paranoid, hired a detective to follow his family, and finally shot his wife with a revolver in front of their infant daughter. Having spent a few months in an insane asylum, he escaped, only to be stopped by Serbian border guards. After a brief struggle, Csáth took poison and killed himself. He was thirty-one. The writing was on the wall for the postwar period. In his short story "Opium"—subtitled "from a Neurologist's Mail"—Csáth delivers a lovely, gloomy eulogy to the fin-de-siècle opium culture:

> Opium, horrible and blessed connection of pleasure, destroys our organs and senses. The healthy appetite and the bourgeois sensation of feeling good and tired have to be sacrificed. The eyes water, the ears ring. Objects, printed words, people look faded. Sounds

and words wander randomly in the tiny mechanisms of the organs of hearing.

Stop those miserable, inferior little contraptions![148]

During World War I, the Harrison Laws in the United States, and a variety of similar laws in other nation-states regulating the sale of narcotics, along with cocaine, came into effect. To what degree did literature play a role in the cascade of events that led to these changes? In general, the role was probably minor, one factor in a much larger network of causes: fear of the "criminality" of the underclasses; the perceived racial threat from outsiders, whether black, Chinese, or Turkish; excessive use by the military, by women, by the medical profession—fueled by overproduction of drugs and disingenuous marketing by pharmaceutical companies; and the reorganization of the boundaries that define private and public life at every level.

Writing played a role in the pathologization and medicalization of the narcotics user, via the theory of decadence and degeneration. According to this theory, literary works that explored Novalis' realm of the night were symptomatic of diseased minds, indications of the degeneration of the middle and upper classes in European and American society. The sickness they presented was also contagious, and presented a threat to women and other people with weak wills who had the leisure time to indulge in reading such books.

Charles Terry and Mildred Pellens' *The Opium Problem* (1928), a mammoth, thousand-page American review of studies of narcotic use, provides a good overview of attitudes toward narcotic use during the period of criminalization. De Quincey is discussed in the history section as one of those "intellectual adventurers" during the Romantic period who would stimulate "among their readers a morbid curiosity that not infrequently led to hazardous experiments." The authors go on:

> It is probable that even today of most of those who have come in
> contact with a considerable number of individuals suffering from
> chronic opium intoxication, there are few who have not known one
> or more who owed their first introduction to the drug to a perusal
> of De Quincey's sorry masterpiece. Not only has it influenced indi-

viduals of suitable psychologic make-up to fall under the sway of the drug but also it was the forerunner of a host of other morbid and ill-conceived creations on the part of misleading writers who have chosen to apply what mediocre or other gifts they have had to the stimulating of exploitable desires and weaknesses.[149]

The authors cite William Blair's homage to De Quincey, "An Opium Eater in America," as evidence of the book's pernicious influence and go on to discuss other works that cite De Quincey as an inspiration. A few pages later they note the appearance of morphine and the syringe as plot devices in sensational novels in the second half of the nineteenth century.[150] Beyond Blair, however, the authors' own review of the literature on the etiology of narcotic addiction does not substantiate any claims that literature was a major cause of narcotic addiction: according to their analysis, narcotic use was associated primarily with medical exposure (especially in the case of morphine) and exposure to criminal types and foreigners, in particular "Chinamen."

The practice of blaming writers like De Quincey for introducing people to opium had its origins in the pathologization of addicts as a specific type, which occurred at the end of the nineteenth century. When H. H. Kane set up one of America's first rehabilitation clinics, he named it the De Quincey Home. But it was only when medical and recreational drug use were legally separated that the image of the drugged writer became a common one. The deputy commissioner of the New York State Narcotic Board, Sara Graham-Mulhall, decried the influence of De Quincey on the young in *Opium: The Demon Flower* (1926). Jeanette Marks, a writer, reformer, and head of the English Department at Mount Holyoke College, studied the literary symptoms of narcotic addiction in *Genius and Disaster: Studies in Drugs and Genius* (1925). "The chemistry of minds is worth something," she observed of Coleridge. "Repetition, color, motion, sound, effects of nature, even the flexing of the line, all reveal the bodily disturbances of drug-taking . . . The whole body of his poetry is drug work, shows drug mentality, bears the stigmata of the drug imagination."[151] Regarding Poe, who, as I have noted, was probably not a regular opiate user, she asked, "What but a drugged imagination would have thought of 'Dark-eyed violets that writhe?' . . . Where, but in drug work, do we get such broken structures, such inconsistent and unlooked-for endings?"[152]

De Quincey's *Confessions* was used as a case history in medical studies of narcotic use well into the twentieth century. Louis Lewin, for example, in his *Phantastica* (1924), quotes De Quincey in a section entitled "The Observable Internal Process in Morphinists and Opiumists." Quoting the "O just, subtle and all-conquering opium!" passage, Lewin notes "an opium-eater who arrived at this stage has expressed his sensations in an emphatic style which we must consider as corresponding to his real impressions."[153] But why should this "emphatic style" correspond to "real impressions"? If De Quincey's Miltonic evocations of the sublime, or Coleridge's use of color, are the symptoms of opium addiction, then the literary imagination itself must be considered pathological. Lewin indicates as much when he notes, in the same section: "The beginning of the process finds the morphinist in a state of delusion with regard to the value of his faculties, his work and his agreeable sensations. The ego bases itself on a false valuation with respect to the personality itself and the rest of the world."[154]

In a sense, the Romantics and the physicians and lawmakers were in agreement about this pathology—but where society saw pathology as something to be eradicated, the artists wanted to cultivate it, as the only authentic source of meaning. This embrace of pathology led to a certain lack of discrimination when it came to modes of rebellion.

I do not think that the medical critique of De Quincey and company should be rejected out of hand. It is likely that books about drugs do influence those who read them. But this concern about influence is itself the result of a crisis in how we understand the relationship between the self and the world, a crisis in which both science and literature are implicated. For Terry and Pellens and for Lewin, literature either speaks the truth via "personal observation" or tells lies that seduce the unwary into trouble (the realm of the imagination). One inhabits either the real world or an illusory one. But psychoactive drugs by definition inhabit both worlds: they have both subjective and objective elements—as, to some degree, do all human activities. De Quincey's *Confessions* has elements of truth in it, but the book is not a case history, even when it adopts the rhetoric of one. It is a story, a fabrication that inhabits a no man's land between fiction and reality. Not so easy, perhaps, to say where one begins and the other ends, even though we have to make such judgments many times each day.

The narcotics users of the nineteenth century were a relatively diverse crowd. Even the most dogmatic of the alienists, obsessed with detecting crime and pathology everywhere, noted the presence of military men, doctors, women of society, men of letters, and so on, among the host of users. This diversity was also reflected in nineteenth-century literature. When the first set of national laws regulating narcotic use was introduced in World War I, particular locations in the big cities—Montmartre in Paris, Soho in London, and 42nd Street in New York—became associated with narcotic use. These were the great racial, sexual, and class melting pots at the centers of modern cities: home to red-light districts, nightclubs, theaters, and cinemas; places of hybridity, mixture, danger. The press focused on such places as the source of tantalizing stories and from them a series of mythical characters emerged (or reemerged): the innocent victim, the corrupter of youth, the fiendish Oriental, the sexually potent black man, and so on. A consensus emerged in the 1920s that such places were full of drug users, despite the evidence from fact-finding missions, such as those of the Rolleston Committee in 1926 in Britain, showing that the typical narcotics user of the period was not a wide-eyed, thrill-seeking young person, but usually a middle-aged or elderly person who had become addicted in the course of medical therapy.

In literature, the most popular narratives of drug use shifted from a focus on the downfall of upper-class members of society for whom narcotic use was a symptom of their preexisting depravity to an obsession with the seduction of the innocent. An example of the former genre is Aleister Crowley's *Diary of a Drug Fiend* (1922), a book that clearly belongs to the old regime. In the book, the protagonist, a World War I hero, and his lover go on a cocaine binge that eventually results in their becoming addicted to heroin. This addiction they escape in a suspiciously didactic way through a crash course in Crowley-style mysticism (Crowley himself had a considerably more prolonged struggle with heroin, during which his doctrine of the unassailability of the Will was severely challenged.[155]) The later genre is well represented by the figure of Sax Rohmer, author of the popular Fu Manchu series of novels, as well as the classic *Dope* (1919). Rohmer was the nom de plume of Arthur Henry Ward, who claimed that he discovered his vocation when he asked the Ouija board how to make a living and it replied with the letters "C-H-I-N-A-M-A-N."[156] *Dope*, based on the tabloid story of the drug-related death of the actress Billie Carleton in 1918, is the story of an aspiring actress, Rita Irvin, who becomes entangled in London's glamorous West End world of show business, late nights, and rootless cosmopolitans.[157] She is introduced to drugs by Sir Lucien Pyne, an upper-class Englishman—similar to Crowley—and moves quickly from cocaine to opium, which she purchases from a mysterious dream-reading Oriental called Kazmah. Inspector Kerry of Scotland Yard, when told about this, exclaims: "It's bad enough in the heathens, but for an Englishwoman to dope herself is downright unchristian and beastly."[158]

From the West End, the trail leads east to the opium dens of the East End, a world of "Jews and Jewesses, Poles, Swedes, Easterns, dagoes, and half-castes"[159]—and further, because "drug-takers form a kind of brotherhood, and outside the charmed circle they are secretive as members of the Mafia, the Camorra, or the Catouse-Mengant. In this secrecy, which indeed, is a recognized symptom of drug mania, lay Kazmah's security."[160] Kazmah turns out to be a wax dummy, and behind the ancien régime of exotic Orientals and West End playboys, Rohmer reveals the new regime: international drug smuggling rings, usually run by a Machiavellian foreigner, such as Rohmer's most popular creation, the nefarious Dr. Fu Manchu. Such rings had become an increasing focus of popular and legislative attention in Great Britain, following the imposition of restrictions on the import and export of opium and cocaine, which were included in the 1920 Dangerous Drugs Act, bringing British drug policy in line with agreements made in the Versailles Treaty. But fictitious figures such as Fu Manchu conveniently obscured the fact that it was actually Britain that was exporting both opium and morphine to China, via the plantations in India, and that most of the opium that reached Britain was therefore a British product.

Books like *Dope* were very popular and constituted the beginning of the vast literature devoted to narcotics smuggling. In France there were the thrillers of Francis Carco and Pierre Mac Orlan. Later on there were cinematic investigative exposés like *The French Connection* (1969) or literary thrillers like Robert Stone's *Dog Soldiers* (1974), the tale of an "innocent" American journalist in Vietnam who naively tries to smuggle heroin back into the United States.

World War I dealt a fatal blow to Decadent aesthetics. Men returned from the trenches traumatized, angry, disgusted. Narcotic use after the war reflects this fatalism. The hostility of the Surrealist André Breton to drug use had its origins in the fate of his wartime comrade Jacques Vaché, whom he had befriended in a neurology clinic at Nantes in 1916. Vaché was found dead on Jan-

uary 6, 1919, in a hotel room in Nantes, overdosed on opium, apparently a suicide.[161] This led Breton to include a feature in the first *Révolution Surréaliste*
entitled "Suicide: Is It a Solution?" One of those who replied "yes" was the poet
René Crevel, who, along with Jacques Rigaut, another Surrealist narcotic user,
later killed himself. Rigaut was obsessed with suicide, going so far as to open a
"suicide bureau" while he plotted his future death in minute detail. But for the
Surrealists who toed Breton's line, the world of dreams was to be accessed directly, rather than through "false" or "pathological" means such as drugs.

And yet Breton was clearly conflicted on the subject. In the first "Manifesto
of Surrealism" (1924), he noted that "there is every reason to believe that it
[Surrealism] acts on the mind very much as drugs do; like drugs it creates a
certain state of need and can push man to frightful revolts. It also is, if you like,
an artificial paradise, and the taste one has for it derives from Baudelaire's criticism for the same reason as the others . . . In many respects Surrealism occurs
as a *new vice*."[162] But the fact that surrealism was like drugs did not mean that
it endorsed them. Surrealism existed as an alternative to drugs. The same year,
in his preface to the first issue of *The Surrealist Revolution*, Breton spelled this
out: "Surrealism is the place where the enchantments of sleep, alcohol, tobacco, ether, opium, cocaine, and morphine meet; but it is also the breaker of
chains; we don't sleep, we don't drink, we don't smoke, we don't snort, we don't
shoot up, and we dream."[163]

Curiously though, it was two regular opium users, René Crevel and Robert
Desnos, who displayed the most talent for automatic writing, the Surrealists'
celebrated method of exploring the unconscious through the direct and spontaneous recording on paper of unconscious thoughts while the person was in a
trance state. Crevel and Desnos, who were in competition with each other for
the automatic-writing crown and Breton's attentions, both increased their
drug use in the hope that drug-induced altered states would help them create
ever more extravagant examples of "automatisme" while in the trance state. As
with so many aspects of modernism, this supposedly pure method of exploring the unconscious in fact relied on the use of specific material aids such as
drugs to make it effective. When he realized what was happening, Breton,
clearly appalled, terminated the experiments.[164]

The post–World War I writers did not expect visions or pleasant dreams
from opium. They firmly embraced the discourse of addiction that had formed
at the end of the nineteenth century. Aside from the works of Cocteau, it is

rare to find the aesthetic pleasures of narcotic use discussed after World War
I. Writers who used narcotics viewed themselves as social rebels for whom
narcotic use was an entrée to the criminal underworld that sprang up as soon
as narcotics were not legally available. In this sense, there was an accord between the national agencies in Europe and America that issued laws during
the war period restricting opium use, those artists like Breton who opposed
narcotic use, and many of the users themselves, who also saw narcotics as
"bad." "Bad" is of course an aesthetic term as well as a moral one, and as we
shall see, the act of transgression involved in taking illegal substances would
itself become an important part of aesthetic practice.

In France, some of the writers from the opium era, such as Claude Farrère,
spoke out against the new laws. Elsewhere however, with the exception of figures such as Crowley in England, few writers cared. Drugs were simply not a
topic of major concern to most writers of this period. The trajectory of Surrealism moved from dreams to leftist engagement on the streets. It was left to
the "untimely" writers, those whose reputations would blossom only in the
1960s, such as Antonin Artaud, to speak out.

In his early incendiary statements on narcotic use, such as "General Security: The Liquidation of Opium," which was published in the second issue
of *La Révolution Surréaliste* in 1925, Artaud declared the rights of the sick to
pain relief. He acknowledged that opium was a poison or a vice, but argued
that this did not mean that it should not be used when someone was suffering. Moreover, "prohibition, which causes increased public curiosity about
the drug, has so far profited only the pimps of medicine, journalism and literature . . . all the campaigns against narcotics will only succeed in depriving all
the most destitute cases of human suffering, who possess over society certain
inalienable rights, of the solvent for their miseries, a sustenance for them more
wonderful than bread, and the means of finally reentering life . . . Only an idiot . . . would claim that we should let the sick stew in their own sickness."[165]
Although some of Artaud's most revealing writing takes the form of correspondence with doctors and literary critics, he believed that no outsider could
measure or judge the suffering of the sick, whose intimate knowledge of sickness made them the best judges of their condition:

> We whom pain has sent traveling through our souls in search of a
> calm place to cling to, seeking stability in evil as others seeks stabil-

ity in good. We are not mad, we are wonderful doctors, we know the dosage of soul, or sensibility, of marrow, of thought. You must leave us alone, you must leave the sick alone, we ask nothing of mankind, we ask only for the relief of our suffering.[166]

Artaud's work is one long meditation on the suffering and sickness of body and mind, and on the possibility of transforming them. As with many of the writers discussed in this chapter, the cause of Artaud's sickness is unclear, but he suffered from meningitis as a child and it is likely that there was organic damage to his brain as a result. Many of Artaud's descriptions of the lack or absence felt at the heart of his psychic state read like the perception of such damage.

Certainly, Artaud was drawn to narcotic use for pain relief. But as with many of the nineteenth-century Romantics, this pain had a number of levels that reached beyond the physiological or the psychological. Artaud had a gnostic drive to escape from the sufferings of body and mind into some other world. In one of his most extraordinary texts, "Appeal to Youth, Intoxication—Disintoxication" (1934), he says that opium is "the most formidable invention of nothingness that has ever fertilized human sensibilities. But I can do nothing unless I take into myself at moments this culture of nothingness. It is not opium which makes me work but its absence, and in order for me to feel its absence it must from time to time be present."[167] Negative piles up upon negative. Opium is the "invention of nothingness," which is to say that it comes from Novalis' realm of night, the negative realm. But it is the absence of this taste of nothingness that makes Artaud able to work. Artaud goes on: "As for that state outside of life to which opium does not do justice but with which it seems to have some very singular affinities, there are no words to describe it but a violent hieroglyph which designates the impossible encounter of matter with mind."[168] This would be the flash of gnosis itself, impossible because it suggests a moment in which the material world and its negation, its other, that "state outside of life" are one and the same. This, as we have already seen, is the paradox of opium, which is at once a material substance and a producer of transcendental experience that dissolves all materiality. Thus opium becomes the double of the gnosis that Artaud is searching for—a "false" double to be sure, but somehow also a necessary one. Opium, like literature (or the theater he envisaged) is a "violent hieroglyph," a phenomenon at once corporeally inscribed and metaphysical. Thus drugs and writing come together for Artaud, as markers of the same paradox.[169]

Artaud was the apotheosis of Novalis' gnostic speculation on narcotics. In fits of cosmic paranoia he demanded of his friends that they bring him all the opium in Paris. Writing to his former lover Génica Athanassiou from an institution in 1940, he said that she should be ready to kill to procure heroin for him, observing that "you must find heroin at any cost and if necessary be killed in order to bring it to me here . . . if it's difficult to get hold of opium or heroin, it's solely because of me and because it is known that it's the only thing that will give me back my strength and restore me to a state in which I can battle evil."[170] Artaud waged a war against the materialist forces of darkness that he claimed had trapped him in his miserable body. Heroin, returning him to "Night," would allow him to access the power of "that state outside of life" in which he believed truth resided.[171]

Artaud's ideas about narcotics were seconded by Roger Gilbert-Lecomte in his *Monsieur Morphée, empoisonneur public* (*Mister Morpheus, Public Poisoner,* 1930). Gilbert-Lecomte, along with René Daumal and Roger Vailland, was the driving force behind the group Le Grand Jeu, which was briefly allied with the Surrealists in the late 1920s before Breton excommunicated its members for a variety of offenses. All of the Grand Jeu members were narcotics users at one time or other. Gilbert-Lecomte personified the narcotic drive as Mister Morpheus, a faceless mythological figure of Novalis' gnostic night, "before all else, may I present myself as the industrious spirit of death-in-life. I am the master of all natural and induced states which "prefigure" or symbolize death, and therefore, participate in its essence."[172] Like Artaud, Gilbert-Lecomte denounced the absurd drug laws and the journalists who exploited them for stories that do nothing but repeat clichés about the nature of drug use. No drug law, he thought, can stop people who want to commit acts of self-destruction from doing so—one way or another. For Gilbert-Lecomte, drugs provide a method of introducing or manifesting death-in-life in a slow, measured way— an idea that Daumal explored more directly (and rapidly) in his experiments with carbon tetrachloride to induce near-death states. As Michel Random notes, there was no sentimentalization of the pleasures of narcotic use. Gilbert-Lecomte spoke with contempt of the nineteenth-century notion of drugs:

> And now acknowledge this principle, which is the sole justification
> for the taste for drugs: what drug users ask for, consciously or un-

consciously from drugs, is never these dubious sensual delights, this hallucinatory proliferation of fantastic images, this sensual hyper-acuity, stimulation, or all the other nonsense which those who know nothing about "artificial paradises" dream about. It is solely and very simply a change of state, a new climate where their consciousness will be less painful.[173]

Drug use, for the Grand Jeu writers, was not literary in the bourgeois sense of offering a phantasmagoric spectacle, but part of a program of pain relief for the sick. The precise nature of the sickness was left vague—because it was so metaphysical: *to be* was in itself *to be sick*. Gilbert-Lecomte was writing a manifesto for what he, along with everyone else, thought were pathological, aberrant states—but he implicitly universalized them. Drug use became a spiritual practice of asceticism that was again highly gnostic in character. Narcotics became a form of starvation, of withdrawal from the world, of escape.

Gilbert-Lecomte's life was as chaotic and miserable as his views suggest it would be. Vailland and Daumal underwent rehabilitation cures after the demise of Le Grand Jeu in 1930, but Gilbert-Lecomte found it harder to give up morphine. He was arrested in 1937 and 1939 for dealing drugs and spent a month in jail. For a while he lived with a German-Jewish woman who was taken away to a concentration camp during the war and died at Auschwitz. Gilbert-Lecomte moved to cheap hotel rooms and relied on friends to procure supplies of laudanum for him. He died in December 1943 of tetanus.

Artaud and the Grand Jeu writers carried Novalis' plans for narcotic exploration of the gnostic darkness/light through to their gruesome conclusion. Emanating from them is the peculiar stench of abandoned, decaying bodies leaving hardly a trace of any discovered light. The exception is Daumal, who gave up drugs to become a disciple of the Armenian mystic Georges Gurdjieff, but still died far too young.

The post–World War I period saw the rise to prominence of the disintoxication diary and the addiction memoir. These genres predate the war: Léon Daudet's *La lutte* (*The Struggle*, 1907) described the struggle of a tubercular young doctor addicted to morphine, and involved in a relationship with a woman named Nina Sem, morphine and ether addict, Jew—cosmopolitan and decadent. The book features descriptions of Daudet's work as an intern in a German rehabilitation clinic. Such clinics had existed since the 1870s in Germany, when the German "alienists" established a scientific basis for addiction.

Cocteau's *Opium: journal d'une désintoxication* (*Opium: A Detoxification Diary,* 1930), the most famous book of this genre, is an anachronism (but a brilliant one), both in its choice of drug, opium, and in its neo-Decadent aestheticization of the drug, which belong to the pre–World War I years (he calls opium smoking "anti-medical"). But whereas the Decadent celebration of narcotics was fervent, willfully ignorant, and wholly convinced of itself, Cocteau, like the Surrealists, writes in a direct dialogue with the public prosecutors of the new antinarcotic laws, and with the doctors at the hospital where he is being cured as he writes. The law and medical discourse are inescapable in twentieth-century narcotic literature. Cocteau's tone remains somewhat precious; he sneers at the vulgarity of the foolish doctors who wish to cure him, but glows with self-satisfaction when they tell him that he's the most intelligent patient they've ever seen.

Cocteau had been smoking opium on occasion since before World War I, and after the publication of *Opium,* he continued to smoke for the rest of his life.[174] If this seems surprising for the author of a disintoxication book, it should be recalled that most of the classics of narcotics literature, De Quincey's *Confessions,* Burroughs' *Junkie,* and, seven years later, *Naked Lunch* begin or end with claims to a cure that prove to be unfounded. As David Ebin notes sagely regarding this phenomenon:

> The need seems to be there: to make a verbal frame of reference intelligible to themselves as well as to readers not familiar with the drug-experience. It may be that some return to drugs out of a need to comprehend their experience. Some may return out of a need for something else. It may be that all men are familiar with the taste of a pear, but how easy is it to describe what a pear tastes like? How much distance from the action is implied in the use of the word "like"; and how much distance is there in the drug-experience? It may be that words reflect the effort of the writer to be rid of the drug-experience, to put himself outside of it. It may be that this effort is only partially successful and that this explains why in some

writings the sound of two voices is heard simultaneously; that of the observer and that of the experiencer.[175]

There was a rumor that Cocteau had run away from home at the age of fifteen to Marseilles, where he lived in the port and smoked opium with sailors there.[176] In the 1920s, he underwent two cures after extensive periods of opium use, which were apparently connected to the death of his lover, Raymond Radiguet, and his growing friendship with the sinologist and philosopher of the fumerie Louis Laloy. Opium was a regulator for Cocteau, producing an artificial calm in which he could work. But even Cocteau's disintoxication periods were productive—in the clinic visit that produced *Opium,* he also wrote a novel, *Les enfants terribles,* leading some, including Igor Stravinsky, to suggest that the "cure" was nothing more than a ruse to allow him to do more work.

Like those of the other interwar writers, many of Cocteau's meditations on opium are related to death. "Opium leads the organism towards death in a euphoric mood."[177] "Everything one achieves in life, even love, occurs in an express train racing towards death. To smoke opium is to get out of the train while it is still moving. It is to concern oneself with something other than life or death."[178]

Opium equals excess: time squandered luxuriously. Like much of the narcotic literature, *Opium* is an attempt to find value or meaning in a period of time that has been "wasted." Cocteau moves between defiant affirmation of the pleasures of opium and regretful acknowledgment that it is time to stop taking the drug. The open, aphoristic form of *Opium* suggests the difficulty of drawing anything other than the most provisional, contingent conclusions during a period of disintoxication. The book is "a wound in slow motion."[179] Time is measured out in terse, aphoristic paragraphs, each of which seems to be written by a different person.

A final key French interwar narcotics book is Pierre Drieu la Rochelle's *Le feu follet* (*Will o' the Wisp,* 1931), a gloomy account of the last day of a drug addict wandering the streets of Paris. During World War II, Jean-Paul Sartre accused Drieu la Rochelle of seeking to escape reality in opium, because he assumed that the book was autobiographical. In fact, when he was writing the novella Drieu probably had in mind his friend Jacques Rigaut, who had died following a period of narcotic addiction in 1929. Drieu, who had flirted with Dadaism and Surrealism in the early 1920s before allying himself with the fas-

Figure 2. "Through the mouth of his wound." Drawing by Jean Cocteau, 1928, from *Opium*.

cists in the 1930s, wrote a series of novels denouncing the decadence of post–World War I France. In all of these books, deviant sexuality is portrayed as the primary symptom of decadence: "sterility, masturbation, homosexuality are spiritual sicknesses. Alcoholism and drugs are the first steps that lead to this failure of the imagination, to this decadence of the creative spirit, when a man prefers to submit rather than to assert himself."[180] In other words, drug addiction is a sign of sexual corruption. *Will o' the Wisp* is often very funny, in a nasty, sardonic way that anticipates Burroughs' novels. It oozes with loathing for the decadence of modern France. The protagonist is a young addict called Alain, who is in debt, has no regular employment, and supports himself by taking money from wealthy American women. One of his friends, Dubourg, observes that Alain has turned his back on life in disgust. While he agrees with Alain that there is plenty in modern life to be revolted by, he sees the Romantic attitude toward narcotics as a trap:

> To yield to this disposition was to fall back into a protestation of mysticism, into the adoration of death. Drug addicts are the mystics of a materialist age, who, no longer having the strength to animate things and sublimate them into symbols, undertake the inverted task of reducing them, wearing them down and eating them away until they reach a core of nothingness. They sacrifice to a symbolism of darkness to combat a sun-fetishism which they hate because it hurts their tired eyes.[181]

Drug addicts are the modern mystics because they attempt to negate the world without any counterbalancing affirmation. Breton affirmed "the marvelous" before turning to revolutionary socialism; Drieu, already quite the crypto-fascist, affirms a force, whether sexual, will-driven, or cosmic, that can dominate things. With narcotics, revolt turns in on itself in an act of negation that sends it toward the death-drive, the zero state, a life spent sharing cheap hotel rooms with Nietzsche's weird guest, nihilism. Even a solar fetishist such as Georges Bataille remained caught in this "labor of the negative" until after World War II. To abandon the negative in the interwar years meant either fascism or revolutionary socialism, even for those who were constitutionally unsuited to either. Neither ideology had much use for drugs, except as further evidence of the degeneracy of modern culture, ground upon which to build their own positivist claims to health.

By the end of World War II, the memory of the legal nineteenth-century drug culture was long gone; the addicts were now aging or dead. And yet, at that

very time, there was a flurry of newspaper articles and novels describing a return of the narcotic menace in a new form, that of the delinquent youth: in the
United States Nelson Algren's *The Man with the Golden Arm* (1949), in England Raymond Thorp's *Viper: The Confessions of a Drug Addict* (1956), along
with the pulps.[182] This literature was similar to the one that flourished in
France at the end of the nineteenth century, but where the principal focus of
the French books was the moral decay of formerly decent citizens, the new exploitation literature featured addicts as a biological type—as though Lombroso's lessons in criminology had been swallowed whole and had become
accepted dogma. The postwar addict has always been sick; in fact he often has
no history whatsoever; he's a type of animal or, if you like, the incarnation of
evil—a "fiend."

The focus on addiction itself was something new. The earlier French literature discussed addiction and formulated the notion of the addict as a type, but
for the most part the dissipation of the addict was marked by a series of symptomatic acts of degeneracy, whether they were attractions to Symbolist poetry,
crime, or lesbianism. The word "hooked," ubiquitous in postwar America, indicates a situation where addiction itself is the crime. One of the functions of
this literature was to dramatize the victimless crime of addiction through a
physiognomy of evil in which the degeneration of the addict's body became a
symptom of addiction, which became in its turn symptomatic of the addict's
criminal nature. Mental illness functioned in a number of often contradictory
ways within this paradigm: the "psychopathic" nature of the addict that psychiatrists like the post–World War I narcotics policy architect Lawrence Kolb
referred to could be used to argue against the notion that addicts were criminals who should be put in jail, while at the same time being touted as offering
further "symptoms" of the deviance of the addict.[183]

Among the proliferation of pulp narcotics paperbacks was one issued by
Ace Paperbacks in 1953 called *Junkie—Confessions of an Unredeemed Drug Addict,* by William Lee. It was published back to back with Maurice Helbrant's
autobiography, *Narcotics Agent* (1941), so as to diplomatically present "both
sides of the story." A coolly observed account of a young man's initiation into
"junk," beginning with a wartime connection who leads him into the hustler's
culture around 42nd Street in New York, the book also contains some passages
that might have confused the average pulp reader: descriptions of insect-like
men loitering around junkies and sucking their energy to transmit to un-

known masters, speculations on telepathy, notes on the orgasm-death of a hanged man. *Junkie* was in fact the literary debut of William S. Burroughs, a Harvard-educated man from a wealthy midwestern family for whom narcotics provided a gateway into the criminal underworld. For Burroughs, junk was "a way of life," which came complete with its own language (the book has a glossary of hipster junky expressions) and rituals: this way of life was the morally neutral inversion of the pulp and medical depictions of the addict. As with most of the post–World War I literature about narcotics, the scenarios described in *Junkie* were more the product of the antinarcotic laws than of the drug itself. Junk was a way of life, and an addict was a type of person rather than a person suffering from an addiction, because narcotic use had been separated off from the rest of life, so that, where once a user would simply go to a pharmacy and purchase laudanum like any other commodity, the user now had to adopt a whole new regimen of activities in order to purchase the same substance: finding a dealer, evading narcotics agents, looking out for stool pigeons, taking to petty crime or dealing in order to pay for the narcotics, and so on.

The Beats appropriated the addict or junkie into their outsider mythology. Allen Ginsberg's *Howl* (1957), for example, begins with "I saw the best minds of my generation destroyed by madness, starving hysterical naked, dragging themselves through the negro streets at dawn looking for an angry fix/ angelheaded hipsters burning for the ancient heavenly connection to the starry dynamo in the machinery of night."[184] In a word, with the Beats, the rebellious gnostic narcotic user, craving the night again, becomes a *saint.* This apparent canonization of the junkie by Ginsberg, who was not himself a regular narcotics user, is best understood in the context of the later sections of *Howl*, in which the holy madness of the first section is healed through a peyote-inspired vision of universal compassion. But it is likely that such subtleties were lost on most people—including the Beats themselves.[185]

In *Junkie*, Burroughs presented addiction within a scientific framework (albeit one that would not necessarily have been acceptable to doctors at the time). Addiction was physiological, a cellular craving. In *Naked Lunch* (1959), Burroughs extended the model into speculative realms, where narcotic addiction becomes a powerful metaphor for the processes of control that order and run our societies. Burroughs speaks of "the algebra of need." Every place in the human body where there is communication, exchange between the inside

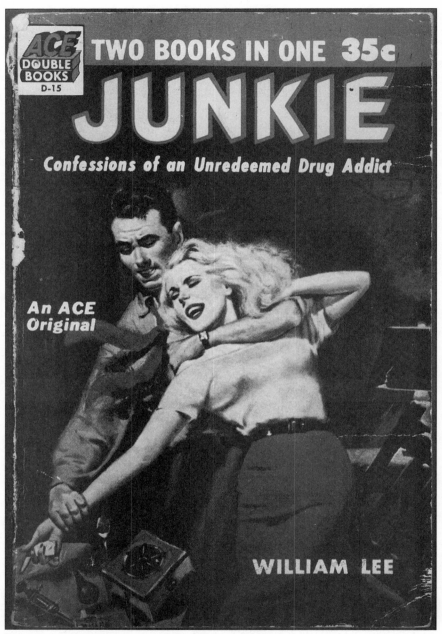

Figure 3. *Junkie,* by William Lee (William Burroughs), 1953.

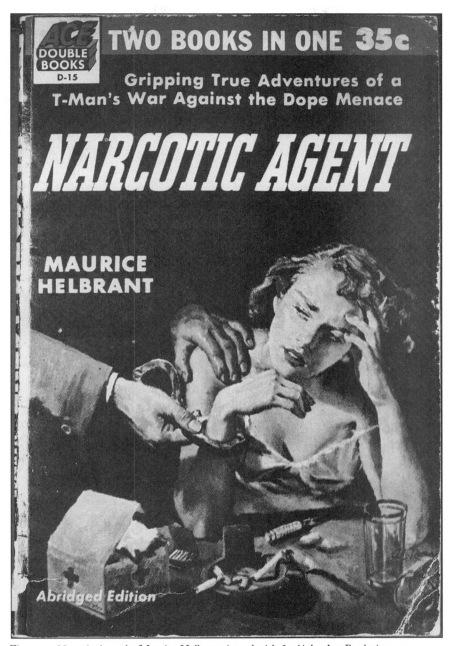

Figure 4. *Narcotic Agent,* by Maurice Helbrant, issued with *Junkie* by Ace Books in 1953.

and outside, is a potential place of addiction. Everywhere where desire exists, where the organism wants something, is a potential node of control that can be incorporated into an economic structure.

Between *Junkie* and *Naked Lunch* there lies an abyss. *Junkie* ends in Mexico, where Burroughs moved in 1949 to avoid standing trial for possessing narcotics, a charge that carried a minimum two-year sentence in the Louisiana state prison if he was convicted. Burroughs left Mexico in November 1952, after shooting his wife dead in the forehead in a drunken game of William Tell (note that the death was alcohol, not junk, related). He finally settled in Tangier, where he lived quietly, using prescription narcotics and writing the comic routines that would later be incorporated into *Naked Lunch*, until the political climate in Morocco made it increasingly difficult to obtain drugs there and Burroughs decided to kick the habit.

Burroughs made contact with addiction specialists in the summer of 1956, in particular Dr. John Dent, a British doctor who played an important role in the study of alcohol and substance abuse in the United Kingdom from the mid-1930s to the 1960s.[186] Dent had first introduced the apomorphine treatment as an aversion therapy for alcoholism in the mid-1930s. Throughout his literary career, Burroughs proselytized for Dent's apomorphine cure, even though apomorphine never was accepted as a mainstream addiction treatment; methadone, a synthetic opiate introduced in the late 1950s, was to fulfill the same function, though, unlike apomorphine, methadone offered maintenance rather than a cure. Burroughs himself quit narcotic use many times, the longest time being the period he lived in London, from 1960 to 1973 (though there were relapses). He began taking methadone in 1980 in New York, and remained on it until his death in August 1997.[187]

For Burroughs, part of the attraction of apomorphine and of Dent's work in general was its broadly antipsychological thrust. A number of psychologists had entered into an alliance with the state in pathologizing the drug user and in providing a medical justification for antinarcotic legislation. While the interwar writers more or less internalized this model of narcotic use, Burroughs and those who came after him were highly critical of it—the nefarious Dr. Benway in *Naked Lunch* works at the Ministry of Mental Hygiene and Prophylaxis, where he "cures" homosexuals. Burroughs saw addiction within a biological framework and defined it as a cellular craving, a disease of exposure similar to a viral infection, rather than a disease of character. Timothy Leary, who was a professor of clinical psychology in the 1950s, also rejected psychotherapy in favor of neurochemistry.

This alliance between literature and the antipsychological trends in postwar psychiatry, a very fragile, illegitimate one, can be observed in the structure of *Naked Lunch*. The book begins with a personal explanation of narcotic use (accompanied by trial testimonies testifying to the book's value), and ends with a letter to the *Journal of Addiction* (which Dent edited at the time the book was written) describing the author's experiences with various methods of narcotics withdrawal, and an "atrophied preface" retroactively instructing the reader how to navigate the nonlinear shape of the book. Psychiatry and personal testimony provide a protective shell for the cauldron of excess within the main part of the book. Burroughs claims that the sex-death passages he has written are Swiftian satire about capital punishment, but this is merely a rationalization. *Naked Lunch* contains passages of raw, uncensored, Dionysian excess: funny, frightening, beyond reason. As in Bataille's postwar writings published in Paris at around the same time, the limited, controlled economy proposed by both capitalism and communism in the shadow of the ruins of World War II is illuminated in its ferocious, destructive aspect as part of a general economy of unlimited consumption, creation, and destruction. Narcotics provide a path into the delimited spaces of cosmic excess, but are also, as McLuhan suggests, an anesthetic that blocks the full realization of that same excess. The "junkie" is an outsider, a no-man in flight from society and its rules. At the same time, narcotic use becomes an identity, with a new set of rules for behavior and action that exerts its own discipline (scoring, fixing, kicking, going to jail).

The pleasure of narcotic literature lies in the imposition of a highly predictable grid of activity on utter chaos. This is the function of the diary (day by day), of Marlowe's alphabetization of her notes on heroin, of De Quincey's listing of the pleasures or pains of opium, or of the journey to hell and back narrative that dominates the genre, however much its authors disguise it with amoral posturing. At a micro-level we find the same thing. The narcotic literature is full of highly precise descriptions of the act of scoring, fixing, kicking, and so forth

> I had $^1/_{16}$ ounce of junk with me. I figured this was enough to taper off, and I had a reduction schedule carefully worked out. It was supposed to take twelve days. I had the junk in solution, and in another

bottle distilled water. Every time I took a dropper of solution out to use it, I put the same amount of distilled water in the junk solution bottle. Eventually I would be shooting plain water. This method is well known to all junkies.[188]

The attention to detail suggests the sublime: a frame, in this case of quantity, scientific precision, imposed on the immense, the overwhelming, the terrible, so as to make it pleasurable. Even the personality of the junkie has sublime qualities. The arrogance of much of the narcotic literature—De Quincey's and Marlowe's repeated references to their education, Cocteau's feelings of superiority over his doctors, the obsession of the jazz musician and narcotics user Art Pepper with his beauty and talent in his autobiography, *Straight Life*—serves the same function: to provide a pretty frame for chaos. The same theory could easily be applied to supermodels and heroin chic in the 1980s and 1990s. Indeed, the narcotics literature is full of scenes in which first-time users look at themselves in the mirror and are struck by their own beauty.[189] Allen Ginsberg said of Burroughs that what junk did for him was give him some subject matter. This was also true of De Quincey, who was floundering as a writer when he turned to writing about his opium use. For all drugs' ability to disrupt and dissolve the ego, the temporary nature of narcotic use (of all drug use) is such that it inevitably involves a regrouping of the ego. Burroughs suggests something similar when he says that the youthfulness of addicts can be attributed to the repeated cycle of shrinking and expanding of the organism, and the discarding of junk-dependent cells during withdrawal. He speculates that if one could continuously kick, one would live forever.

The counterpoint to this sublime ordering is arbitrariness, Marlowe's A–Z organization of her reminiscences of heroin use or Burroughs's "method" of composing *Naked Lunch*:

> When Paul Bowles visited [Burroughs'] room in the Muniria, the floor was covered with hundreds of yellow foolscap pages. Many of them had been stepped on; you could see sole and heel marks on them. They were covered with rat droppings and bits of cheese sandwiches. Obviously, Burroughs ate at the same table where he typed. "What is all this?" asked Bowles, who, being meticulously neat, was put off by clutter. "That's what I'm working on," Burroughs replied. "Do you make copies before you throw it on the

floor?" "Nope." "Then how are you going to read it?" "Oh, I figure it'll be legible."[190]

It was left to the speed-freak typist Jack Kerouac and the arch-organizer Allen Ginsberg to assemble the final text of *Naked Lunch*. This arbitrariness is no accident, however: it is strategic and spectacular. All displays of entropy, of negligence and debris, serve to provide an intense backdrop for opium-based transcendence. Burroughs in particular is enamored of those moments in which all meaning appears to drain from a human form, and this lack of meaning itself becomes the basis for the junkie's experience, of himself and others: "Doolie sick was an unnerving sight. The envelope of personality was gone, dissolved by his junk-hungry cells. Viscera and cells, galvanized into a loathsome insect-like activity seemed on the point of breaking through the surface. His face was blurred, unrecognizable, at the same time shrunken and tumescent."[191] In *Naked Lunch* human beings are constantly melting down into blobs of protoplasm as the narcotic craving triggers a Lamarckian transformation of their bodies to better adapt to the new reality. The material world is a repugnant place, and its repulsive qualities are actively cultivated, so as to justify gnostic flight from the trap of corporeality and all that comes with it.

Narcotics addiction, for Burroughs, is merely the crudest example of a matrix of techniques of control that addiction to being human, to being itself, makes possible. This would include language and literature. In *Nova Express* (1964), a book in which Burroughs used the arbitrariness of the "cut-up" montage method devised by Brion Gysin to break through these deeper addictions, he declares: "What scared you all into time? Into body? Into shit? I will tell you: *'the word.'* Alien Word *'the.'* *'The'* word of Alien Enemy imprisons *'thee'* in Time. In Body. In Shit. Prisoner, come out. The great skies are open. I Hassan I Sabbah *rub out the word forever.*"[192]

Much of the most important recent writing about narcotics is necessarily concerned with crime or time spent in institutions—such as the brutal, poetic first-person account of Lexington's Federal Narcotics Hospital in Clarence Cooper's *The Farm* (1967), and Art Pepper's *Straight Life*, an autobiographical roam from the U.S. Public Health Service Hospital at Fort Worth to jail in San Quentin and the rehabilitation community of Synanon. But it would be wrong to think that only the underworld defined narcotic experience and writing even after World War II. In the nineteenth century, women were more likely than men to be narcotics users, and a number of female writers have written about their narcotic use, often in milieus very different from those considered typical of the period.[193] Accounts of narcotic addiction by women proliferated in the twentieth century. In America, *No Bed of Roses* (1930), by the anonymous O.W., was the first best-selling drug memoir describing a familiar trajectory from cocaine use to morphine addiction. The French pop writer Françoise Sagan described her disintoxication from morphine in the Cocteau-inspired *Toxique* (1962).

Several twentieth-century female writers were addicted to morphine in a medical setting—the most important is Anna Kavan (1901–1968). Kavan was the daughter of an English physician who became addicted to heroin in her twenties (in the 1920s) at a time when recreational use of narcotics was still quite popular among the upper classes in Britain.[194] Because the British version of the drug laws allowed a physician to prescribe narcotics for maintenance of a habit, Kavan, who was not lacking in funds, was able to take heroin for most of her life without being exposed to the black market and the law, especially after she developed a friendship with Dr. Karl Bluth, who advised her to legally register with the Home Office as a heroin addict. Interestingly, when Kavan died at the age of sixty-seven, many people assumed she had died of an overdose—in fact she died of a heart attack.[195]

The short story "High in the Mountains," from Kavan's *Julia and the Bazooka* (1970), begins with a homage to amphetamines, which allow the narrator to win a tennis tournament. Kavan contrasts the vulgarity and social disruption of alcohol and cigarettes with those of pharmaceuticals: "What I do never affects anyone else. I don't behave in an embarrassing way. And a clean white powder is not repulsive; it looks pure, it glitters, the pure white crystals sparkle like snow."[196] These snowlike crystals are the key to Kavan's masterpiece, her science fiction novel *Ice* (1967), which never actually mentions heroin, or any other opiates. It is the tale of an ice age that engulfs a woman, a marriage, and a world. The ice grows both inside and outside—in the woman's imagination and in the outside world, where her naked body manifests itself in/as the snow. The "cool" of narcotics, their ability to contrast the harshness of the exterior world with the glowing self-sufficient body of the narcotics user is the source of a much more intimate apocalypse than Burroughs', but one no less extreme. "Outside there was only the deadly cold, the frozen vacuum of an ice age, life reduced to mineral crystals; but here, in our lighted room, we were safe and warm."[197]

Images of projection and introjection abound in Kavan's work. In "Among the Lost Things" it is a "new star" that is responsible for the narrator's metamorphosis into a genderless being. In other stories, houses and cars regulate an environment that is always threatening to turn dark, cold, and stormy. *Ice* obsessively depicts the trope of freezing over in a linear narrative that continually loops back to the same scene—an ever deeper entrapment in the material world, through which gnostic, narcotic pulses of luminescence move.

As Kavan notes concerning herself in *Julia and the Bazooka*, "she is most unlike the popular notion of a drug addict. Nobody could call her vicious."[198] But even so, imagery of violence and self-destruction (the bazooka, of course, is her syringe) remains as prevalent in her work as it is in Burroughs'. In the short story "High in the Mountains," she summarizes her situation: "I know I've got a death-wish. I've never enjoyed my life, I've never liked people. I love the mountains because they are the negation of life, indestructible, inhuman, untouchable, indifferent as I want to be."[199]

The "pathos" that accompanies the transformation of the naive exuberance of the first-time opiate user into the bitter world-weariness of the recovering addict has kept the narcotic literature going for two hundred years now; Novalis formulated the concept of gnostic revolt and then died before he had the chance to destroy himself using it. Others since have unfortunately managed to align theory and practice more tightly. The fact that people still become addicted to narcotics, after generation upon generation of writings of addicts, suggests that for many people, only personal testimony wrought through experience leads to knowledge.

But even this is far from assured—it may be merely the humanist promise that literature appears to offer to the drug user: that of profiting from his or her experience. What if this is not possible? What if the promise that literature offers is nothing more than the flip side of the transcendental promise made by drugs? When the attempt to escape the plastic fakeness of the modern world into the real through drugs fails, one turns to literature to reincorporate the failure of the transcendental into a narrative of worldly experience. But what if worldly experience itself is nothing more than another mirage, another strategy in the modern subject's desperate search for a means of validating itself? This would explain the otherwise puzzling fact that many authors cannot abandon the discursive repertoire of the addict, and his or her outsider status, even long after they have abandoned the drug itself—or, in many cases, even if they never took the drug in the first place.

There has been no major advance in the narcotic literature since the 1950s— or even the 1930s. The same genres, confession, addiction, and disintoxication narratives, continue to be written. New generations of people become addicted to opiates, in either medical or recreational settings; these settings are diverse and often interesting in their own right (the jazz scene, the Lower East Side, Harvard, Edinburgh in the 1980s, milieus special to women or minorities), but the story is the same one.[200] Pleasure, suffering, redemption, and/or loss. I am not saying this because I think Burroughs and Cocteau are better, more original, or more important than recent authors who have explored narcotic addiction, such as Irvine Welsh, Jim Carroll, and Ann Marlowe. But we have heard the same story over and over again for more than fifty years. The reason is partly that the situation of addicts is roughly the same as it has been since World War I, both pharmacologically (no new opiates of any note, except for methadone) and socially (opiates remain forbidden), with minor variations in how the state treats addicts. And partly the reason is that, as Burroughs says, there's not much variation in narcotic addiction itself. All the action comes from the state's method of dealing with the problem. "*I Don't Want To Hear Any More Tired Old Junk Talk And Junk Con.* . . . The same things said a million times and more and there is no point in saying anything because *NOTHING Ever Happens* in the junk world."[201] All the italics and capitals should alert the reader that the author himself is struggling desperately when he says that, but the truth of the statement remains. And after writing *Naked Lunch* Burroughs did move on from writing about narcotic addiction.

Ann Marlowe makes a similar point in her memoir *How To Stop Time* (1999):

> Dope is antifiction. A novel about heroin is weighed down by the inherent consistency of everyone's experience of the drug in a way that a novel about love or revenge is not; those experiences are universal but not identical. Few writers are skilled enough to overcome this obstacle. So heroin demands nonfiction, memoir, truth-telling, but even here the trick is to outwit the drug, to introduce what the drug will not: surprise.[202]

But is nonfiction about narcotics really less prone to this repetition than fiction? The only difference is that the "truth" that nonfiction claims to speak legitimizes and adds a little more pathos to the act of repetition. At any rate, the state has been much more inventive than writers in producing surprises for those who wish to take narcotics.

The narcotic "darkness" that Voltaire confronted on his deathbed is ancient; it was already apparent in ancient Greece, in the poppies growing by the banks of the Lethe, the river of death. But the meaning of this darkness, with its resonances of painless sleep and death, was transformed by the Enlightenment and the Industrial Revolution. When Voltaire tasted the narcotic draught, he felt himself invaded by that ever-present darkness and struggled against it, as though it was a newly discovered alien force, roaming the landscape of Enlightenment Europe. Twenty years later, when Novalis wrote *Hymns to the Night*, the "alien" nature of the narcotic force was already incorporated into the Romantic rebellion against the profane world of science and industry. Writers celebrated the gnostic darkness of opium as part of an aesthetic revolt against rationalist, scientific force, even though opium was made available to them by the very forces that they decried. Pathologists and states reinforced and developed this view of narcotics as alien, and created laws and institutions whose apparent purpose was to neutralize or eradicate their darkness, but whose real effect was to institutionalize it. This new institutionalized darkness of rehabilitation clinics, prisons, addicts, and narcotics agents was itself a highly aestheticized one—and was taken up as such by writers. Clarence Cooper describes his institutional time as being done in "Dante's County jail."[203] The cover of the recent junkie best seller *Trainspotting* (1993), by the Scottish writer Irvine Welsh, has refined many of these elements still further. Printed in black and white on a metallic silver paper, the cover features a photo of two men wearing skull masks, the epitome of "death in life" as Coleridge and Gilbert-Lecomte called it, while a quote from "Rebel Inc." proclaims that the book "deserves to sell more copies than the Bible," thus once more linking opiate use to a transcendence of religion through an act of negation, a performance of death.

Far from acting as a deterrent to narcotic use, as groups like the Partnership for a Drug-Free America assume, the linking of narcotics and death has been commodified, and is now packaged in the belief that the association is attractive to many people. Opium is, and always has been, a product of the marketplace. As the volume of opium imported and exported from Europe increased in the nineteenth century, and the new knowledge of alkaloids and industrial refinement techniques resulted in highly concentrated, potent products such as morphine and heroin being sold, a crisis developed in which the marketplace threatened to destroy itself. Writers acted as an avant-garde for this market, as they have for many others—packaging the pleasures and dangers of excessive narcotic use in their formulations of the sublime. Without feeding this brutal machine any further by vilifying addicts and writers, or by creating new forbidden territories that become the site of new ecstatic narcotic transgressions, we must ask whether this particular construction of narcotic use serves any purpose at this stage of the game. If I add the word "positive" or "real" or "useful" to the word "purpose" in the last sentence, I immediately fall back into the clutches of the gnostic machine, and the necessary opposition that rises up to meet the endless claims for the real, the useful, and the positive that are made in our cultures. It has been the function of literature, for better or for worse, to articulate this opposition for the last two hundred years, in part through the vehicle of narcotic transcendence.

How do we avoid this trap? Not necessarily by avoiding narcotics—or literature. In fact, opiates are used for pain relief all the time in hospitals, without any reference to criminality or gnostic vision, as was also the case for the most part in pre-Enlightenment Europe. But the goal of gnosis, which has been so solidly connected to opiates, by writers, legal authorities, and other experts, will not go away either. We must acknowledge this goal, as Burroughs does repeatedly in his "post"-narcotic period, by a call for a proliferation of alternative methods of attaining gnosis: "This is the space age. Time to look beyond this run-down radioactive cop-rotten planet. Time to look beyond this animal body. Remember anything that can be done chemically can be done in other ways."[204]

THE VOICE OF THE BLOOD

Anesthetics and Literature

A young man, a Mr. Davy, at Dr. Beddoes, who has applied himself much to chemistry, has made some discoveries of importance, and enthusiastically expects wonders will be performed by
the use of certain gases, which inebriate in the most delightful
manner, having the oblivious effects of Lethe, and at the same time
giving the rapturous sensations of the Nectar of the Gods! Pleasure
even to madness is the consequence of this draught. But faith,
great faith, is I believe necessary to produce any effect upon the
drinkers, and I have seen some of the adventurous philosophers
who sought in vain for satisfaction in the bag of Gaseous Oxyd
and found nothing but a sick stomach and a giddy head.

MARIA EDGEWORTH,
letter to Margaret Ruxton, May 26, 1799

In 1799, the young Humphry Davy, who worked with
Thomas Beddoes at his Medical Pneumatic Institution on the outskirts of
Bristol, conducted a series of experiments using nitrous oxide, also known as
laughing gas, on a group of volunteers and patients, including the poets Coleridge and Southey. Coleridge's own descriptions of taking nitrous oxide are
rather reserved, but there is evidence that his 1799 trip to Germany, in which
he was converted to the Idealist philosophy of Kant and Fichte, was not lost on
Davy, who described his experience after inhaling nitrous oxide for more than

an hour and a quarter in terms that seemed to provide experimental verifica-
tion of the new philosophy:

> I felt a sense of tangible extension highly pleasurable in every limb;
> my visible impressions were dazzling, and apparently magnified, I
> heard distinctly every sound in the room, and was perfectly aware
> of my situation. By degrees, as the pleasurable sensations increased,
> I lost all connection with external things; trains of vivid visible im-
> ages rapidly passed through my mind, and were connected with
> words in such a manner, as to produce perceptions perfectly novel.
> I existed in a world of newly connected and newly modified ideas.
> I theorised—I imagined that I made discoveries. When I was
> awakened from this trance . . . I exclaimed to Dr. Kinglake, "Noth-
> ing exists but thoughts!—the universe is composed of impressions,
> ideas, pleasures and pains!"[1]

I have already suggested that the transcendental impulse, the desire to go beyond matter and mind and experience the whole, forms one of the principal
reasons that people take drugs. This definition of "transcendental" would have
been unacceptable to Kant, for whom transcendence was by definition *beyond*
experience. It was a quality of mind—indeed it defined mind in its separation
from the world and from objects, and in its orientation toward them. Although Kant claimed that the transcendental, in the sense of the divine, was
accessible through faith, by positing it as something beyond experience, he essentially thought it out of existence.[2]

Can something that exists disappear merely because a persuasive but incon-
clusive argument is made for its nonexistence—an argument that ends up being believed by a number of people? How would such a something manifest
itself to a group of people who had already refuted, to their own satisfaction,
its existence? The case of transcendental experience is an instructive one in
this regard—and of decisive importance for understanding what "drugs" are in
the modern world. Ever since Kant, we have struggled with the problem or
question of the possibility of transcendental experience. And yet even at the
very moment that Kant boldly claimed to eradicate it, we find Davy, a young
Englishman who has just learned about Kantian philosophy from his friend
Samuel Taylor Coleridge, claiming to experience, by taking a drug, precisely
that structure of Idealist thought which denies the very validity of experience
as a trigger for transcendental states.

The anesthetics, with their ability to shut down the body and mind in a single swift movement when administered at the appropriate doses, resonate in a special way with the notion of transcendence, a way that was apparent almost from the moment that Kant's thought began to spread itself throughout the world at the beginning of the nineteenth century. The literature on drugs is full of doubles, doppelgängers. In this chapter, we shall see how successive generations of philosophers and writers, grappling with the Kantian worldview, became acquainted with these substances, and experienced the strange double of the transcendental—or perhaps *the thing itself*—an experience made all the more puzzling, and perhaps humiliating, because of the anesthetics' incredible utility and ubiquity as a source of pain relief in surgery after the mid-nineteenth century.

As the historian of anesthesia A. J. Wright has shown, the discovery of nitrous oxide's psychoactive properties was the result of a complicated set of connections between the arts and sciences in the second half of the eighteenth century.[3] The self-taught chemist and nonconformist minister Joseph Priestley had conducted experiments on the effects of inhaling various kinds of "airs," including oxygen (which he discovered) and nitrous oxide, beginning in the 1770s. He was a member of a loose alliance of intellectuals known as the Lunar Society, which included James Watt, Erasmus Darwin, and Josiah Wedgwood, that was involved at least peripherally in most of the scientific and technological activities in England in the eighteenth century.

Priestley's work was continued by his fellow Lunar Society member Thomas Beddoes, a physician and political radical with a strong interest in chemistry. Beddoes was married to the sister of Maria Edgeworth, a gothic novelist who introduced Beddoes to literary circles. Coleridge and Beddoes both moved to Bristol in 1794 and became involved in politics, with Beddoes contributing material to Coleridge's newspaper *The Watchman*. Meanwhile, Beddoes planned an institute to continue Priestley's work on "airs" and to pursue Brunonian therapy—Beddoes being the English editor of Brown's *Elementa Medicinae*.

The idea of a gas as something composed of simple substances was a novel one at that time. Johann Baptista Van Helmont, one of the founders of the science of chemistry, had coined the word "gas" in the seventeenth century,

taking it from the Greek word *khos,* meaning chaos, but Priestley did not discover oxygen until the mid-1770s. Davy was taking a leap into the chemical
unknown when he inhaled oxygen and nitrous oxide. Others warned of terrible dangers: an American scientist named Samuel Mitchill had written a didactic poem, *The Doctrine of Septon* (1797), in the style of Erasmus Darwin,
denouncing nitrous oxide and other nitrogen compounds as causes of contagious disease. Mitchill spoke of "Grim Septon, arm'd with power to inter-
vene / And disconnect the animal machine."[4] But for Davy, the possibility
that these "aeriform fluids . . . presented a chance of useful agency" was tantalizing enough for him to proceed.[5]

The Pneumatic Institution was opened in 1799 with Davy at the helm. Nitrous oxide therapy was given for treatment of paralysis, rheumatism, and depression, as well as for more experimental purposes. Robert Southey, one of
the first participants, wrote to his brother in July of that year:

> Oh Tom! such a gas has Davy discovered, the gaseous oxyd! Oh
> Tom! I have had some; it made me laugh and tingle in every toe and
> finger tip. Davy has actually invented a new pleasure, for which lan-
> guage has no name. Oh, Tom! I am going for more this evening; it
> makes one strong, and so happy! so gloriously happy! and without
> any after-debility, but, instead of it, increased strength of mind and
> body. Oh, excellent air-bag! Tom, I am sure the air in heaven must
> be this wonder-working gas of delight![6]

Southey's rapture about nitrous oxide diminished rapidly, and in his contribution to Davy's 580-page book, *Researches, Chemical and Philosophical, Chiefly
concerning Nitrous Oxide, or Dephlogisticated Nitrous Air, and Its Respiration,*
published the following year, he noted that "the quantity which I formerly
breathed, would now destroy me."[7] Indeed, many of those involved with the
experiments, including Davy himself, concluded that used in excess, the gas
could prove to be toxic. Some biographers have concluded that Davy's relatively short lifespan (he died at the age of forty-eight) can be attributed to the
effects of his extensive self-experimentation with nitrous oxide. Coleridge's
and Davy's publisher in Bristol, Joseph Cottle, noted that "the laughable and
diversified effects produced by this new gas on different individuals quite ex-
orcised philosophical gravity and converted the laboratory into the region of
hilarity and relaxation."[8] He observed that there were no cures and that pa-

tients quickly became disenchanted with the wonder gas and had to be paid to continue taking it.[9] Experimentation with psychoactive substances in Davy's circle was not confined to anesthetics: Coleridge, in imitation of Davy, spoke of studying the effects of bhang (hashish) and other plant extracts, while a number of people associated with the institute were addicted to opium, which was liberally prescribed by Erasmus Darwin and Beddoes, among others.

During this period, Coleridge was fascinated by chemistry, which he saw as an important part in the "divine scheme" by which "all can become each and each all."[10] He dreamed of writing a master philosophical epic poem (never written) about the medieval alchemist Michael Scott, conceived in self-consciously Faustian fashion, about how Scott's lust for power through knowledge led him to witchcraft, where "he learns the chemistry of exciting drugs and exploding powders" and has an encounter with the devil.[11] Later, Coleridge asked for Davy's assistance in setting up a chemical laboratory with Wordsworth, and attended Davy's lectures hoping to find fresh metaphors for his poetry.[12] Coleridge told Davy, "As far as words go, I have become a formidable chemist."[13]

Chemistry was a popular metaphor among European intellectuals at the beginning of the nineteenth century. The emerging new science resonated for them as computers or the Internet do at the end of the twentieth century, and provided a model for understanding what mind or poetry or words were, by reducing them to sets of "elements," as Kant had done with his categories. At the same time, writers like Novalis and Coleridge offered their own contributions to chemistry, by viewing it from the perspective of poetry. Anticipating the advances in organic chemistry that would come later in the nineteenth century, Coleridge sniffed, "I find all power and vital attributes to depend on modes of arrangement, and that Chemistry throws not even a distant rushlight glimmer upon this subject."[14]

Literary experimentation with drugs had its birth in the friendship between Davy and Coleridge and the momentary possibility of a rapprochement between experimental chemistry, German Idealism, and Romantic poetics. The first writers to discuss drug experiences were all familiar with the new German Idealist philosophy, which revealed a hitherto ignored intellectual significance in the altered states that drugs produced and provided a vocabulary for describing those states. The philosophical dictum that "the world is nothing but

thoughts," announced by Berkeley earlier in the eighteenth century, but sys-
tematized in various ways by Kant, Fichte, Schelling, and Hegel, became a
lived experience for De Quincey and Coleridge in the dream worlds that
opium and hashish opened up, and for Davy, in the total shutdown of sensory
perception that anesthetics like nitrous oxide offered. The German Idealists
themselves had little interest in this application of drugs.[15] It was the British
Romantics, empiricists at heart, who sought out experimental models for the
study of the transcendental subject, whether it actually existed or not. The Romantics may have misunderstood Kant—indeed many of the aspirations that
have driven modern interest in drugs may depend on some version of this mis-
understanding—but through their philosophizing of their experiences with
opium and nitrous oxide, they created "drugs" as we now know them.

Despite Davy's Kantian epiphanies, and his friendship with Coleridge, his
book on the nitrous oxide experiments, *Researches, Chemical and Philosophical,
Chiefly concerning Nitrous Oxide,* is chiefly notable for its careful documentation of these wild experiments. Davy went on to play a major role in the development of chemistry, but he continued to pursue chemistry within a very
broad and open field, writing books about "chemical philosophy" that viewed
Lavoisier's chemical revolution from the perspective of a kind of Naturphilosophie. Davy also wrote poetry and philosophical treatises and oversaw
the publishing of the second edition of Wordsworth's *Lyrical Ballads.* According to Molly Lefebure, his notebooks from the Bristol period contain descriptions of "experiences of interplanetary space travel, in the course of which, as
he flew or floated amongst heavenly universes, he encountered all manner of
incredibly strange beings"[16]—all of which would be reported by other, later
experimenters with anesthetics.

Aside from Davy's more lyrical moments and some dream visions that Davy
persuaded Southey to include in his *Curse of Kehana,* nitrous oxide made little
impression on the Romantic literature of the day. While opium had a history as
a motif in literature, as well as powerful associations with the mysterious Orient,
nitrous oxide was something new that grew out of a strictly scientific milieu,
which the Romantics, whether they believed themselves chemists or doctors, either ignored or mistrusted. This was not the case in the more popular literature
of the day, which gleefully celebrated the mysterious powers of the gas.

Figure 5. A group of poets carousing and composing verse under the influence of nitrous oxide. Etching by R. Seymour, 1829.

In May 1800, the nitrous oxide trials at Bristol ended, and the following March, Davy moved to the Royal Institution in London, where he lectured and gave demonstrations of the properties of nitrous oxide. These lectures were popular enough to merit a satiric poem, "The Pneumatic Revellers—An Ecologue," that ridiculed Davy and company. A number of satirical drawings from this period also survive. In 1820, a book entitled *Doctor Syntax in Paris* was published, in which the hero takes his wife, Molly, to a Parisian dentist called Le Charlatan. After using galvanism on Molly to detect and remove the offending tooth, Le Charlatan offers her and Syntax some nitrous oxide for pain relief:

> Said Syntax, "I have often heard
> Philosophers with high regard
> Speak of this nitrous inhalation,
> and of its gay exhilaration.
> Now, as my wife and I have been

To view a dismal, deadly scene,
the place you call the Catacombs,
Where millions rest in their last homes,
We're both in hypochondriac mood,
and I don't think a mouthful would
Do me much harm, although my mind
And not my body, is, I find,
The seat of this my melancholy."
"This will dispel it, Monsieur, wholly,"
Replied Le Charlatan; "so come
With me into the ajoining room,
Where you shall see the grave and wise
Enjoy an earthly Paradise.
The Othman's opium is vile fare,
Compared to this our heavenly air.[17]

Le Charlatan notes that Southey praised nitrous oxide and Syntax and Molly each take a lungful from the airbag, whereupon they are transported to a realm of pleasure. This book was one of a popular series of illustrated verse books and would appear to contain the earliest known record of dental anesthesia. Since it was published in 1820, one year before De Quincey's *Confessions,* it also contains one of the earliest references to a poet's interest in psychoactive substances.

The public was fascinated by this strange new scientific magic, whereby the invisible air itself could produce such transformations of behavior and mood. Demonstrations of the powers of nitrous oxide and, a little later, ether soon became a major attraction in the United States and England. Traveling lecturers invited members of the audience to inhale ether or nitrous oxide and then entertain the audience with their intoxicated staggering. Christian Schoenbein, a German naturalist, has preserved a description of one of these events for us. He attended a demonstration of nitrous oxide at the Adelphi Theatre in London in the 1820s:

> When the curtain was raised, you could see on the stage, in a wide semicircle, a dozen or more large caoutchouc bladders with shining metal taps, filled with the laughing gas. The "Experimentator" appeared in a simple dress suit, and made a short opening speech in

which he described the properties of the gas, and its preparation, in a way which would have done credit to a professor of chemistry. At the end of his lecture he asked for someone from the audience to come on the stage and to inhale from one of the bladders . . . The volunteer—sitting in a chair—put the tap to his mouth, compressed his nose, and inhaled the laughing gas while the "Experimentator" held the bladder. The tap was then closed while the subject breathed out through the nose. The tap was opened again, the nose compressed, and some more gas inhaled through the mouth. He continued in this way until the bag was emptied. Now the "Experimentator" retired; but the "luft-trunken" man remained sitting in his chair for a few minutes, while he stared straight ahead, holding his nose. You can imagine how this comical posture sent the audience into roars of laughter which increased when the intoxicated man leapt smartly from his chair and then made astonishing bounds all over the stage.

When the audience had had its fill and the man had sobered up, a voice called out: "All nonsense and humbug!" "All nonsense and humbug!" echoed immediately from hundreds of throats. "No! No!" came the emphatic reply. When the protests continued, the "Experimentator" appeared and shouted at the top of his voice: "Ladies and Gentlemen." When he obtained a hearing, he assured the audience that the experiment was genuine and he invited the man who had first voiced his doubts to try the experiment himself. The man responded with alacrity and displayed his incredulity by demanding to empty the largest bladder. His request was immediately complied with, and the effect of the gas upon the disbeliever was so great that he beat around him like a madman and assaulted the "Experimentator."[18]

Violent reactions to anesthetic gases were common in the nineteenth century. In 1808, William Barton observed that he became violent after inhaling the gas and "beat with indignant resentment every person that attempted, vainly, to impede my progress." Describing symptoms similar to those of a PCP-induced frenzy, he continued, "All my muscles seemed to vibrate, and I felt strong enough to root out mountains and demolish worlds, and, like the spirit of Milton, was 'vital in every part.'"[19] At a public demonstration in

Philadelphia a few years later, the audience members closest to the front of the stage fled when an exceptionally large man stepped up to inhale the gas after witnessing the violent displays of other affected audience members.[20] Later in the century, in a burlesque sketch called "Laughing Gas" (1874), the dramatic comedy revolves around the dangers of giving laughing gas to a potentially crazy "nigger."[21]

Schoenbein also reported an afternoon garden party at which a group of young men inhaled a lot of the gas, damaging the surrounding flower beds. "Maybe," commented Schoenbein, "it will become the custom for us to inhale laughing gas at the end of a dinner party, instead of drinking champagne, and in that event there would be no shortage of gas factories."[22]

In the popular culture of the early nineteenth century, the transcendental vacation of the body under anesthesia was prized not as a source of sublime logic but as the source of a theater of states of intoxication. Lacking an interest in Kantian philosophy, the crowd conducted their own analysis of transcendental experience—according to its visible effects. The descriptions of public demonstrations of anesthesia stress the effects on the body and the interaction of the anesthetized subject with the crowd. Unimpressed by what they saw on stage, the London crowds teased the presenters by shouting, "All nonsense and humbug!" The problem of how to validate transcendental experience is a fundamental one—as William James would acknowledge at the end of the century—and the crowd appears gleefully aware of this fact. The laughter of the crowd is a recognition of the impossibility of measuring the truth value of transcendental states through language or gesture. It's a malicious laughter—but one that contains its own affirmation of intoxicated experience in all its ambiguity.

Scientific interest in nitrous oxide in Europe actually declined after Davy's work, and Davy's comments about the pain-killing properties of nitrous oxide, which he speculated would be of use in surgery, were ignored for nearly fifty years. News of the gas slowly diffused across the world via other avenues. In 1791, a mob had destroyed Priestley's house and laboratory, after discovering his sympathies for the French Revolution. Three years later, he emigrated to America, where he settled in Pennsylvania, taking with him his work on nitrous oxide.[23] Although Priestley himself was no longer directly involved, others such as James Woodhouse, dean of the Pennsylvania Medical School, continued to study the gas. One of Woodhouse's students, William Barton, wrote his dissertation on nitrous oxide in 1808 and described its effects on him in great detail. After approving Southey's comments about the ecstasy the drug induced, he described the characteristic feeling of transcendence that resulted: "I seemed to be placed on an immense height, and the noise occasioned by the reiterated shouts of laughter and hallooing of the bystanders appeared to be far below me, and resembled the hum or buzz which aeronauts describe as issuing from a large city, when they have ascended to a considerable height above it."[24]

The public demonstrations of ether and nitrous oxide had one unexpected result. When visiting members of the medical profession attended the shows, several of them observed that people under the influence of nitrous oxide or ether felt no pain when they fell off the stage or were beaten by others. From this observation, and subsequent self-experimentation, the idea of surgical and dental anesthesia developed.[25]

Successful anesthesia was first achieved by Crawford Long in 1842, in a series of operations he conducted in Georgia using ether. Since he did not publish his results, news of successful anesthesia was spread around the world by the series of demonstrations of ether's anesthetic properties conducted by William Morton at the Massachusetts General Hospital in 1846. Ether, a highly volatile liquid prepared by mixing sulphuric acid with alcohol, was known as far back as the thirteenth century, and was described by the alchemist Valerius Cordus under the name of sweet oil of vitriol. It was named ether, or spiritus aethereus, by Frobenius in 1730 and was used as an industrial solvent and pharmaceutical from the eighteenth century on.

Before Long's and Morton's work, surgery had been a grim last-resort intervention for both patient, owing to the intense pain, and surgeon, who had to attempt to perform precise procedures on a screaming, writhing body. The change in surgical ambience that resulted from the introduction of general anesthesia is captured by John Collins Warren, a colleague of Morton, who wrote in 1847: "Who could have imagined that drawing a knife over the delicate skin of the face, might produce a sensation of unmixed delight? That the turning and twisting of instruments in the most sensitive bladder, might be accompanied by a delightful dream? That the contorting of anchylosed joints should coexist with a celestial vision?"[26]

Ether was known as "letheon" at that time—a reaching back to the water of Lethe, the stream of oblivion running through classical hell. The poet, physician, and Boston Brahmin Oliver Wendell Holmes, who first suggested the term "anesthesia" to Morton in a letter in 1846, celebrated the "lethe-al" properties of ether in an essay called "Mechanism in Thoughts and Morals": "Inhale a few whiffs of ether, and we cross over into the unknown world of death with a return ticket; or we prefer chloroform, and perhaps get no return ticket."[27]

Meanwhile, the Transcendentalist philosophers of Boston also paid attention to the new discoveries. With their omnicultural curiosity about transcendental experience, one might expect that the New England writers would be excited by these substances. On May 12, 1851, after receiving ether during a visit to the dentist, Henry David Thoreau recorded in his diary:

> If I have got false teeth, I trust that I have not got a false conscience. It is safer to employ the dentist than the priest to repair the deficiencies of nature . . . By taking the ether the other day I was convinced how far asunder a man could be separated from his senses. You are told it will make you unconscious—But no one can imagine what it is to be unconscious: how far removed from the state of consciousness and all that we call "this world"—until he has experienced it. The value of the experiment is that it does give you experience of an interval as between one life and another—a greater space than you have ever travelled. You are a sane mind without organs—groping for organs—which if it did not soon recover its old senses would get new ones. You expand like a seed in the ground. You exist in your roots, like a tree in winter. If you have an inclination to travel, take the ether: you go beyond the furthest star.
>
> It is not necessary for them to take ether, who in their sane and waking hours are ever translated by thoughts; not for them to see with their hindheads, who sometimes see from their foreheads; nor listen to the spiritual knowings, who attend to the intimations of reason or conscience.[28]

Margaret Fuller had a tooth extracted in Paris in 1847 under ether anesthesia; she noted that the impression was as in the Oriental tale, where the man has his head in the water an instant only, but in his vision that same sense of an immense length of time and succession of impressions; even now, the moment my mind was in that state seems to me a far longer period in time than my life on earth does as I look back upon it. Suddenly I seemed to see the old dentist, as I had for the moment before I inhaled the gas, amid his plants, in his nightcap and dressing gown; in the twilight the figure had somewhat of a Faust-like, magical air, and he seemed to say, "C'est inutile." Again I started up, fancying that once more he had not dared to extract the tooth, but it was gone. What is worth noticing is the mental translation I made of his words, which my ear must have caught, for my companion tells me he said, "C'est le moment," a phrase of just as many syllables, but conveying just the opposite sense.[29]

Fuller complained afterward that "neuralgic pain," whether from the anesthetic or the operation, persisted for several days and was only finally alleviated by a performance of *Don Giovanni*. In true Transcendentalist fashion, she concluded, "if physicians only understood the influence of the mind over the body, instead of treating, as they do, their patients as machines."

Finally, the *New American Cyclopedia* of 1857, edited by George Ripley, leader of the Transcendentalist Brook Farm commune, contained a long article on anesthetics, which mostly dealt with their uses in surgery and for pain relief, noting that the use of a vapor for anesthetic purposes had no precedents outside the use of mandrake and hashish in the East. The article observed that outside of medicine anesthetics had been used "for nefarious purposes in cases of violence where a struggle or noise was feared," and described the initial effect of these vapors as "exhilarating and intoxicating as from any diffusible stimulant."[30]

The Transcendentalists were sufficiently close, both geographically and philosophically, to the anesthetic revolution that their recordings of their encounters and experiments are hardly surprising. Yet Fuller and Thoreau very clearly rejected anesthetics as having any direct relationship to their own concerns. However alluring the cosmos revealed by ether, it contained nothing that the mind could not achieve directly, or through a direct connection to nature. Thoreau never spoke of ether again; nor did Fuller. Ralph Waldo

Emerson, in "The Poet," summed up the Transcendentalist position on intoxicants:

> The poet knows that he speaks adequately then only when he speaks somewhat wildly, or "with the flower of the mind"; not with the intellect used as an organ, but with the intellect released from all service and suffered to take its direction from its celestial life; or as the ancients were wont to express themselves, not with intellect alone but with the intellect inebriated by nectar . . . This is the reason why bards love wine, mead, narcotics, coffee, tea, opium, the fumes of sandalwood and tobacco, or whatever other procurers of animal exhilaration . . . which are several coarser or finer quasi-mechanical substitutes for the true nectar, which is the ravishment of the intellect by coming nearer to the fact. These are auxiliaries to the centrifugal tendency of a man, to his passage out into free space, and they help him to escape the custody of that body in which he is pent up, and of that jailyard of individual relations in which he is enclosed. Hence a great number of such as were professionally expressers of Beauty, as painters, poets, musicians and actors, have been more than others wont to lead a life of pleasure and indulgence; all but the few who received the true nectar; and, as it was a spurious mode of attaining freedom, as it was an emancipation not into the heavens but into the freedom of baser places, they were punished for that advantage they won, by a dissipation and deterioration. But never can any advantage be taken of nature by a trick. The spirit of the world, the great calm presence of the Creator, comes not forth to the sorceries of opium or of wine. The sublime vision comes to the pure and simple soul in a clean and chaste body. This is not an inspiration, which we owe to narcotics, but some counterfeit excitement and fury. Milton says that the lyric poet may drink wine and live generously, but the epic poet, he who shall sing of the gods and their descent unto men, must drink water out of a wooden bowl.[31]

For Emerson, as well as many others, narcotics offered a false, materialist experience of transcendence—"the freedom of baser places" he says, in a veiled reference to the popular use of drugs as intoxicants. Drugs are "quasi-mechanical substitutes" for true transcendental experience, which could only occur through the mind's union with nature or the divine. The question remains though: Why should the experience of narcotics be more false than "water out of a wooden bowl" as a means of attaining "sublime vision"?[32]

Fitz Hugh Ludlow, whose *The Hasheesh Eater* (1855) remains the great nineteenth-century American statement on the subject of drugs, responded to Emerson by offering his own radical reading of how the transcendental impulse could fulfill itself in man. He claimed that although one should beware of stimulants, absolutely condemning them was akin to criticizing someone for building a shelter rather than choosing to live in the wilderness that God had given. Ludlow located the significance of narcotics, notably opium and hashish, precisely in their ability to suggest a path through the labyrinth that connected matter and spirit, until the user gained a perception of Kant's "thing in itself."

But Ludlow was not so impressed by the anesthetics. He named them in his survey of substances that can give "grander views of Beauty, Truth, and Good," but decided that "ether, chloroform, and the exhilarant gases may be left out of the consideration, since but very few people are enthusiastic or reckless enough in the pursuit of remarkable emotions to tamper with agents so evanescent in their immediate, so fatal in their prolonged affects."[33] Hashish and opium exerted their effects at a tempo that revealed a path that was still human: Ludlow uses the metaphor of habitation, to suggest that the worlds revealed by these narcotics are habitable. The anesthetics, however, so rapidly sent the user "beyond the furthest star"—they so literally doubled the transcendental movement from matter to spirit—that they could be dismissed from consideration. It is this doubling of transcendental experience that made anesthetics more problematic than "water out of a wooden bowl." The austerity of water forced the Transcendentalist thinker to rely on his or her own resources. Anesthetics threatened that self-reliance—they allowed self-transcendence, but subtly instituted a new form of reliance: on the drug itself.

It was not only the Transcendentalists who expressed doubts about the value of anesthesia, either from a spiritual or a medical point of view. In France Balzac claimed that "should my leg be cut off, I would never be chloroformed.

I would never want to abdicate my self."[34] There were others who believed that transcendence of pain was a form of heresy, since pain was given by God, and, as Christian Scientists maintain to this day, could only be taken away by him too. The French physiologist François Magendie, one of the developers of experimental science (though, as Jean-Jacques Yvorel notes, not a surgeon), declared in 1847 that "the loss of moral sense, of consciousness of real life, has something degrading and shameful about it . . . whoever has a little courage and energy prefers to suffer for a minute, rather than see themselves annihilated by drunkenness, however transitory."[35]

The German toxicologist Louis Lewin, who grouped ether, nitrous oxide, and chloroform together with alcohol as "Inebriantia" in his ground-breaking *Phantastica* (1924), claimed that ether was especially popular with women, because it was "not considered becoming . . . [for them] to consume large quantities of concentrated alcohol habitually."[36] In 1847, Auguste Barthélemy wrote of women who used ether for childbirth: "Oh, what a doubly mysterious, ineffable power / At the moment she gives birth, she believes she conceives."[37]

The possibility of women taking pleasure (ether was also said to turn women into nymphomaniacs) in childbirth, or at least avoiding pain, gave rise to predictable cries of outrage.[38] In one of the first books advocating the use of chloroform, the Scottish surgeon Sir James Simpson responded to charges that anesthesia contradicted Genesis, chapter 3, verse 16, where God says to Eve: "in sorrow thou shalt bring forth children." Simpson's reply (like Ludlow's above) was that if one took these words literally, one also had to take other parts of God's curse literally, including not weeding the "thorns and thistles" that grow in the fields where man grows food. The use of chloroform in childbirth gained some legitimacy in 1853 when Simpson's most famous patient, Queen Victoria, gave birth to her eighth child under partial anesthesia, a method that became known as "the Queen's Chloroform."

Anesthetic administration of ether to women caused other problems. Laurence Turnbull's late-nineteenth-century anesthetic manual warned, in the "Medico-Legal" section, that because of repeated claims by women that they had been raped under anesthesia, male anesthetists should always make sure that they had a witness present during surgery and after. Turnbull's explanation for this phenomenon was that "women are subject to conditions and sensations identical to the sexual act, which arise quite subjectively and without any extrinsic stimulus."[39] When women were anesthetized, the pleasurable sensation caused by ether led them to think that they had had intercourse while unconscious, and to afterward accuse the physician or dentist. Turnbull admitted no exceptions to this explanation.

Ether was also given to women who found intercourse physically painful or impossible. O. P. Dinnick describes a case in late-nineteenth-century Scotland where, "suffice it to say that it became the business of the physician to repair regularly to the residence of this couple two or three times a week to etherize the poor wife for the purpose above alluded to. They persevered, hoping that she would become pregnant and that delivery would cure her. This etherisation was continued for a year, when conception occurred."[40] The physician was in attendance throughout this period.

In Europe, ether was primarily used not for exploration of mystical states but as an intoxicant. It was popular in Ulster in the second half of the nineteenth century, where it was sold in chemists' shops, grocers' stores, and bars as a cheap and effective substitute for alcohol. "The atmosphere of Cookstown and Moneymore was 'loaded' with ether; hundreds of yards outside Drapers-town a visiting surgeon detected the familiar smell; market days smelt 'not of pigs, tobacco smoke or of unwashed human beings'; even the bank 'stoved' of ether, and its reek on the Derry Central Railway was 'disgusting and abominable.'"[41]

The vogue for ether drinking in Ulster was probably a result of Father Theobald Matthew's highly successful temperance campaigns, which began in the 1840s, along with a decline in illicit liquor distillation. As with most nineteenth-century intoxicants, medical arguments were produced in ether's favor, notably that the liquid, which boils at body temperature, produced a powerful amount of wind when it entered the stomach and thus "cleared the pipes"; the success of ether in anesthesia also enhanced its reputation. Ether was popular throughout Europe, and its use was not restricted to the poor. Dr. Norman Kerr, the British authority on "inebriety" and president of the Society for Promoting Legislation for the Control and Cure of Habitual Drunk-ards, had cases that were "'persons of education and refinement' . . . mostly women; the men were all doctors."[42]

In France, ether was part of the pantheon of substances associated with the fin de siècle. Proust apparently used it on occasion. According to the French neurologist Dominique Mabin, from the age of eighteen on Proust had used a variety of drugs to help him sleep and to control his asthma. These included at various times the sedatives Trional and valerian, the newly discovered barbiturates Veronal and Dial (though these restricted his breathing, an effect that was difficult for an asthmatic to tolerate), and opium, morphine, and heroin (mainly taken for his asthma, though he never seems to have become addicted to them). He also smoked a variety of preparations to relieve his asthma, inhaled a "syrup of ether," and sucked various pastilles that included aspirin, theobromine, and the poisons belladonna and aconite. To counteract the drowsiness caused by many of these substances, he used caffeine and subcutaneous injections of adrenalin.[43]

For Proust, drugs were a way of inducing different types of sleep and dream, to be savored—and written about. In *Guermantes' Way* (1920) Proust speaks of "the private garden where, like unknown flowers, the sleeps, so different from one another, of datura, of Indian hemp, of multiple extracts of ether, the sleep of belladonna, of opium and valerian grow, flowers which will stay closed until the day when that predestined unknown person comes to them, opens them up, and sets free for long hours their particular scents and dreams in a marveling and surprised being."[44]

All the attention that is given to Proust's madeleine, as the trigger of memories and altered mental states—an attention that supports the idea of the modernist literary imagination as being purely a product of mental activity, since a madeleine is not, in itself psychoactive—obscures the fact that Proust's mind and body were constantly awash in a sea of chemicals that produced precisely the kind of cognitive movements that he describes in his books. The extreme form of literary transcendence that Proust, sitting in his cork-lined room for years, exploring his own interiority, was a mascot for, could not be sustained without some level of chemical support. Nor was it.

Guy de Maupassant used a variety of drugs, including ether, which he took to soothe his migraines, precursors of his descent into insanity. His work, which contains abundant references to altered states, makes almost no mention of drugs. In classic tales like "La horla" it is madness that induces hallucinations. There are two exceptions: "Rêves," the story of a dinner conversation between a doctor, a writer, and three bachelors in which the doctor extols the virtues of ether, and "Sur l'eau," ("Afloat," 1888) an autobiographical story in which the narrator sniffs from a flask of ether in order to rid himself of a migraine attack. Soon after he inhales, a sensation of "void" spreads from the narrator's chest to his limbs and he experiences an "intensification of my mental faculties":

It was not a dream like that of hashish, it was not the rather sickly visions of opium; it was marvellously keen reasoning, a new way of seeing, judging, appreciating things and life, with the certainty, the complete awareness, that this way was the right one.

And the old image from the Scriptures suddenly came into my mind. It seemed to me that I had tasted of the Tree of Knowledge, that all the mysteries had been unveiled, so much did I find myself under the sway of a new, strange, irrefutable logic. And arguments, reasonings, proofs came to me in hordes, immediately reversed by a stronger proof, reasoning, argument. My head became a battlefield of ideas. I was a superior being, armed with invincible intelligence, and I experienced marvellous pleasure at the recognition of my power.[45]

Once again, ether is a philosopher's drug that triggers arguments, reasonings, judgment, proofs, ideas, knowledge, irrefutable logic—the whole apparatus of Kantian cognitive transcendence. It is also a medicine—a Socratic one, no doubt—for it is the doctor in "Rêves" who extols the virtues of the drug to the curious but ignorant writers.

As Ernst Jünger points out in his essay "On Maupassant's Tracks," ether inhalation results in "an acoustic revelation." Jünger says of Maupassant's ether experience that "he describes it like a dialog which one listens in on with the spirit's ear. But this attention of the ear cannot be separated from the participation of the listener, who assumes sometimes one role, sometimes the other ... the man who speaks begins to hear himself and is surprised by his interior dialectic."[46]

This appears to be true of anesthetic experience in general. In "Afloat," Maupassant hears conversations, voices, just as Dr. Vatabeel, the anesthetized patient in Theodore Dreiser's play *Laughing Gas* (1915) hears The Rhythm of the Universe chanting "Om! Om! Om! Om! Om! Om! Om! Om!" when he is anesthetized. Sound itself has transcendental qualities—and is used to this day as a marker and conduit for transcendental experience in religious music. Anesthetics, in producing something similar to transcendental experience, trigger a heightened sensitivity to sound at certain doses—and acoustic phenomena provide one of the best metaphors for what it feels like to move from the embodied, typically visually ordered world to that which lies beyond. This may even be the key to the otherwise puzzling appeal of ketamine to late-twentieth-century ravers; ketamine synergizes with the sonic battery of the disco sound system to produce "K-holes," sudden black-outs of consciousness on the dance floor.

Sound is also crucial to some of the writings of the undisputed king of ether in fin-de-siècle France, the Decadent writer Jean Lorrain. Lorrain started using ether when he moved to Paris in 1885. He was fond of drinking ether and eating strawberries dipped in it at Parisian dinner parties—with predictably catastrophic results for his health. In 1893, although he had already given up the pleasures of the volatile liquid, he was operated on for nine intestinal ulcers. In 1900 he moved to Nice, where he died in 1906 from a fatal perforation of his intestinal wall, which could not be operated on due to its fragility.

In the short story "Un crime inconnu" ("An Unknown Crime") which reprises the Decadent theme of the Circean femininity of drugs with a queer twist, the narrator has given up ether use but is still tortured by "nervous troubles." Haunted by the ghostlike presences in his apartment, he takes to living in hotels. One night, during Mardi Gras, two butchers, one looking suspiciously aristocratic, take the room next to the narrator and prepare for a night of costumed revelry. They return from dinner and the narrator overhears their conversation through the wall. One of the two men, furious that the other is too drunk to go out to the ball, changes into his masque costume: green silk robes and a metallic mask. He also changes to a "she" at this moment, as well as to the embodiment of the spirits haunting the narrator in his apartment. Shifting his perspective from an acoustic to a (highly constrained) visual one, the narrator creeps up to the keyhole of their room and watches as the drunken man writhes in the other's silk robes until finally he passes out "with the black hole of a long scream, strangled in his large open mouth."[47] "She" then takes off her robes and brings forth "a glass mask , a hermetic mask without eyes and mouth, and this mask is filled to the edges with ether, the liquid poison."[48] She smothers her drunken friend's face with the mask and, after he slumps to the floor, becomes a "he" again and leaves.

The chief proponent of the philosophical use of ether was Benjamin Paul Blood (1832–1919). Blood lived all of his life in the small town of Amsterdam, New York, where he worked variously as a boxer, weight-lifter, gambler, business speculator, mill worker, farmer, and inventor.[49] He was also a prolific writer, publishing his work privately or in local newspapers. In a thirty-seven page pamphlet entitled *The Anaesthetic Revelation and the Gist of Philosophy*, published privately in 1874, Blood described the experience that he had first had after being given ether in a dentist's office in 1860. After many years of self-experimentation, Blood claimed that "there is an invariable and reliable condition (or uncondition) ensuing about the instant of recall from anaesthetic stupor to sensible observation, or 'coming to,' in which the genius of being is revealed."[50] The anesthetic revelation contained within it the solution to philosophical questions about the relationship of the self to the universe.

Somewhat disappointingly, most of Blood's work is devoted to the history of these questions, with little direct writing about his experiments or their results. The general trajectory of Blood's thought is captured in the title of another of his pamphlets: *Plato! Jesus! Kant!* though it was Hegel, Fichte, and the German Idealists, whom he had encountered via the *Journal of Speculative Philosophy*, that he referred to most often. Although he wrote about philosophy, Blood was ultimately a mystic; the revelation of being was beyond philosophical categories and language. As Blood states at the end of *The Anaesthetic Revelation*, only through direct experience of anesthesia could it be had: "No poetry, no emotion known to the normal sanity of man can furnish a hint of its primeval prestige, and its all but appalling solemnity . . . Nor can it be long until all who enter the anaesthetic condition (and there are hundreds every secular day) will be taught to expect this revelation, and will date from its experience their initiation into the Secret of Life."[51]

Philosophically, Blood was a pluralist who believed in a multiplicit universe, irreducible to a single cosmic principle, yet the cosmos revealed to him under anesthesia was monistic. Blood tried to resolve this (Hegelian) problem in his posthumously published opus *Pluriverse* (1920), by describing the revelation as an "unequivocal *impasse* whose obstruction can be neither obviated nor defined."[52] Pluralism functioned in the everyday universe—the anesthetic revelation defined this universe's transcendental limit.

Pluriverse has passages of a uniquely homespun American materialist mysticism. Blood compares the anesthetic revelation to the voice of the blood that tells God that Cain has murdered his brother Abel:

> The dwellers in cities may live and die with no pathetic suggestion
> from this incident . . . but it undoubtedly grew out of a peculiarity
> well known to every plainsman, and which shall have been ob-

> served, however carelessly, by many a farmer's boy—a peculiarity of
> the following character: Where the blood of an animal has been
> freshly shed upon the ground . . . any member of the herd passing
> over the fatal spot will be arrested and entranced, seemingly by
> some exhalation of the vital fluid. The animal stares, with a rapt and
> distracted expression, moaning and pawing the ground . . . This ab-
> straction may last for several seconds; but any noise or intrusion
> which would ordinarily call attention will break the spell, which, as
> in the case of "bearing pain," seems to be instantly gone and for-
> gotten.[53]

Blood says that this may be the animal's "supreme moment," "the monad's
most palpable connection with an unseen world." The voice of the blood is an
ecstatic but sensuous experience of the invisible, as are anesthetics. In particular, the voice of the blood is the voice of death, the invisible, transcendental
force par excellence.

Blood carried on a considerable correspondence with authors, including Alfred, Lord Tennyson, and William James, regarding the revelation, and in
Pluriverse he cites various parts of it to back up his case. Sir William Ramsay,
a professor in London, had published an account of his experiments with
ether in 1893 that was similar to Blood's in some respects, but also expressed
disappointment afterward:

> My feelings are sometimes those of despair at finding the secret of
> existence so little worthy of regard. It is as if the veil that hides
> whence we come, what we are, and what will become of us, were
> suddenly rent, and as if a glimpse of the Absolute burst upon us.
> The conviction of its truth is overwhelming, but it is painful in the
> extreme. I have exclaimed—"Good heavens! is this all?"[54]

Ramsay rebuffed Blood in correspondence, and that led Blood to declare
somewhat petulantly concerning the revelation:

> There is nothing imminent in it for one whose outlook is expectant
> of a royal and monistic explanation . . . Sir William's depression un-
> der the commonplace and secular tone of the world-mystery ac-
> cords very well with our democratic multiverse, which dispenses
> with the brazen general Absolute, and the tape-tied Infinite, whose

quasi prestige is that it is unlimited; but just therefore it has no def-inition, and consequently it has no practical use.[55]

Anesthesia was a *democratic* mystical revelation, available to all, whenever they wanted, with no secret elite holding the key to its mysteries. Blood was self-consciously American, with, in the words of his biographer Robert Marks, "no little of the frontiersman's quality transported to the prairies of dialectic."[56]

Blood's work made little impact during his lifetime or after. It has chiefly come to light through his long-term correspondence with William James, who gave several accounts of Blood's work, most famously in his lecture on mysticism in *The Varieties of Religious Experience* (1902). James introduced Blood in a section devoted to the use of intoxicants to achieve mystical states of consciousness. "Sobriety diminishes, discriminates, and says no; drunken-ness expands, unites and says yes. It is in fact the great exciter of the *Yes* func-tion in man."[57] After describing Blood's experience, he observed that even if all that remained of these experiences was the vague memory of something profound, they nevertheless indicated the existence in the mind of multiple states of consciousness, each awaiting its trigger. "No account of the universe in its totality can be final which leaves these other forms of consciousness quite disregarded." These states were discontinuous with one another, but, un-der the influence of anesthetics, could be reconciled and "melted into a unity." This is "something like what the Hegelian philosophy means."[58]

In a note attached to an earlier essay, "On Some Hegelisms" (1882), James described in detail how his own experiences with nitrous oxide had illumi-nated the flaws in the Hegelian system, which was at the height of its popu-larity in the Anglophone world at the end of the nineteenth century. In Hegel, the apparent plurality of phenomena in the world is produced by a dialectic in which things attain their separate existence through their relationship to that which is their opposite. This separateness can be synthesized into a unity at a higher level of reasoning. Viewed cosmically, all human thought—indeed the whole universe—is finally synthesized as transcendental Spirit in which mind and matter are one. Under nitrous oxide, James claimed that he had directly experienced the process of thinking whereby this became apparent.

> With me, as with every other person of whom I have heard, the keynote of the experience is the tremendously exciting sense of an intense metaphysical illumination. Truth lies open to the view in

depth beneath depth of almost blinding evidence. The mind sees all
the logical relations of being with an apparent subtlety and instan-
taneity to which its normal consciousness offers no parallel; only as
sobriety returns, the feeling of insight fades, and one is left staring
vacantly at a few disjointed words or phrases, as one stares at a
cadaverous-looking snow-peak from which the sunset glow has just
fled, or at the black cinder left by an extinguished brand.[59]

James saw that "every opposition, among whatsoever things, vanishes in a
higher unity in which it is based; that all contradictions, so-called, are but differences; that all differences are of degree; that all degrees are of a common
kind; that unbroken continuity is of the essence of being; and that we are literally in the midst of *an infinite,* to perceive the existence of which is the ut-
most we can attain."[60] These oppositions revealed themselves in the words he
wrote in the state of intoxication:

> What's mistake but a kind of take?
> What's nausea but a kind of -ausea?
> Sober, drunk, -unk, astonishment.
> . . . . .
> Reconciliation of opposites; sober drunk, all the same![61]

Oliver Wendell Holmes performed a similar experiment, probably around
the same time:

> I once inhaled a pretty full dose of ether, with the determination
> to put on record, at the earliest moment of regaining consciousness,
> the thought I should find uppermost in my mind . . . The one great
> truth which underlies all human experience, and is the key to all the
> mysteries that philosophy has sought in vain to solve, flashed upon
> me in a sudden revelation . . . As my natural condition returned . . .
> I wrote . . . "A strong sense of turpentine prevails throughout."[62]

Similarly, James's excitement at his experience of the final unity soon turned
to a disgust when he realized that "the identification of contradictories, so far
from being the self-developing process which Hegel supposes, is really a self-
consuming process, passing from the less to the more abstract, and terminat-
ing either in a laugh at the ultimate nothingness, or in a mood of vertiginous

amazement at a meaningless infinity."[63] Rather than being a genuine description or explanation of the universe, it was a kind of intellectual process that fed upon itself: "what is the principle of unity in all this monotonous rain of instances? Although I did not see it at first, I soon found that it was in each case nothing but the abstract *genus* of which the conflicting terms were opposite species."[64] Anesthetics, and Hegel, offered a false vision of the infinite that remained entirely in the realm of thought, without ever actually engaging the phenomenal world.

Some writers have disparaged James's interest in Blood and nitrous oxide as being nothing more than a psychological curiosity.[65] But although it is hardly the core of his philosophy, James's interest in chemical revelation was a natural part of his attempt to synthesize scientific, psychological, and religious points of view, and marked the coming full circle of the departure that Transcendentalist and Idealist philosophy made from empiricism at the end of the eighteenth century. It was entirely in keeping with Jamesian pragmatism that if there were such things as mystical or transcendental states, they should be verifiable through a repeatable experience. Indeed, in opposition to Kant, James argued that without taking experience into account, there could be no such thing as actual transcendence; there could only be its intellectual simulation. At the same time, experience itself could not be the only measure of the validity of transcendental experience. James never entirely resolved what the criteria for measuring this validity are. But he remained open to the anesthetic revelation: his last major published article was an homage to Blood and his doctrine of pluralism.

A number of other writers at the end of the nineteenth century wrote descriptions of mystical anesthetic revelations.[66] Most intriguing of these is an unsigned letter that James published in *The Psychological Review* that appears to have been written by Oscar Wilde. In this letter, Wilde (if it was he) euphorically described his dental anesthesia experience: "My God! I knew everything! A vast inrush of obvious and absolutely satisfying solutions to all possible problems overwhelmed my entire being . . . I seemed to have reconciled Hegelianism itself with all other schools of philosophy in some higher synthesis."[67] Wilde resolved to bring this news back to suffering humanity, but on his return to consciousness, could only shout out to the "little pink man" who was his dentist the words: "That would have been a tough job without the elevator."

❖

After World War I, the focus of chemo-philosophical mind exploration shifted to the psychedelic plants. Sartre, for example, chose to be injected with mescaline when he wanted to experience a hallucination. Ether was not one of the substances that came under the drug laws issued around the time of World War I. A document produced by the French Commission de l'Hygiène during discussion of the drug law notes: "I have put aside the question of ether because this product is currently used by industry and any regulation of its sale in pharmacies would have no effect on ether addicts, who could always procure it by other means without the least difficulty."[68] French workers in plastics factories during the period were exposed to ether fumes for eighteen hours at a time, and were so intoxicated by the end of the day that special train compartments were set aside for them to travel home in.[69]

Anesthetics continued to be used as a tool for exploration of mystical states in certain circles. Aleister Crowley wrote an essay entitled "Ethyl Oxide" (1923) in which he suggested that ether could be used for uncovering the system whereby specific thoughts or consciousness comes into being. Experimentation with anesthetics was also pursued by several figures associated with the mystic Georges Gurdjieff, including his chief disciple, Peter Ouspensky.[70] Gurdjieff affirmed to Ouspensky the potential value of research with psychoactive chemicals, "to take a look ahead, to know their possibilities better, to see beforehand, 'in advance,' what can be attained later on as the result of prolonged work." He also warned of the dangers of undiscriminating and unstructured use. Although Gurdjieff maintained the separation between drug-induced and "work"-induced transcendental experiences, he repeatedly invoked his own version of scientific method and practice, speaking of a "special chemistry" that could be used to manipulate the "human machine," as well as proposing a more general cosmic chemistry that reached back to the speculations of Schelling, Novalis, and German Naturphilosophie.[71]

Ouspensky described his own drug studies in Russia in a chapter of his *New Model of the Universe* (1931) entitled "Experimental Mysticism." Although he does not name the substance(s) he used, claiming that to do so would distract people from the real matter at hand (the nature of the human mind), his biographer, James Webb, believes that he used both hashish and nitrous oxide.[72]

Ouspensky's discussion of his experiences is highly reminiscent of accounts given by other anesthetic philosophers discussed in this chapter. He found that although new states of consciousness were easily achieved, "these new and unexpected experiences came upon me and flashed by so quickly that I could not find words, could not find forms of speech, could not find concepts, which would enable me to remember what had occurred even for myself, still less to convey it to anyone else." Like James and others, he tried to write down his insights while high, with little luck. He experienced a hierarchy of mental states at different dose levels—at first a clamor of voices offering revelations that he came to mistrust, and beyond that, a complex set of mathematical relations, which drew him toward an experience of infinity, both threatening and fascinating. Ouspensky determined that it was all a question of how one approached infinity. Finally, he abandoned his experiments, concluding that although they were useful, they foundered in the face of "the impossibility of conveying in the language of the dead the impressions of the living world."[73]

A founding member of the Surrealist group Le Grand Jeu, René Daumal, who later studied the mystical path with Gurdjieff in Paris, first experimented with carbon tetrachloride when he was sixteen. He was an insect collector, and one of his teachers had advised him that carbon tetrachloride was the best substance to use to kill and preserve the insects. He inhaled some himself, "to see what would happen" and discovered, in subsequent experiments, a way of inducing a deathlike state that he came to view as one of his fundamental experiences.[74] It is highly likely that Daumal, who died at the age of thirty-six from tuberculosis, did significant damage to his lungs through these experiments.

Daumal published two versions of his experiments. "L'asphyxie et l'évidence absurde" ("Asphyxsia and the Absurd Evidence," 1930) used a mostly profane, philosophical vocabulary to show how carbon tetrachloride revealed to him, in a particularly intense way, the absurdity of everyday life. The second essay, "Le souvenir déterminant" ("The Determining Memory," 1943), written after Daumal's immersion in Sanskrit studies and his work with Gurdjieff, abandons the proto-existential vagueness of the earlier essay for a more precise phenomenological analysis of the dissolution of identity under anesthesia. Daumal's account of the way that the finite, temporal ego struggles to maintain itself in the face of infinity was influenced on the one hand by Western ideas and thinkers from non-Euclidean geometry, to William James, Oscar

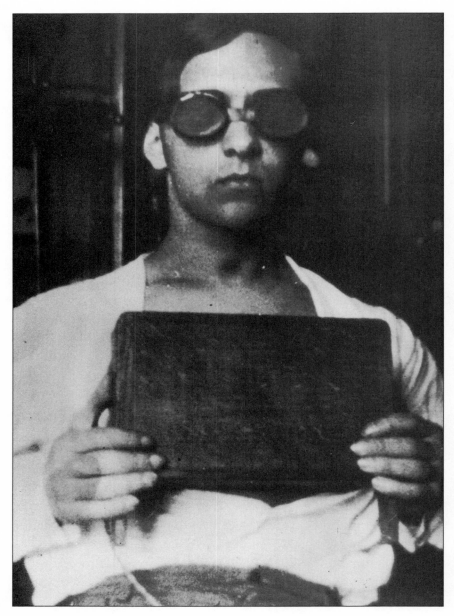

Figure 6. René Daumal at the age of fifteen conducting an experiment with "paroptic vision" at the home of his teacher René Maublanc.

Milosz's[75] and Blaise Pascal's visions, and a variety of Eastern mystical texts, including the *Bhagavad-Gita* and *The Tibetan Book of the Dead.*

The core of Daumal's carbon tetrachloride experience was the revelation of a higher-level world, which he called the *certainty,* that contained this one within it.

> And this "world" appeared in its unreality, because I had abruptly entered another world, intensely more real, an instantaneous world, eternal, a fiery inferno of reality and evidence into which I was thrown, spinning like a butterfly in a flame. At that moment, there is *certainty,* and it's here that words must be content to circle around the bare fact.[76]

In this world, Daumal experienced "the total nothingness of my particular existence within the undifferentiated substance of the Immobile." This was the "cause of a cancerous proliferation of moments," which we experience as time, space, personal identity, and so on.[77] Like other anesthetic voyagers, Daumal experienced his identity in this other world as being made of sound: "I sustained my existence by emitting this sound. This sound expressed itself in a formula which I had to repeat faster and faster, to 'follow the movement'; this formula (I am recounting the facts without trying to disguise their absurdity) came down to something like this: 'Tem gwef tem gwef dr rr rr' with the main stress on the second 'gwef'; and the last syllable blending back into the first one, to give a perpetual pulsation to the rhythm which was, I repeat, that of my life itself."[78]

Like Ouspensky and Crowley, Daumal sought to distinguish his "experimentation" from mere "experiences," because he saw it as revealing a truth that was both mathematical and experimental: mathematical because it could be conceptualized in terms of relationships between the finite and the infinite; repeatable because, rather than just happening, the experience could only occur through a continuous act of concentration that maintained the experimental conditions. Daumal believed that ether and nitrous oxide produced the same results as carbon tetrachloride, but that

> there are many ether addicts who totally ignore this revelation, no doubt because, having reached this critical point, they can no longer think and fall asleep. Otherwise, this despair, this more than human suffering would heal them quickly of their addiction. This

is why the possibility, for a man, of having an experience such as I
am describing quite contradicts the desire for drugs.[79]

In these terms, "addiction" would be the compulsive act of falling unconscious at the sight of one's own death or nothingness, a ritual that Daumal
would explore more fully in his satirical novel *La grande beuverie* (*A Night of
Serious Drinking*, 1938), in which the assembled drinkers will go to any lengths
to maintain their constant state of intoxicated drowsiness, whether they obtain it through booze, books, or ideologies. To wake up, in Daumal's terms,
means to break through the intoxicated sleep of ordinary consciousness by
coming closer to the source of this willful drowsiness—fear of death.

Daumal's work raises the question as to whether anesthetics should even be
considered psychoactive in the traditional sense, since they are literally transcendental in their effects, inducing at the most potent doses unconsciousness
rather than hallucinations. Insight comes from exposure to the realm of unconsciousness itself rather than from chemical modulation of the structures of
consciousness. Anesthetics produce a deterioration of the organism and its
functions, which then results in unusual mental experiences, which can be
linked to other experiences of the limits of consciousness, including concus-
sion, exhaustion, and a variety of near-death experiences.

Daumal's approach to the problem of transcendence abandoned Kantian
models of subjectivity for a phenomenological approach: he does not assume
that there is a subject who structures worldly experience through his or her
faculties; he says there is merely a set of structures that gives this impression.
He then demonstrates how these structures can be disrupted—not merely in-
tellectually, but through an event, an experiment. For Daumal, transcendence
is decisively experiential—"the certainty" itself stands at the limit of the possibility of phenomenological inquiry and of experience itself, as the condition
of its possibility. The act of inhaling carbon tetrachloride provided a repeatable procedure for experiencing the impermanence of conventional states of
mind, including those "faculties" by which we, following Kant or the phe-
nomenologists, define experience. The drug itself was unimportant though,
since what it revealed existed before and without the drug, and could be experienced by other means.

Medical anesthesia developed only incrementally between the middle of the nineteenth century and the middle of the twentieth. The agents used (nitrous oxide, ether, and to a lesser extent, chloroform) remained the same, and inhalation continued to be the main method of induction, even after the development of the syringe. The two world wars provided extensive opportunity for experimental work in anesthesia. Jünger recalled going on an ether binge while convalescing from a war wound in Hamburg in 1918, during which he was stopped by an officer who told him he smelled like a hospital.[80] Seeing Jünger's gold medal of honor, he let Junger continue his stoned wander through the wartime city.

The intravenous anesthetic sodium pentothal, "truth serum," was used in the 1930s in the United States to make thieves confess to crimes.[81] The use of anesthetics to achieve mind control or to extract a confession indicates the subtle persistence of the belief in a Hegelian theory of anesthesia. If lower states of consciousness are drawn up and synthesized into higher ones, then the criminal who is given a powerful anesthetic should submit to the power of the chemical and its administrators, allowing them access to the "lower"-level secrets that he hides. The notion that sodium pentothal can be used in this way to divine truth has by now been thoroughly discredited. It does, however, reveal a fantasy about power indulged in by Hegelian philosophers as well as the ghoulish control addicts of the Cold War national states: that higher levels of organization necessarily control lower, more disorderly structures. Interestingly, sodium pentothal is now used as part of the lethal injection in the administration of the death penalty. Once again, we see a movement from truth to death and back again.

Nitrous oxide and ether had their place in the pantheon of 1960s drugs, alongside solvents and other cheap, legal, and brain-damaging substitutes. Whippets (small canisters of nitrous oxide used for making soda water fizzy) were inhaled out of balloons at frat boy parties. Poppers (capsules of amyl nitrate) became a fixture of gay culture in the 1970s, used to add a peak buzz to orgasm. Quaaludes, a type of muscle relaxant, were also used as a sex drug, mainly by women, while phencyclidine, known as PCP or angel dust, enjoyed a vogue in American barrios and ghettoes. The use of anesthetics by liberation movements can be connected to an observation of McLuhan's, that the waves of socio-technical transformation striking America in the 1960s required some form of anesthesia to allow the success of the "social surgery" taking place.

It is in the dance scene, with its multiple cultures of liberation through heightened corporeality and ecstatic chemical and sonic transcendence, that the drug ketamine has emerged in the 1990s. A powerful anesthetic developed in the 1960s by Parke-Davis, ketamine is currently used mainly for veterinary purposes, but was available to people by prescription until August 1999, when it was added to the list of controlled substances. Ketamine has a brief but striking history of use for exploring the same transcendental dimensions that I have described in the rest of this chapter. In *Journeys into the Bright World* (1978), the yoga teacher and theosophist Marcia Moore with the help of her husband, the anesthesiologist Howard Altounian, described their experiences using the drug for "samadhi therapy"—samadhi being the term for the ultimate state of enlightenment in yoga, the state beyond all forms. Moore, whose zeal for anesthesia is reminiscent of Blood's, claimed that "the Goddess ketamine" was "the democrat of drugs" and "might well blur the distinctions between the aristocrats of holiness and the common crowd of seekers who simply wish to expand their conceptual horizons."[82]

In *Journeys into the Bright World*, Moore pursued a peculiar split logic: she was critical of the drug culture but a solid believer in the powers of ketamine; she understood the concept of addiction, yet justified her compulsive use of the drug as a form of meditation or nourishment. She recognized the dangers of paranoia, yet was convinced that the world would come to an end unless world leaders were given ketamine. At the end of the book, Moore visited the ketamine researcher John Lilly in his Malibu Hills home. Lilly, who had recently abandoned his own experimentation with the drug because of two fatalities among his own ketamine research group, warned Moore about the dangers of continuing to use it. Moore ends the book by describing her negotiations with the Food and Drug Administration (FDA) to continue her experimentation with the drug. Shortly after the book was published, Moore disappeared from her home in Seattle. Her remains were found two months later, at the base of a tree where she apparently liked to take ketamine.

Lilly has described his own research with ketamine in his "novel autobiography" *The Scientist* (written in a highly dissociated third person). Lilly, a neuroscientist and physician who had previously been studying dolphins, conducted much of his experimentation in Esalen, California, in a sensory deprivation tank, which allowed access to "inner reality." His compulsive use of the drug in the external world led to repeated institutionalizations, after he passed out in airports. He became convinced that he should alert the President to the dangers of "solid-state propaganda"[83] being projected at earth by solid-state-technology–based beings in their war with water-based life forms (like human beings) for dominion over the universe.

Lilly developed a model of the universe as a result of his ketamine experimentation (the development of such models has been a hallmark of anesthetic use, from Davy through Blood and Daumal). At low levels, the drug caused changes in visual perceptions and, with the eyes shut, the appearance of an inner reality. At higher doses, "he began to experience interaction with the strange presences, strange beings, and began to communicate with them. I have left my body floating in a tank on the planet Earth. This is a very strange and alien environment. It must be extra-terrestrial . . . I am in a peculiar state of high indifference. I am not involved in either fear or love. I am a highly neutral being, watching and waiting."[84] Lilly was able to converse with these beings. At still higher doses, "'I' as an individual disappears,"[85] and Lilly experiences himself as a universe creator connected to a multiplicity of possible universes. At the highest doses, he found that he "had become the void beyond any human specification. In returning from the void, he went through the creative network, the extraterrestrial reality, the internal reality, back into his body in the tank. He realized that, as a human being, he would be unable to use these larger-dose regions. He would be unable to describe what happened, so he labeled this high-dose threshold U, the Unknown."[86]

Finally, Lilly had a serious accident while bicycling when he was high on ketamine and returned to his research on dolphins. The book ends with a dialogue about Lilly between three beings and with his own questions regarding their reality. As with Philip K. Dick's post-visionary experience books, *The Scientist* uses fiction as a device for describing a world that the author at least partly believes to be real, while allowing for the possibility that it is not.

Anesthetics remain an anomaly in the history of drug use: the only drugs for which the major cultural reference points are Hegel and transcendental philosophy. Philosophers have experimented with other drugs—Coleridge and De Quincey considered themselves philosophers, though neither of them got around to actually articulating what a philosophy of opium would be; Foucault took LSD in Death Valley; Heidegger is rumored to have taken LSD with Jünger—but none of them used their experiences to articulate or analyze a philosophy, the way Blood, James, and Daumal—or for that matter Davy— did with nitrous oxide and ether.

Anesthetics opened up the possibility of an experimental philosophy in which the problem of transcendence could be approached through a repeatable, specifically scientific method, and that was also subject to "mathematicological" operations—mainly the relationship of "A" to "B." Anesthetic experience, with its dose-dependent hierarchy of cognitive states and its curious lack of emotion and affect, mirrored the structure of transcendental idealism with varying levels of success. James believed that rather than allowing a true description of the transcendental structure of the universe, the flow of thought on anesthetics reproduced the rhetoric of philosophical analysis, while containing little or none of the content of the experience of transcendence itself, which remained ineffable. Daumal, going a stage further, believed that his experiences illuminated the relationship between the Real, or "the certainty" as he called it, and the time-bound world of language and identity— which is also the world of the many philosophical schemes that cluster around the void. From Davy to Lilly, these schemes are strikingly similar: a movement from everyday reality to an inner reality where "nothing exists except for thoughts and ideas." At higher doses, this world of ideas gives way to the transcendental realm of the "anesthetic revelation," or Daumal's certainty—the final Hegelian synthesis.

But why were these schemes so often dialectical? Even if Hegel was wrong in his description of the cosmos, his description of the extreme tension between mind and matter, the rapid movement back and forth between them that is suddenly lifted and resolved into a higher unity, provided the closest analogy for anesthetic experience, where mind suddenly transcends sensation in one rapid, relatively clean movement. How could matter disappear into the "ether" so smoothly? Blood captured this materialist paradox in his synesthetic notion of the "voice of the blood"—a sound that is simultaneously a *smell* and also the movement of *matter* itself. The dialectic is the simplest way of describing the structural relationship between a here and a there that the anesthetic experimenters all allude to.

It must be said that this attempt at an experimental philosophy was a failure, despite the initial enthusiasm of many of its proponents. The synthesis of the worlds of mind and matter proved difficult, as Moore discovered when she tried to find ways of remaining simultaneously in this world and the "bright" one. The word "seems" appears in the anesthetic literature more often than in the literature on other drugs, because it was so difficult to connect what occurred under anesthesia with everyday life. The third level of the drug's action, in which it blotted out the world of mind and matter, rather than transforming it, left the user no wiser as to what to do with his or her life, after the inevitable return to everyday consciousness—except, as Daumal believed, that it demonstrated that transcendental experience per se was possible. The laughter produced by the rowdy exhibitions of anesthesia in the early nineteenth century, in which the snickering and hostility of the crowd was directed at the intoxicated staggerings of stage volunteers, was also a laughter at the impossibility of validating transcendental experience through use of a drug—a laughter that finally has its source in the impossible itself.

Why does "laughing gas" make people laugh? In his play of the same name, Dreiser suggests, through the voice of Demyaphon, the spirit of nitrous oxide who appears to the anesthetized Dr. Vatabeel during surgery, that the intensely linear time-trajectory of human events is embedded in an ocean of eternal recurrence, and that human beings experiencing these events are merely mechanical puppets, manipulated by eternal forces. It is this revelation of the mechanical nature of human activity, guided by transcendental forces that is the source of laughing gas's laughter.[87] Dr. Vatabeel awakes from anesthesia racked with this laughter—but he soon forgets what Demyaphon has told him when the drug's effects wear off.

The problems with anesthetic revelation are evident if we consider the traces such revelations leave in language. Where the use of psychedelics often results in rapturous descriptions of luminous patterning and mystical experiences that are highly lyrical, the anesthetic literature has left us very little writing that could be described as poetic, aside from records of conversations conducted with alien beings. The anesthetics encourage a clinical, or rather a philosophical, attitude, since they allow a rapid movement through the language function to a place beyond, and then back again. But attempts to carry back a message from this transcendental zone, whether Daumal's chant of "tem gwef" or Wilde's "that would have been a tough job without the elevator" are something of a disappointment, both to the experimenter and to the reader. For the anesthetics user, language exists not as an absolute marker of reality, but as a zone of activity through which one passes on the way to something more fundamental. Nevertheless, Daumal believed that anesthesia illuminated identity as something maintained in and against infinity by language, not necessarily in its semiotic aspect, but as a pure mantra-like sonic refrain: that of the moth circling a flame. Hence the repeated return to sound and rhythm that many anesthetics users describe.

Anesthetics have remained legally available for most of their history, and thus free of the exotic (and Manichean) trappings of dealer and junkie, smuggler and narcotics agents. This may be because few people, with the exception of Benjamin Blood, choose to repeatedly tolerate the throbbing headaches that accompany the other effects of the drugs, or because, in the case of Daumal, Lorrain, and possibly Davy, these substances evidently resulted in permanent damage to the body or the mind. Perhaps, as Daumal says, it would be more accurate to call them poisons rather than drugs. The ultimate reference point for transcendence within modern paradigms is death, and the literature that most resembles the anesthetic literature is that of near-death experiences. Blood was a pharmaceutical Captain Ahab, single-minded in his pursuit of the Revelation, and James was his Ishmael, flexible enough to try his hand at worshipping any God that came along. Mysticism means dying to the world, to experience the Everlasting Life now. Anesthetics, at least for a time, captured in a strangely literal way that desire to create the conditions of death experimentally, go there, and return to tell the story.

3

THE TIME OF THE ASSASSINS

Cannabis and Literature

This drug is as old as civilization itself. Homer wrote about it, as a drug which made men forget their homes, and that turned them into swine. In Persia, a thousand years before Christ, there was a religious and military order founded which was called the Assassins, and they derived their name from the drug called hashish which is now known in this country as marihuana. They were noted for their acts of cruelty and the word "assassin" very aptly describes the drug.

HARRY ANSLINGER, testimony to Congress regarding the
Taxation of Marihuana Act, April 27, 1937

One should always be on guard when statesmen start citing poets, and Harry Anslinger, commissioner of the Federal Narcotics Bureau, giving testimony to the House Ways and Means Committee of Congress in 1937, is no exception to this rule.[1] Anslinger, speaking in favor of a taxation system that would effectively prohibit all use of the cannabis plant in the United States, told Congress a story about the origins of cannabis. Hardly an innocent or neutral story, it referred to two myths: first that of the psychoactive drugs of *The Odyssey,* the lotus and Circe's magic; second, that of the Assassins, a medieval Islamic group mentioned by Marco Polo whose name has been repeatedly connected to the use of hashish, the resinous extract of the cannabis plant. Neither of Homer's plants has any known connection with cannabis, but the reference served to establish the drug's evil effects: it made men forget home and turned them into animals. The Assassins, who Anslinger, in his frenzy for origins, dates to a thousand years b.c.e. rather than c.e., as is actually the case, provided evidence that cannabis products predispose their users to acts of cruelty and violence. Anslinger deliberately stressed the foreign nature of the drug, playing on racist associations of foreignness with crime and degeneracy, even as Works Progress Administration (WPA) brigades were being dispatched to cut down the extensive growths of hemp that grew along the Potomac River outside of Washington, D.C.

How did this extraordinary situation came about, in which two literary works, Homer's *Odyssey,* the first masterwork in the Western canon, and *Marco Polo's Travels,* that marvelous concoction of fact and fable which fired the Western literary imagination for centuries, were effectively cited as evidence that would determine American law regarding the cannabis plant for the last sixty years of the twentieth century? Criminality has been associated with many classes, qualities, and uses of psychoactive drugs. In the chapter on opiates, I explored the way in which nineteenth- and twentieth-century writers made use of the narcotic properties of the opiates as part of a gesture of negation that embodied a transgression against nature, culture, and God. This revolt was ultimately a private affair, and if it involved crime, it was, according to Artaud and others, a "victimless crime." The case with cannabis is somewhat different, not least because cannabis is not physiologically addictive, and is not fatally toxic to human beings.[2] What precisely then is it about cannabis that has made it a matter for courts of law? And how did literature become part of the evidence?

As I detail the history of writing about cannabis, you will notice a tendency in my writing toward digression, not the digressive overdrive of stimulant use, which can be measured quantitatively as page upon page of unsolicited insight and opinion, but a subtler tendency to drift from hashish to politics, horticulture, mysticism, semiotics, and back, as the subject seems to require. Patterns of great beauty, rich with meaning, will appear, only to disappear with the next historical text or event, which will often be concerned with something apparently unrelated. Although it is easy enough to summarize the physiological effects of the drug, the challenge that the historian of cannabis faces is that of unifying an extraordinarily diverse body of literature and anecdote about the drug. In David Lenson's words, "cannabis is a drug that alters a relationship without predetermining that relationship's altered form."[3] How do we find a framework for discussing something that can be defined only as causing frameworks to shift? That will be the challenge.

In 1809, Sylvestre de Sacy, one of the originators of European Oriental studies, read a paper at a meeting in Paris concerning the legend of the Old Man of the Mountain, Hasan-i Sabbah, founder of the Assassins.[4] Sabbah was a medieval Ismaeli renegade warlord who is believed to have lived in an area close to the current Turkish-Iranian border in a castle known as Alamut.[5] From this castle, Sabbah sallied forth to make war against both the Turks and the Crusaders, and he was said to have sent forth his warriors on missions to spread terror in Christian Europe. In explaining the origin of the word *Assassins*, Sacy suggested that it has its etymological root in the word *hashish*. Sacy noted that hashish

> causes an ecstasy similar to that which the Orientals produce by the use of opium; and, from the testimony of a great number of travelers, we may affirm that those who fall into this state of delirium imagine they enjoy the ordinary objects of their desires, and taste felicity at a cheap rate; but the too frequent enjoyment changes the animal economy, and produces, first, marasmus, and then, death. Some, even in this state of temporary insanity, losing all knowledge of their debility, commit the most brutal actions, so as to disturb the public peace.[6]

To counter the objection that hashish-intoxicated men would make poor Assassins, Sacy recalled Marco Polo's story about Sabbah, who was said to have recruited young men to fight for him by inviting them to his castle, where he would give them a drug and bring them to paradise-like gardens. They would awake, believing they had been reborn in a paradise to which Sabbah held the key, which they would be readmitted to only if they carried out his commands. This story was quite well known in Europe: both Boccaccio and Dante used it in their works.[7] But no specific identification of the "potion" used by Sabbah was made until Sacy identified it as hashish.

The etymological connection between *Assassin* and *hashish* on which Sacy's theory rests is generally believed to be false nowadays; "hashish" in Arabic was a nickname for cannabis and roughly translated, means herb, grass, or weed.[8] If Sabbah did indeed use a potion to seduce followers, it may have contained hashish—but there is no evidence that anyone prior to Sacy believed that.[9] One suspects that Sacy, eager to demonstrate that modern Oriental studies was a science, latched on to a tale with the kind of sensationalist allure that he hoped would appeal to both specialists and nonspecialists—not unlike Anslinger, who also used the story of the Assassins to build up the power of the Federal Bureau of Narcotics.

Cannabis products were well known throughout much of Islamic history, although hashish was only one of the names used. Banj was also a popular name, reflecting the plant's long association with the Indian subcontinent, where to this day cannabis is used under the name of bhang, by followers of Siva, the god of destruction, asceticism, and renunciation.[10] The word "cannabis" itself comes from the Greek "qunbus" (hashish was known in the Muslim world as ibnat al-qunbus—daughter of cannabis), yet the drug does not appear to have been very important in ancient Greece, where, if we can believe Herodotus, it was already associated with barbarian outsiders such as the Scythians, who, after building a kind of sweat lodge, "take some hemp seed, creep into the tent, and throw the seed on to the hot stones. At once it begins to smoke, giving off a vapour unsurpassed by any vapour-bath one could find in Greece. The Scythians enjoy it so much that they howl with pleasure."[11]

Because the prophet Mohammed forbade intoxication with alcohol in the Koran, many Islamic legal authorities argued that all other intoxicants were banned; others argued that since hashish (along with tobacco and coffee) was not mentioned by name, it should not be subject to the ban.[12] Throughout most of Islamic history, hashish use was subject to regulation and repression by the law. Nor was it merely a question of how to interpret the *Koran*. Many of the criticisms leveled at drug users now were leveled at the users of hashish: it made people lazy; the mental changes turned people into animals or drove them insane; and, some said, it killed people or made them killers.

Hashish was associated with the Sufis, with esoteric religious sects on the margins of Islam, along with the poor, scholars, and, curiously, the judiciary. Many of the qualities of hashish that more orthodox society reviled were praised in such circles. There were hedonistic invocations of the drug:

A pound of roast meat, a few loaves of bread
A jug of wine, at least one willing boy,
A pipe of hashish. Now the picnic's spread
My garden beggars paradise's joy.[13]

The Sufi literature contains a number of poems in which hashish, the "green parrot," is praised for its "many meanings" and "the Secret" that it holds—and it is often contrast with profane (and proscribed) wine:

Swear off wine and drink from the cup of Haydar,
Amber-scented, smarigdite green.
Look: it is offered to you by a slender Turkish gazelle
Who sways delicate as a willow bough.
As he prepares it, you might compare it
To the traces of fine down on a blushing cheek
Since even the slightest breeze makes it move
As if in the coolness of a drunken morning
When silvery pigeons might whisper in branches
Filling its vegetal soul with their mutual emotions.
How many meanings it has, significances unknown to wine!
So close your ears to the Old Censor's slander![14]

These many esoteric "meanings" and "significances" form the basis for a ritual, cultic use of cannabis, whose aim is a state of illumination.[15] This state of illumination can be differentiated from the ritual use of psychedelics precisely because its level of intensity corresponds to a shift in cognition and perception rather than a total, if temporary, dissolution of the ego. Meaning and significance still exist for the cannabis user—and are articulated in ritual or poetic form—even when that which they point to is beyond words. This may be one of the principal reasons why the hashish user gets into trouble: he or she is not content to rest in the transcendental state, as do opiate, anesthetic, and psychedelic users, but wants to and is capable of introducing esoteric secrets into the domain of the social.

There are at least two hashish stories in the *Thousand and One Nights* collection of folktales. It is difficult to date these stories, but they give an indication of what was believed about hashish in some sectors of the Islamic diaspora—as well as in nineteenth-century Europe, where these stories were very popular.[16]

"The Tale of the Hashish Eater" is a relatively simple story about a man, reduced to poverty by his pursuit of beautiful women, who eats hashish, becomes convinced he is a powerful ruler, and dreams that he is making love to
a woman, only to wake up in a public place, naked, "his prickle at point," to use
Sir Richard Burton's translation.[17] "The Tale of Two Hashish Eaters" develops
a similar theme, this time about "a fisherman by trade and a hashish-eater by
occupation. When he had earned his daily wage, he would spend a little of it
on food and the rest on a sufficiency of that hilarious herb. He took his
hashish three times a day . . . Thus he was never lacking in extravagant gaity."
After taking hashish one evening, he becomes convinced that the light of the
full moon reflected on the road is a river and decides to start fishing. A dog
catches his bait and an almighty struggle occurs, waking up the neighborhood.
The fisherman is arrested, but the judge he is brought before is also a hashish
eater, and the two become friends. One night, as the two dance around the
judge's garden, naked and intoxicated, the Sultan and his Wazir appear in disguise. The fisherman proclaims himself Sultan and threatens to piss on the
real Sultan, who leaves laughing, shouting, "God's curse on all hashish eaters!"
The next day, he teases his judge about the incident; the judge immediately re-
pents, but the fisherman responds: "And what of it? You are in your palace this
morning, we were in our palace last night." The Sultan takes the fisherman on
as a storyteller and forgives the judge.[18]

Anslinger conflated the asocial character of the lotus eater with the criminal antisocial activities of the Assassins. Something similar happens with the
hashish user in the *Thousand and One Nights*. Hashish, like other drugs, allows
access to the dream world. But in contrast to the passivity of the opium
smoker, who simply lies in his den and dreams, the hashish-intoxicated one in
the *Thousand and One Nights* exists simultaneously in both the dream and the
real world. He dreams, and he reveals his dreams in public, waking up with an
erection in the marketplace, or creating a racket as he "fishes" in the street at
night. Thus his dreaming becomes a matter of political concern, which is handled with great subtlety by the Sultan. Rather than punishing the offending
fisherman, he converts the explosion of the hashish eater's laughter, gaiety, and
immoderation in the city, which is supposedly under his control, into a social
function: that of the storyteller, at once liberated from the rules and restrictions that bind everyday life, yet subservient to the Sultan. As in our own
world, the subversive quality of dreams is quickly turned into entertainment.

Hashish and hashish users make excellent subject matter for stories—and the tale is the literary genre par excellence for cannabis. It is not necessarily the storyteller who gets high, but, as in the *Thousand and One Nights,* the storyteller tells a story that involves hashish. Anslinger, as we shall see, was fascinated by the stories that could be told about hashish, by it's potency as a metaphor and as an agent.

The earliest account of cannabis intoxication to appear in Europe was that of a Moroccan Christian convert named Leo Africanus, who in 1510 described to the pope the giggling of Tunisian fakirs who were using hashish.[19] A few decades later, Rabelais, that master of intoxicated laughter, devoted three chapters of *Gargantua and Pantagruel* to "the good herb Pantagruelion." It has been argued that, with a knowing wink to his audience, Rabelais wrote these chapters as an homage to the psychoactive properties of the good weed.[20] There is little doubt that Pantagruelion is the cannabis plant. And Pantagruelion is indeed an allegorical plant, half real, half myth. But the purpose of the myth is not to suggest getting high. Instead, Rabelais plays with the plant's use for making rope and cord, sails and hangman's nooses, and its medicinal properties, which he culled from Pliny and other classical authors. Although nooses and sails were no doubt potent items in the Renaissance imagination, it feels as if Rabelais devotes too much time to Pantagruelion for it to be merely about string. Mikhail Bakhtin argues that Rabelais, who was himself a physician, is paying homage to Pantagruelion so as to satirize the medical quacks who sold panaceas in Renaissance marketplaces. This satire is also a celebration of the Renaissance marketplace, in which a rowdy folkloric culture gives expression to its dreams of transformation of the world through jokes about the magical potency of Pantagruelion: "from the marketplace style and folklore Pantagruel's announcement acquires its utopian radicalism and its deep optimism, completely alien to the pessimistic Pliny."[21] Although Bakhtin sees Pantagruelion's potency only in social terms, its utopian political power is derived from nature also, for it is nature, and man's relationship to nature, that gives birth to myths. Nature is an ally of the inhabitants of the marketplace and provides a set of magical tools to aid those who wish to transcend or their transform social conditions. In this sense, Pantagruelion is strongly linked to the history of cannabis, in which the plant, whether plucked on the roadside or bought in a pharmacy or Mexican bar, brings together groups of people (Beats, Sufis, Hashishins, pornographers, criminals) who meet in secret, away from the eyes of the state, to pursue their dreams of utopia.

We know very little, alas, about the actual use of cannabis in Renaissance Europe, although there are references to the psychoactive properties of the plant in writings about witchcraft and in travelers' accounts.[22] It is to the Romantic period that we must look, once again, for a specifically literary cannabis culture in the West. But even here, we encounter a tale with a curiously cannabinoid twist. In a recently discovered manuscript, whose existence was announced in an Austrian newspaper, a text attributed to Johann Wolfgang von Goethe describes a visit to Johann Schiller in Jena in the autumn of 1797, during which the two writers and three of Schiller's students smoked pipes of hemp resin (hashish) together to see whether the experience could shed any light on the plant principle as it applies to human beings.[23] To Goethe's displeasure, the students embarked upon experiments in poetry, which he dismissed as of little worth. Goethe commented: "I was in the most singular condition: all kinds of dark thoughts swirled around me like cold goldfish in a jar, but I was not able to catch any of them and remained bored, a boredom that became increasingly mixed with an ever stronger indignation." Afterward the five intrepid explorers retired to a local bar, where they devoured plates of sausages with "amazing appetites"—possibly the first recorded case of "the munchies." Goethe attempted to expound upon the experience, only to find that Schiller had fallen asleep with his face in his empty plate.

Can this text be considered authentic? Schiller's interest in intoxication is well known,[24] as is Goethe's interest in science; besides his own writings and collaborations, he was instrumental in the development of scientific research in Weimar and Jena. Goethe's skepticism about the creativity-enhancing possibilities of hashish is also plausible, given his antipathy to Romanticism, as is his curiosity. What is less likely is the theory that "in each person, a trinity of the human, the animal, and the plant reigns," and that the plant consciousness could be stimulated by smoking the resin. This hypothesis—which does not appear anywhere else in Goethe's work—reads suspiciously like a distortion of Goethe's doctrine of the "ur-phenomenon," according to which plants, animals, and man all have an ideal form that provides the blueprint for all variations thereon. However, this theory relies on the notion that men, animals, and plants are different from one another, rather than being the same. Furthermore, even if the trinity theory was truly Goethe's, it is difficult to see why smoking hashish would be a better case study than smoking tobacco or, for that matter, drinking wine, beer, or tea. The notion that the wonders of smoking and growing hemp were discussed by university students in Jena in the 1790s is also doubtful, since hemp products were for the most part *eaten* in the nineteenth century—the 1970s is a much more likely date. If the text is a prank, what is important is to observe the way that the text destabilizes the linear flow of the history I am telling in a characteristically cannabis-related way, turning it back into a story whose date of origin is indeterminate (1800 or now?), a parody of the kind of "official" literary documentation that would interest a scholar like me, or a reader in search of "facts" about the history of cannabis. The cannabis user knows that history too is a kind of dream world.[25]

Hashish did have a brief vogue among the English Romantics though. In 1803, one of Humphry Davy's chief patients, Thomas Wedgwood, requested that Coleridge help him find some "Bang" (bhang, or hashish). Sir Joseph Banks, master botanist, colonialist, and president of the Royal Society, forwarded some to Wedgwood, noting that it was in use throughout the East, where it was taken "by Criminals condemned to suffer amputation."[26] Banks added that it was beyond question that Bang was the main constituent of the Homeric drug nepenthes.[27] Coleridge wrote with relish to Wedgwood: "We will have a fair trial of *Bang* . . . Do bring down some of the Hyoscyamine pills, and I will give a fair Trial of opium, Hensbane, and Nepenthe. Bye the bye, I always considered Homer's account of the *Nepenthe* as a *Banging* lie."[28] In 1807, Coleridge wrote about his Bang experience:

> I have both smoked & taken the powder [Bang] . . . the effects in
> both were the same, merely narcotic, with a painful weight from the
> flatulence or stifled gas, occasioned by the morbid action on the
> coats of the Stomach. In others however it had produced, as we
> were informed by Sir J. Banks, almost frantic exhilaration. We took
> it in the powder, and as much as would lie on a Shilling. Probably,
> if we had combined with opium and some of the most powerful essential Oils, to stimulate and heat the stomach, it might have acted
> more pleasantly.[29]

The word "probably" gives a clear indication of where Coleridge's interests really lay. De Quincey also obtained a sample of bhang in 1845, although he never described its effects on himself.[30] It is often said that the first-time pot smoker does not actually get high—"Nothing's happening." It takes a few attempts to get used to what *high* means, and to experience it. Perhaps, in this case, it was true of Europe as a whole.

It was a group of French psychiatrists in the first half of the nineteenth century who first took a real interest in the drug's psychoactive uses. Most French sources link the discovery of hashish to Napoleon's invasion of Egypt in 1800; the drug is said to have been brought back to France by Napoleon's soldiers. But, as with opium, it was through medicine and not Oriental infiltration that hashish was disseminated in Europe and America. Figures such as Jean Etienne Esquirol, who wrote the first scientific study of madness, *Des maladies mentales* (*On Mental Illness,* 1838), were fascinated by the notion of hallucination. Esquirol and his colleagues defined hallucinations as "external sensations which the patient believes he experiences, even though no external agent has acted materially on his senses."[31] Louis-Francisque Lélut and Alexandre Brierre de Boismont used this concept to reinterpret "supernatural" phenomena, such as accounts of demonic possession, religious visions, and "récits fantastiques" by Charles Nodier, George Sand, and De Quincey, as records of historically based, psychological phenomena. Mental states that were previously given a religious, magical, or poetic meaning were now explained scientifically. Hashish became of great interest to the pioneers of psychiatry, because it appeared to be a material agent capable of producing such altered states. No one, with the possible exception of Davy and Coleridge, had thought of using drugs to study psychological phenomena in a scientific way before.

There were Orientalist connections too. Jean-Jacques Moreau de Tours, who in 1845 published an entire book devoted to the psychiatric use of hashish, was a pupil of Esquirol. Moreau was sent abroad with mentally ill patients on voyages of convalescence. Between 1837 and 1840, he visited Egypt, Syria, and Asia Minor, where he started using hashish and became interested in using it to study mental illness. Louis Aubert-Roche, another early hashish researcher, also traveled in the Middle East, reporting on hashish use in his *De la peste et du typhus d'Orient* (*On the Plague and Oriental Typhus,* 1840). On his return Moreau became a doctor at Bicêtre asylum, where he began his research.[32]

Moreau's *Du hachisch et de l'aliénation mentale* (*On Hashish and Mental Alienation,* 1845), the seminal nineteenth-century medical text on the subject, opened with an impassioned defense of personal experience as the criteria for judging the effects of hashish. Besides his own experiences, Moreau presented two case studies, one the account of an unknown person, the other that of Théophile Gautier, published in the newspaper *La Presse.* Through hashish, the doctor claimed to study the "mysteries of madness," because for Moreau, madness and the dream state were absolutely identical and hashish offered "dream without sleep."[33]

Moreau focused on the hallucinations triggered by hashish use as he struggled with the paradox that, subjectively, hallucinations are experienced as being real by the senses, while, objectively, they are unreal. According to the dogma of nineteenth-century rationalism, such a confusion should have been impossible. Drugs like hashish were quickly seized on by psychiatrists as materialist "tools" to study the irrational. Even though the days of biochemical models of mental illness were still far away, drugs still appeared to offer some kind of mechanism by which mental disturbance could be triggered and controlled. Madness, the dream state, and hashish intoxication: all, according to Moreau, occupied a space between the real and the unreal, which would also become the space of literature.

Moreau reviewed Davy's experiences with nitrous oxide and De Quincey's with opium, as well as recounting his own experiences with various poisons such as belladonna, aconite, and thorn apple:

> Invariably, at least at the beginning, the results of their actions are identical to those of hashish; disassociation of ideas, daydreams that seem to be the prelude to a more complete dream state in which new, more or less bizarre associations of ideas, perceptions without external stimulus, and so forth, are formed; associations and perceptions that, transported into real life, will become obsessions, extraordinary beliefs, and hallucinations.[34]

He concluded by suggesting hashish as a therapy for madness, one that works by substituting hashish visions for madness, thereby displacing the disease.

Although a group of Milanese physicians and chemists continued Moreau's work with hashish, not everybody was convinced by it.[35] The Académie des Sciences received it with polite disinterest. The psychologist Alphonse Esquiros, who claimed to have repeated Moreau's hashish experiments on patients without success, observed that "to displace madness is not to heal it."[36] Boismont argued in his book on hallucinations that the various mental effects of hashish, "far from being signs of madness are for us the necessary conditions of ferment for the creations of the spirit."[37] Nor did the criticism come exclusively from scientists: in a footnote to his essay on wine and hashish, Baudelaire commented: "the doctor who invented this beautiful system is not in the least a part of the world of philosophy."[38] But although Moreau was wrong in just about all his major hypotheses, he did make several major contributions to medical history: the beginnings of a phenomenological (and experimental) study of altered mental states and some of the first explicitly psychopharmacological experiments using drugs.[39] He also introduced hashish to the artistic world of Paris at the famous Club des Hashishins.

The club met between 1845 and 1849 for monthly "fantasias" in the room of the painter Francois Boissard at the Hotel Pimodan, on the Ile Saint-Louis, a hotel where Baudelaire and Gautier, on occasion, lived. Moreau de Tours and Aubert-Roche presided over the gatherings; among the artists who attended were Honoré de Balzac,[40] Gérard de Nerval, Eugène Delacroix, Honoré Daumier, Alphonse Karr, Gautier, and Baudelaire.[41] Along with the group around Davy and Coleridge at the Pneumatic Institution in Bristol in 1800, Walter Benjamin's and Ernst Bloch's studies with Ernst Joël in Berlin in the 1920s, and various examples in the history of psychedelics, the club provides a fascinating example of a collaboration between writers and scientists.

Perhaps the closest thing to documentary evidence that we have of the club is a snooty letter from its host, Fernand Boissard, to Théophile Gautier:

> My dear Théophile, hashish will be taken at my house, Monday, September 3rd [1845], under the auspices of Moreau and Aubert-Roche. Do you want to participate? If so, arrive between 5 and 6 at the latest. You will have your share of a light dinner and await the hallucination. You may bring with you whatever bourgeois that you wish to inject; since strangers are already being brought to my home, one more will make no difference. I ask only to be forewarned so that food can be ordered accordingly. It will cost 3–5

francs per head. Please reply yes or no—if you are afraid of impure contacts, I think I can suggest a method of isolation, the hotel Pimodan makes it possible.

Always yours, F. Boissard[42]

The club owes its fame principally to Gautier, whose short story "Le Club des Hachichins" ("The Hashishins' Club") was published in the *Revue des Deux Mondes* on February 1, 1846.[43] Gautier was probably introduced to opium around 1834, when he was friendly with the painter Prosper Marilhat, who had traveled in Syria and Egypt; Gautier's first story on the subject, "La pipe d'opium," appeared in *La Presse* on September 27, 1838. He met Moreau in the early 1840s and, having sampled the drug, a paté of hashish and almonds known as dawamesk, or "la confiture verte," wrote his first essay on the subject, "Le hachich" (1843), which was cited in Moreau's book. "Le Club des Hachichins" begins:

> One December evening, obeying a mysterious summons, composed in enigmatic terms that were comprehensible only to initiates, and unintelligible to all others, I arrived in a far-off quarter, a kind of oasis of solitude in the center of Paris, which the river, wrapping it in its two arms, seemed to protect against the incursions of civilization; for it was in an old house on the Ile Saint-Louis, built by Lauzun, the hotel Pimodan, where the bizarre club that I had recently joined held its monthly meetings . . . Surely, those people who had seen me leave my home at the hour when ordinary mortals take their food would not have believed that I was heading to the Ile Saint-Louis, a virtuous and patriarchal place if ever there was one, to dine on a strange dish that had served, centuries ago, as a means of stimulation for an imposter sheikh to use to push his disciples to acts of assassination. Nothing in my perfectly bourgeois demeanor could have made me suspected of such an excess of Orientalism.[44]

Gautier transplanted the myth of Sabbah's medieval warrior cult to a group of nineteenth-century literati, who get together in a secret location in order to dream together. This collective embodies the paradox of most literary collectives, not to say most groups of cannabis smokers, at least in the modern

world: that dreaming has become an act of individual introspection, not a social one, as perhaps it was for Rabelais or the Sufi poets. Only the storyteller,
who orally transmits his or her tale to a group, bridges the gap between the interiority of literary experience and the social group that wishes to share a
dream. And this is perhaps why so many of the literary texts about cannabis
are tales—because the tale mimics the act of collectively sharing a dream.
Gautier struggles with this problem. There is little or no dialogue in his tale—
the Hashishins quickly sink into their own private worlds of fantasy, only occasionally bumping into one another, as if by accident. Hashish invaded the
body in the form of hallucination, "that strange host," allowing the artist to
break down and catalog many of the components of Romantic subjectivity in
an almost Kantian fashion. The hashish user discovered time and space as categories of experience along with shape, color, number, sound, taste, and so on:

> Then, suddenly, a red flash passed under my eyelids, countless can-
> dles were lit up by their own flames, and I felt myself bathed in a
> warm, golden light. The place where I found myself was certainly
> the same one, but different, the way a sketch is different from a fin-
> ished painting: everything was larger, richer, more splendid. Reality
> served only as the point of departure for the magnificence of the
> hallucination.[45]

Gautier's hashish intoxication unfolded in a theater, a *fantasia*—names to
describe the parameters of the subjective imagination. The opium visions of
the English Romantics were also concerned with subjectivity, but De Quincey
and Coleridge explored history and memory as building blocks of dream experience, while hashish allowed Gautier to examine how whatever he was
feeling or experiencing directly contributed to his visions. The imagery in
these dreams was also different: with opium, seas, faces, and architecture pre-
dominated, where Gautier saw geometric patterns, extensions of senses. With
opium, the dream world existed as an autonomous space, appearing out of the
mysterious darkness of sleep, while for the Hashishin, the dream vision was
mapped back to, or contrasted with, the grid of the user's body, and the space
he was in. Each of the senses could be stimulated, and even be confused with
other senses, but subjectivity itself was never transcended. Gautier reiterated
this point in a preface to Baudelaire's work, published in 1868: hashish can only
exaggerate or develop what is already there in consciousness, it cannot "give

visions." The limits of the drug-induced state are the limits of subjectivity it-self, as defined by Kant and others. If subjectivity itself were porous, if "vi-sions" spontaneously appeared that had no preexisting basis in the psyche, then drugs would cease to be of interest, since drug visions would be no more remarkable than any other kind of mental visitation, whatever its source.

"The Hashishins' Club," contrary to many accounts, is a work of fiction; as a record of what occurred at the Pimodan or the nature of hashish intoxica-tion, it can take us only so far. Gautier, the French disciple of E. T. A. Hoff-mann, and the French master of the fantastic tale, blurs reality and dream while winking at the reader. The figure of Daucus-Carota, orchestrator of the hallucinations in "The Hashishins' Club," is taken from Hoffmann. But this literary blurring serves the serious purpose, as it did for Hoffmann, of allow-ing the fantastic, a necessary dimension of human experience, to enter into modern life.

Other attendees of the club gave their writings about hashish a more ex-plicitly Orientalist tone. Alexandre Dumas's *Le comte de Monte-Cristo* (1844–45) features a young nobleman called Franz, who is taken by some smugglers to the supposedly uninhabited island of Monte Cristo in the Mediterranean, where a mysterious man, the Count, an escaped Bonapartiste prisoner who travels around Europe under a variety of assumed identities, lives under the name of Sinbad in a hidden Oriental palace worthy of a James Bond movie. After dinner, the host invites Franz to take some of the "green jam": "If you are a pragmatic man and if gold is for you, taste this, and the mines of Peru, Gujurat, and Golconda will open for you. If you are a man of the imagination, a poet, again taste this and the limits of the possible will dis-appear; the fields of the infinite will open up."[46] The host recounts the story of Hasan-i Sabbah, warns Franz that dream will become reality and reality dream, and gives Franz some of the hashish. It triggers a succession of erotic, musical, and visual experiences of ecstasy, and Franz awakens in a cave, unable to find the mysterious Oriental palace again.

A further variation on this theme can be found in Gérard de Nerval's story "Histoire du Calife Hakem" ("The Tale of the Caliph Hakim," 1847), which later became a part of his semifictional account of his travels in the Middle East, *Voyage en Orient* (1851). The tale begins when the Caliph Hakim, ruler of Cairo, pays an incognito visit to a poor Sabean fisherman's *okel* (a dive where hashish and other intoxicants are used) on the banks of the Nile. There, he meets a youth called Yousef, who invites him to take hashish. The two men become intoxicated and the Caliph is seized with the belief that he has become the true God. After returning to his palace, he declares his intention to marry his sister, while the people in the city suffer because of a dreadful famine. The Caliph is arrested by his scheming Vizier while in disguise on another visit to the okel, and is put in the madhouse. There he is visited by his sister and the Vizier, who claim not to recognize him. A mysterious double of the Caliph takes over the rule of the state and wages war against the enemies of Cairo, while the Caliph rouses the criminals and the madmen whom he has been imprisoned with, to revolt and break out of prison. Through the resulting insurrection, the Caliph regains control over Cairo, but is thwarted in his desire to marry his sister, who has fallen in love with Yousef, who now appears as a jewel-bedecked double of the Caliph. The Caliph's sister persuades Yousef to kill Hakim in an ambush, which he does, before realizing that the Caliph is in fact his hashish-eating partner from the okel.

Nerval certainly visited the Hotel Pimodan, and no doubt would have had the opportunity to take hashish during his travels, but equally important to "The Tale of the Caliph Hakim" are a number of literary sources, including Hoffmann's *Devil's Elixirs* and Sacy's *Exposé de la religion des Druses*. Nerval was already predisposed to seeing the world in the same way as the Caliph. In 1841, he spent nine months in a mental institution, diagnosed by his doctors with "theomania" or "demonomania"—precisely what Hakim "suffers" from. And Nerval's work is full of meditations on the nature of dreams, and the double life they give access to.[47] In both the Caliph Hakim tale and other stories like "Aurelia," Nerval linked this dream state, whether caused by hashish or not, to what Moreau and others would have called madness. But although Nerval believed that the dream state was irrational, he saw it as more than a form of pathology; it was also potentially a state that could reveal truth.[48] Hashish became a cipher for this dream state, one which allowed for two possibilities: mental derangement caused by the drug, or initiation into knowledge of the truth. "Is it possible," the Caliph wonders, "that there is something more powerful than the Almighty and that a mere weed could work such wonders?"[49]

"The Tale of the Caliph Hakim" can also be read as an allegory of postrevolutionary France's turbulent political life, in which medieval Cairo, like modern Paris, seethes with angry crowds, demanding bread and leadership.

Hashish is a "foreign substance" used by the Sabeans, which reveals to the Caliph the deeper forces that shape the swarming metropolis. The story is awash with references to Oedipus' crimes, which determined the fate of Thebes. The Sphinx watches from across the Nile while the Caliph proposes incestuous marriage with his sister. The city's destiny is shaped by the configuration of the stars—but hashish, because it gets him admitted to the madhouse, also reveals to the Caliph the poverty and suffering of the people, and puts him back on the path of righteousness.

Nerval's political allegory has a predecessor—François Lallemand's *Le Hachych* (1843). An anonymously published utopian treatise on social progress, written by a doctor, the book was quite popular when it came out (a second edition, published under the author's name, has the unlikely title of *The 1848 Political and Social Revolutions Predicted in 1843*). The book's narrator, a doctor who has traveled in the Middle East, brings forth a sample of hashish at a pan-European dinner party, claiming that when he took it "instead of erotic visions or warlike furies, I experienced political ecstasies."[50] When the European diners take hashish, they are inspired with visions of social, political, and scientific progress. An engineer invents "a new electrical engine capable of driving all machines"; a young Greek speaks lovingly of the rise of the workers' movement; and "a professor of zoology speaks up, describing the internal organization of prehistoric animals."[51] Meanwhile, the narrator travels through time and space to 1943, where he discovers an enlightened and peaceful Europe.

Even Baudelaire's first essay on hashish, "Du vin et du hachish" (1851) has a utopian flavor.[52] Baudelaire, still mildly intoxicated by the 1848 revolution (in which he urged the masses to march on his stepfather, General Aupick), praised wine as a social beverage, beloved of "the divine Hoffmann" and Balzac; he linked intoxication through wine to acuity, powers of penetrating thought, and solidarity with the suffering of others. Hashish, although offering pleasures, was antisocial, lazy, "a suicide weapon." "In short, wine is for the people who work and who deserve to drink it. Hashish belongs to the class of solitary joys; it is made for miserable idlers. Wine is useful; it produces fruitful results. Hashish is useless and dangerous."[53] Baudelaire noted the prohibition of hashish in Egypt and gave it his approval:

> A reasonable state could never survive with the use of hashish,
> which produces neither warriors nor citizens. It is forbidden for

man, under penalty of his downfall and intellectual death, to de-
range the primordial conditions of his existence, and to disturb the
equilibrium between his faculties and his environment. If a government existed that was interested in corrupting its people, it would
have to do no more than encourage the use of hashish.[54]

It remains unclear whether Baudelaire, hardly a paragon of civic virtue, actually preferred the "fruitful" to the "useless and dangerous." We do know that
outside of his experiences at the Pimodan, Baudelaire was not a regular user of
hashish (nor, it seems, were any of the other participants); alcohol and opium
were the substances that he returned to throughout his life.

Baudelaire developed his ideas about hashish in his book *Les paradis artificiels* (*Artificial Paradises*).[55] He is deeply ambiguous concerning hashish. The
repeated moral denunciations of the drug, begun in the earlier essay, are un-
dercut by the lyricism of his descriptions of hashish visions. A passage in
praise of the sensitivity to allegory ("that most spiritual of genres") produced
by hashish leads directly to one of Baudelaire's greatest poems, "Correspon-
dences," with its forest of symbols and its synaesthetic pleasures. Likewise, one
of the testimonies to the powers of hashish that Baudelaire brings forth recalls
that beautiful prose poem "La chambre double," with its superimposed imagery of paradise and a sordid hotel room. Baudelaire presents picturesque images and unusual experiences only to deny their value.

Baudelaire, a great admirer of Nerval, adapted his ideas about theomania to
his own thinking about hashish. Baudelaire's principal criticism of hashish was
that it turned a human being into *l'homme-Dieu*. But where Nerval's use of
this conceit was personal and somewhat idiosyncratic, Baudelaire slyly turned
it into a quite specific allegorical (and therefore moral) statement about the
dangers of intoxicated creativity in general. The hashish-intoxicated artist
mistakes the projection of his self and its desires for true creativity. He believes
himself to be God; he desires to "carry off paradise in one go," but courts a
subtle ruin when he mistakes this fantasy for reality, and the diabolic powers
of the material world for God-given, serendipitous but elusive, true happiness.

The phrase "artificial paradise" serves to describe a fundamental myth un-
derlying nineteenth-century Euro-American civilization; another name for it
would be "progress." Hashish was part of the crude bourgeois utopia of com-
modities and Baudelaire had little but scorn for it, even though, as Walter

Figure 7. Charles Baudelaire, self-portrait, 1844. In this watercolor painted while Baudelaire was under the influence of hashish, he towers over the statue of Napoleon in the Place Vendôme.

Benjamin has observed, it is possible that through his use of hashish, Baudelaire was able to see the bourgeois utopia of the commodity for the hallucination that it was and is, right at the moment that the first department stores and advertisements were appearing in Paris.[56]

Baudelaire wanted to escape from the nineteenth century's artificial utopias, but not through Romantic flight into nature. His position was a gnostic one; "anywhere, out of this world" was the only place where happiness or truth could be found. How did one get there? Baudelaire suggested, unconvincingly (even to himself), through work and prayer. The act of negation was more important to him than any positive solution. Hashish, at any rate, was incapable of transporting people beyond themselves. But, as Jünger has pointed out, Baudelaire's attack on the idea of a pharmacological paradise was hardly likely to be the last move in this particular game; the aspirations of the psychonauts of the 1960s, gnostic or not, are evidence of the "urgent need" driving the search for paradise.[57]

We know very little about the broader reception that *Artificial Paradises* or for that matter hashish itself had in mid-nineteenth-century France, outside of the milieu of the artists and writers who attended the Club des Hashishins. According to Benjamin, a Brussels pharmacist tried to make a deal with the book's publisher: in return for an order of two hundred copies of the book, the pharmacist wanted to advertise in the back of the book a marijuana extract that he had produced. However, Baudelaire vetoed the idea.[58]

Gustave Flaubert wrote an enthusiastic letter to Baudelaire in 1860 praising the book but criticizing his insistence on "the spirit of evil."[59] Baudelaire wrote a polite but defiant reply, saying that he would maintain his opinion, even if the whole of the nineteenth century were gathered against him. Around this time, Flaubert drew up plans to write a hashish-related novel called *La spirale*.[60] The book, which was never developed beyond note form, would have been about a painter who after traveling in the Orient becomes habituated to the use of hashish, has visions that after a while occur even without ingestion of the drug, leading him to a state of "permanent somnambulism." The novel was to conclude that true happiness consisted of what ordinary people called madness—having visions, considering works of the imagination more real than everyday life. Many of the themes recall the hallucinations of *La tentation de St. Antoine*, which Flaubert worked on for most of his adult life. Flaubert's enthusiasm for hashish was surprising, since he himself probably never actually tried it. "If I wasn't so afraid of hashish, I'd stuff myself with it as though it were bread," he wrote.[61]

We know that Arthur Rimbaud "tried" hashish.[62] Rimbaud took up and developed the Baudelairean aesthetics of intoxication in a way that the Decadents who followed him were hardly capable of doing. In the famous "Lettre du voyant" Rimbaud had already announced the process of alchemical transformation that the poet of the future would go through: "a long, immense and systematic *disruption of all the senses* . . . he exhausts in himself all poisons, so as to keep nothing but their quintessences . . . he becomes among all men the great sick one, the great criminal, the great cursed one—and the supreme Sage!—for he arrives at the *unknown!*"[63]

These poisons were by no means exclusively metaphorical. Rimbaud envisioned a scientific alchemy that would arrive, through the use of those poisons, at direct knowledge of the unknown. This project was still in Rimbaud's mind when he wrote "Matinée d'ivresse" ("Drunken Morning"), of all his poems the one most clearly related to hashish:

> Oh *my* Good! O *my* beautiful! Terrible fanfare in which I never stumble! Magical rack! Hurrah for the miraculous work, and for the marvelous body, for the first time! This all began with the laughter of children and it will end with them. This poison will remain in all my veins, even when, the fanfare ending, we are returned to the old disharmony. O now may those of us so worthy of these tortures fervently reassemble this superhuman promise made to our bodies and our created souls: this promise, this madness! Elegance, science, violence! They promised us that they would bury the tree of good and evil in the shadows, to deport tyrannical respectabilities, so that we could bring forth our very pure love . . .
>
> Brief, holy night of intoxication! Even if there was nothing more to it than the mask with which you favored us. We affirm you, method! We won't forget that yesterday you glorified each one of our ages. We have faith in the poison. We know how to offer up our whole life every day.
>
> Now is the time of the ASSASSINS.[64]

Flaubert wrote to Baudelaire that his work on hashish was part of the inauguration of a new science. When Rimbaud cries, "We affirm you, method!" he celebrates the ability of scientifically developed "poisons," such as Dr. Moreau's hashish, to induce states of excess, poetry, and violence, states that will turn the scientist or sage into something new, something unknown. This enthusiasm was apparently short lived. The poet was not otherwise that impressed by the powers of hashish (or poetry). When Paul Verlaine found him stoned on hashish in the Hotel des Etrangers, he asked him to describe what was happening. Rimbaud replied, "Well, nothing much at all . . . white moons, and black moons which are chasing them."[65]

Why did a group of writers living in Paris in the middle of the nineteenth century become so fascinated by the story of Hasan-i Sabbah and the Assassins? Sabbah provided the blueprint for a modern, bohemian counterculture, complete with secret castles in which conspirators gathered to overturn all the rules of bourgeois life. The hyperaestheticized style of the despot became a model for the nineteenth-century artist, a strange mixture of aesthetics and threats of violence, of luxurious fabrics, mysterious glances, intoxicating magical substances, flashing lights and music, linked to a mind that, in Baudelaire's words "dreams of scaffolds." The Oriental despot was embraced by Gautier and others as a medieval dandy who, in the receding tide of revolutionary fervor, satisfied his fantasies of total revolt through acts of aesthetic terrorism, and through the use of hashish. This figure has remained with us to this day in the dope-smoking radicals of the 1960s, decked out in caftans while plotting the overthrow of the state, and the blunt-smoking thugz of gangsta rap, dressed in gold and making videos for MTV in which they pose as crime lords. The Romantic writers believed that the despot could overcome the force of materialist power (whether capitalist or colonialist) through the sheer power of aesthetics—supplemented by a little materialist magic courtesy of Dr. Moreau.

I have already dwelled on cannabis' long history of esoteric religious associations, which can be traced back as far as the remains of cultic ritual chambers found in Central Asia by Russian archeologists, dating back as far as the third millennium B.C.E.[66] This cultic significance, which we find in Herodotus' comments on the Scythians, and in the Sufi and Ismaeli groups, was maintained in the nineteenth century, in the literary culture of the Club des

Hachichins, but more specifically it found a place in the mystical-spiritualist peripheries of the avant-garde, and in their various attempts at organizing collective rituals, groups, and experiments, often undertaken with the aid of hashish and other drugs. One of the earliest European writers to discuss the spiritual use of hashish was a French disciple of Emanuel Swedenborg named Louis-Alphonse Cahagnet. In his *Sanctuaire du spiritualisme* (1850), Cahagnet, who espoused a neo-Platonic doctrine of man as microcosm of the universe, wrote that hashish allowed him entrance to the spirit world. Cahagnet criticized the use by psychiatrists and literati of words like "hallucination" to describe what he saw as the "sacred truths" revealed by hashish visions.

The most famous spiritualist of her age, Helena Petrovna Blavatsky, founder of the Theosophical Society, was apparently an enthusiastic user of hashish, and claimed privately that it increased her mental powers a thousand fold—although it never played an explicit role in theosophical doctrine.[67] Others associated with the group, such as F. K. Gaboriau, founder of the Lotus Society, and Jules Giraud, who made a career out of traveling around France lecturing about hashish, made similar claims.[68] Stanislas de Guaita, whose story I told in the narcotics chapter, was interested in hermeticism and said in *Le temple du Satan* that hashish was "a first-class magical herb" that allowed the travel of the astral body, although he did not recommend it.[69] Hashish appears a number of times in his poetry as the source of dark pleasures.

It was in these circles in Paris in the 1890s that William Butler Yeats had smoked hashish, as he records in his *Autobiography*.[70] He and Maud Gonne conducted experiments in extrasensory communication using hashish, and some of the occult flavor of the stories collected in *The Secret Rose* (1897) is the result of his hashish use. Yeats was one of the writers associated with the Hermetic Order of the Golden Dawn, as well as its literary offshoot, The Rhymers Club, which met in the 1890s in London.[71] In self-conscious imitation of the Club des Hachichins and their French symbolist heroes, British fin-de-siècle writers such as John Addington Symonds and Ernest Dowson experimented with hashish. In 1910 the mystery writer and Rhymer Algernon Blackwood published "A Psychical Invasion," about a psychic doctor-detective named John Silence, who is called to investigate the case of a traumatized young comic writer who takes a cannabis extract to make himself laugh. Instead, the comic writer is haunted by ghostly visitations, which threaten to drive him mad. Silence offers the following diagnosis: "the hashish has partially opened another world to you by increasing your rate of psychical vibration, and thus rendering you abnormally sensitive. Ancient forces attached to this house have attacked you."[72]

The republication of Fitz Hugh Ludlow's *Hasheesh Eater* in London in 1903 also stimulated a renewed interest in the drug. Curiously, it was the dark side of Ludlow's experiences that writers like Blackwood focused on. The supernatural horror writer H. P. Lovecraft, whose literary style is very similar to that of Ludlow in his most gothic moments, said that Ludlow's "phantasmagoria of exotic colour . . . proved more of a stimulant to my own fancy than any vegetable alkaloid ever grown or distilled."[73]

The occultist and magical practitioner Aleister Crowley criticized Ludlow's dependence on De Quincey and his sentimentality, but printed extracts from his book in his journal *The Equinox*. He also published an essay there on his own experiments called "The Psychology of Hashish" (1909). Having traveled in India, where he observed that some yogis use hashish, Crowley decided to try the drug, hoping to interrupt what he called the dryness of meditation and speed up the process of mystical insight to "a few hours." He dismissed the enhancement of sensuality noted by other writers: "I have no use for hashish save as a preliminary demonstration that there exists another world attainable—somehow."[74]

Crowley had approved the ritual use of drugs in his revealed scripture, *The Book of the Law* (1904), and used hashish in some of his attempts to attain the yogic Samadhi (enlightenment). But the difficulty of disentangling the "real" mystical experience from the "false," drug-induced one exasperated him: "the hashish enthusiasm surged up against the ritual-enthusiasm; so I hardly know which phenomena to attribute to which."[75] In a later diary entry he sarcastically observed: "there are only two more idiocies to perform—one, to take a big dose of Hashish and record the ravings as if they were Samadhi; and two, to go to church. I may as well give up."[76]

Crowley offered a quite sober appraisal of the effects of the drug, developing Baudelaire's and Ludlow's thoughts on hashish's ability to bring out the symbolic potential of objects into a complete semiotic system:

> Simple impressions in normal consciousness are resolved by hashish
> into a concatenation of hieroglyphs of a purely symbolic type.

Just as we represent a horse by the five letters h-o-r-s-e, none of which has in itself the smallest relation to a horse, so an even simpler concept such as the letter A seems resolved into a set of pictures, a fairly large number, possibly a constant number, of them. These glyphs are perceived together, just as the skilled reader reads h-o-r-s-e as a single word, not letter by letter. These pictorial glyphs, letters as it were of the word which we call a thought, seem to stand at a definite distance in space behind the thought.[77]

Crowley explained the expansion of time and space experienced by hashish users as a result of the multiplication of the units of perception involved in perceiving any object, or "glyph." Consciousness appeared to expand because of the time and space needed to process this excess of perception.

A number of other writers of the time also developed spiritually based semiotic systems through experimental drug use—for example, William James with his use of nitrous oxide. Indeed, at the beginning of the twentieth century, in the shadow of Saussurean linguistics, there lurked a whole semiotic underworld, rich with connections to esoteric doctrine and psychoactive substances. Baudelaire saw nature as a vast synaesthetic "forest of symbols" that emitted mystical words. Rimbaud sought to break down conventional semiotic systems through derangement of the senses and experimented with a synaesthetic alchemy of words that aimed at finding the truth that lurked behind signs. The use of hashish encouraged such ideas. The repeated references to synaesthesia in the hashish literature express a semiotic anomaly: signs that have their source in something that they should not—a smell in a sound for example.

The hashish user's fascination with masks, those brittle outer semiotic layers that obscure the "real" person, point to something similar. Any object under the hashish user's gaze became double—both the cluster of signs under which it maintained a name and identity, and something else which this exterior only hints at. Henri Michaux would later call hashish a "first-class spy" and use it to study what was "behind words."[78] Walter Benjamin, who took the drug in the 1920s, observed while high that "things are only mannequins and even the great world-historical events are only costumes beneath which they exchange glances of assent with nothingness, with the base and banal."[79] Benjamin's notion of "aura," which he defined variously as the ability of objects to look back at one when looked at, or the historical presence of the object outside of the reproducible signs of its existence, can be directly related to the peculiarities of hashish-influenced perception.[80]

Benjamin took hashish for the first time in December 1927 with the Berlin doctors Ernst Joël and Fritz Fränkel.[81] Benjamin had known Joël when they were in college in Berlin, where they had headed rival student organizations. Joël became a doctor during World War I, in the course of which he apparently became addicted to morphine, and after the war he returned to Berlin to set up a psychiatric clinic, where he treated the poor and formulated what he called "social psychiatry." In the 1920s, along with Fränkel, he conducted a series of experiments using a variety of psychoactive substances, stressing phenomenological and gestalt methods of recording the effects of hashish (as opposed to treating research subjects like laboratory animals), with the aim of producing and studying abnormal and pathological states of mind. Benjamin, along with the philosopher Ernst Bloch and others, participated in informal experiments that involved opiates, mescaline, and possibly cocaine, as well as hashish.[82] About these experiments, Benjamin said: "The notes I made, in part independently, in part relying on the written record of the experiment, may well turn out to be a very worthwhile supplement to my philosophical observations, with which they are most intimately related, as are to a certain degree even my experiences while under the influence of the drug."[83]

In 1932, Benjamin described his intention to write a book about hashish,[84] but he actually published only two pieces of work directly related to his experiences with hashish: the short story "Myslowitz-Braunschweig-Marseilles" (1930) and the anecdotal autobiographical essay "Hashish in Marseilles" (1932), which contains material very similar to that in the short story. Benjamin's insightful but undeveloped notes on his experiences were published in the 1970s in Germany under the title *Über Haschisch*.

In his experiments with hashish, Benjamin examined the links between aesthetic activity and the hashish "Rausch," a word best translated as "intoxication," but having no exact English language counterpart.[85]

> To begin to solve the riddle of the ecstasy of trance [Rausch, or intoxication], one ought to meditate on Ariadne's thread. What joy in the mere act of unrolling a ball of thread! And this joy is very deeply related to the joy of trance [intoxication], as to that of creation. We

go forward; but in so doing we not only discover the twists and turns of the cave, but also enjoy this pleasure of discovery against the background of the other, rhythmical bliss of unwinding the thread. The certainty of unrolling an artfully wound skein—is that not the joy of all productivity, at least in prose? And under hashish we are enraptured prose-beings of the highest power.[86]

Ariadne unwinds her ball of thread in the maze of that death symbol, the minotaur. To be high is to enter into a certain relationship with death, to let consciousness rhythmically unwind itself and to take pleasure in the process, which is both a deferral of and a step toward death. Prose is the material trace of this unwinding (literally "wrapping" itself around the page). Such a meditation resonates with the work of a number of other Surrealist fellow travelers living in Paris in the 1930s: Artaud's incorporation of death into his body through opium, Daumal's carbon tetrachloride–driven experiments on his own death (see Chapter 2), and Bataille's exploration of death and excess. Benjamin concludes "Hashish in Marseilles" with a beautiful image of the excess (cosmic, semiotic, or otherwise) to which hashish opens the door: "I should like to believe that hashish persuades nature to permit us—for less egoistic purposes—that squandering of our own existence that we know in love. For if, when we love, our existence runs through nature's fingers like golden coins that she cannot hold, and lets fall to purchase new birth thereby, she now throws us, without hoping or expecting anything, in ample handfuls to existence."[87]

Benjamin's short story "Myslowitz-Braunschweig-Marseilles" plays with a different version of utopian excess, the fantasy of becoming a millionaire. The narrator is given an opportunity to make a potentially profitable investment minutes after ingesting some hashish. On his way to execute orders for the investment, he becomes so distracted by the sights of the city around him, transformed under the power of the drug, that he misses his opportunity. The tale, told with Hoffmannesque irony (from Hoffmann's favorite bar in Berlin, Lutter & Wegener's) is one in the great tradition of stoned bungling. Like other such tales, it reveals the deeper truth of bungling: that the enraptured apprehension of beauty must win over practical considerations every time. For nothing else constitutes winning in this life—everything else is merely survival.

Benjamin's most significant discussion of hashish is found in his essay on
Surrealism (1929), in which he discusses the idea of "profane illumination,"
similar to the experience that the spiritualists were looking for with hashish,
but turned back on itself, so as to illuminate and revolutionize everyday life,
rather than transcend it.[88] "The true, creative overcoming of religious illumination certainly does not lie in narcotics. It resides in a profane illumination, a
materialistic, anthropological inspiration, to which hashish, opium, or whatever else can give an introductory lesson. (But a dangerous one; and the religious lesson is stricter.)"[89] The tension between mysticism, materialism, and
aesthetics is readily apparent here, and like every good modernist, Benjamin
believed that any hint of a mystical experience had to be subsumed and redi-
rected toward specific social, political, or aesthetic goals. Benjamin claimed
that the Surrealists aimed "to win the energies of intoxication for the revolution," but warned against Romantic notions of the power of intoxication or
mysticism.

> Histrionic or fanatical stress on the mysterious side of the mysteri-
> ous takes us no further; we penetrate the mystery only to the degree
> that we recognize it in the everyday world . . . the most passionate
> investigation of the hashish trance will not teach us half as much
> about thinking (which is eminently narcotic) as the profane illumi-
> nation of thinking about the hashish trance. The reader, the
> thinker, the loiterer, the flaneur, are types of illuminati just as much
> as the opium eater, the dreamer, the ecstatic. And more profane.
> Not to mention that most terrible drug—ourselves—which we take
> in solitude.[90]

Benjamin turned the flickering between trance or dream state and sober
consciousness that we have seen in many of the hashish narratives into a dialectical maneuver, which he believed would reveal the truth of everyday life.
Hashish was an excellent choice for this purpose, since it rarely produces the
deeper experiences of transcendental alterity that the psychedelics or anesthetics do. True transcendence was to be deferred until a future moment of total revolution—until then there could only be what Benjamin's colleague
Theodor Adorno called "negative dialectics," the flickering back and forth between opposing states, with the utopian promise of synthesis always beyond
reach.

Even though Benjamin was inspired to write the passage quoted above by his experiments with hashish, he decided to erase the drug itself from the very thought process that it had initiated. Scott Thompson argues that Benjamin's interest in hashish was connected to his interest in unlocking cosmic energies to drive the proletarian revolution.[91] Although it is true that Benjamin's interest in drugs has been effaced owing to aesthetic and political squeamishness on the part of his disciples, Benjamin himself was rather reticent about discussing his experiences, begging correspondents to keep their knowledge of his experiments to themselves.[92] Perhaps he experienced the same disappointment as Baudelaire did at hashish's inability to provide an experience that went beyond the parameters of the self. Benjamin's notes on mescaline plunge quickly into the metaphysical depths, but his hashish writings are more interesting for the way he exposes his loneliness, fear of the future, and desire for a colleague's wife. As the political crisis of the 1930s deepened, and demanded a more orthodox Marxist critique of social reality, Benjamin's interest in writing the hashish book clearly dwindled.

The first American writer to report on his own experiences with cannabis was the travel writer and diplomat Bayard Taylor, who took the drug while in Damascus and published a chapter about his experiences, "The Visions of Hasheesh" in *The Lands of the Saracen* (1855). Taylor gives one of the clearest descriptions of the doubling phenomenon that repeatedly manifests itself in the literature on cannabis:

> My enjoyment of the visions was complete and absolute, undisturbed by the faintest doubt of their reality; while, in some other chamber of my brain, Reason sat coolly watching them, and heaping the liveliest ridicule on their fantastic features. One set of nerves was thrilled with the bliss of the gods, while another was convulsed with unquenchable laughter at that very bliss. My highest ecstasies could not bear down and silence the weight of my ridicule, which, in its turn, was powerless to prevent me from running into other and more gorgeous absurdities. I was double, not "swan and shadow," but rather Sphinx-like, human and beast. A true Sphinx, I was a riddle and a mystery to myself.[93]

This is not the first time that we have encountered the Sphinx in this chapter—she watched from across the river in Nerval's tale of the Caliph Hakim, published in France eight years earlier. The constellation of man-beast and crime was also one that Anslinger used in describing the supposed effects of cannabis. Why Sphinx and not "swan and shadow"? The answer is connected to the unquenchable laughter that is one of the most well known effects of cannabis intoxication. This laughter is something profane, earthy, intimately concerned with mortality. Transcendental swans do not laugh, at least in the Christian world. Animality has a fundamental connection to crime in human culture, whether incestuous sexual crime or the crime of turning citizens into animals, which medieval Muslims believed hashish use could do. Animality in fact functions as the ignoble, materialist double of transcendental flight. Any movement beyond the realm of the human risks being labeled animal—and criminal.

Doubles and doppelgängers: think of the fisherman pretending to be the Sultan in the *Thousand and One Nights,* or the Assassins, masquerading as courtiers. In *Artificial Paradises,* Baudelaire criticized drug-induced ecstatic states as doubles of "real" states of illumination. This notion could be applied, rightly or wrongly, to all drug experiences, depending on how one defines "real"—are work or prayer, Baudelaire's proposed alternatives, really more "real" than hashish? But such issues aside, the image of the doppelgänger, and the experience of a doubled-up reality, have a particular affinity with cannabis, as they do with literature, which also functions as a double of life, connected but at the same time separate.

This doubling is an essential feature of Ludlow's *The Hasheesh Eater*—the book that inaugurated writing about drugs in America. As a young man, Ludlow was exhaustively sampling the curious substances kept by his friend the local apothecary when he came across "a row of comely pasteboard cylinders inclosing vials of the various extracts prepared by Tilden & Co."—one of them containing an extract of *Cannabis indica*.[94] In a series of chapters devoted to different hashish-triggered visions, Ludlow describes how he becomes addicted to the use of cannabis, and finally how he breaks the addiction, in the following curious way.

Ludlow says that he was inspired to quit taking hashish by an anonymous article in *Putnam's* entitled, oddly, "The Hasheesh Eater."[95] The author of this article purports to be a lawyer who spent five years in Damascus, during which time he became a habitual user of hashish. With great suffering he broke the habit and returned to Connecticut, only to receive a gift from the East, containing a box with hashish in it. Urged on by his fiancée, he takes the drug again, and experiences a fantasy of killing everyone around him. Ludlow claims that he contacted and corresponded with the author, who gave him much useful advice about hashish. Lester Grinspoon has suggested that this article was in fact written by Ludlow himself, plagiarizing some of Taylor's work and adding Ludlow's moralistic tone and the idea of the hashish habit, possibly to drum up enthusiasm for the book that he was completing.[96] Given that this article and Ludlow's book are the only ones ever to suggest a hashish habit, and that Ludlow subsequently published his own essay, "The Apocalypse of Hasheesh" in *Putnam's,* this supposition certainly seems reasonable. Doubling phenomena abound: Ludlow reinvents himself as a double of Taylor, whose writing first introduced him to the drug, and produces a fictional text by him that helps him break his own addiction to a drug that is not addictive. And through the device of the box mailed from the East, hashish itself returns as a mysterious doppelgänger, and the murderous frenzy attributed to hashish in Asia now manifests itself in Connecticut.

The other double that looms over *The Hasheesh Eater* is De Quincey's *Confessions,* which clearly structured Ludlow's mind-set in his hashish experiments. Ludlow acknowledges his debt to this book, his inspiration. One of the major tropes of the cannabis literature is the citation of someone else's experience so as to explain one's own, as though there were always a need to import a framework of understanding from the outside, just as the drug itself comes from "outside."[97] *The Hasheesh Eater* is a disappointment, albeit a brilliant one. Blasé hipsters often claim that there is nothing more dull than reading about other people's drug experiences. For the most part, this is merely a rhetorical strategy employed by those who wish to valorize their own experience—been there, done that. But the cannabis literature is often dull, narcissistic, and peculiarly earthbound, never quite reaching the altered states that the psychedelics and anesthetics provide access to. I feel that I ought to admire Ludlow's achievement in writing such a long, idea-packed book about hashish, and yet I find it hard to finish the book, and cannot remember much of what I have read the next day.

The Hasheesh Eater was published in New York in 1857 to generally positive reviews, but was not especially popular at the time. It went out of print during the Civil War and was not republished until 1903.[98] Ludlow himself became a journalist and moved in New York bohemian circles with Walt Whitman and others. He went on to publish books about his travels in the West, before dying at the age of thirty-six from tuberculosis.

A number of medical and literary accounts of cannabis use were published in America after Ludlow's, including a short story by Louisa May Alcott.[99] But the other key hashish text of this period, Marcus Clarke's short story "Cannabis Indica" (1868), was written and published in Australia.[100] In it, Clarke, an Englishman who emigrated to Melbourne in 1863, proposed an experiment: he would write a story while under the influence of hashish, in the presence of a doctor who recorded Clarke's comments while high and made notes on his physiological state during the experiment. In order to provide a complete map of the sources of the imagery in his story, Clarke also described the room in which he took the drug. By doing this, he hoped to provide a materialist map of his imaginative processes, almost like a whodunnit detective story—just as Henri Michaux was to do in the 1960s in *Connaisance par les gouffres*, in which he published a long poem written under the influence of hashish, following it with a long analysis of how each line came to be written. For Clarke, as for many others, hashish was an agent of doubling effects, a translator of physiological processes and sensory perceptions into texts and dreams.

At the end of the nineteenth century, the first newspaper accounts of popular cannabis use in the United States began to appear—and with them, a wave of paranoia about the drug. The immediate results of this fear were few. The Harrison Anti-Narcotic Act of 1914 did not include cannabis products, chiefly because there was little perception of use of cannabis in the United States at that time, little evidence of adverse effects, and a strong lobby from industry, which wanted to protect its right to grow hemp products.

Nevertheless, a number of anti-cannabis laws were passed in at the state level in the early twentieth century. These were mostly driven by the perception that Mexican immigrants fleeing the Mexican revolution of 1910 into Texas and other border states, or blacks in the southern states, were committing violent crimes under the influence of the drug, which now went by the

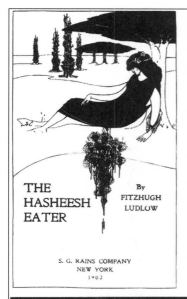

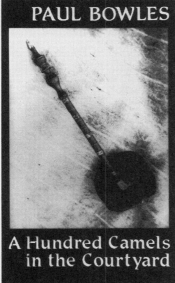

Figure 8. Cannabis book images. Clockwise from the upper left: title page of the the 1903 edition of *The Hasheesh Eater* by Fitz Hugh Ludlow, illustration by Aubrey Beardsley; cover of *Assassin of Youth! Marihuana,* by Robert James Devine, published in 1943; cover of *Pot and Pleasure,* by James Simpson, published in 1972; and cover of *A Hundred Camels in the Courtyard* by Paul Bowles, with a photo by Paul Bowles, published in 1962.

new name "marihuana" or "marijuana"—cannabis' own sinister double. The drug was now smoked rather than eaten, which removed it from the medical context, although, ironically, smoking generally led to a much milder experience than the heady chunks of resin consumed in the nineteenth century. And of course, the new name linked the drug to the world of the new immigrants. Marijuana was certainly used in Mexico. The followers of Pancho Villa sang:

> The cockroach, the cockroach
> Is unable to walk
> Because he doesn't, because he doesn't
> Have any pot to smoke.

Similarly, marijuana was used in black communities, especially in New Orleans, where it was associated with the jazz culture of the brothels. This was not the first time that fears of a link between crime and cannabis had come up: there was considerable debate in medieval Islamic society as to whether hashish use led to crime, and the Indian Hemp Drugs Commission of 1893–94 in England had been formed precisely to address the question of whether cannabis drugs were "dangerous" (the commission concluded that they weren't).

With the new fear came the return of an old myth—that of the Assassins. The myth, which already had considerable potential as a racist one, was transported to America and fused with the fear of Mexican immigrants, those "doubles" of Americans, with their mysterious vices. According to Ernest Abel, the Harlem-based physician Victor Robinson, in 1912, was one of the first to make the link between cannabis and crime, and the supposed link between hashish and assassin.[101] The etymology was repeated afterward in medical journals, in legal decisions, and by the commissioner of the Bureau of Narcotics, Harry Anslinger, as part of his justification for banning the weed.

Anslinger's role in the passing of the 1937 law against cannabis products and his subsequent demonization of cannabis users has received considerable attention.[102] Here I would like to emphasize how Anslinger used literary elements to craft and carry out the policies of the Federal Narcotics Bureau. I began this chapter by discussing Anslinger's use of the legend of the Assassins in arguing the case against marijuana before Congress. In *The Murderers* (1961) Anslinger again discusses the medieval Islamic group, noting that "they made homicide a high ritualistic art. Their name itself is today a synonym for murder."[103] Anslinger, like the writers of the Club des Hashishins, saw the Assassins as turning crime into an aesthetic act—through the taking of the drug.

Anslinger goes on to give a reasonable description of the effects of cannabis—euphoria, loss of space-time relations. But then he discusses those "vivid kaleidoscopic visions, sometimes of a pleasing sensual kind, but occasionally of a gruesome nature," that he believes cannabis produces. This was probably a fantasy originating in nineteenth-century literature. In the next paragraph, Anslinger claims that "those who are accustomed to habitual use of the drug are said eventually to develop a delirious rage after its administration during which they are temporarily, at least, irresponsible and prone to commit violent crimes . . . much of the most irrational juvenile violence and killing that has written a new chapter of shame and tragedy is traceable directly to this hemp intoxication."[104]

Anslinger usually brushed aside scientific work on cannabis—either ignoring it completely or, when this was impossible, calling into question the credentials of the scientists responsible. He understood the power of the media—that is, the power of story-telling. One of his first actions, after the passing of the 1937 Marihuana Tax Act, was to discourage media stories about cannabis, other than those originating from his own office. He protested Robert James Devine's pamphlets *The Menace of Marihuana* and *Assassin of Youth! Marihuana—Feeding the God Moloch* (1943) and also criticized Earle Albert Rowell, a California-based temperance lecturer who wrote a series of books including *Battling the Wolves of Society: The Narcotics Evil* and *On the Trail of Marihuana—the Weed of Madness* (1939). Deemed too sensationalist in his anti-weed rhetoric, Rowell was arrested in 1938 by Bureau of Narcotics agents for possession of opium and other narcotics he used in his lectures.[105] He quickly disappeared from public view.

At the same time, Anslinger wrote several pulplike books about drugs, wrote and oversaw articles for newspapers and journals, and shopped script ideas to Hollywood directors. Independently made Hollywood movies, including *Reefer Madness, Assassin of Youth,* and *Marihuana, Weed with Roots in Hell,* appeared. In 1947, Anslinger appeared in a cameo role in *To the Ends of the Earth,* starring Dick Powell as a narcotics bureau agent hot on the trail of international opium smugglers.[106] Anslinger, according to Larry Sloman (who examined his archives), was a big pulp fan with a substantial collection of sensationalist crime magazines such as *True Detective, True Crime,* and *True Po-*

lice Cases. Much of his knowledge of cannabis in fact came from the collection of press clippings on the subject that he had amassed.

Marijuana quickly became a symbol for everything middle-class white America was afraid of; its smell was the smell of crime and poverty, its user either a desirable but corrupt Mexican or black woman or a male criminal, seedy and deranged. These images were quickly incorporated into pulp fiction.[107] Chester Himes's short story "Marihuana and a Pistol," published in *Esquire* in 1940, gives a brief, grim description of a depressed man who smokes two joints, plans and forgets a series of crimes, goes to the corner store with a pistol in his pocket, eats some candy, then realizes that he's just murdered the store clerk. Thurston Scott's *Cure it with Honey* (1951) features a "brain screw"—a prison psychologist—who hooks up with a Mexican American woman. When they get home, he pours himself the obligatory scotch and water while she produces three marijuana cigarettes. He watches her smoke, full of desire for her, and reflects on the recently issued La Guardia Commission report on marijuana: "Marijuana grows half-wild in the rural slums and at harvest time they bring it up to sell in the city slums; cool dreams, two sticks for a dollar, like looking down the wrong end of a telescope. It isn't toxic, the way alcohol is toxic. Nobody staggers or goes crazy or commits a crime because of marijuana. It's a clean quiet way out."[108]

James Hadley Chase's *The Marihuana Mob* (1951) features a strung-out blonde, who is already bruised and decayed when the narrator meets her: "she gave me that silly, meaningless smile reefer smokers hand out when they suspect they should be sociable and the effort is too much for them." Her smile was "fixed"; "I doubted if she heard what I said, let alone understood what was happening," but she was also "surprisingly strong" when she became aggressive. Her companion is a petty criminal called Barratt who plays "strident jazz" in his room. "From the look of his eyes, he was full of reefer smoke," and "the enlarged pupils of his eyes gave him a blind look"; "he came on, slowly, rather like a sleepwalker."[109] Meanwhile, in another room across town, "there was a distinct smell of marijuana smoke . . . Not new, but of many months' standing. It had seeped into the walls and the curtains and the bed and hung over the room like a muted memory of sin."[110]

And so on.

Much has been said about drug use being a victimless crime. In the case of marijuana, the peculiar doubling effect that the drug can set in motion, allowing shifts of perception between dream and sober states, appears to have affected nonusers too. In the absence of any causal connection between marijuana and crime, marijuana became a symbol or, more precisely, a symptom of crime. If, as Anslinger says, the Assassins turned murder into a ritualistic art, then modern marijuana users, with their rituals, must also be criminals. And after 1937, when possession of cannabis products became illegal, users *were* criminals. Marijuana use became a symptom of itself, a sign of a sign—a crime because its use indicated that the user was willing to break the law. The gateway theory of cannabis, in which the drug, even if proved relatively harmless, "leads" to more harmful activities, is a variation of this theme—if cannabis use in schools is a gateway to "harder" drugs, it is for the most part because the drug is illegal, and legitimizes other illegal activities through association with its own relative harmlessness.

One of the narcotics bureau's earliest targets was jazz musicians—another of those secret, cultic groups devoted to ecstatic illumination that keep recurring in the history of cannabis. Marijuana, known as "moota" or "muggles," was associated with jazz from 1900 on in New Orleans whorehouses. By the 1930s, there were a number of jazz songs about marijuana; and "tea-pads," where people went to get high and listen to a record player or jukebox, proliferated in Harlem. Musicians such as Louis Armstrong have spoken (positively) about their use of marijuana, but there is no record of marijuana use among the Harlem Renaissance writers.

The most detailed account of marijuana in Harlem and among jazz musicians appears in a 1946 autobiography, *Really the Blues,* written by the self-proclaimed "White Mayor of Harlem," the Jewish jazz musician Milton "Mezz" Mezzrow. Mezzrow was not the first white man to imitate blacks, but he was one of the first to write about his experiences. Mezzrow was turned on to marijuana as a jazz musician and claimed that smoking made him play better. He compared the life of a viper (slang for weed-smoking hipster), one of peaceful coexistence and relaxation, with that of the "lush-hound," who brawls and becomes angry as soon as he gets intoxicated. After finding a connection who could sell him good-quality Mexican gold-leaf grass ("Poppa, you never smacked your chops on anything sweeter in all your days of viping"), Mezzrow started to deal to his friends, "and pretty soon all Harlem was after me to light them up."[111] In 1933, a successful radio-booking agent even proposed to Mezzrow that they set up a company to sell his marijuana cigarettes nationally, but Mezzrow declined.[112] Mezzrow bristled at the notion that he was a "pusher" and claimed that he simply sold marijuana to friends who asked him for some—"sort of everybody to their own notion, that was the whole spirit." In 1940, Mezzrow was busted and spent three years in jail for possession of marijuana, leading him to conclude somberly that the one dangerous side effect of the drug was the prison sentence it now carried.

Although Mezzrow was obviously inclined to hyperbole regarding his own place in history, his descriptions of marijuana highs are much more recognizable than those of earlier writers. Mezzrow's fascination with jive set the scene for the Beat appropriation of black culture in the 1950s. This appropriation can in itself be seen as part of the culture of doubles and doppelgängers that surrounds cannabis: a culture of copying that has been endlessly productive of new social forms, not merely in "white" Bohemia, but within jazz, as a mutant West African music form appropriating European musical instruments and structures.

For the Beat writers, cannabis held the utopian promise of escape from white America, just as use of the drug by mid-nineteenth-century French writers held out the promise of escaping from bourgeois Paris. Burroughs grew a marijuana crop in Texas in the 1930s, both as a money-making scheme and a perverse gesture. In Jack Kerouac's *On The Road* (1957), his protagonist Sal Paradise tries to score in a black jukebox joint in Los Angeles, with his Mexican girlfriend. Later in the book, Paradise and Dean Moriarty, a thinly veiled verson of Kerouac's friend Neal Cassady, score from a young Mexican boy while on a road trip through Mexico, and Kerouac has a vision of Moriarty as God. (Cassady would later spend two and a half years in San Quentin jail, after he had given a couple of off-duty cops a joint in exchange for a ride to work in San Francisco in 1959.)

Although Kerouac is known principally as a drinker and amphetamine user, several of his books were written with the assistance of marijuana, notably *Mexico City Blues* (1959) and *Doctor Sax* (1959), both of which were written in part during a trip to Mexico City, where Kerouac had ready access to marijuana (and occasional hits of morphine courtesy of Burroughs). According to Allen Ginsberg, Kerouac wrote *Mexico City Blues* by drinking coffee, smoking a joint, and writing down whatever came into his head, blending Buddhist apprehensions of *sunyatta* (open, spontaneous, luminous emptiness) with jazz improvisation and Proustian memory flashes.[113] *Doctor Sax* can be seen in a similar way, as a series of phenomenological diagrams of the experience of remembering a childhood in Lowell, Massachusetts, alternating passages of remembrance with a mythological fantasy of a comic book superhero fighting the cosmic forces of darkness. Dream and reality alternating again, in other words.

Allen Ginsberg first started smoking marijuana in 1945 or 1946 in New Orleans, but ascribed his involvement with the weed to "picking up this story among criminals, prostitutes, musicians, movie people, circus and legit theater people, 42nd Street, Times Square, 1945."[114] It was also a self-conscious continuation of the tradition of Rimbaud and the European nineteenth-century literary experimenters. For Ginsberg, being high in New York in the 1940s meant being part of a gnostic conspiracy, secretly committing a heretical act in order "to resurrect a lost art or a lost knowledge or a lost consciousness."[115] Some of Ginsberg's poems, such as "Marijuana Notation," were written under the influence. But Ginsberg's most eloquent statement about marijuana is his essay "First Manifesto to End the Bringdown" (1966). The first part of the essay was written while he was smoking a joint. Ginsberg contrasts the abuse heaped on marijuana by the narcotics bureau with the actual experience of the drug: "the paradoxical key to this bizarre impasse of awareness is precisely that the marijuana consciousness is one that, ever so gently, shifts the center of attention from habitual shallow purely verbal guidelines and repetitive secondhand ideological interpretations of experience to more direct, slower, absorbing, occasionally microscopically minute, engagement with sensing phenomena during the high moments or hours after one has smoked."[116]

In truth, Ginsberg meanders, but as he says, this meandering is harmless enough. The second half of the essay was written while he was not high, and presents in a forceful and coherent way some of the major arguments in favor of decriminalization of marijuana: that the law is racist, constructed by people who have no first-hand experience of the drug as a way of justifying their own bureaucratic existence; that marijuana can aid perception and was used by most of the poets and artists that Ginsberg knew; that public interest in marijuana signaled boredom and a turning away from the ideological frenzy of the Cold War to other levels of experience.

Ginsberg played a major role in breaking the wall of silence that Anslinger had skillfully constructed around marijuana. On February 12, 1961, Ginsberg was scheduled to appear on a TV talk show hosted by John Crosby to discuss "Hips and Beats" with Norman Mailer and the anthropologist Ashley Montagu. Ginsberg proposed to Mailer that they discuss the harmlessness of marijuana, and Mailer, although he had had a bad experience with the drug, went along with that plan. Ginsberg discussed his experiences in India and Tangier on the show and everybody agreed that the current marijuana laws were too extreme. The broadcast was received with surprise by the media, and with even greater surprise by the Bureau of Narcotics. Against the wishes of the show's host, Anslinger demanded and was granted equal time on the show to issue a rebuttal; a bureau spokesman claimed that, among other things, marijuana was so damaging to dogs in tests that they had to be destroyed. Nevertheless, the door to public dissent from Anslinger's position was open.

Ginsberg observed that although Anslinger's fictions about marijuana were undoubtedly successful in the short term in persuading society that marijuana was harmful, when people actually tried the weed and discovered its real qualities, it led them to question whether the whole state apparatus and its ideology was also a fiction. This cynicism about Bureau of Narcotics dogma concerning cannabis also led to a certain hubris concerning the positive qualities of the weed in the 1960s. It was claimed, for example, that the weed made people incapable of fighting wars even though marijuana use was probably as prevalent in Vietnam as it was at home.[117] Meanwhile, Ginsberg was arrested in his hometown of Paterson, New Jersey, in 1966 for smoking marijuana (the charges were dropped), and Bureau of Narcotics intrigues aimed at framing him as a drug dealer surfaced in the press. Nor was he the only one: Timothy Leary was arrested on charges of marijuana possession in 1965 in Texas, and given a thirty-year sentence. The conviction was overturned by the Supreme Court in 1969, but Leary was retried early in 1970 in Texas, and on new possession charges in California, and given a ten-year sentence in each case. Later that year, he escaped from the minimum security prison he was being held in, only to be caught again in 1973 in Kabul, Afghanistan. He was granted parole after two years in prison. Nor were literary critics immune. In 1967 Leslie Fiedler, who had helped to found LeMar, a group advocating the legalization of marijuana use, was arrested for "maintaining premises where marijuana was used" and given a six-month sentence.[118]

And as public consciousness of alternative culture grew, a market for books exploring the hidden history and culture of drug use developed. A small group of English-language independent presses, Calder and Owen in London, Grove in New York, Olympia in Paris, and City Lights in San Francisco, published much of the new literature, often under threat of prosecution on charges of obscenity, until Burroughs' *Naked Lunch,* the last book prosecutors accused of obscenity in the United States, was deemed not obscene by a Massachusetts court in 1965. "Secret" histories and the "science" of cannabis were revealed in collections such as *The Marijuana Papers* (1966) and *The Book of Grass: An Anthology of Indian Hemp* (1967), and in 1970, Michael Horowitz and some of his friends in San Francisco founded the Fitz Hugh Ludlow Memorial Library, devoted entirely to the history of books about drug use, again demonstrating the ability of cannabis aficionados to form social groups around the plant.

As a mass culture of cannabis use evolved in the 1960s, new genres of books appeared, describing the sexual antics of stoned bohemians,[119] the folklore of dope farmers, smugglers, and dealers,[120] and a homegrown crop of horticultural wisdom issued in the shade of the hydroponically powered success of *High Times* magazine, which began publication in 1974.[121] Weed culture in the 1960s and 1970s was full of Rabelaisian laughter: the political satire of Paul Krassner's magazine *The Realist,* the clowning antics of The Fabulous Furry Freak Brothers, Robert Crumb, and Cheech and Chong.[122] Pot-smoking audiences gathered to watch and laugh at Anslinger-era movies like *Reefer Madness. High Times* published *Playboy*-parodying glossy centerfold photos of budding sensimilla plants. As in Rabelais' medieval marketplace, where official pronouncements were turned into objects of ridicule, the cannabis users of the 1960s and 1970s parodied conventions and dogma, creating a "counter"-culture out of the doubled up, secret meanings, the slippages between dream and reality that are so connected with the drug.

There is one further twist to this tale, which brings us back full circle to the Orient, which fueled the early European notions of cannabis. In 1947, the writers Paul and Jane Bowles moved from New York to Tangier, Morocco. Paul had experimented with ether while a student at the University of Virginia and had tried marijuana in 1934 in Mexico. Tangier, at that time, was part of an international zone in the north of Morocco in which just about anything was for sale and, in the words of Hasan-i Sabbah, anything was permitted—a utopia, in other words. The Bowles made their home(s) there and served as the focal point for an expatriate literary and artistic scene through which a number of major literary figures passed in the following decades. One of the delights of Tangier, and a draw for writers such as William S. Burroughs, who lived there from 1954 to 1958, was the easy availability of various drugs. For Burroughs of course, the principal attraction was pharmaceutical-grade narcotics, available over the counter. The local drug of choice however, was cannabis, which was used in a variety of preparations. Bowles soon became familiar with majoun, a very potent hashish candy,[123] and used the visions it triggered as material for the hallucinatory death scene of Port Moresby in *The Sheltering Sky* (1949) and the "hashish delirium" at the end of his second novel, *Let It Come Down* (1952).

Even though Bowles's wife and companion, Jane, was a drinker and loathed hashish, Bowles enthusiastically explored the world of Moroccan cannabis drugs, and served as a somewhat dubious guide to visitors. Bowles was apparently fond of offering unsuspecting visitors hashish candy and then scaring them with tales of permanent mental damage when they became nervous; among those who had this experience were Robert Rauschenberg, Christopher Isherwood, and Ned Rorem.[124] "Oh he was a real ministering angel when you were having the horrors," noted Burroughs sardonically.[125]

Burroughs was initially avoided by many of the Tangier expatriates, partly because of his narcotic addiction. But by the late 1950s, he and Bowles had become friends. The arrival of Ginsberg, Kerouac, and others in 1957, to assist in preparing the manuscript of *Naked Lunch,* cemented the whole North African Beat scene. It should be remembered that although the subject matter of *Naked Lunch* is narcotic addiction, large sections of the book were written in Tangier after Burroughs had gone through one of his frequent withdrawals. During these periods, Burroughs ate majoun (which he prepared himself) and kept a row of pre-rolled joints by his writing desk. "Unquestionably this drug is very useful to the artist, activating trains of association that would otherwise be inaccessible, and I owe many of the scenes in 'Naked Lunch' directly to the use of cannabis."[126] Much of the atmosphere of *Naked Lunch,* the turbulent blocks of association and intense paranoia, along with the constant shifting between hard-boiled pulp realism and experimental dream writing, have more in common with the cannabis literature than with anything written about narcotics. Burroughs was also obsessed with the legend of Hasan-i Sabbah, occasionally signing his work with the warlord's name and developing a complicated myth of Sabbah as a blend of mystic and Nietzschean superman.

Meanwhile, in 1955 Bowles had started smoking cannabis in a pipe, in the preparation known locally as kif.[127] Unlike majoun, which was potent enough to be considered a hallucinogen, kif conveyed a gentler experience. Bowles began recording stories told by Moroccans high on kif, some of which later became the basis for books of short stories that he compiled, such as *Five Eyes* (1979). In a 1961 article published in the American Beat magazine *Kulchur*, Bowles linked the use of hashish to traditional Islamic culture, which was being destroyed by global modernization:

> In Africa particularly, the dagga, the ganja, the bangui, the kif, as well as the dawamesk, the sammit, the majoun and the hashish, are all on their way to the bonfires of progressivism. They just don't go with pretending to be European . . . a population of satisfied smokers or eaters offers no foothold to an ambitious demagogue . . . you can't even get together a crowd of smokers: each man is alone and happy to stay that way . . . The user of cannabis is all too likely to see the truth where it is and to fail to see it where it is not.[128]

Once again, this is not the asocial passivity of the opiate user who is oblivious to social reality. The cannabis user is aware of what is going on around him or her. He or she rejects it in favor of something else that is seen simultaneously.

In 1962, at the urging of Ginsberg, Bowles published a set of hashish-related stories with City Lights Press. *A Hundred Camels in the Courtyard*—the title taken from a Moroccan proverb, "a pipeful of kif before breakfast gives a man the strength of a hundred camels in the courtyard"[129]—is an oddly clinical, almost mathematical series of exercises, in which, as Bowles says in the preface, he tries to bring together the everyday world, governed by natural law, and the world of the kif smoker, taking unrelated elements and stories from the former, and connecting them using the power of kif. The stories radiate paranoia, or, if you like, the ambience of black magic.

Three of the stories are relatively traditional in style. The fourth, a cryptic tale called "He of the Assembly," sets Burroughs-style associative prose within

a musical, almost mathematical structure of points of view. Bowles also taped
and translated a book of hashish-related stories related by his friend Mohamed Mrabet: *M'Hashish* (1969). Most of the stories compare the crudity and
misfortune of the drinker with the wisdom and luck of the kif smoker. Where
Bowles exposes (or invents) webs of black magic, most of Mrabet's stories
have a more subtle and direct explanation of kif's effects. Allah favors the kif
smoker, who, through smoking, is more in touch with the unseen world and
more willing to allow it to determine the way in which events unfold.

I would like now to return to the problem of framework, with which I began
this chapter. As we have seen, the use of cannabis has been framed in an extraordinary number of ways. What if cannabis' ability to trigger relational
shifts, and a doubling up of consciousness, is fundamentally meaningless, and
therefore value neutral? That is to say that the mental states triggered by pot
have no particular meaning, but that meaning is added by the user in his or her
particular set and setting. In Sufi culture, the shift in consciousness is one that
leads to illumination; in nineteenth-century literary culture it is associated
with a sensitivity to symbols and signs; for a law enforcement officer in America in the 1930s, it suggests a deviation from the order of the human and the
law, into crime; for lovers, it acts as an aphrodisiac; for insomniacs, it is a sleep
inducer; and so on and so forth. In recent years, cannabis advocates have become quite prolific in creating compelling new frameworks for the use of
cannabis: medical marijuana; the hemp fiber industry; cutting-edge hy-
bridization techniques producing ever more potent strains.

Whether or not one is persuaded by every one of these frameworks, the
subtle shifts in perception, the switching back and forth between the everyday
and dream worlds that cannabis triggers, clearly lend themselves to utopian
musings on the transformation of this world. Utopias are not merely impossible dreams or fantasies. They are visions of the transfiguration of our own
world—visions that are often acted on, as we have seen. The literature on
cannabis is filled with such utopias: secret societies like the Assassins and the
Club des Hashishins, heretical sects like the Sufis, Nerval's madhouse and the
prison, Rabelais's herb vendors, the marginal worlds of Times Square hustlers,
jazz musicians, the Mexican peasants eulogized by the Beats. All of these ex-

ist as fractal social spaces, whose existence is either denied, threatened, or forced into hiding by political or religious orthodoxy, but that appear in the popular imagination as utopias which offer an already visible model of a transformed society.

The ultimate fractal social space is that of dreams. The dreams of the cannabis user are not gnostic; they do not withdraw into the darkness of another world, like those of the narcotic user. These dreams are developed out of the social space that the user finds himself or herself in. Of course, it is likely that the user will simply giggle at these dreams, or run from them in a fit of paranoia. But there also exists the possibility of acting on them. The erotic potential of marijuana is entirely connected to this point. Cannabis connects, even if some of the connections the cannabis user sees render him incredulous. "Surely you don't really mean to look that way!" exclaimed Walter Benjamin during one hashish experiment.[130]

From the *Thousand and One Nights* to Paul Bowles's work, the short story or tale is the cannabis literary genre par excellence—a short story that is somehow lacking the traditional, rich weaving of the tale, however. Many of the cannabis-inspired short stories bring together an associational block and give it narrative continuity in much the same way that a dream, recalled and described the morning after, gives shape to the dream material. Baudelaire's *Prose Poems,* which he gleefully described as a serpent from which individual elements could be removed or replaced at will, without affecting the structure, achieve a similar effect. There is something arbitrary, unconvincing about this—and Baudelaire knew it, ironically celebrating the modern reader and writer's short attention span. At the same time, the process by which thoughts and sensory data are turned into a narrative under the influence of cannabis has a more general significance, and was used by writers like Gautier, and later Crowley and Benjamin, to provide early descriptions of how the mind structures experience into coherent cognitive structures. Hashish, with its tendency to amplify preexisting thoughts, was an ideal tool for this work—but the cognitive processes it revealed are universal.

From the beginning, the history of cannabis has been a history of clashing interpretations, clashing names. When Linnaeus named the hemp plant *Cannabis sativa* in 1753, there were immediate protests. The French naturalist Jean de Lamarck proposed that a differentiation be made between the Asian and European plants, because of their different qualities: *Cannabis sativa* (tall and fibrous, European) and *Cannabis indica* (short, bushy, resinous, psychotropic, Asian). Twentieth-century Soviet botanists later proposed a third species: *Cannabis ruderalis* (a wild species). This dispute remains unsettled.

The same problem has cropped up in defining the active principle in cannabis. Although the active alkaloids of many other psychoactive plants were quickly discovered in the nineteenth century, the cannabis alkaloid proved highly elusive. In the 1890s, T. B. Wood and his colleagues at Cambridge University discovered the parent active molecule—cannabinol (not in fact an alkaloid) at the cost of two lives lost in laboratory explosions.[131] Tetrahydrocannabinol (THC), one of the main physiologically active molecules in cannabis, was finally discovered in the 1960s, but there are in fact a family of more than sixty cannabinol molecules present in every plant. It would appear that the mix of these molecules determines the activity of the drug.

Even the spelling of the word "hashish" has fragmented into many differently spelled, differently defined subwords: hashish, hasheesh, hachych, hachich, hachisch, hachish, haschisch. This linguistic flickering is itself reminiscent of a phenomenon known to cannabis users, who, when high, can become highly sensitized to the microscopic cognitive fluctuations that usually go unnoticed but that are in fact characteristic of consciousness at all times. It is this sensitivity to detail, to tiny differences, that has given cannabis its reputation as a creative tool. It also has a political significance: One of the major indications of the shift in attitude toward cannabis in the early twentieth century was the renaming of the drug as "marijuana," a word free of medical or nineteenth-century cultural associations, but rich with associations with despised minority groups. Recently, groups like the National Organization for Reform of Marijuana Laws, which advocates decriminalization of cannabis use, have gone back to calling the cannabis plant "hemp," to emphasize its "NORMLity" and its links to industry.

From a practical point of view, Anslinger's vilification of cannabis remains mysterious: the data to back up his claims of the dangers of the drug simply do not exist. The literary and cultural associations of the cannabis plant, and its strange propensity for creating secret, cultic phenomena around it, were not epiphenomena in Anslinger's war against the weed. They were essential to it, and provided both the rhetoric with which the plant was condemned and some of the "evidence." Cannabis advocates repeatedly had to disavow the literary culture that had grown up around the plant. During the early initiatives in the United States to place restrictions on marijuana, Charles West, chairman of the National Wholesale Druggists' Association, defended the sale of marijuana by maintaining that the idea that the substance was harmful was based on literary fantasies, such as *The Count of Monte Cristo*.[132] The La Guardia Commission claimed that "romanticist" nineteenth-century writers exaggerated the powers and dangers of hashish, and because of the respect that European society had for them, people avoided the drug.[133]

Although it was disingenuously convenient for Anslinger and company to exploit this literature regarding cannabis, and to create out of it a framework of criminality, it was no less disingenuous for writers to use cannabis as a way of framing and selling the realm of the imagination in which they were so heavily invested. Cannabis served as a vector for bringing dreams to the marketplace. This hawking of dreams was always going to be a risky business, likely to blow up in the faces of those who initiated it. The materiality of cannabis, which made it such "fantastic" magic, also made it the material trace by which those dwelling in the worlds of the imaginary could be fingered. They were highly visible, and a peculiar smell could be detected emanating from the rooms they hung out in. In this respect, it is important to note that there have been very few writers about drugs whose books have actually been targeted by prosecutors for contravening the obscenity laws.[134] There have, however, been a number of cases where writers have been arrested for possession of cannabis, in part as a consequence of writings that identified them as cannabis users.

It was Allen Ginsberg who first drew attention to the need to simultaneously defend the realm of the imagination and its material traces, among them drugs and literature—and to the fact that a marketplace is something more than a place to sell things in. A photograph from 1965 shows Ginsberg standing at a demonstration on a street in Manhattan, his hair covered with a dusting of snow. The silhouetted cops that are watching him trigger a flashback to the statue of Napoleon that lurks behind Baudelaire in the poet's self-portrait under the influence of hashish: a reminder of the constant presence of the state in the dreams of the cannabis user. But hanging from Ginsberg's neck is a cardboard sign that, with three words, takes us back to the laughter that tears through Rabelais's marketplace when the vendor of Pantagruelion arrives: POT IS FUN.

4

INDUCED LIFE

Stimulants and Literature

All speedfreaks are liars; anybody that keeps their mouth open
that much can't tell the truth all the time or they'd run out of things
to say.

—LESTER BANGS, "Kraftwerkfeature," *Creem*, 1975

I am using a caffeine-containing liquid, prepared by im-
mersing the dried leaves of the tea bush in boiling water for several minutes,
as I write these words. I believe that drinking this liquid is helping me to
write—and yet I do not think of the resulting text as having anything to do
with caffeine. This transparency is characteristic of our attitude to stimulants,
the most ubiquitous, yet least understood, of the psychoactive drugs used in
modern life. Although my definition of stimulants is quite straightforward—
substances that "make people feel more alert and energetic by activating or exciting the nervous system"[1]—many different substances with different effects
have been called stimulants at various times, and other drugs that are quite
clearly stimulants to us have been considered otherwise. Opium was considered the stimulant par excellence in the eighteenth and early nineteenth centuries. Even De Quincey, who significantly contributed to the destruction of
the stimulant view of opium, claimed that the primary effect of the drug was
"in the highest degree, to excite and stimulate the system," and liked to take
nocturnal walks around London while high.[2] Cocaine, which clearly acts as a
stimulant in the sense above, was classified by Louis Lewin in his *Phantastica*

as a euphoriant, like morphine. Tobacco acts as both a stimulant and a depressant. In writing this chapter, however, I have confined myself to the history of the drugs currently believed to be stimulants: caffeine, cocaine, and the amphetamines.

What is the effect of stimulants on writing? In order to answer this question we must consider the way in which drugs have come to function in the modern world as technological aids to writing, whether it be the conceptualizing activity of the scholar, the code production of the computer programmer, the persuasive rhetoric of the advertising executive, or the imaginative work of the poet, all of which have been associated with stimulant use. All drugs are, in Heidegger's definition of the word, technologies, because they "posit ends and procure and utilize the means to them."[3] We can speak of opiates as technologies of pleasure, cannabis as a technology of dreaming, anesthetics as technologies of transcendence. But the stimulants, which appear to offer us an almost mechanical increase in productivity, in focus, in the ability to think, pose the problem of technology at a more fundamental level. To use McLuhan's terminology, they are "extensions of man," extensions of our capabilities. Taken at high, intense doses, they can certainly be used to induce euphoria, to get high, but we still describe their action in a quantitative rather than a qualitative way. There is a conscious recourse to machine metaphors, to a whole rhetoric of material production.

Stimulants introduce the problem of speed to our discussion of drugs and writing. "All drugs fundamentally concern speeds, and modifications of speed," say Gilles Deleuze and Félix Guattari.[4] Thus the slowing down of the gastrointestinal system with narcotics or of time perception with DMT are modulations of speed as much as the loquacity of the cokehead or speedfreak. The speed of literature itself, however, is hard to quantify. We can talk about how fast a book was written, printed, or distributed, but this tells us little about the speed of the text itself. How does an increase or decrease in the speed of cognitive functioning inscribe itself in the writing or reading of a text? This is a question that has scarcely been asked before. The French philosopher of technology Paul Virilio has suggested that every technology programs its own accident that is specific to it. Just as we cannot give an account of the place of the automobile in our society without including the automobile crash or the spectacular forms of 1950s U.S. convertibles, we should expect that stimulants, rather than just acting as vehicles that transport us speedily through the act of

writing a text, should carry with them their own set of side effects, of accidents, whose traces are revealed in the lives and writings that I will examine.

A Chinese legend tells us that Bodhidharma, the Indian monk who brought
Buddhism to China, struggled not to fall asleep during long meditation ses-
sions. Finally, in exasperation, he tore off his eyelids and threw them away so
that he would remain perpetually awake. Where they fell to the ground, tea
plants are said to have sprouted. In the Middle Eastern world, coffee, a plant
indigenous to Ethiopia, first appeared circa 900 c.e. in medical works like
those of Rhazes and Avicenna.[5] The drink was used as an aid to prayer in the
Eastern Christian church in Ethiopia, by the Sufi dervishes, who introduced
it to Islamic culture in the middle of the fifteenth century, and in European
Christian monasteries.[6] Coca leaves were given to sacrificial victims by Inca
priests at the moment before their sacrifice to the sun, but they were also
chewed by Andean villagers to promote endurance on long journeys by foot.
In each of these cases, it is a question of developing endurance through the
drug, as an antidote to the limits of the human body, whether for sacred or
profane purposes: not a shift in cognition, as with hashish, not a transcending
of the body and the world, as with anesthetics and psychedelics, not a narcotic
triggering of dreams or sleep, but "simply" a continuation of awakeness, of activity, of whatever sort. In other words, stimulants acquired a *technical* meaning, as far back in human history as we can trace them.

Coffee first appeared in European literature in the accounts of travelers to
the Near East in the sixteenth century, and it was mentioned more frequently
after the drink was introduced to Europe in the seventeenth century. It was
quickly recontextualized away from its connections with Islam: Pierre Della
Valle argued that coffee was in fact the Homeric nepenthe, while other European writers linked coffee to various passages in the Old Testament.[7] Coffee
became associated with literature in two ways: through the social act of drinking coffee at a coffee house and through its pharmacological effects, which
promoted clarity of thought and sobriety.

The first coffeehouses appeared in Mecca at the end of the fifteenth century
and evolved out of the sacred use of the beverage by the dervishes. Throughout the Islamic world in the sixteenth century, the spread of the coffeehouse

was accompanied by a wave of clerical furor, and coffeehouses were shut down for promoting intoxication and for being a social institution that rivaled the mosque. The controversy about coffee resulted in a copious literature devoted to arguments for and against coffee.[8] The coffeehouses of Constantinople, besides being places where politics were discussed, gambling and sexual liaisons conducted, were places of entertainment where storytellers plied their trade. In other words they were, at least potentially, secular and aesthetic institutions.

The first European coffeehouses opened in Venice in 1645 and in London in the 1650s, and quickly replaced taverns as places where business and discussion of politics, literature, and business were conducted.[9] Besides offering coffee, the coffeehouse provided other amenities, notably newspapers and lights. The coffeehouse was plundered as an image by writers of the time. The early issues of Sir Richard Steele's *Tatler* (1709–1711), one of the first literary journals to be produced, were organized as follows: "All accounts of gallantry, pleasure and entertainment shall be under the article of White's Coffee House; poetry under that of Will's Coffee House; learning under the title of Grecian; foreign and domestic news you will have from St. James' Coffee House, and what else I shall on any other subject offer shall be dated from my own apartment."[10]

Various British writers, including Jonathan Swift, Henry Fielding, John Dryden, Alexander Pope, and Oliver Goldsmith, were associated with particular coffeehouses and a number of authors, including Carlo Goldoni, Voltaire, and Fielding wrote dramatic comedies entitled "The Coffee House" in the eighteenth century.[11] According to Wolfgang Schivelbusch, the coffeehouse made possible a culture of conversation that, through the introduction of colloquial language and argumentation, took literature out of the library and resulted in the abandoning of the conceit and cliché as the foundations of literary style.[12]

Poetic homages to coffee—"all bad" as Stewart Allen observes[13]—were quite common in seventeenth- and eighteenth-century Europe; coffee was often brought forth as an antidote to the soporific qualities of opium or wine.[14] It was "sober," promoting health, moderation, clarity of thought, and energy. Pope, in the *Rape of the Lock* (1714), wrote that:

> Coffee (which makes the politician wise,
> And see through all things with his half-shut eyes)
> Sent up in vapors to the baron's brain
> New stratagems, the radiant lock to gain.[15]

In the nineteenth century, Jules Michelet linked the acceleration and intensification of French intellectual life in the age of the Enlightenment to the
consumption of increasingly potent coffee: "Coffee, the sober liquor, potently
cerebral, which contrary to spirits, augments clarity and lucidity—coffee
which suppresses the vague and heavy poetry of the smoke of the imagination,
which, seeing reality in plain view, makes the sparkle and clarity of the truth
shine forth." Michelet spoke approvingly of how coffee from "our Indian island," Réunion, was responsible for the "torrent of sparks which the light
verses of Voltaire and the *Persian Letters* give us a feeble idea of," and how the
strong coffee from the Antilles nourished the age of the *Encyclopedia,* being
drunk by Georges Buffon, Denis Diderot, and Jean-Jacques Rousseau, who
"added their light to the penetrating insight of the prophets assembled "in the
den of the Procope," [those] who saw, at the bottom of the black brew, the future ray of '89."[16]

Honoré de Balzac, probably the most famous coffee-drinking intellectual of
the nineteenth century, devoted a section of his *Traité des excitants modernes*
(1838) to coffee. The essay was first published as a postscript to Jean-Anthelme
Brillat-Savarin's highly popular work *Physiologie du goût* (1826), in which the
author, after observing that "it is beyond doubt that coffee greatly excites the
cerebral powers," goes on to attribute specific literary qualities to the drink:
"Voltaire and Buffon drank a great deal of coffee; perhaps the former owed to
this habit the admirable clarity which ones senses in his works, and the latter
the enthusiastic harmony which is found in his literary style. It is plain enough
that many pages of ESSAYS ON MAN, about the *dog,* the *tiger,* the *lion* and the
horse, were written in a state of extraordinary cerebral exaltation."[17]

Balzac expands on Brillat-Savarin's comments, by praising the modernity of
coffee and the other "stimulants": tea, liquor, tobacco, and chocolate. Although
the energy contained in the body and mind is finite, excitants can change the
speed at which energy is consumed and work is done, since "for social man, to
live means to spend oneself, more or less quickly."[18] Coffee, unlike tea and
liquor, which contribute to the brutishness of the British character, makes the
blood move faster, and produces a "stimulation which aids digestion, chases
away sleep, and allows the exercise of the cerebral faculties to be maintained
for a longer duration."[19] For strong spirits such as himself Balzac recommended drinking strong undiluted coffee on an empty stomach: "Everything
stirs: ideas set off like the battalions of a great army over a battlefield, and give

battle. Memories come in at the charge, colors flying; the light cavalry of metaphors spreads out in a magnificent gallop; the artillery of logic rushes in with its supplies . . . witticisms arrive as skirmishers; figures rise up; the paper is covered with ink, for this waking state begins and ends with torrents of black water, like a battle with its black powder."[20]

The writer brews the coffee a second time in his stomach, and then it pours forth as black ink on a white page.[21] This image contains one of the primary themes of stimulant literature, that of a technologically assisted dictation that becomes possible through use of a stimulant. The writer's body disappears as his mental faculties accelerate and the paper covers itself with ink. This acceleration involves a kind of violence, which, according to Virilio, is characteristic of the culture of speed.[22] This violence was already apparent in my first example of stimulant use: Bodhidharma tearing off his eyelids in order to stay awake. Balzac gives the violence a characteristically modern, military form: coffee is part of a logistical organization of forces, a rapid concentration and forceful, accelerated deployment of them, which results in a text. It is a rational form of violence. The comfort with which we now experience acceleration (padded seats, soothing music, hostesses—in airplanes and coffeehouses!) serves to obscure the violation of our bodies and minds that is fundamental to stimulant use. But Balzac, standing at the birth of modern speed culture, was able to describe it, without making it seem like an accident or side effect of coffee, as an integral part of its properties.

Balzac was one of the first writers to discuss the importance of the speed and volume of what he wrote—for financial reasons and because of the "reality of the marketplace," no doubt. In the early part of his career he wrote novels in two to three weeks and kept up a curious work schedule that consisted of going to bed in the early evening, awaking at midnight, and, fueled by strong coffee that he brewed himself, working through the night to the morning, when he took an hour-long hot bath and then edited proofs until lunch. Afternoons were taken up with social calls. It is said that Balzac drank 50,000 cups of coffee in his life.[23] He complained about stomach pains and abscesses caused by his excessive coffee drinking, and according to his long-term physician, Dr. Nacquart, his early death, whose actual cause is hard to determine since Balzac by that time was suffering from many different ailments, was hastened by his nocturnal work habits and his abuse of coffee.[24]

During the nineteenth century, coffee ceased to be a drug worthy of discussion, even though its use for the purpose of mental stimulation became even more prevalent. We know that Marcel Proust drank large quantities of coffee, to rouse himself from barbiturate-induced sleep. In the twentieth century, F. Scott Fitzgerald wrote while drinking coffee, presumably before and after his alcohol binges. Sartre washed down his pep pills with coffee. And coffee accompanies the cigarette in many a writer's armament. But coffee has been so thoroughly absorbed into the structure of the modern workplace that it has become transparent, a tiny mechanical cog in the machinery of everyday life.

The history of cocaine has been reviewed many times, a surprisingly large number of times in fact. The first *History of Coca* (1901), 576 pages long, was written by an American doctor and enthusiast named W. Golden Mortimer. Mainly concerned with the coca plant, as opposed to one of its alkaloids, cocaine, the book reviews at great length the story of coca use in Andean civilizations, discusses the effects of the European invasion on coca consumption, and gives very detailed information on the harvesting and production of coca, its pharmacology, and its physiological effects. Many other books on cocaine include similar information, with a discussion of the plant and its use in South America followed by a description of the discovery of one of its alkaloids, cocaine and its use by Freud and Sherlock Holmes, and so on. No such history books were written about other drugs until much later in the twentieth century unless we include tea and coffee, which had history books written about them in the twenties, sponsored by manufacturing companies, trying to position them as "temperance beverages." It is likely that Mortimer's intention was to situate coca as a food substance similar to tea or coffee—a plea for coca's legitimacy written at the very moment when public and institutional distrust of the substance was growing, and its image as a "tonic" or food was shifting to that of "drug." A similar vogue for histories of hashish and opium accompanies the current attempts to legalize these substances.

But something more specific is at work here too, because the histories continued after cocaine was made illegal, in both the twenties and the seventies. Opium, hashish, and the psychedelics have until recently had no history, even though all were known to Europeans at least as long as cocaine was. They were written about ethnographically, the books containing descriptions of the habits of peoples who were believed to have no history, such as the barbaric Turks who used hashish and opium, or savages, living eternally within nature, like the Native American peyote eaters. Cocaine, by contrast, is a social drug, and wherever people gather together to take a substance, they like to talk about its qualities. Cocaine aficionados, at least until the advent of crack, liked to think of themselves as connoisseurs, and cultural history added a value, an aura of sophistication, to the drug, one which could be talked or written about. At great length.

Coca was used by the Indians of the Andes for thousands of years, and for a variety of purposes before the arrival of men such as Pedro Cieza de Leon, a soldier in the Spanish campaign against the Incas, who wrote the first European account of the plant in his *Chronica del Peru* (1550). Its ritual use was quickly banned, while its uses for military and economic purposes, notably to invigorate slave laborers in the mines of Peru, were tacitly encouraged. In the eyes of the "modern" European conquistadors, the stimulative qualities of coca leaves made them excellent fuel for what they saw as subhuman machines.

A hundred years after the first European accounts of Andean coca use began to appear, the British poet and physician Abraham Cowley spoke of "the divine plant of the Incas" in his *Books of the Plants* (1662), a long poem in which Venus hosts a convention of gods who deliver homages to the plants over which they preside. After being forced to taste the wine of Bacchus, a South American deity named Pachamama brings forth the coca plant:

> Behold how thick with Leaves it is beset;
> Each Leaf is Fruit, and such substantial Fare,
> No Fruit beside to rival it will dare.
> Mov'd with his country's coming Fate (whose Soil
> Must for her Treasurers be exposed to spoil),
> Our Varichocha first this Coca sent,
> Endow'd with leaves of wond'rous Nourishment,
> Whose Juice succ'd in, and to the Stomach tak'n
> Long Hunger and long Labor can sustain:
> From which our faint and weary Bodies find

More Succor, more they cheer the drooping Mind,
Than can your Bacchus and your Ceres joined.[25]

For Cowley, coca was the antithesis of the Bacchic wine, not an intoxicant,
but food provided by the Gods for those who would have to work like slaves
under colonial rule. A hundred years later, at the beginning of the Industrial
Revolution, a Jesuit priest named Antonio Julian suggested in his *Disertacion
sobre hayo o coca dans la perla de la America* (1787) that coca would be a blessing
to the poor of Europe, sustaining them in their labors. Other writers con-
curred. In *Travels in Peru* (1846) the Swiss naturalist Johann Jakob von Tschudi
gave an account of the effects of chewing coca leaves, while the Italian doctor
Paolo Mantegazza, who had experimented with coca while living in Peru,
claimed in his 1859 thesis on the drug that "God is unjust because he made
man incapable of sustaining the effect of coca all life long. I would rather have
a life span of ten years with coca than one of 1000000 . . . (and here I had inserted a line of zeros) centuries without coca."[26]

Mantegazza, who went on to make significant contributions to the fields of
pathology, anthropology, photography, and sexology, articulated a number of
the more important themes of the cocaine literature: the craving for an intensification of time through use of the drug; the "injustice" of a world in which
it is impossible to maintain coca-induced pleasure indefinitely; the unfocused,
directionless acceleration of thought processes and writing, which sends zeros
shooting off the page. But while the motor activity of writing on a piece of paper came easily to him when he was under the influence of the coca leaves, no
corresponding complexity of mental imagery or idea accompanied it: "while
my pen would run quickly and impatiently over the paper, I would not be able
to either conceive new ideas or imagine a harder or more exalting task that
might better suit the exceptional state of my brain."[27] We are once again in the
territory of the Balzacian stimulant-fueled writing-machine.

Coca's entry into European society was effected in 1863 by a Corsican
chemist named Angelo Mariani, who made a wine with a cocaine base that he
called Vin Mariani, "the athlete's wine." This wine was the prototype for the
numerous cocaine-based patent medicines, tonics, and "soft drinks" that proliferated in the United States at the end of the nineteenth century, the most
famous of which was Coca-Cola.

Mariani, an early user of advertising techniques, published an album each year with signed testimonies as to the virtues of his wine from many nineteenth-century luminaries, including Pope Leo XIII, the tsar of Russia, Jules Verne, Emile Zola, Henrik Ibsen, Louis-Adolphe Thiers, Léon-Michel Gambetta, Alexis Carrel, Léon Daudet, Colette, Henry Bordeaux, Joseph-Simon Gallieni, Victor Hugo, Thomas Edison, and William McKinley. Auguste Rodin did drawings for the album and Charles Gounod composed a hymn: "Honor! Honor! Honor to Mari-a-ni wine!" Cardinal Charles Lavigerie wrote a note to Mariani saying that "your coca gives my white Fathers the strength to civilize Asia and Africa." Claude Farrère, a former military officer and one of the chief French eulogists of opium at the end of the nineteenth century, wrote slyly to Mariani: "A long time ago, I had the idea of writing a novel about a man who drinks lots and lots of Mariani wine . . . and I will write it."[28] But Farrère, perhaps because of his devotion to opium, did not write this book. Still, the implicit warning sounded by Farrère regarding the addictive potential of Mariani wine was heeded: the matrix of stimulant, exoticism, advertising, and worldwide distribution invented by Mariani was carried forward into the twentieth century by Coca-Cola—but coca itself was replaced by the everyday stimulant par excellence of the West: caffeine.

Cocaine, one of the active alkaloids in coca leaves, was isolated in 1859 by Albert Niemann, but it was not until the early 1880s that it had its day as a wonder drug. That was the period when a number of technological innovations contributed to a sense that the pace of life in Europe and America was accelerating. Over the following thirty years, the automobile, the telephone, the first metropolitan subway systems, the motion picture, and the airplane all contributed to a radical shift in what McLuhan calls sense perception ratios. There was little interest in speed per se as a useful quality, however. The talk of the day was of fatigue, *épuisement*, and what people wanted was a drug that would banish exhaustion.

The first accounts of cocaine by medical specialists confirmed its reputation for alleviating fatigue. Some of them undertook Alpine hikes, in imitation of the Peruvian Indians who were said to measure distance according to how far one could walk under the influence of a mouthful of coca leaves. Coca was, then, a unit of time.[29] Speed equals distance divided by time. Distance equals speed times time. Distance equals coca-induced speed of walking times number of coca mouthfuls chewed. In 1883, a Bavarian physician, Theodor Aschenbrandt, discovered its military applications, when he gave some soldiers

cocaine before maneuvers and was impressed by their astonishing energy.[30]
The euphoria and acceleration of mental processes that accompanied this
newfound vigor were seen as epiphenomena.

Sir Arthur Conan Doyle, whose detective, Sherlock Holmes, was a famous
cocaine user, probably learned about cocaine during a period of medical studies in Vienna in the 1880s. Even so, in "A Scandal in Bohemia" (1886), where
the drug first makes its appearance in Doyle's work, the author appears to con-
fuse cocaine with morphine. He speaks of Holmes "alternating from week to
week between cocaine and ambition, the drowsiness of the drug and the fierce
energy of his own keen nature." "The Sign of Four" (1888) contains the most
fully elaborated description of Holmes's cocaine use:

> Sherlock Holmes took his bottle from the corner of the mantel-
> piece and his hypodermic syringe from its neat morocco case. With
> his long, white nervous fingers, he adjusted the delicate needle and
> rolled back his left shirtcuff. For some little time his eyes rested
> thoughtfully upon the sinewy forearm and wrist, all dotted and
> scarred with innumerable puncture-marks. Finally, he thrust the
> sharp point home, pressed down the tiny piston, and sank back into
> the velvet-lined armchair with a long sigh of satisfaction.
>
> Three times a day for many months I had witnessed this
> performance, but custom had not reconciled my mind to it. On
> the contrary, from day to day I had become more irritable at the
> thought that I had lacked the courage to protest . . .
>
> "Which is it today," I asked, "Morphine or cocaine?"
>
> He raised his eyes languidly from the old black-letter volume
> which he had opened.
>
> "It is cocaine," he said, "a seven-per-cent solution. Would you
> care to try it?"
>
> "No indeed," I answered brusquely. "My constitution has not got
> over the Afghan campaign yet. I cannot afford to throw any extra
> strain upon it."
>
> He smiled at my vehemence. "Perhaps you are right, Watson," he
> said. "I suppose that its influence is physically a bad one. I find it,
> however, so transcendently stimulating and clarifying to the mind
> that its secondary action is a matter of small moment."

"But consider!" I said earnestly. "Count the cost! Your brain may, as you say, be roused and excited, but it is a pathological and morbid process which involves increased tissue-change and may at least leave a permanent weakness. You know, too, what a black reaction comes upon you. Surely the game is hardly worth the candle. Why should you, for a mere passing pleasure, risk the loss of those great powers with which you have been endowed? Remember that I speak not only as one comrade to another but as a medical man . . ."

He did not seem offended. On the contrary, he put his fingertips together, and leaned his elbows on the arms of his chair, like one who has a relish for conversation.

"My mind," he said, "rebels at stagnation. Give me problems, give me work, give me the most abstruse cryptogram, or the most intricate analysis, and I am in my own proper atmosphere. I can dispense then with artificial stimulants. But I abhor the dull routine of existence. I crave for mental exaltation."[31]

The hypodermic syringe marks the modernity of Holmes's pastime, and cocaine provides a double for the stimulation of solving a crime. It unleashes the same set of "intricate" or "abstruse" mental phenomena and provides that sense of "exaltation" that comes from finding an order in them.

Richard Ashley in his history of cocaine suggests that Holmes's obsession with conspiracies is a possible symptom of cocaine abuse; another way of saying this is that Holmes's sensitivity to signs and traces could be linked to substance abuse. It is a characteristic of late-nineteenth-century modern culture in general to be concerned with developing a microperception of signs—as is evidenced in Charles Pierce's theory of semiotics, Nietzsche's mobile army of metaphors, Freud's symptomatology of the unconscious, the early years of the detective novel, the quantum theory in physics, Louis Pasteur's discovery of the germ theory of disease, and Saussurean linguistics. Paranoia, one of the symptoms of excessive stimulant use, consists in finding an order in sign systems where none exists.

As societal disapproval of cocaine grew in the 1890s, Holmes's cocaine use was gradually phased out, until in "The Adventure of the Missing Three-Quarter," Dr. Watson speaks of having cured Holmes of "drug mania," leaving him with only tobacco. This disapproval is already apparent in the other great nineteenth-century cocaine book, Robert Louis Stevenson's *Strange Case of Dr. Jekyll and Mr. Hyde* (1886). We know that Stevenson wrote the first draft of the book in three days during a period of sickness, and in the late 1960s, a doctor suggested that the book was written under the influence of cocaine.[32] Although there is little material evidence to support that theory (and Stevenson of course never specifies what the potion that Dr. Jekyll cooks up in his home laboratory is), the major theme of the book is one that crops up a number of times in the cocaine literature: that of man's dual existence as a good and evil being, and the use of a drug to bring this duality to crisis point. Stimulants, and cocaine in particular, with its measured pulses of pleasure, often trigger these moral ruminations. Freud, in a letter to Martha Bernays written the same year as *Dr. Jekyll,* says, "the bit of cocaine I have just taken is making me talkative, my little woman. I will go on writing and comment on your criticism of my wretched self. Do you realize how strangely a human being is constructed, that his virtues are often the seed of his downfall and his faults the source of his happiness?"[33] The highs and lows that a stimulant user experiences suggest a quantitative, almost mathematical relationship between cause and effect, euphoria and depression, and other emotional and moral states. Dr. Jekyll's goodness, based as it is on his scientific research, is intimately connected with the unrestrained animality of Mr. Hyde. The link is made through the mediating drug.

The period during which cocaine enjoyed medical respectability was brief. In 1885, the young Freud suggested that cocaine was an antidote to morphine addiction. At the same time, Carl Koller, a Viennese physician, discovered cocaine's use as a local anesthetic. For a few years, cocaine was hailed as a panacea. By 1885, however, a number of reports had appeared in the medical press about the negative consequences of overprescription of cocaine. By the end of the 1880s, cocaine was being swept into the same category as opium, morphine, and hashish, as a symptom of sickness rather than a cure, part of the armory of Decadent aesthetics.

Although there are few literary references to cocaine outside of Conan Doyle before World War I, cocaine does appear in some popular literature from the period. George Normandy and Charles Poinsot's *La mortelle impuissance* (*Mortal Impotence,* 1903) is the story of Georges Daussones, who seeks to cure his morphine addiction by using cocaine. As he becomes habituated to the drug, "he writes Alexandrins which are perhaps brilliant. No fatigue, no hesitation, no failure of memory. His mental faculties multiply. Finally, the work is born. Nevertheless, the sickness slowly wells up from the bottom of his being—already! His hyperaestheticized auditory sense perceives the noise of a mosquito that he sees, or believes he sees, on a page where ink has fixed marvelous writings. This gets on his nerves."[34] He begins to hear voices, and, as insanity overtakes him, is overcome with the sensation of "a vast and spontaneous generation of vermin who obstinately refused to leave him. He believed he was a corpse invaded before its time by the parasites of coffins. And this devouring drove him mad."[35] Like many of the novels purporting to examine drug use among the Decadents in Paris at the end of the nineteenth century, the book reads as though the authors were copying symptoms and case histories straight from a medical journal.

Indeed, if we are to find evidence of cocaine use in literature before World War I, we must look to the scientific literature. As with many of the psychotropic substances of the nineteenth century, there were a large number of doctors and others with access to medication who became habituated to cocaine—probably because, as Burroughs says, addiction is a disease of exposure.

In his published work, Freud echoed many of the contemporary ideas about cocaine: that it alleviates fatigue and makes "long-lasting mental or physical work" possible. He also spoke of its aphrodisiac qualities. In a letter of 1884 to Bernays, he wrote, "Woe to you my Princess, when I come. I will kiss you quite red and feed you till you are plump. And if you are forward, you shall see who is stronger, a gentle little girl who doesn't eat enough or a big wild man who has cocaine in his body. In my last severe depression I took coca again, and a small dose lifted me to the heights in a wonderful fashion. I am just now busy collecting the literature for a song of praise to this magical substance."[36]

The German psychoanalyst Jürgen vom Scheidt argues that cocaine played a significant role in the self-analysis that Freud performed in the mid 1890s, which resulted in *The Interpretation of Dreams* (1900). Cocaine, according to vom Scheidt, put Freud in touch with the unconscious by amplifying his sexual and aggressive drives in such a way that they were brought to consciousness. In this sense, the dream of the mid-nineteenth-century French psychologists who hoped to discover and study madness through use of psychoactive drugs may be said to have been realized—except that it was ordinary consciousness, not madness, that cocaine and psychoanalysis revealed.[37] Freud was humorously aware in his private correspondence of the effects that cocaine had on him. In another long letter to Bernays he exclaims, at the end of a long digression, "Oh, how I run on! I really wanted to say something quite different." He recognized that "it is the cocaine that makes me talk so much,"[38] and used the drug "to untie my tongue" before an important meeting with Charcot in Paris in 1886.[39] Freud also prescribed the drug for a variety of medical conditions, including the morphine addiction of his friend Ernst Fleischl in 1884. The following year, reports began appearing that cocaine was addictive, and it soon became apparent that Fleischl too had become addicted to the drug. Freud was forced to back down rapidly from his advocacy of the drug. It is believed, however, that he privately used the drug from time to time into the 1890s.[40]

Freud was not the only person with medical training to display such enthusiasm for cocaine. William Halsted (1852–1922), one of the founders of modern surgery, had first come into contact with cocaine in 1884, during experiments that led to his discovery of nerve-block anesthesia. He subsequently became addicted and was only able to escape the drug via a year-long sailing trip in the Caribbean and the acquiring of a life-long morphine habit. Halsted wrote a paper about cocaine for the *New York Medical Journal* in 1885 that begins with the following sentence:

> Neither indifferent as to which of how many possibilities may best explain, nor yet at a loss to comprehend, why surgeons have, and that so many, quite without discredit, could have exhibited scarcely any interest in what, as a local anaesthetic, had been supposed, if not declared, by most so very sure to prove, especially to them, attractive, still I do not think that this circumstance, or some sense of obligation to rescue fragmentary reputation for surgeons rather than the belief that an opportunity existed for assisting others to an appreciable extent, induced me, several months ago, to write on the subject in hand the greater part of a somewhat comprehensive paper, which poor health disinclined me to complete.[41]

Halsted's literary style, so reminiscent of Dean Moriarty's way of speaking in Kerouac's *On the Road*, contains the characteristic stimulant-induced features of extension, elaboration of, and digression from an idea, whether in a particular sentence, or a paragraph, or a page, somewhat in the way that I, for a very specific reason, a good one in fact, am writing, though in fact it would be more accurate to say *typing*, this sentence. The sentence is fragmented into a number of smaller, semiautonomous phrases that modify each other in a way that suggests a desire for ever increasing precision. Thought moves too fast to settle on any particular relationship between thinker and object of thought. By the time a thought has been uttered, consciousness has already moved and views the previous thought from a "subtly" changed perspective. This evolution of thought is experienced with a sense of joy at the ability of the thinker to achieve such microscopic levels of precision in speech and perception—and with a sense of growing bewilderment by the reader who rapidly loses the confidence that the writer artificially maintains throughout.

One of the few writers before World War I who we can link directly to cocaine is the Austrian poet Georg Trakl. Trakl's mother was an opium addict, and he tried to kill himself a number of times when he was a boy.[42] In high school, Trakl began carrying a flask of chloroform with him, and also cigarettes dipped in opium. In 1905 he became an apprentice in a Salzburg pharmacy called the White Angel, which gave him access to all the pharmaceuticals he wanted: chloroform, ether, Veronal, morphine, opium, cocaine, and possibly mescaline. The influence of these substances on Trakl's poetry has been discussed, but it is hard to draw solid conclusions, since there are few direct mentions of substances in the poems, and Trakl's fascination with the French Symbolists could in itself have resulted in many of the druglike effects found in his writing.[43]

Trakl moved between the army and the pharmacy, achieving some literary success in the meantime. In the summer of 1914 he volunteered for active service in the recently declared Austrian war against Serbia, and left Innsbruck for Galicia. Having been placed in charge of a large group of severely injured soldiers at the end of the bloody battle of Grodek, he became overwhelmed by the levels of death and carnage around him, had a mental breakdown, and attempted to kill himself again. He was moved to a garrison hospital in Cracow, where on November 3, 1914, he killed himself with an overdose of cocaine.[44]

During World War I, cocaine replaced opiates as the most fashionable psychoactive substance, both in artistic circles and in the mythical spaces of bohemia and the criminal and racial underworlds. In this sense, Trakl's suicide by

cocaine overdose was not entirely coincidental; the world of the "long nineteenth century" died on battlefields such as Grodek. Where opiates were linked
to decadence, to imaginative excesses and retreat from the world of industry,
cocaine was linked to the machinic hyperdrive of twentieth-century culture, a
world of exponential development of potentialities and fatalities, of shining
machines and traumatized human bodies, struggling to keep up with them.

Aleister Crowley's *Diary of a Drug Fiend* (1922), written in twenty-eight
days on commission for the publisher William Collins, captures this new
world well. The narrator, Sir Peter Pendragon, is a decorated World War I
fighter pilot who returns to London, where he meets and falls in love with an
eccentric, passionate woman called Lou, on the same night that he first tries
cocaine. After dancing for a while in a nightclub with her, he leaps into a car
with her and drives in an unknown direction, until he runs out of gas and (simultaneously) reaches the sea. Once again we are in the territory of the man-
machine. The acceleration of human life at the beginning of the twentieth
century, through the automobile and the plane accompany the discovery of
cocaine and later, amphetamines. In order for a human being to keep up with
or operate these machines, supercharged fuel is necessary. Man becomes a
man-machine, running on a fuel of cocaine until he drops. Pendragon observes that cocaine gives a person the same courage that the British used to
gain their Empire.

The book describes the narrator and his wife's "honeymoon" with cocaine
and their subsequent addiction to heroin. Crowley himself became addicted to
heroin, which he was given as an analgesic, without understanding its addictive properties. Predictably, Crowley's mystical-magical formulas, which always lurk under the surface of the otherwise conventional narrative, serve as a
way to free the heroes from addiction.

Crowley offers a theory of cocaine's action that encompasses the drug's
anesthetic and stimulant properties. "Cocaine is in reality a local anaesthetic
. . . One cannot feel one's body . . . It deadens any feeling which might arouse
what physiologists call inhibition. One becomes absolutely reckless . . . The
sober continuity of thought is broken up. One goes off at a tangent, a fresh,
fierce, fantastic tangent, on the slightest excuse. One's sense of proportion is
gone; and despite all the millions of miles that one cheerily goes out of one's
way, one never loses sight of one's goal."[45] It is worth noting that Crowley
makes no claim that this goal is ever actually reached.

Diary of a Drug Fiend was reasonably popular in its time, but had the unfortunate effect of triggering the full wrath of the British tabloid press, which had a field day with Crowley's mythological brew of "sex-magick," drugs, and the occult. Crowley was forced to emigrate, and his departure foreshadowed the flight of Timothy Leary from the United States in the 1960s—one more Waterloo for self-styled media manipulators, playing with the collective unconscious.

Cocaine was also associated with the post–World War I revolutionary period, which was when it became broadly used in European and American society. Hans W. Maier, in his lengthy monograph *Der Kokainismus* (*Cocainism,* 1926) commented that

> in Germany and Austria, the revolutionary period of the years 1918–1921 was particularly favorable for the propagation and spread of cocaine addiction by nasal inhalation for two reasons. In the first place, the psychopathological state that affected all segments of the population, especially in large cities, constituted a favorable terrain and gave rise to the need for drugs. Second, the chaos that prevailed in the distribution of army stocks had made available to the population a large number of pharmaceuticals, especially alkaloids, the trade in which was soon totally beyond control.[46]

This surplus was fueled by the extraordinary level of industrial production of cocaine by German pharmaceutical companies during the period. In Berlin after the war, cocaine was sold in packets of 4–6 grams known as "koks" or "gramophone disks"—an early link between cocaine and the "hot" electronic auditory space of post-World War II culture that McLuhan celebrates.[47]

We know very little about drug use in Russia during the revolutionary period beyond what we learn from Mikhail Bulgakov's novel *Morphine* (1927). But M. Ageyev's *Novel with Cocaine* (1934), a Dostoyevskian book set in Moscow about a student's coming of age precisely during the period of the revolution, gives us some valuable information. The text was published pseudonymously in an issue of the Parisian Russian émigré journal *Numbers* in 1934, but we have no conclusive information as to the identity of the author. Vladimir Nabokov and George Ivanov, another member of the *Numbers* group, have been suggested as authors, but there is little basis for the claim.

According to sources who rediscovered the text in Paris in the 1980s, the author was a Russian living in Istanbul named Mark Levi, who, emboldened by the *succès de scandale* that the text caused, later sent another story to *Numbers*, along with his passport, apparently in the hope of moving to Paris. That story, however, remains unverified too.[48]

The book sounds a number of familiar cocaine-related motifs. The narrator, Vadim, goes through a series of educational but traumatic experiences, including a fumbling sexual relationship with a married woman, the failure of which serves as a prologue to his induction into cocaine use in a dark café with vaguely disreputable colleagues. Like Pitigrilli after him and Crowley before, Ageyev, who speaks of losing one's nasal virginity, eroticizes the act of sniffing. The trajectory here is important: what begins as a search for pleasure, which often results in heightened experiences of sexual intensity, ends when that which is beyond the pleasure principle—the death drive—is revealed. Accordingly, Vadim dies at the end of the book.

Vadim speculates that cocaine has taught him that what goes up must go down; that feelings of happiness are inevitably replaced by feelings of exhaustion and depression. The moral consequence he draws is that every good act in the world presupposes an evil act as its inevitable consequence—an idea I have already noted in Freud's and Stevenson's writing. There is a lot of moral speculation in the stimulant literature—perhaps because the religious dimension of most psychoactive drug experiences is absent.

But Ageyev also goes further. The association of cocaine with the period of the revolution is hardly an accident, and on pages 177–181, Ageyev explains why. According to Vadim, the end of all human existence is the inner experience of happiness. All external events are aimed at producing this inner experience. Revolution and cocaine, along with sexual love, are merely different means of achieving the same ends.

At the beginning of the book, Vadim's schoolmate, a nervous, acne-prone student named Burkewitz, is publicly humiliated in class when a large gob of snot falls from his nose just as he is about to speak. As a result he decides to "become a man," and through his rapidly developing political consciousness in the prerevolutionary period, he is quickly elevated by the revolution to the status of hero. The narrator, on the other hand, who is more concerned with picking up girls and arguing with his mother, falls through all the spaces opened up by the war and revolution and dies from exposure, in a state of mental derangement brought on by cocaine addiction.

The moral of the story is more ambiguous than this description makes it sound. Although the novel appears to pay homage to the revolution, the fact that Burkewitz, a mere teenager, is now in charge of the hospital that Vadim is admitted to indicates the arbitrariness of the revolution, and of the sentiments that drive it. The unspoken message that the reader is left with is that the revolution is another kind of cocaine addiction, governed by drives and impulses it remains completely unaware of: Burkewitz's destiny is decided by something falling out of his nose; Vadim's by something entering his nose. The likely fate of the revolution can be predicted from what happens to Vadim.

The European aesthetic revolutionary movements that came into being around World War I also dabbled in cocaine. The Italian Futurists, with their love of speed and machinery, might seem like obvious candidates for stimulants, but the Italian Futurist Fillipo Marinetti condemned drugs in his "Manifesto of Tactilism" in January 1921: "The intellectual minority . . . no longer enjoying the ancient pleasures of Religion, of Art, of Love . . . abandons itself to refined pessimism, sexual inversions, and to the artificial paradises of cocaine, opium, ether, etc. . . . Almost everyone proposes a return to a savage life, contemplative, slow, solitary, far from the hated cities. As for us Futurists, we who bravely face the agonising drama of the post-war period, we are in favour of all the revolutionary attacks that the majority will attempt. But, to the minority of artists and thinkers, we yell at the top of our lungs: Life is always right! The artificial paradises with which you attempt to murder her are useless. Stop dreaming of an absurd return to the savage life."[49] The Futurist poet Sofronio Pocarini in his poem "Cocaine" wrote: "I took cocaine and I wandered in the countryside, racked by an infantile savagery, seized by a strange sobriety." The poem ends: "I fell into some cowshit."[50] Ernst Jünger, who offered his own version of Futurism in his homage to mechanized warfare, *Storm of Steel* (1920), was not enchanted by cocaine either: "This intoxication had brought me neither images nor dreams, nothing more than the abstract narcissism of the spirit, the nocturnal review of its immense but anonymous power. Which had been brought about by an enormous expenditure."[51]

The Futurists were fascinated by speed as a form of violence that could be unleashed on the environment. Marinetti had defined Futurism as "a violent attack on unknown forces." Although this theme is a constant throughout the stimulant literature from Balzac to Philip K. Dick, the form it takes is a violence that is turned in on itself; Balzac, for example, talked of coffee's effects

as a kind of warfare, but conducted inside the body. This view was offensive to
the Futurists, who considered any examination of their own interiority a sign
of weakness, and who looked for an experience of speed that was completely
externalized, a pure violation of the environment that would leave them un-
touched.

Like the Futurists, the French Surrealists, at least those following Breton's
dogma, also disapproved of drugs. However, both René Crevel and Robert
Desnos wrote about their cocaine use.[52] According to Jean-Louis Brau, Hugo
Ball and Emmy Hennings, founders of the Dadaist nightclub the Cabaret
Voltaire in Zurich, tried various drugs, including cocaine and heroin. In
post–World War I Berlin, Johannes Baader and Rudolf Schlichter also used
cocaine.[53] The Expressionist Walter Rheiner, who was later to die of an overdose of morphine, wrote a grim novella called *Cocaine* in 1918, one of a cluster
of such texts appearing during the post–World War I period.[54]

The German physician, poet, and essayist Gottfried Benn wrote a poem entitled "Kokain" ("Cocaine") in 1917, after a period in 1916 working as a doctor
for a prostitutes' clinic in Brussels, where, like Jünger in World War I, he had
plenty of time on his hands to "experiment":

> The disintegration of the self, sweet, yearned-for,
> that you give me: my throat is already raw,
> already the foreign sound has reached
> the foundations of the unmentioned structures of my ego.
>
> No longer at the sword that sprang from the mother's
> scabbard to carry out an act here and there,
> and with a steely stab: sunk in the heather,
> where hills of barely revealed shapes rest!
>
> A luke-warm flatness, a small something, an expanse
> And now the Ur arises for breaths of wind
> Rolled into a ball. Those who are not its
> Quake, brain-spectators of crumbling transience.
>
> Shattered self—O drunk-up ulcer!
> Scattered fever—sweetly burst open weir

Come forth, O come forth! Give
blood-bellied birth to the misformed.[55]

Benn describes a strange violence that is interior and exterior at once, a violence that results in the destruction of the Freudian ego, and its world of love
and work, replacing it with a strange, monstrous birth—of the poem.

"Kokain" has much in common with the generalities of Benn's essay "Provoziertes Leben" ("Induced Life"), in which he defines the position of drugs in
relationship to human existence: "*Existence is nervous existence,* that is, irri-
tability, discipline, enormous factual knowledge, art. To suffer means to suffer
consciousness, not bereavements. Work is intensification of consciousness for
the making of intellectual forms. In short: *Life is induced life.*"[56] To live, in
other words, is to be stimulated. Benn's essay, which goes far beyond cocaine,
develops a vitalist theory of intoxication, in which artificial means are used to
spur the development of the human nervous system to higher states of creativity and consciousness. These states are not merely the utilitarian ones of
science, but spiritual and aesthetic states as well. In this sense, all drugs are
stimulants: Benn discusses mescaline, hashish, coca, opium, and pervitine (an
amphetamine).

Benn gives this theory a disturbing racial spin. Meditating on the difficulty
of discovering a single psychoactive plant in a confusion of toxic ones, he
notes: "probably countless people died of poisoning before the race had
achieved its goal: intensification, expansion—induced life."[57] Benn argues that
this goal is not decadent, but primary: "defense against the beginnings of consciousness, against its senseless imperative projects—hence the urge to alter
the spatial dimensions, to extinguish time, to blow out the horrible flow of its
hours."[58] These states are clearly achieved at the expense of social existence
(love and work)—as in the poem "Kokain."

"Induced Life" was written in 1943, at a moment when the German "race"
was "racing" against Russia for lebensraum, when German soldiers were being
given amphetamines in order to achieve the Third Reich's goals. For Benn, the
intensities of drug use are either asocial, occurring in a private space where the
will engages in an existential struggle with its environment, or racial, and concerned with racial goals. The space in between these two levels of experience,
that of the individual as a part of society, is to be abandoned as soon as possible. The desire to escape the social does not have to be a fascist one. When

Benn speaks of "the mythical collectivity as a vital foundation," the appeal to Timothy Leary and his friends, who printed "Induced Life" in the *Psychedelic Review* in the 1960s, is clear. But in the context of Germany in 1943, Benn's notion of stimulating such a collectivity through drugs, whether for war or for peace, does not escape fascist ideology.

Benn speaks of "religious physiology." As I have already noted, the stimulant literature is strikingly lacking in a spiritual dimension. This is true of Benn's essay, where he speculates on the existence of a "muscle soul" and views the history of religion as a compendium of techniques of physiological and psychic manipulation whose goal he almost completely ignores. In "Kokain," the "yearned-for disintegration of the ego" gives rise not to an experience of divine power, but to a material monstrosity. "Induced Life" continues this line of thought by proclaiming that "God is a substance, a drug! It's certainly possible, and at any rate more likely than his being an electrostatic generator or a Spemannian triton larva developed by transplanting tadpole tissues into the mouth region."[59]

Cocaine was associated with journalists even before World War I. In 1910 the American journal *Current Literature* published its own study of the "Influence of Cocaine on Contemporary Style in Literature." The article reported on the work of the addiction specialist Dr. T. D. Crothers, bringing together a number of familiar ideas about decadence and the arts under the name of "cocainism," but adding some very specific points:

> Cocoaine or cocaine, as it is variously spelled, is responsible for much of the smooth and flowing sentences now so characteristic of the magazine writing of this period . . . Writers of fiction for the magazines seem to this expert to show cocainism most completely when their style is easy or, as some critics call it, "graceful." The brilliance of an imagination or the restless play of a subtle fancy are attainable through cocaine and sometimes in no other way, for the demands made upon the popular writer force him to do his work under the influence of this drug.[60]

No names are named, and there is no direct evidence to support what Crothers believed, but stimulants have always been connected, from the introduction of tea and coffee to Europe, with writing as labor, production. The use of the telegraph at the end of the nineteenth century to transmit stories quickly forced journalists to simplify and economize in their choice of language—much to the dismay of certain writers. Any sign of adaptation to the speeds of machines could become a symptom of cocaine use.

The hero of Pitigrilli's *Cocaina* (1921), as well as its author, is a journalist. Pitigrilli was a pseudonym of Dino Segre, an Italian journalist who wrote several books in the twenties. The novel describes the rise and fall of Tito, a young Italian who moves to Paris to become a journalist. There his first assignment is to write a story about cocaine. He goes to Montmartre and is given his first experience of coke by a one-legged dealer who hides his stash in his wooden leg, while four women around him beg for more cocaine. As in much of the literature of the time, he almost immediately becomes addicted. Tito sits in his room at the Hotel Napoleon, doing cocaine, and has the idea that God is a form of cocaine: "to give life to man He breathed the breath of life into his nostrils." As Tito's journalist colleague observes, "when you make biblical comparisons, it means that you have a few grammes of cocaine up your nose."[61] This is about as close as the stimulant literature gets to a connection with the divine.

Tito's theory of cocaine's toxicity is that it damages through splitting the personality. "I believe that in every intelligent person there are two persons of opposite ideas and tastes; and I believe that in the artist these two persons are so distinct that one can criticize the other, suggest remedies to him and cultivate his vices if they are attractive and his virtues if they are not boring. The effect of cocaine is to make the splitting of the personality take the form of an explosion of revulsion. The two persons inside me criticize each other, corrode each other, in a way that results in my hating myself."[62]

This split takes an interesting form in the novel, when one of Tito's mistresses (the book is full of sage and dubious advice about how to seduce someone—not entirely a coincidence in a book about cocaine), Maud, turns into a "white-skinned" woman known simply as Cocaine. Ageyev and Crowley also hint at this personification of cocaine as a woman—continued after World War II in African American hipster circles, where cocaine was known simply as "girl."

The novel builds to a frenzied climax wherein Tito and Maud, after being separated, are reunited in Dakar, Senegal. In a cocaine frenzy, they decide to end it all by letting the intercontinental train run over them: "Think how exciting it will be to lie down on this endless track with our cheeks against the cold steel, to feel for the last time our bodies clinging to each other, trembling with fear . . . in our last embrace, which will be the most exciting in our lives, we shall hear the clatter of the train and see its shadow approaching, we shall shrink like beaten dogs, but the black monster will be on us, crushing us and mixing our blood for ever."[63] This erotic act anticipates J. G. Ballard's 1972 novel *Crash,* with its ironic fetishization of the automobile accident. The literature on stimulants is rife with the image of humans as parasites, insects, bugs, which usually serve as the metaphors for machines. The ultimate act of cocaine-fueled eroticism is annihilation by a machine. *Cocaine* is full of images of machinic or biochemical disassembly: "I'm sick of knowing that my body's a laboratory designed to nourish and renew my protoplasm. I'm nothing but phosphorus, nitrogen, hydrogen, oxygen and carbon. I'm sick of looking at myself, of looking down on myself as if I had eyes outside myself. And I'm sick of being in love, that is of using up my phosphorus, nitrogen, hydrogen, oxygen, and carbon."[64]

In the stimulant literature, all emotional or moral states are merely chemical or electrical fluctuations, dependent on the presence or absence of drugs. Virilio uses the term "metabolic vehicle" to describe the human organism when it is seen merely as a technological apparatus, carrying out purely technical functions, in situations such as slavery or service in the army.[65] With stimulant use, the metabolic vehicle of the body is to some degree produced and controlled by its "owner," who treats his or her body as if it could be programmed, through stimulants, for work—or for pleasure. Emotions are a waste of atoms that could be put to other "uses."

Lurking behind each image, each lunge at pleasure, is the notion of the death drive:

> Cocaine, as pale as the powder that intoxicates and kills; Cocaine, passive woman, as irresponsible as a lifeless being, a pinch of poison that seeks out no one but kills when swallowed; Cocaine, the inert creature who had been willing to die when Tito suggested it, but agreed to live when he no longer wanted to die; Cocaine who gave herself to anyone who wanted her and refused no one, because refusing is an effort; Cocaine, woman made of white, exquisite poison, the poison of our time, the poison that lures one to sweet death.[66]

Virilio has observed that acknowledgment of the catastrophic side effects of any technology implies "a certain relation to death, that is, the revelation of the identity of the object."[67] Although all drugs are technologies, this statement applies particularly to stimulants and narcotics, for which the sensation of pleasure is intimately connected to the knowledge of that pleasure's finitude. Was Freud thinking about the fatigue that comes with excess stimulant use when he proposed precisely this relationship between pleasure, exhaustion, and death in *Beyond the Pleasure Principle* (1920)?

The world that Segre's book describes was one of the set pieces of post–World War I journalism: locations such as Soho, Montmartre, New York, and Berlin; a cast of perverted aristocrats, naive students, progressive women, African and Chinese pimps, prostitutes and journalists, all speeding down the road to ruin, fueled by fast money and "snow." Newspapers dished out righteous indignation and sensationalist accounts, which were closely followed by popular fiction writers, who gave their own hyperbolic accounts of cocaine use.[68]

Although popular literature was quick to exploit cocaine's associations with crime and sexual excess, there is little evidence that many writers in the interwar years used cocaine. Walter Benjamin, for example, who experimented with hashish and mescaline in Berlin with Joël and Fränkel, authors of a monograph on cocaine, never mentions cocaine. Cocaine thrived in the McLuhanesque world of electronic media, while the interwar avant-garde remained secretly committed to the nineteenth-century world (and its drugs); thus at the end of "Ode a Coco," Robert Desnos wrote dismissively of the superiority of opiates to the white fairy:

> I have fields of shifty, pernicious poppies
> Which, more than you, Coco! will turn my eyes blue,
> On Sodom and Gomorrah, and their profound ruts,
> I have spilled the fertilizing salt of the shadows.
>
> I wanted to ravage my intimate countrysides,
> Forests have shot up to recover my ruins
> Three superimposed lives, working daily
> Would not be enough to wreak havoc on the empire.
>
> The poison of my dream is voluptuous and sure
> And the heavy phantasms of the treacherous drug

Will never produce in a lucid spirit
The terror of too much love, too much horizon
Which for me, the traveler, brings to birth songs.[69]

Amphetamines were developed in the 1920s as a result of a search for a cheap synthetic version of ephedrine, an alkaloid from the ma huang plant that has stimulant properties. They were first sold in the United States in 1935 by Smith, Kline, and French. By 1946, Benzedrine (amphetamine sulphate) was being prescribed for thirty-nine medical conditions, including obesity, epilepsy, schizophrenia, alcoholism, excessive anesthesia administration, morphine and codeine addiction, and migraine headaches. For a period of thirty-five years, the same years that cocaine use rapidly declined, amphetamines were legally available, and were prescribed to cause weight loss, as a "pick-me-up," and to increase concentration. They were also widely used in World War II by the German and British armies and, unofficially, by the U.S. Army Air Force, which bootlegged and distributed the drug to troops in Africa, Europe, and the Pacific.[70] Amphetamines were distributed during the Korean War and from 1966 to 1969, the U.S. Army consumed over 225 million tablets, mostly Dexedrine—more than the entire British or American armed forces during World War II.[71]

When a substance is widely distributed and legally available, it becomes difficult to document the number of people using it or its effects. Legal substances are often almost transparent—think of coffee, alcohol, and tobacco in our own culture—lacking the law of the forbidden fruit that leads to fascination and myth making. At first glance, amphetamines must have seemed tailormade for modern military-industrial society. The Russians experimented with giving amphetamines to factory workers; similar experiments are carried out to this day by workers who wish to stay awake for prolonged periods of time. As Jünger caustically observed of cocaine use among fighter pilots, "this could not continue for long without an accident."[72]

Amphetamines have never become a formal part of the workplace—nor are they often used by today's military forces. The exhaustion that follows amphetamine use is debilitating and ill suited to the regularity of nine-to-five work. And the long-term effects of amphetamine use—as of cocaine use—

make regular work habits almost impossible. For writers, for whom the act of writing often occurs during a period of heightened intensity injected into an irregular work schedule, the appeal of stimulants is obvious. Faust sells his soul for a life of intensely heightened activity—he is unconcerned about what happens afterward. The writer on amphetamines makes a similar deal—to finish something fast, efficiently. According to Jünger, it is all a question of dosage, and of time, with the danger of some mental or physical error increasing with the duration the intoxication is sustained for.

The most famous literary association amphetamines have is with the American Beat writers, principally through the writing of Jack Kerouac, but also through stories of William Burroughs' wife, Joan Vollmer, his son, William Burroughs Jr., and the hero of *On The Road*, Neal Cassady. Kerouac first used amphetamines in the mid-forties while he was at Columbia University. He would buy the Benzedrine inhalers that were available over the counter in drugstores, remove the soaked paper inside, roll it into a ball, and wash it down with a cup of coffee or a glass of Coke. Kerouac used Benzedrine as a tool for writing, cranking out rough drafts of three novels in a two-week period. Although he was proud of the large quantities of Benzedrine that he could take (Kerouac was a former football star and in pretty good shape), he was hospitalized in December 1945 with thrombophlebitis caused by excessive amphetamine and alcohol use.[73]

According to legend, Kerouac wrote a draft of *On The Road* in 1951, in a period of two or three weeks, by feeding a roll of shelf paper into a typewriter. Clellon Holmes remembers that "when I visited him a few days after that, I heard his typewriter (as I came up the stairs) clattering away without pause, and watched, with some incredulity, as he unrolled the manuscript thirty feet beyond the machine in search of a choice passage. Two and a half weeks later, I read the finished book, which had become a scroll three inches thick made up of one single-spaced, unbroken paragraph 120 feet long."[74] A cocker spaniel belonging to Lucien Carr apparently chewed up the last few feet of the manuscript. *The Subterraneans* was completed in even more epic fashion in three nights in 1953, with a similar trinity of Benzedrine, teletype roll, and typewriter. Kerouac later boasted that he was as "pale as a sheet and had lost fifteen pounds and looked strange in the mirror" from the writing of it.[75] *Vanity of Duluoz* was also written while Kerouac was on amphetamines.

Little actual mention is made of amphetamines in *On The Road*, although Sal Paradise's only advice to Dean Moriarty when he asks how to become a writer is that "you've got to stick to it with the energy of a benny addict."[76] The book swings between wild euphoria and deep depression and is full of amphetamine-induced conversation. As he prepares to leave San Francisco for New York, Sal observes that "my stay had lasted sixty-odd hours. With frantic Dean I was rushing through the world without a chance to see it."[77] He hitches a ride with Dean to Denver, "buzzing." In the car, they talk ("I never talked so much in all my life"),[78] while sweat pours off their bodies and they sway "to the rhythm and the IT of our final excited joy in talking and living to the blank tranced end of all innumerable riotous angelic particulars that had been lurking in our souls all our lives."[79]

On The Road celebrates speed as a value in itself. Sedentariness is connected to dull, archaic American conformity, except when it is linked to third world peasants and poor blacks who are in touch with the land. Although amphetamines existed before World War II, the culture of speed that exploded in the United States (bikers, rock and roll, the Beats) occurred after large numbers of American men were exposed to the machinic accelerations of World War II, often with the assistance of amphetamines and other drugs. As Hunter S. Thompson reveals in *Hell's Angels: A Strange and Terrible Saga* (1966), these soldiers brought the speed and intensity of military life back to the peacetime spaces of the United States. If, as Herman Melville envisioned in *Moby Dick,* the Pacific formed a final frontier in space, then American exposure to technological and pharmacological modes of acceleration in World War II made possible a new frontier in time, which was quickly settled by the hordes of men who had been exposed to this world. Dean Moriarty rants that "we know what IT is and we know TIME and we know that everything is really FINE."[80] The new importance of music, with its intense, immersive relationship to the present moment is a characteristic of this new culture of speed.

Kerouac's "spontaneous prose" method can be interpreted as a manifesto for writing under the influence of amphetamines: "sketching language is undisturbed flow from the mind of personal secret idea-words, blowing (as per jazz musician) on subject of image." It is the relationship of music to time that provides the model for writing. Kerouac's objective is to accelerate writing until it approaches the speed of thought. Sentence structure is to be replaced by "the vigorous space dash . . . separating rhetorical breathing." "Not 'selectivity' of expression but following free deviation (association) of mind into limitless blow-on-subject seas of thought, swimming in sea of English with no discipline other than rhythms of rhetorical exhalation, and expostulated statement, like a fist coming down on a table with each complete utterance, bang! (the space dash)." Writing was if possible to be "without consciousness . . . in semi-trance."[81]

Allen Ginsberg, who was also associated with the creation of "spontaneous prose," saw this method as primarily a fusion of jazz and Buddhist aesthetics. He disapproved of Kerouac's amphetamine use, believing that it had a deleterious effect on his writing, and was one of the main instigators of the "Speed Kills" countercultural anti-amphetamine campaign in the 1960s.[82] But there are striking similarities between Kerouac's words and those of other stimulant users, who also aimed through stimulant use at an automated transcription of thought, as we shall see. "Spontaneous prose" was a misnomer, since Kerouac's spontaneity was for the most part mediated through chemicals. And let us not overlook the importance of the typewriter in all of this. Although the typewriter was commercially available in the United States from 1874 on, and touch-typing dates to the end of the nineteenth century, the linking of writer with typewriter was a post–World War I phenomenon.[83] Ernest Hemingway advised potential writers to "learn to type"; Truman Capote dismissed Kerouac's work as typing, not writing. The typist is another kind of man-machine and amphetamines act as fuel or lubrication to facilitate the interface of human brain and the machinery of production.

Although the image of the man-machine sits quite comfortably within popular literature, which is after all supposed to be a tainted or corrupted copy of "pure" aesthetic form, we still think of the high culture writers of the twentieth century as existing beyond the hybrid world of mediating machines— hence Capote's "insult." But inevitably, the actual writing practices of the high modernists bear witness to the same reliance on material "aids" to writing true of everybody else. From some time around the World War II, Jean-Paul Sartre used speed in the form of orthedrine and later corydrane, a mixture of amphetamine and aspirin, alternating them with barbiturates when he had insomnia. According to Annie Cohen-Solal, one of his biographers:

> as soon as he was up, after a heavy meal and just a few hours of bad
> sleep, artificially induced by four or five sleeping pills, he had a cup

of coffee and some corydrane: first one tablet, then two, then three, which he chewed while working . . . By the end of the day, he had emptied a whole tube and produced thirty to forty pages of Sartre. When calm and smoothly linear—words clinging to one another— his spidery blue handwriting would unfold with vigor, slightly leaning to the right, often stretching upward, or dipping, but always under control. But, at times, it was like a storm, utter chaos, unfettered madness, monstrous words, twisted every which way, stretched to the breaking point, shrunk, bloated, unruly, drunk. This is how he wrote *The Critique of Dialectical Reason:* a wild rush of words and juxtaposed ideas, pouring forth during crises of hyperexcitement, under the effect of contradictory drugs, that would zing him up, knock him down, or halt him in between . . .

"You see, my trusting in corydrane," he told Beauvoir in 1974, "was to some extent the pursuit of the imaginary. While I was working, after taking ten corydranes in the morning, my state was one of complete bodily surrender. I perceived myself through the motion of my pen, my forming images and ideas. I was the same active being as Pardaillan." And he added, "I thought that in my head—not separated, not analyzed, but in a shape that would become rational—that in my head I possessed all the ideas I was to put down on paper. It was only a question of separating them and writing them on the paper. So to put it briefly, in philosophy, writing consisted of analyzing my ideas; and a tube of corydrane meant 'these ideas will be analyzed in the next two days.'"[84]

In his "complete bodily surrender," Sartre becomes a disembodied transcendental consciousness, able to manifest itself on paper through an act of dictation to the pen in his hand and the paper in front of him, his amphetamine-fueled body a writing machine.

Several of Sartre's works show the influence of speed, including the abovementioned *Critique of Dialectical Reason* (1960); his sprawling, mammoth, incomplete five-volume biography of Flaubert, *L'idiot de la famille* (1971–72); and *Saint Genet* (1952), which, according to Susan Sontag, began as a 50-page preface to Genet's writings, and ended up an 800-page book.[85]

Sartre's amphetamine use reveals itself in two ways: first, in the sheer, or "mere" quantity of words; and second, in the lack of control that Sartre exercised over the size and scope of some of his later projects, which are often large but incomplete, with ideas proliferating without reaching closure or conclusion. Of course, many modern texts display these characteristics—because modernity as a whole is fascinated by the same set of effects that the stimulants trigger: heightened intensity, increased duration, the subtle interplay of large systems of ideas and the will to power. Stimulants are both an example of modernity's preoccupations and a catalyst for further reconfigurations of the modern.

The number of italicized words and phrases in *The Critique* is also very striking. It is as though Sartre is trying, through sheer force, to make his ideas cohere, to amplify them in such a way that they become persuasive. The words themselves buckle under the excessive force that he brings to their inscription. One can almost see Sartre's pen scraping holes in the paper he is writing on, just as one can imagine the machine gun rattle of Kerouac's typewriter. Kerouac himself preferred the image of a jazz drummer pounding on a snare, a more organic, but no less stimulant-driven image.

Sartre and Kerouac attempted to organize vast multiplicities of ideas and images through some form of totalizing structure. This was Sartre's project in *The Critique,* and it was also the function of the theory of spontaneous-bop poetics. Sartre used Hegel and Marx to try to achieve a "theory of practical ensembles"; Kerouac and the other Beat writers used jazz or Mahayana Buddhism to work through spontaneity or improvisation to produce self-organizing texts. In both cases, the writers tried to find a way of going beyond the entropy of random, machinic word production toward a higher, unifying meaning. This was the great challenge of cybernetic culture—the idea of "the net" being its most current form. Sartre and the Beatniks stand on two sides of the great divide opened up by post–World War II civilization: Sartre trying to hold on to rationalism, even as that rationalism decimates larger and larger human populations, while the Beats flee into the transcendental East—both fueled by over-the-counter stimulants.

Amphetamines have been associated with New York, the twenty-four-hour city, ever since the Beats. Stimulant use in bohemia appears paradoxical at first. After all, stimulants have been traditionally associated with the virtues of work, sobriety, and so on. Clearly, in post–World War I Paris, or in Kerouac's frenzied drives across the United States, this was no longer the case. Stimulant use is a very active form of the culture of excess, of unproductive expenditure. Instead of the world of dreams or cosmic spirituality, it produces the all-night coffeehouse, the late-night jam session, the all-weekend party. When you are freed from the rhythms of day and night, sleeping and going to work, in a city where you can (or could) do anything at any time of the day or night, all kinds of novel reconfigurations of excess and expenditure became possible.[86]

The classic amphetamine novel is William Burroughs Jr.'s *Speed* (1970), a strange speedball-like blend of Kerouac's spontaneous prose poetics with the senior Burroughs' dry observation techniques in *Junkie*. Much of the speed ingestion in *Speed* takes the form of injecting crystal methedrine, which causes a very rapid acceleration of both the pleasurable and the destructive effects of amphetamines. Burroughs Jr. (1947–1981) himself burned out rapidly, like many crystal users. As a result of these chemical surges of energy, Burroughs Jr.'s prose constantly takes off in strange flights of lyricism that are alien to the smoother flow of Kerouac. Discontinuity is everywhere apparent, and there are also strange surges of time, with passages of expansive detail and then sudden leaps, blanks, captured with haiku-like brevity. It is hard to tell which is more disrupting to the narrative: the speed-freak jabbering or the constant punctuation of everyday New York city life by police busts and arrests, friends passing out or freaking out.

The following passage from *Speed* illustrates several of the important motifs of speed literature. After borrowing and then selling his friend's record player, the narrator notes:

> So, with my frayed morals, I was in the debt of one person or the other most of the time. I had speed, however, and hadn't slept or eaten for two weeks which was a bright spot. There were two sores on my sides where my ribs were stretching through, and strange strange, I'd started seeing faces everywhere. No matter where I looked, someone was there. Tiny people slept in my ashtray and a giant slouched, sulking, against the Chrysler Building . . . In the mirror, my own face crawled with a dozen others making positive identification impossible, but none of this was anything to worry

about I thought because it was just a drug reaction . . . At every abscess or miss, Chad would say, "You're all fucked up, man, you're a skeletal frame, ha, ha." And I'd call him blind babe in mad world. He was a hollow framework to my eyes, like an erector set wrapped in cellophane, and every time he'd hit, I'd watch the electricity that kept him running crack and sparkle from forearm to elbow to shoulder and then to his brain, where sparks would flicker from his black eyesockets in a reek of electrical fire. I myself, labored under the illusion that I had died weeks ago at 1,000 mph ta ra! ta ra! and was running headlong on accumulating momentum into the approaching Fall.[87]

Lack of control over facial gestures is one of the main symptoms of an out-of-control drug experience in Burroughs, and the multiplication of faces within a single face is reminiscent of the scramble suit Bob Arctor wears in Philip K. Dick's *A Scanner Darkly*, which flickers its way through thousands of images of faces every minute, to safeguard the anonymity of its wearer. The human body is reduced to a twitching, robotic frame, driven by pulses of "electric" amphetamine. At the end of the passage we sense an inexorably accelerating disaster that is both about to happen *and has already happened*, presaging the inevitable crash, a trope that is repeated in the stimulant literature from Pitigrilli's work to Dick's.

In the 1960s, amphetamines were used by a number of people associated with Andy Warhol's salon, The Factory.[88] Warhol himself produced *a, a novel* (1968), 451 pages of what looks like transcriptions of taped amphetamine conversations, which he followed with *From A to B and Back Again* (1975), a masterpiece of interminable digressions and trivia that concludes with a 26-page transcription of a phone call in which a B describes her "morning" wake-up routine. The Warhol "superstar," the debutante Edie Sedgwick, who, like many of the Factory crowd paid frequent visits to Dr. Charles Roberts to receive shots of vitamins and methedrine, has her story told in *Edie* (1982), an oral history. "As told to" books are the perfect genre for amphetamine users.[89]

Which brings us to rock and roll. Stimulants have a long association with music, going back to Bach's "Coffee Cantata," cocaine in turn-of-the-century New Orleans, Irving Berlin's "I Get a Kick Out of You," Leadbelly's "Cocaine Blues," and on to the Grateful Dead's "Casey Jones," and the early seventies'

L.A. rock-star culture and disco. In the case of amphetamines, the connections include Elvis Presley and many of the early rock and rollers, Bob Dylan, The Velvet Underground, the English mod scene, and punk. Popular music is not literature and it does not need to shelter under literature's wing, so I do not intend to offer up any lyrics for interpretation. What is worth noting is that for the speed culture, rock and roll was an alternative to literature. Nobody has to become a writer. When the typewriter became too slow to keep up with modernity's acceleration, a return to the Dionysian form of the folk song, the oral tradition, was perhaps inevitable. Rock critics worldwide have continued the link between stimulants and the written word though.

Amphetamines were embraced as an anti-hippie (and anti-cocaine) drug according to various writers and musicians associated with the the history of punk/new wave: notably the Velvet Underground, Lester Bangs, Julie Burchill, and Tony Parsons. Hunter Thompson also contrasts the Benzedrine-chewing Hell's Angels to the proto-hippies hanging out at Ken Kesey's ranch. Burchill and Parsons trace speed's links to music back to Elvis. Their book, *The Boy Looked at Johnny* (1978), reads like a latter-day document of the Spanish Inquisition written by a couple of speed freaks, dividing the world up into those who do good drugs (Johnny Rotten, Elvis, mods) and those who do bad drugs (hippies, Americans in general)—a paranoid division highly characteristic of speed culture. Burchill and Parsons theorize that speed gave working-class kids the confidence to break through the inhibitions of the British class system:

> Speed has always been an essentially proletarian drug . . . speed is the only drug which acts as a spur; the only social mobility drug. It is the only drug that can make a prole realise that to make it you don't need more intelligence, just the confidence to flaunt that sharpness in the faces of those who would have dismissed you because of your background, the confidence to look down on them. Speed is the only thing that can take the place of elocuation [*sic*] lessons.[90]

Through punk, amphetamines became a weapon in a putative class war, and carried with them a set of associations with violence that are highly characteristic of the technological discourse that surrounds stimulant use. However, this violence, as so often with stimulants, was often ultimately turned back on the user himself, often through recourse to heroin or alcohol, in a gesture of negation.

The American rock critic Lester Bangs, whose work appeared in *Rolling Stone, Creem,* and the *Village Voice* in the 1970s and 1980s, has a lot to say about speed. When he was teenager, Bangs's drug of choice was Romilar, a cough syrup containing the synthetic morphine analog dextromethorphan (DXM). In the 1970s, Bangs used amphetamines, along with a smorgasbord of other substances (notably alcohol), both to help him write and for recreational purposes. His death, at the age of thirty-four, appears to have been the result of an overdose of the sedatives Darvon and Valium.[91]

At the beginning of his article on the German electronic group Kraftwerk (1975), he notes:

> As is well known, it was the Germans who invented methamphetamine, which of all accessible tools has brought human beings within the closest twitch of machinehood, and without methamphetamine we would never have had such high plasma marks of the counterculture as Lenny Bruce, Bob Dylan, Lou Reed and the Velvet Underground, Neal Cassady, Jack Kerouac, Allen Ginsberg's "Howl," Blue Cheer, Cream and *Creem* . . . so it can easily be seen that it was in reality the *Germans* who were responsible for *Blonde on Blonde* and *On the Road;* the Reich never died, it just reincarnated in American archetypes ground out by holloweyed jerkyfingered mannikins locked into their typewriters and guitars like rhinoceroses copulating. Of course, just as very few speedfreaks will cop to their vice, so it took a while before due credit was rendered to the factor of machinehood as a source of our finest cultural artifacts.[92]

Lou Reed's hour-long noise/drone extravaganza *Metal Machine Music,* which was dismissed by many listeners as being an unlistenable act of nihilist provocation when it was first issued in 1975, inspired some of Bangs's finest insights into speed culture. Bangs playfully defended what he saw as Reed's amphetamine-fueled act of negation, producing a two-page parody of a speed-rant constructed out of digression, hyperbole, defensiveness, pseudo-scientific speculation about amphetamines as a possible source of immortality, and a castration fantasy in which somebody's penis is replaced with a horse doctor's syringe. This last sequence relates to another of Bangs's observations: he believed that one of the hallmarks of mid-seventies culture was the fact that drugs had replaced sex as the main reason for getting out of bed, and that they had effectively overwritten the sexual drive: "Everybody knows that drugs come in sexes. Downs are feminine, speed is masculine. Downs make you all nice and sweet and pliant and tenderized like with E-Z Bake, whereas speed makes you aggressive and visceral and forthright and a real take-charge kind of guy/gal. (Makes no difference, because all humans are the same sex, except albinos. It is the drugs that, obviously, determine the gender of the being.)"[93]

When Bangs said of the Velvet Underground that they ushered in a revolution in the relationship of men to women, this is what he was referring to: the dissolving of biologically determined gender and identity in an ever shifting flux of chemical vectors. Aside from Julie Burchill, the stimulant literature is, however, overwhelmingly written by males—and obsessed with defensive demonstrations of male hyper-potency that will cancel out the fantasies of castration or becoming woman.

Bangs's most profound theme was the wholesale abandonment of emotion and feeling in 1970s culture, which he explored in articles on noise, disco, and the swinging 1970s cult of pleasure. Immersive sensation replaced or, rather, drowned out emotion—as it did for Pitigrilli's narrator in the 1920s—as cocaine's anesthetic and pleasure-inducing properties came together. In his diaries, Bangs went to extraordinary lengths to recall what it felt like to be a human being, reminding one of perhaps the greatest amphetamine-driven writer: Philip K. Dick.

Dick went through periods of intense involvement with a variety of substances. He took depressants, antidepressants, and various other psychiatric medications from the mid-1950s on and experimented with LSD in the early sixties, but he also liked to raid his mother's medicine cabinet to try other medicines.[94] Dick used Semoxydrine, a brand of methamphetamine, both as a mood elevator and to crank out pulp science fiction novels and stories, for which he was paid by the unit. In 1963–64, Dick wrote eleven science fiction novels, along with a number of essays, short stories, and plot treatments in an amphetamine-fueled frenzy that accompanied or precipitated the end of one of his marriages. The most remarkable of these novels is *The Three Stigmata of Palmer Eldritch* (1965).

Three Stigmata showcases Dick's signature obsession with machinic traits in human beings. Palmer Eldritch's steel jaws in particular recall the grinding, frozen jaw of the stimulant abuser. Dick's work is full of this motif, the most famous example being *Bladerunner, or Do Androids Dream of Electric Sheep?* where the line between android and human is so blurred that nobody can be sure that he is not a machine. Although the book describes a struggle for intergalactic market dominance between two hallucinogen manufacturers, the theme of cosmic paranoia that drives the story is amphetamine related. One hallucinogen (Can-D) allows users to visit a clearly simulated version of California in the 1950s; the other one, introduced by Eldritch from another galaxy, permanently disrupts the user's sense of reality, so that he can never again be sure whether or not he is in the clutches of the drug—except by the appearance of the machinic stigmata (artificial hand, eye, and jaw). In fact, the novel's plot disintegrates at the moment when paranoia becomes so strong that it is no longer possible for the reader to distinguish the real from the virtual, or drug-induced, event.

In Dick's later work, these structural flaws become more and more the real subject matter, especially in *VALIS* (1981), a book that wavers between being a first-person or third-person narrative of spiritual apotheosis, and *A Scanner Darkly* (1977), a portrait of Bob Arctor, an undercover narcotics agent living in California in 1994, who is ordered to infiltrate his own undercover identity as a small-time narcotics dealer of Substance D ("D is for death"!). When going to meet his superiors, Arctor wears a scramble suit, which blurs his identity into the images of millions of other people. As he proceeds to spy on his own activities, using scanners installed in his own house, his own identity breaks down as he becomes increasingly unable to account for his own activities. Finally, an empty shell, he is carted away to a rehabilitation clinic, where, in a moment of typical Dickian apotheosis, he discovers the source of the cosmic conspiracy by which Substance D, death, rises from the earth itself.

As Dick indicates in the famous afterword to *Scanner,* the book has its roots in autobiography, recalling a period (1970–1972) when Dick opened his house in Santa Venetia, California, to his friends after the end of his fourth marriage. There was a refrigerator full of protein milkshake mix and amphetamines that Dick would consume by the handful, spending three or four days awake, followed by forty-eight-hour sleeps. He did not get much writing done during that period. Taking a thousand or more methedrine tabs a week, Dick developed various conspiracy theories about the CIA tapping his phone and breaking into his home, and was admitted to a series of psychiatric clinics, until, in 1972, after a suicide attempt, he was admitted to a Canadian rehabilitation clinic.

What makes Dick's work so satisfying is that the drug-related delusions in his work become material in a gnostic struggle for transcendence over the fallen world. Substance D is the agent both of fallen consciousness and of a gnostic realization—that the material world as a whole is a trap. In the most developed version of the fatalism often found in stimulant-related books, events in Dick's stories are the retelling or outcome of a disaster that happened long before the beginning of the book, ultimately because, according to gnostic thought, the creation of the universe, an error of the Divine, is itself the primary disaster.

In most of the stimulant literature, as I have noted, there is no spiritual content. Dick makes this absence the basis of his own intense desire for transcendence. The world of amphetamines becomes an amplified version of everyday reality and its problems:

> Maybe inside the terribly burned and burning circuits of your head that char more and more, even as I hold you, a spark of color and light in some disguised form manifested itself, unrecognized, to lead you, by its memory, through the years to come, the dreadful years ahead. A word not fully understood, some small thing seen but not understood, some fragment of a star mixed with the trash of this world, to guide you by reflex until the day . . . but it was so remote.[95]

Dick's writing has been acknowledged as a key influence on the development of the cyberpunk aesthetic, which fetishizes many of the elements of the stimulant world: the notion of the body as hardware, the mind as software, and the eroticization of violence, machinery, and alienation. William Gibson's *Neuromancer* (1984) reprises many of the amphetamine-related themes that I have discussed:

> Two blocks west of the Chat, in a teashop called the Jarre de Thé, Case washed down the night's first pill with a double espresso. It was a flat pink octagon, a potent species of Brazilian dex he bought from one of Zone's girls . . . At first, finding himself alone in Chiba, with little money and less hope of finding a cure, he'd gone into a kind of terminal overdrive, hustling fresh capital with a cold intensity that had seemed to belong to someone else. In the first month,

he'd killed two men and a woman over sums that a year before would have seemed ludicrous. Ninsei wore him down until the street itself came to seem the externalization of some death wish, some secret poison he hadn't known he carried . . . A part of him knew that the arc of his self-destruction was glaringly obvious to his customers, who grew steadily fewer, but that same part of him basked in the knowledge that it was only a matter of time. And that was the part of him, smug in its expectation of death, that most hated the thought of Linda Lee.[96]

In cyberpunk, amphetamines are again linked to a projected death wish, an accelerated act of self-destruction that has its origin in an armed revolt against a libidinal impulse—"the thought of Linda Lee." *Neuromancer* is full of stimulants—there is hardly a scene in the book where coffee is not present, not to mention cigarettes and cocaine. Drugs gain a prestigious value, when, as Jacques Derrida has said, the door to the transcendental heaven previously provided by religion is shut.[97] The fantasy of the Matrix, that "cyberspace" which dominates *Neuromancer*, is a fundamentally materialist one, and precisely blocks this doorway to transcendence: "The body was meat," Gibson observes. "Case fell into the prison of his own flesh."[98] In cyberpunk, stimulants appear as markers of an existential relationship between man and machine—they mechanically sustain the cyborg in the voidlike Matrix that he or she has constructed, and act at the same time as a Trojan horse for the necessary, but veiled transcendental impulse. However, in *Count Zero*, Gibson's follow-up to *Neuromancer*, the Matrix is swiftly invaded by voodoo deities, and, aside from coffee, the drugs, deprived of their source of prestige, disappear again, never to reappear in subsequent works. Neil Stephenson, author of the celebrated *Snow Crash* (1992), playing with this dynamic or perhaps confused by it, ambiguously balances different definitions of what cyborg consciousness is, social, biotechnical, or spiritual:

> "I have another question. Raven also distributes another drug—in Reality—called, among other things, Snow Crash. What is it?"
>
> "It's not a drug," Juanita says. "They make it look like a drug and feel like a drug so that people will want to take it. It's laced with cocaine and some other stuff."
>
> "If it's not a drug, what is it?"

Figure 9. Stimulant book images. Clockwise from the upper left: cover of *Cocaina*, by Pitigrilli, 1923; jacket of *Dealer: Portrait of a Cocaine Merchant*, by Richard Woodley, published in 1970; cover of *Speed*, by William Burroughs Jr., published in 1971; and cover of *A Scanner Darkly*, by Philip K. Dick, published in 1977.

"It's chemically processed blood serum taken from people who are infected with the metavirus," Juanita says. "That is, it's just another way of spreading the infection."

"Who's spreading it?"

"L. Bob Rife's private church. All of those people are infected."

Hiro puts his head in his hands. He's not exactly thinking about this; he's letting it ricochet around in his skull, waiting for it to come to rest. "Wait a minute, Juanita. Make up your mind. This Snow Crash thing—is it a virus, a drug, or a religion?"

Juanita shrugs. "What's the difference?"[99]

Cocaine returned to the public eye (and nose) at the beginning of the 1970s and became one of the main symbols of the post-sixties "me" generation. The drug's newfound popularity can be connected to the appropriation of black pimp mythology by white rock musicians at the end of the sixties. Cocaine had had a connection with pimps and prostitutes since the turn of the century in New Orleans and in Paris since post–World War I period. In the United States, it should be added, one of the principal concerns leading to the banning of cocaine was the fear of cocaine-crazed black men raping and killing white women. In his *Autobiography* (1967), Malcolm X describes being introduced to cocaine in the Harlem hustlers' world and in Boston. He noted that "cocaine produces, for those who sniff its powdery white crystals, an illusion of supreme well-being, and a soaring over-confidence in both physical and mental ability. You think you could whip the heavyweight champion, and that you are smarter than anybody. There was also that feeling of timelessness. And there were intervals of ability to recall and review things that had happened years back with an astonishing clarity."[100] He mentions a number of drugs in the *Autobiography:* Benzedrine, heroin, marijuana, tobacco, and alcohol; in jail, nutmeg and Nembutal (a barbiturate). All of these substances are used to suppress consciousness of what blacks have to do to survive—but the stimulants are also weapons in a race war, just as they were elements of a class war for punks—part of a militarization of the body.

This war also took on a sexual form. The Los Angeles publishing group Holloway House made cocaine-snorting pimps one of the mainstays of its highly successful line of blackploitation pulp fiction in the late 1960s and early 1970s. One of them, Iceberg Slim's *Pimp: The Story of My Life* (1969), begins as follows: "Dawn was breaking as the big Hog scooted through the streets. My five whores were chattering like drunk magpies. I smelled the stink that only a street whore has after a long, busy night. The inside of my nose was raw. It happens when you're a pig for snorting cocaine."[101]

The narrator is a high-rolling pimp who gets his nickname, Iceberg, when he is able to stand impassively throughout a barroom shoot-out, thanks to the cocaine that he's snorted. Cocaine is an anesthetic. "I was so frosted with cocaine I felt embalmed."[102] At other times, it is an orgasmic pleasure drug. The first time Iceberg shoots cocaine, "it was like I had a million "swipes" [that is, penises] in every pore from head to toe. It was like they were all popping off together in a nerve-shredding climax . . . I looked down at my hands and thighs. A thrill shot through me. Surely they were the most beautiful in the Universe. I felt a superman's surge of power."[103] The whole book is a larger than life, epic tale of black male hyper-potency, moving between extremes of anesthetic cool and orgiastic pleasure seeking, in a search for power. The pimp, like the big-time cocaine dealer of Brian De Palma's *Scarface,* is a pop-culture Superman. Power is a differential, according to Nietzsche and physics. The power of the "cocaine-crazed man" (to quote Freud) is felt in the differential between the ice of anesthesia and the heat of pleasure. Similar imagery pervades Richard Woodley's *Dealer: Portrait of a Cocaine Merchant* (1971), the first of a series of books about cocaine dealing—a profession that clearly attained a level of literary acceptability that heroin dealing never would.

By the early 1970s, following a fashion set by rock musicians copying black hustler culture, cocaine became a fashionable substance for hip, white middle-class America, part of a mellow, leisure, pleasure- (and self-) centered culture. The atmosphere of this culture is captured in Bruce Jay Friedman's novel *About Harry Towns* (1974), notably in a chapter devoted to cocaine called "Lady." Harry Towns initially goes to bars with friends where the social ritual of waiting to score and talking about cocaine is as important as taking the drug itself, about which all he can say is that it is "subtle" (this is either a very cocaine or a very 1970s thing to say). At a certain point, Towns makes the decisive move of cutting out his friends and buying an ounce of cocaine for himself. This maneuver puts him in more direct contact with the world of the dealers, whom he feels both superior to and intimidated by, as well as the co-

caine itself. He uses the cocaine as bait to pick up girls and all goes well until he's forced to choose between going to his mother's funeral and keeping an
appointment to score some extra-fine Peruvian. He half successfully manages
to do both, while remaining uncomfortably aware that he has moved one step
further across some invisible line. This affectless search for pleasure was also
used by Jay McInerney in *Bright Lights, Big City* (1984), the effect amplified
by the highly dissociated second-person narrative ("you do this, you do
that.")

The most sophisticated cocaine book of the 1970s is Robert Sabbag's *Snowblind* (1976): a dealer's-eye account of the cocaine trade, set in New York City,
Long Island, and Colombia.[104] Sabbag, and his subject, a college-educated
former sales executive named Zachary Swan, are very convinced of their own
cleverness; the book is full of archly described characters, sophisticated scams,
highly ambiguous moral positions. Everything in the book is overembellished,
almost to the point of parody. Dealing or taking drugs, as Hunter Thompson
most famously claimed, is another version of the American dream. "Cocaine
is merely the metaphor," Sabbag notes with a leering wink. *Snowblind* is a
"subtle" book, in other words. "These are felonies practiced by professionals,
do not attempt them at home."[105] A professional is one who is not taken in by
the drug, who can see the drug as "merely a metaphor." But cocaine is more
than a metaphor: dealer, user, and pimp all use the same rhetoric of knowledge
and control to distinguish their activities from those of the naive or uniniti-
ated, yet this rhetoric is itself "subtly" propped up by the drug.

As the 1970s turned into the 1980s, and the casualties of long-term cocaine
use mounted, nonfictional addiction narratives began to appear, written by
wealthy middle-class swingers or media figures. These books typically begin
with ironic hindsight-driven descriptions of a cocaine-fueled Eden of sensuality and prosperity, pass through a hell where everything that has been gained
and more is lost, and end somewhere between redemption and destruction.
Richard Smart's *Snow Papers* (1985) is one of the most articulate of these
books. Smart says the vogue for cocaine resulted from the collapse of the social consciousness of the 1960s into a mixture of affluence and a narcissistic
search for "realizing human potential" through pleasure. Although Smart's
self-loathing, like that of most former coke users, is hard to take, he is full of
insight about the ambition and pretensions to style and sophistication that go
with a certain use of cocaine. This style is not particularly literary, but literature could be one of its emblems, literature being a way of setting down all

those amazing thoughts that occur to the cocaine user (even if he or she is utterly incapable of editing them into a finished text):

> All inhibitions were gone, brains were reeling with great truths that just had to be shared, hearts were bursting with feelings, and six well-lubricated tongues were poised to launch the inevitable nonstop, free-form pronouncements that, floating on undammed streams of consciousness, would flood the room with wisdom . . . if the sequential arrangement of our sentences sometimes exhibited less than a logical symmetry, the defect went unnoticed since what we were now about was not dialogue but the simultaneous presentation of six very earnest monologues.[106]

Included in this genre must be the books by and about Hollywood stars and their dalliance with the drug, such as Carrie Fisher's fictional addiction narrative *Postcards from the Edge* (1987) and Bob Woodward's popular biography of the comedian John Belushi, *Wired* (1984)—one of a group of stimulant-abusing comedians from Lenny Bruce through Richard Pryor and Robin Williams.

The prestige of cocaine declined in the eighties, partly as a result of the various well-publicized lives destroyed by the infamous "Bolivian marching powder," and partly because of the explosion of the use of crack, smokable cocaine, packaged to be sold in small, cheap quantities on the street to the underclasses of the world. The masterwork of crack literature (so far) is Lee Stringer's *Grand Central Winter* (1998), which opens with the author, at that time a homeless crack user, spending the winter living in an abandoned pipeline somewhere deep under Grand Central Station in New York. Stringer was in the habit of using a pencil to get at the caked crack resin that was stuck to the sides of his pipe, so that he could smoke it up. One day, "sitting there in my hole with nothing to smoke and nothing to do . . . I pull the pencil out just to look at the film of residue stuck to the sides . . . and it dawns on me that it's a pencil. I mean it's got a lead in it and all, and you can write with the thing." He finds an old composition book and begins writing in an ever mounting fit of excitement "until it's like I'm just taking dictation . . . It's just like taking a hit."[107]

This chapter has been a tiring one to research and write. It has been hard for me to keep up with the relentless pace and volume of many of the writers who have used stimulants. The two or three cups of English Breakfast tea I drink every day are not enough for me to maintain concentration for all the hours that I need to go through every page of Balzac's collected writings or Sartre's *Critique of Dialectical Reason,* or to reach a conclusion about whether Isaac Asimov's enormous oeuvre suggests amphetamine use. Can it be possible that James Joyce's *Ulysses* or Robert Musil's *The Man without Qualities* were written without the aid of stimulants?

It is not just the volume of words that is fatiguing in stimulant literature, but the volume of ideas, each of which is in itself somewhat interesting and original, and which appears to be connected to the ideas that precede and follow it. As I have shown, each thought is interrupted by the next one in such a way that the final text is more like a montage of phrases forced into coexistence than an organic whole. Of course, it could be argued that all texts are like this, but a sonnet, or a novel with its dialogism, formalizes the organization of fragments into a unit. In post-Mallarméan writing, this organization of fragments is replaced by a strategic use of absences. In the cannabis literature, which is also packed with ideas and images, the narrative form of the tale gives form to the assembled fragments.

Such a strategy is lacking in much of the stimulant literature. In fact the goal of Kerouac's thirty-foot long single spaced sentence is to avoid or delay the inevitable onset of the space at the end of the sentence, paragraph, or page. Or day. Sherlock Holmes's use of cocaine is a part of this fantasy of ever active consciousness, an infinitely subtle apprehension of the world of signs that remains objective, logical, but can never stop, because, as William Burroughs Jr. observes: "what most people take for silence is really a grotesque bedlam of creaks and groans and distant howling thunder."[108]

But since continuous consciousness is impossible, discontinuity finds other ways to manifest itself. Virilio uses the word "picnolepsy" to describe tiny lapses of consciousness that occur, little sleeps or deaths that happen without our even being aware of them. This phenomenon accounts for the peculiar swerve that can be found in the stimulant literature, from productive clarity into paranoia, delusions, depression, and exhaustion.

The accident that gives cocaine and speed literature its sense of drama is often prefigured in the first sentences of the book, an exhaustion that will follow exhilaration with utter predictability. Are there stimulant works that are produced in this state of exhaustion? If so, they are often produced under the influence of other drugs: Burroughs Jr.'s *Kentucky Ham,* with its grim evocation of the Federal Narcotics Hospital in Lexington, Kentucky; Kerouac's depressing, alcoholic West Coast pastorals; and the darker, more gnostic side of Philip K. Dick's work.

I have repeatedly referred to the notion of the man-machine that recurs in the stimulant literature. In this age of cyborgs, it is easy to use the phrase without really understanding what it means. It implies a body whose soul has vacated it, a body that has become subject to a will—either the owner's or somebody else's. Stimulants augment the will—thus the famous feeling of self-confidence that comes with a stimulant high. Stimulants allow the user's will to temporarily control the body, turning it into a technological vehicle, capable of work, endurance, pleasure. Jünger suggests that the quality of the experience is again a question of dosage. With low doses, a certain tempo is established that is compatible with acts of will and overall coordination of mental and physical faculties. With higher doses, the acceleration of the will causes delusions of grandeur and paranoia. Sartre talks of "complete bodily surrender," but it is not just the body that is affected by stimulant use (only existential philosophy could have allowed Sartre to believe that). Since the will is not itself a mode of perception, the "triumph of the will" over the body through stimulant use results in distorted perception, the projection of the will onto the outside world.

There is an existential quality to the stimulant literature as a whole. Stimulants posit existence in the world as a drama of willpower in an otherwise neutral or vacant space. But the world is not a neutral space, nor are our minds and bodies. Thus the stimulant literature is full of ghosts: unstable sexual energies, godlike entities, overwritten memories, muscles that won't stop twitching. A hallucination involves seeing that which is not there. The ghosts of the stimulant literature are objects that are there, but that become spectral, semivisible, like objects on the side of the road seen from a fast-moving vehicle.

Nietzsche had already explored this drama to its limits with the notion of the will to power, a term that tries to define will itself as an autonomous force. The over-man, an image straight out of the stimulant literature, overcomes the man in "himself," as man has supposedly overcome the animal. In the stimulant literature, this attempt to overcome man results in the creation of monstrosities: Benn's misformed births, Burroughs Jr.'s electrified frames, Freud's patient Fleischl, the sex machines Dean Moriarty and Iceberg Slim, the former football player turned alcoholic Kerouac, and Philip K. Dick's cyborgs, none of them sure whether they are supermen or cripples.

5

THE IMAGINAL REALMS

Psychedelics and Literature

Snakes "too good to be true." Stylization and colors. Pearly tanks of
the Assyrian kings. (I often interrupt the visions in order to write
them down). So many things vanish in this whirl. The portrait of
an old Kossak (hanging in my room) came to life and started to
move . . .

12:55—I am going to try not to write, and to enter more into the
spirit of things. I put out the lights as an experiment. I cannot stand
not writing it down: cross-section of reptile machine (of course this
is hardly a fraction of what I'm seeing).

STANISLAW IGNACY WITKIEWICZ,
note written under the influence of peyote, 1928

In his early masque *Comus* (1637), John Milton tells a tale
about the dangers of taking a walk in the woods—those murky pagan woods
that have haunted the Western imagination since Dante first got lost in them
at the beginning of *The Divine Comedy*. In these woods dwells a spirit named
Comus, the son of Bacchus and Circe, ready to ensnare the unwary traveler.
Comus

> Excels his mother at her mighty art,
> Offering to every weary traveller,
> His orient liquor in a crystal glass . . .
> . . . . . .

Soon as the potion works, their human countenance,
The express resemblance of the gods, is changed
Into some brutish form of wolf, or bear,
Or ounce, or tiger, hog, or bearded goat,
All other parts remaining as they were,
And they, so perfect is their misery,
Not once perceive their foul disfigurement,
But boast themselves more comely than before
And all their friends, and native home forget
To roll with pleasure in a sensual sty.[1]

This sprite, "with power to cheat the eye with blear illusion,"[2] comes upon a virginal nymph called Sabrina, who has gotten lost in the woods, and tries to seduce her with his liquor, which is better than "Nepenthes," a Homeric drug, probably opium:

... One sip of this
Will bathe the drooping spirits in delight
Beyond the bliss of dreams.[3]

Comus takes Sabrina to a pleasure palace, where he traps her and tries to force her to drink the cordial, only to be interrupted by Sabrina's elder brothers, who get wind of his scheme and attack his palace. They are aided by a spirit who gives them another herb to guard against Comus' powers:

... of divine effect ...
. . . . .
... more med'cinal is it than that moly
That Hermes once to wise Ulysses gave;
He called it haemony, and gave it to me
And bade me keep it as of sovran use
'Gainst all enchantments ...[4]

Once liberated, Sabrina is taken to a river nymph, who dispenses "precious vialed liquors"[5] that heal the effects of the black magic.

Thirty years later, Milton transposed the elements of this scenario in *Paradise Lost* (1667) in his retelling of the story of Adam and Eve from Genesis. In his first speech about the tree of knowledge to Eve, Satan begins by invoking pagan wisdom:

> "O sacred, wise, and wisdom-giving plant,
> Mother of science, now I feel thy power
> Within me clear, not only to discern
> Things in their causes, but to trace the ways
> Of highest agents . . ."[6]

This is a tree that offers gnosis—knowledge of the divine. When Eve eats the apple, Milton emphasizes this point:

> . . . such delight till then, as seemed,
> In fruit she never tasted, whether true
> Or fancied so, through expectation high
> Of knowledge, nor was godhead from her thought.
> Greedily she engorged without restraint,
> And knew not eating death: satiate at length,
> And heightened as with wine.[7]

Milton notes that "the power / That dwelt within, whose presence had infused / Into the plant sciential sap, derived / From nectar, drink of gods."[8] As in *Comus,* the tension between the Christian story Milton is telling and the pagan, classical imagery through which it is embodied, is palpable. He returns to the theme when, after Adam and Eve have eaten and made love in their newly fallen state, God sends down the angel Michael to give Adam a vision of the future of man—again using magical plants:

> Michael from Adam's eyes the film removed
> Which that false fruit that promised clearer sight
> Had bred; then purged with euphrasy and rue
> The visual nerve, for he had much to see;
> And from the well of life three drops instilled.
> So deep the power of these ingredients pierced,
> Even to the inmost seat of mental sight,
> That Adam now enforced to close his eyes,
> Sunk down and all his spirits became entranced.[9]

I hope it is not belaboring the obvious to say that Milton is talking about psychoactive substances in *Comus* and *Paradise Lost,* with many of the same qualities that we attribute to hashish or LSD, substances that bathe "the

drooping spirits in delight beyond the bliss of dreams" and allow access to animal states of consciousness. But the Renaissance, not to say all of European
literary history before De Quincey, is generally considered a drug-free zone.
Why have Milton's drugs not been recognized?

Some will respond that the plants that Milton is talking about are not real;
that they are at best vestigial traces of the lost classical world, transformed by
the Renaissance into literary conventions, symbols without substance. But a
look at the medical plant guides known as herbals that were published around
the same time as Milton's poetry suggests otherwise. In 1595, Rembert Dodoens, author of one of the most popular herbals, noted that "moly is also excellent against inchauntments, as Plinie and Homer do testifie, saying, that
Mercurie . . . shewed it to Ulysses, whereby he escaped all the inchantments of
Circe the Magician."[10] Moly was a "real" herb, but one whose medical power
had its roots (according to Dodoens) in the very classical literary tradition to
which Milton refers.

It has even been suggested that Milton's "rue" and Homer's "moly" are actually the same substance—namely a tree called *Peganum harmala*.[11] But
whether or not Milton knew that "rue" had psychoactive properties, the point
remains that Milton makes use of a discourse of psychoactive plants in his
poems.[12] Many other plants served a similar function in Renaissance literature: among them, belladonna, henbane, hemlock, nightshade, aconite, rue,
moly, haemony, ambrosia, poppy, nectar, nepenthe, mandrake, mandragora,
hellebore, the waters of Lethe, and possibly thorn-apple (datura, or Jimson
weed), and lotus.[13] Love potions, poisons, mythical philtres and brews,
powerful herbs, magical stones, and secret powders: all are recognizably "psychoactive" and all play the role of mediating the space between the imagination, with its vectors of desire, intoxication, death, and truth, and the material
world.

Skeptical readers will argue that Milton did not intend the reader to believe
that these were "real drugs"—he intended them to perform the mythopoetic
function of making visible the agents of shifts in moral states through allegory
or metaphor. This may be the case, but drugs remain allegorical in this same
sense in our society too. The set of fears and concerns that people voice about
drug use also concern "shifts in moral states": insanity, sexual excess, crime,
degeneration of the "human" to less evolved (animal) states; or, conversely,
cures for neurosis, sexual liberation, right livelihood, and union with God. We

have not finished living through the confusion between the real and the myth-ical—in thinking about drugs, or in thinking about anything else.

We do this because we are confused as to the nature and meaning of the imagination and all that is touched by it—which is pretty much every aspect of human culture. The imaginal plays a part in our lives at all times, in the most extreme experiences of altered states, in the virtual realities of science fiction films, cartoons, or religious iconography, and in how our perception of everyday objects flickers and shifts in subtle ways, from moment to moment.[14] Of course, there are aspects of human culture that we do not generally think of as involving the imaginal: road building and three-dimensional molecular modeling of proteins, for example. But the imagination is there too, in the way that time and space are shaped into a pattern by the mind.

The imaginal presents itself to us at certain moments as a realm in its own right, separate from our sensory experience, independent of our will, but rich with meaning. I take it (as Plato did) that such imaginal realms are a funda-mental, irreducible part of human experience, however these realms are de-fined, used, or represented in religion, art, psychology, or medical science. Both literature and certain psychoactive substances are strongly associated with such imaginal realms. In fact, they are often made to bear the entire weight of our struggles with the imaginal and its meaning, and many believe that the dangers of the imaginal realms, such as they are, would be forever eradicated if certain methods of accessing them—art and psychoactive sub-stances—were forever banned.

I will use the word "psychedelic" to bring together those substances that open up the imaginal realms in all their complexity. Biochemically speaking, most of these substances are potent psychoactive agents that fall within two chemical families: the phenethylamines and tryptamines. But hashish, some of the anesthetics, and even opium, as De Quincey describes it, could be called psychedelic when taken at certain doses. Let me be clear about it: There is no consensus about psychedelics, and the proliferation of names that they have been given over the years—"hallucinogen," "entheogen," and so on—is testi-monial to this fact. And again, I remind the reader that if we substitute the word "book" for "substance," we have an excellent definition of literature: a text concerned with the imaginal realms.

Psychedelic drugs have been used in religious rituals and as healing agents for thousands of years before Milton wrote about them. Vedic Indian civiliza-

tion used soma, whose exact composition we do not know, as a religious sacra-
ment, fifteen hundred years before Christ. In classical Greece it has been speculated that the Mysteries of Eleusis involved a psychoactive plant—but again,
we know very little about it, because the Mysteries were a closely held secret.[15]
Even during periods of active use, psychedelics retained a necessarily mythological aspect that is connected with the ambiguous quality of their powers.

During the Christian era, European civilization drove the psychedelics substances to its margins, where they existed either in secret as a part of pagan-
ism, or as symbols, lurking in memory, text, and ritual. The transformation of
psychoactive plants into symbols has indeed been one of the principal strate-
gies by which civilization, whether in Judaeo-Christian, classical Greek, or
Islamic form, absorbed the energies of shamanic religious practice, with its
emphasis on the direct experience of the divine, and made them a part of its
own imaginal realm, reconfiguring them as dark, false, satanic forces.

When Greek natural science and literature were rediscovered at the beginning of the Renaissance, the tension between the pagan and Christian imaginal realms increased considerably. This tension inevitably found expression in
European literature, including the Milton passages I cited above. Indeed, the
growth of literature as a cultural form in Europe was fueled by the need to
find a way to express the "dark" but fascinating energies of the pagan, natural
world, while remaining "true" to Christian dogma. The pagan world, and its
imaginal realms, complete with deities, festivities, and vision-inducing plants,
could be celebrated in Renaissance literature, if they were depicted with a vocabulary that at least pretended to separate the fantastic worlds of classical
legend from the real world, and by a moral structure that allowed the representation of intoxicated states, so long as true, Christian, spiritual intoxication
and false, pagan, carnal intoxication were clearly distinguished, and rewarded
or punished as necessary (somewhat as in Hollywood today). What we call literature or art is a very particular negotiation of the ways in which human beings access, configure, and share imaginal space. In this chapter, I will show
how the history of what we now call the psychedelics is intimately linked to
the evolution of literature in the West, insofar as literature provided a set of
maps or blueprints for the imaginary, and a place to situate and explore the
imaginal realms, when this was impossible elsewhere.

◈

The great epic poems of the Renaissance, such as Torquato Tasso's *Jerusalem Delivered* (1586) or Edmund Spenser's *Faerie Queene* (1596), are full of Eden-like gardens hung with exotic, sensuous fruits and mysterious plants, gardens that embody the principle of the earthly paradise; a blending of Eden and Greek mythical locations such as the Hesperides. But these gardens also reflect the discovery of the New World by Europeans—and the extreme ambivalence of Europeans in their confrontation with a formerly paradisal imaginary space suddenly become extremely real. Spenser's *Faerie Queene* in particular, written roughly a century after Columbus first landed in the New World, gives a reasonably accurate account of what a group of ardent European Christian men would do were they ever to encounter the real-life equivalent of one of the Renaissance poets' earthly paradises.

> But all those pleasant bowres and Pallace brave,
> Guyon broke downe, with rigour pittilesse;
> Ne ought their goodly workmanship might save
> Them from the tempest of his wrathfulnesse,
> But that their blisse he turned to balefulnesse:
> Their groves he feld, their gardins did deface,
> Their arbers spoyle, their Cabinets suppresse,
> Their banket houses burne, their buildings race,
> And of the fairest late, now made the fowlest place.[16]

Peyote, ololiuhqui (morning glory seeds), mushroom, and datura use in Meso-American cultures was noted by the Spanish Franciscan monk Bernardino de Sahagún in 1560. Sahagún wrote of peyote (the cactus from which mescaline is derived): "On him who eats it or drinks it, it takes effect like mushrooms. Also he sees many things which frighten one, or make one laugh. It affects him perhaps one day, perhaps two days, but likewise it abates. However it harms one, troubles one, makes one besotted, takes effect on one."[17] He noted that the Chichimeca assembled in the desert to dance and sing when they took peyote, and "they wept; they wept exceedingly. They said [thus] eyes were washed; thus they cleansed their eyes."[18] This openness to the richness of the plant world did not last long, however. In 1620, a decree from the Inquisition was issued in Mexico City:

> The use of the Herb or Root called Peyote . . . is a superstitious action and reproved as opposed to the purity and sincerity of our

Holy Catholic Faith, being so that this said herb, nor any other cannot possess the virtue and natural efficacy attributed to it for said effects, nor to cause the images, phantasms and representations on which are founded said divination, and that in these one sees notoriously the suggestion and assistance of the devil, author of this abuse.[19]

Peyote's "natural efficacy" was denied, and use of peyote buttons could not therefore be seen as part of natural or medical science. As with all New World substances, there was no precedent in classical or biblical tradition for a defense of peyote. But peyote was not seen as entirely ineffective; instead, the imaginal realms that peyote gave access to were false or delusional, and their only meaning a negative one, that of leading people astray from the true faith. The existence of the imaginal realms themselves was not denied; but peyote as an agent capable of accessing them was. The approach to these realms must remain symbolic—as it was for Milton. Thus the Inquisition successfully pushed Peyote into the realm of nonexistence or legend, which is where, to the Western mind, these plants generally resided until the nineteenth century, when the search for pharmaceutical medicines and burgeoning interest in primitive culture necessitated a reassessment of these plants and the practices that accepted their reality.[20]

Europeans also left records of their encounters with Native American and Siberian shamanism. Although the earliest accounts of these practices were often dismissive, explaining shamanic visions as the product of superstition or deluded imagination, by the eighteenth century it was known that the Siberian shamans used the fly agaric mushroom as a part of their rituals. In 1724, Joseph-François Lafitau, a Jesuit missionary to Canada, made comparisons between the sweat lodges in which Herodotus' Scythians inhaled cannabis vapors in the fifth century B.C.E and similar places in use by Native American tribes.[21] Stephan Krascheninnikow, a Russian botanist on one of the Bering expeditions, was one of the first to describe the use of mushroom infusions: "The first symptom of a man's being affected with this liquor is a trembling in all his joints, and in half an hour he begins to rave as if in a fever; and is either merry or melancholy mad, according to his particular constitution. Some jump, dance, and sing; others weep, and are in terrible agonies, a small hole appearing to them as a great pit, and a spoonful of water as a lake."[22]

Later academic expeditions in the second half of the eighteenth century further examined the use of the mushroom. Georg Forster, who had traveled as a child on expeditions in Russia, and as a young man was with Cook on his second voyage around the world, speculated that folk belief, fueled by religious ecstasy, sexual bliss, or intoxicants, was the source of creativity. Accounts of Siberian expeditions were read enthusiastically by European intellectuals and formed part of the basis of a wave of speculation about the origins of man, spanning Giovanni Vico's *Scienza Nuova* (1725) through to the writings of the Encylopedists and the German pre-Romantics, Herder and Goethe. But these speculations focused on the generally aesthetic quality of the shaman's "performance." Although opium and hashish use could be situated, correctly or not, within a framework of millennia of contact between Europe and Asia, the novelty of Siberian shamanism was such that, like other aspects of "primitive culture," it was viewed as a kind of pure, elemental human activity, which could provide the original prototypes of civilized culture and symbolic religion as they had developed in Europe. The significance of the mushrooms, as actual, effective agents of altered states, was dismissed by anthropologists as late as the 1960s as a degenerate aspect of shamanism—since it did not support the symbolic model of ritual that dominated anthropology at that time.

It was through Hoffmann's fantastic tales that nineteenth-century writers brought back the worlds of fantasy and fable, within a new rational and realistic framework that required material agents for journeys into the imaginal realms. Hoffmann used plant potions and mysterious powders in several of his tales to transport people into other worlds. Gautier, Hoffmann's chief French disciple, used hashish and opium in his stories. Lewis Carroll's *Alice in Wonderland* (1865) continued the fantasy tradition, adding the element of childhood to the motifs that protect the fantasy dimension from the inquisitions of the real.

Carroll was familiar with the world of narcotics through friendships with users such as Dante Gabriel Rossetti and Henry Kingsley; he also owned a copy of *Stimulants and Narcotics* (1864), by the English toxicologist Francis Anstie, which reviewed the psychoactive substances available at the time.[23] More specifically, Carroll had read Mordecai Cooke's books on intoxicants, *The Seven Sisters of Sleep* (1860) and *Plain and Easy Account of British Fungi* (1862), with their descriptions of Siberian amanita use:

> At first, it generally produces cheerfulness, afterwards giddiness
> and drunkenness, ending occasionally in the entire loss of con-

sciousness. The natural inclinations of the individual become stimulated. The dancer executes a pas d'extravagance, the musical indulge in a song, the chatterer divulges all his secrets, the oratorical delivers himself of a philippic, and the mimic indulges in caricature. Erroneous impressions of size and distance are common occurrences, equally with the swallower of amanita and hemp. The experiences of M. Moreau with haschisch are repeated with the fungus-eaters of Siberia; a straw lying in the road becomes a formidable object, to overcome which, a leap is taken sufficient to clear a barrel of ale, or the prostrate trunk of a British oak.[24]

With astounding prescience, Carroll took these descriptions of the effects of the amanita mushroom and turned them into a set of mathematical operations, which could be executed on a young girl and the world she perceived. Alice changes size when she drinks from bottles not marked "poison," or eats from cakes which say "EAT ME." "First, however, she waited for a few minutes to see if she was going to shrink any further: she felt a little nervous about this; 'for it might end, you know,' said Alice, 'in my going out altogether, like a candle. I wonder what I should be like then?' And she tried to fancy what the flame of a candle is like after it is blown out, for she could not remember ever having seen such a thing."[25]

Alice encounters a caterpillar perched on top of a mushroom, smoking a hookah, who questions her and then leaves, advising her that she can grow larger or smaller, according to which side of the perfectly circular mushroom she eats from. The games with logic at the Mad Hatter's Tea Party, the tricks played with visual space by the Cheshire Cat, just about any episode in the book in fact, resonate with psychedelic experience. Why?

Carroll's particular genius was to form a fantasy world from the "logical" outcome of a certain number of statements and questions, using the intermediary of the magical potion. Alice knows that "something interesting will happen" when she drinks from another bottle without a label; she knows she will become larger; what she does not know is what the intensity or duration of the effect will be. It is all a question of dosage, as Jünger says. Radically different worlds appear accordingly. Carroll replicated, through logical operations, the chemically triggered alterations of cognitive functioning that users of psychedelics experience, and that had already been described in a book that Carroll had read.

It was thus a properly material, "modern" imaginal space that Carroll created. Rather than belonging to the world of religion—or the world of the fantastic tale—the Alice books found a home in the Victorian world of the "innocent child," as fantastic a place as Elven realms or the impenetrable world of savages. Several books—as well as a host of childrens' television series—have, inadvertently or not, invoked the connection between psychedelic experience and children's fantasy tales.[26] Most recently, *Teletubbies*, with its polymorphous alien beings stumbling through a mescalinian, color-saturated landscape, and the strange doubling/repetition of whole dialogues and scenes, has been "accused" of playing with drug motifs, while being adopted by a generation of Ecstasy-popping students for whom its 9:00 A.M. time-slot makes it perfect late-night viewing.

Another extraordinary fantasy work from the end of the nineteenth century is John Uri Lloyd's *Etidorhpa* (1897).[27] Lloyd grew up in New York state and as an adult moved to Cincinnati, where he became laboratory manager for a drug firm and with his brother established a quarterly journal, *Drugs and Medicines of North America*. *Etidorhpa* is a fantasy novel in which the narrator wanders through a hollow-earth realm until he reaches the land of the drunkards. There he is offered a fungal potion, which sends him into "an extravagant dream of higher fairy land,"[28] where he meets the goddess Etidorhpa ("Aphrodite" spelled backward). The narrator is cautious in his attitude, reviling intemperance as a destroyer of mankind, but affirming that intoxication, if "properly employed, may serve humanity's highest aims." He reviews the various intoxicants of man, lists most of the substances Cooke describes in *Seven Sisters of Sleep*, and speculates about the nature of soma.[29]

The narrator travels through a series of cavernous spaces in which beings deformed by drunkenness tempt him with visions, which he ignores when he perceives the satanic nature of the tempters. Finally, Etidorhpa offers him a vision of transcendental synaesthetic bliss, after which he returns to this world, to muse on the relationship between eternity and time. After this section, the author adds the following note:

> If in the course of experimentation, a chemist should strike upon a
> compound that in traces only would subject his mind and drive his
> pen to record such seemingly extravagant ideas as are found in the
> hallucinations herein pictured . . . and yet could he not know the

end of such a drug, would it not be his duty to bury the discovery from others, to cover from mankind the existence of such a noxious fruit of the chemist's or pharmaceutist's art? To sip once or twice of such a potent liquid, and then to write lines that tell the story of its power may do no harm to an individual on his guard, but mankind in common should never possess such a penetrating essence.[30]

We do not know whether Lloyd himself ever discovered such a chemical, although he was certainly in a position where he could experiment.

Horror, science fiction, fantasy, erotica, travel narratives, and children's literature: all are genres that deal with the "unreal" in one way or another. The unreal is the place where all that is feared or desired, that which cannot be spoken about, resides. Writers have talked about magical plants that produce visions in the spaces opened up by these genres, safe in the knowledge that they pose no danger because they are merely fictional devices. The boundaries around these spaces are rigorously policed, for there is always a danger of leakage, of contamination of the real by fantasy products. The more that motifs like the mushroom or the hookah are used as generic symbols of fantasy worlds, the more emptied of their actual, historical significance as shamanic substances or smoking apparatus they become. At their most hollowed out, the mushroom and hookah are nothing more than "pure conventions." But the intensity with which certain symbols are consigned to the oblivion of the unreal (and the literature on drugs is full of this particular strategy) is itself indicative of an unresolved tension, a fear that that which has been banished may return. Just as the Renaissance poets' use of magical plants was a response to the persistence of pagan plant knowledge, the fantasy space that Carroll and Lloyd explore was informed by knowledge that there were substances that produced precisely the altered states that are to be found in their books.

The reemergence of actual psychedelic plants in Western culture began in the middle of the nineteenth century, with the first detailed ethnographic and travelers' accounts of New World psychedelic plants. The Ecuadorian geographer Manuel Villavicencio tried the Amazonian hallucinogenic brew ayahuasca in 1858, and the British Botanist Richard Spruce conducted a study of ayahuasca around the same time, though his results were not published until the 1870s in a journal, and in book form not until the turn of the century.[31] It is very clear that mere knowledge of the existence of a substance, even personal knowledge of its effects, is no guarantee that attention will be paid to it. Only when a culture finds a way of using the substance do the "discovery" and dissemination of information about the substance actually occur.

Peyote use came to the attention of North American and European scientists as a result of its adoption by North American native groups in the middle of the nineteenth century—during the period of the greatest persecution of native cultures, when the Kiowa and Comanche were driven into Mexico and (presumably) encountered indigenous Mexican tribes such as the Tarahumara and the Huichol. The peyote religion and ritual sprang up along with movements such as the Ghost Dance, a late-nineteenth-century trans-tribal movement whose goal was to restore native life to its form before the European conquest, in the new reservations to which native tribes were confined. Although the peyote religion, whose existence was formalized as the Native American Church in Oklahoma in 1918, lacked the messianic fervor of the Ghost Dance, its adherents stand at the origin of modern psychedelic culture, not as timeless primitives, but as the earliest peoples thrown, through the destruction of their culture, into the rootless, nomadic hyperspaces that open up in the midst of the shattered, yet overcontrolled, geography of the reservation.[32]

The first nonnative American to describe North American use of peyote (or mescal, as it was also known) was an observer from the Smithsonian's newly formed Bureau of American Ethnology named James Mooney, who wrote a coolly observed report called "The Mescal Plant and Ceremony" for the *Therapeutic Gazette* in 1896.[33] Other writers such as Carl Lumholtz, an ethnologist associated with the American Museum of Natural History, had already published articles on the use by northern Mexican tribes such as the Huichol and Tarahumare of peyote, which they called hikuli. Lumholtz notes that "during the Civil War, the so-called Texas Rangers, when taken prisoners and deprived of all other stimulating drinks, used mescal buttons, or 'white mule,' as they called them. They soaked the plants in water and became intoxicated with the liquid."[34] Lumholtz gave an account of an all-night hikuli dance or ritual, culminating in worship of the rising sun (at least as powerful as peyote)—not so far removed from Artaud's "Peyote Dance," though lacking the gnostic revisions and reversals that Artaud makes. Lumholtz also described his own experience with peyote—but he had little to say about it besides the fact that it produced in him "a depression and a chill such as I have never experienced before."[35]

The first account of the effects of peyote ingestion was given in 1887 by John Briggs, a physician in Dallas, Texas. Little attention was paid, however, and thus the account in the *British Medical Journal* of 1896 by the American psychiatrist, physician, and historical romance writer S. Weir Mitchell is usually considered the first one. Mitchell was the first to describe many of the characteristic visual phenomena associated with peyote: heightened sensitivity to light and color, abstract visual pattern formation on closed eyelids. Mitchell's account was rapturous.[36]

Mitchell gave some peyote to William James, whose enthusiasm for nitrous oxide has been discussed elsewhere in this book. James took a button and was violently sick for twenty-four hours (Louis Lewin had a similar reaction). He wrote back to Mitchell that he would "take the visions on trust." Mitchell's account was also read by the British psychologist Havelock Ellis, who, in early 1897, obtained a supply of peyote from the firm of Potter & Clarke in London.[37] Ellis wrote several articles describing his own experience; one appeared in a medical journal, but the better-known one, "A New Artificial Paradise," was published in *The Contemporary Review* in 1898. In it he describes how on Good Friday in his rooms in the Temple in the center of London, he drank a decoction of three peyote buttons, and began to experience the characteristic visual imagery on his closed eyelids: "I would see thick glorious fields of jewels, solitary or clustered, sometimes brilliant and sparkling, sometimes with a dull rich glow. Then they would spring up into flower-like shapes beneath my gaze, and then seem to turn into gorgeous butterfly forms or endless folds of glistening, iridescent, fibrous wings of wonderful insects."[38]

Comparing his visions to the paintings of Monet, he summarized the experience as offering increased sensitivity to "the more delicate phenomena of light and shade and colour." Mescal offered access to an "optical Fairyland." Besides the obvious parallels to developments in contemporary painting (the interest in light of the Impressionists, the heightened color sensitivity of the Fauves, the earliest rumblings of the move toward abstraction), the discoveries of Mitchell and Ellis represent one of the first explorations of visual abstraction in modern culture. Unlike Aldous Huxley, who was also interested in the visual meaning of the mescaline experience, Ellis did not stress the decorative aspects of this abstraction, but described them in more purely phenomenological terms. Future users of psychedelics, including the Mazatec shaman woman Maria Sabina, were to make analogies between psychedelic visions and the movies or television, but the projecting screen of the eyelids is already there in Ellis' writing—only a few years after the first cinematic projections were made (one of Ellis' experimenters compares the experience to going to the theater in the afternoon, "in an artificial light of gas and lamps, the spectator of a fictitious world of action").[39]

Ellis gave some of the peyote buttons to William Butler Yeats in April 1897, but the poet found peyote's effect on his breathing unpleasant, and expressed a preference for hashish.[40] Ellis also gave some to the poet Arthur Symons, who was more enthusiastic, observing at one point that "my eye seemed to be turning into a vast drop of dirty water in which millions of minute creatures resembling tadpoles were in motion."[41] But research was not pursued because of the mixed results obtained (both Ellis and Mitchell gave it to people who experienced fear of dying) and perhaps because of criticism from those like the editors of the *British Medical Journal,* who in an editorial suggested that peyote was in fact a "New Inferno."[42]

Although many of the early experimenters with peyote were aware that Native American use of the drug had a strong religious dimension, they did not share this experience. For them, peyote was experienced as something profane, fascinating, but with aesthetic and scientific implications. In Ellis' account, we are already in the post-print world that McLuhan called electronic space. The peyote visions offer no narratives and very little dream imagery of the sort that De Quincey and Gautier experienced with opium and hashish. The primary referents are the visual arts and music: "mescal intoxication may be described as chiefly a saturnalia of the specific senses, and, above all, an orgy of vision. It reveals an optical fairyland, where all the senses now and again join the play." In this "orgy" there is no sense of linear organization and separation of impressions, no distance of the observer from the observed when the visions are seen with closed eyelids—instead there is an overwhelming, immersive simultaneity. The eye itself, mediating inner and outer vision, has become the locus of the imaginal. At the same time, Ellis felt that mescal was "the most democratic of the plants which lead men to an artificial paradise" because of "the halo of beauty which it casts around the simplest and commonest things."[43]

The use of peyote by writers was rare at the turn of the century. Aleister Crowley is said to have added peyote to a "libation" that was shared at performances of his ritual-theater piece *The Rites of Eleusis,* which was performed privately and publicly in London in 1910. The Manhattan socialite Mabel Dodge Luhan included in her memoir, *Movers and Shakers* (1935), an amusing anecdote about a peyote experiment in New York's Greenwich Village before World War I.[44] Luhan, who cultivated a bohemian salon through which people such as John Reed and Eugene O'Neill passed, offered to host a peyote séance in 1914, at the request of a friend, Raymond Harrington, who had been doing ethnological research among the Kiowa in Oklahoma. Although Harrington tried to maintain a sense of the native rituals he witnessed, the séance quickly deteriorated into bohemian chaos and laughter. Some of those participating panicked and ran out onto the street, while a beatific anarchist called Terry, who had vowed never to work another day in his life, sat in the corner, chain-smoking, and declared "I have seen the universe and, Man, it is wonderful!"[45]

Luhan was apparently appalled by the effects of peyote. In the 1930s, by which time she was living in Taos, New Mexico, presiding over a salon that included figures like D. H. Lawrence and Georgia O'Keeffe, Luhan was a vocal campaigner against the use of peyote by the Native American Church and lobbied for a federal law preventing peyote use. In a letter of 1936, she wrote "The Catholic Church does not recognize the 'Native American Church.' Would you stand for hashish, cocaine, or morphine and defend them on the grounds of liberty?" But thanks to a coalition of anthropologists that included Harrington, Weston La Barre, and Franz Boas, and representatives of native tribes, attempts to introduce the bill in the Senate were defeated in 1937—the same year that the passing of the Marijuana Tax Act effectively made marijuana use illegal.[46]

Pharmacological study of peyote was initiated by the German psychopharmacologist and toxicologist Louis Lewin, who was given a supply of buttons by the firm of Parke Davis and Company in 1887 while on a trip to the United States. Lewin was the first person to extract an alkaloid from the peyote cactus in 1888, although it was another German chemist, Arthur Heffter, who discovered the alkaloid "mezcalin hydrochloride," which he used for purposes of self-experimentation in 1897.[47] It is this molecule, along with the related mescaline sulphate, that is commonly known as mescaline. Unlike morphine, cocaine, or even *Cannabis indica* extracts, neither mescaline nor peyote was marketed as a medication (or intoxicant), although in 1933, a Swiss pharmacy briefly offered "Peyotyl" as a psychological restorative. Indeed, despite having undeniable effects on the human psyche, and in the case of peyote a history of use for religious purposes by "primitives," these two substances appeared to have no obvious utility whatsoever. The problem for psychiatrists then was how to interpret the properties that peyote and mescaline had—and to work out what use they could be put to.

Human experimentation with mescaline was conducted at the Kräpelin Clinic in Munich before World War I, and in the 1920s there were at least three groups that studied the effects of mescaline in human subjects. Lewin himself, although not actually involved in clinical work, devoted a chapter of *Phantastica* (1924), his survey of psychoactive plants, to the psychedelics that were then known, naming them "phantastica." Kurt Beringer, working in a psychiatric clinic in Heidelberg, gave mescaline to approximately sixty doctors and medical students and reported the results in his epic *Der Meskalinrausch* (1927); the book contains over two hundred pages of self-reports. Beringer, who was an associate of Hermann Hesse and Carl Jung as well as Lewin, was, like Moreau in the 1840s, searching for a psychotomimetic that would provide an experimental model for madness. In France, Alexandre Rouhier also studied the effects of mescaline, and produced two books in which, among other things, he described the use of yage, peyote, and other New World plants to predict the future.[48] He spoke of "botanomancy" and of conducting studies of the plants with a group called the Institut Métapsychique International. In 1928, Heinrich Klüver, an American psychologist, published *Mescal: The "Divine" Plant and Its Psychological Effects*, the first English-language monograph on the subject.

In describing the mental states produced by mescaline, researchers searched for analogies in religious experience or literature that would describe the effects of the drug, or they developed what was essentially an aesthetics in order to categorize the effects. Lewin, for example, cited the visions of Ezekiel and Goethe's *Faust* as hallucinatory experiences, equivocating between his own feelings of religious faith and the notion that "visionary states are . . . generally temporarily limited intermediate and transitory states caused by substances produced in the organism."[49] It is certainly surprising to read a scientific monograph that contains passages such as the following one from Klüver:

> An edge of a huge cliff seemed to project over a gulf of unseen depth. My viewless enchanter set on the brink a huge bird claw of stone. Above, from the stem or leg, hung a fragment of some stuff. This began to unroll and float out to a distance which seemed to me to represent Time as well as immensity of Space. Here were miles of rippled purples, half transparent, and of ineffable beauty. Now and then soft golden clouds floated from these folds, or a great shimmer went over the whole of the rolling purples, and things, like green birds, fell from it, fluttering down into the gulf below.[50]

Aesthetics provided the technical tools for the transcription of the mental states induced by mescaline, even though, according to Klüver, "the investigators emphasize that the phenomena defy all description."[51] Klüver developed what he called "form constants"—lattices, spirals, and so on—that would allow him to categorize and generalize about people's experiences.

McLuhan has observed that when a new technology emerges that changes human sense-perception ratios, one effect is that the old structure of perception becomes the content of the new one. Literature, and in particular Symbolist poetry with its fractal, disjunctive temporal organization, became part of the content of the mescaline experience, even though psychedelic experience itself is hardly conducive to the production of literature. There are in fact hardly any poems, novels, or short stories written about psychedelic experience, although the descriptions of the states triggered by the drugs are "poetic" and invoke poetic motifs and figures so as to define the experience.

For the most part, writers who used mescaline and peyote in the inter-war period did so in clinical settings with researchers; at the very least they obtained their supplies of drugs from these sources. Jean-Paul Sartre, for example, was injected with mescaline in January 1935 at the Sainte-Anne Hospital in Paris by an old friend, the psychiatrist Daniel Lagache. Sartre was at that time working on a book on the imagination, later to become *L'imaginaire; psychologie—phénoménologique de l'imagination* (*The Imaginary: Psychology— Phenomenology of the Imagination*, 1940). He was interested in the use of mescaline to explore the nature of the image in hallucinating subjects, as was Lagache, who had just finished writing a book called *Les hallucinations verbales et la parole* (*Verbal Hallucinations and Speech,* 1934). According to Simone de Beauvoir, Sartre had a rather unpleasant experience with mescaline and made only a brief reference to it in *The Imaginary,* toward the end of the book in the section entitled "Pathology of the Imagination":

> I was able to note a brief hallucinatory phenomenon, on the occa-
> sion when I had an injection of mascaline [*sic*] administered to me. It
> presented precisely this lateral character: someone was singing in a
> nearby room, and when I opened my ear to listen, it ceased entirely,
> whereupon I saw before me—three little parallel clouds which ap-
> peared before me. This phenomenon disappeared of course as soon
> I tried to grasp it. It was incompatible with a plain and clear visual
> consciousness. It could only exist *by stealth* . . . there was, in the way
> in which these three little clouds appeared in my memory, as soon
> as they had disappeared, something at once inconsistent and mys-
> terious, which, so it seems to me, had only translated the existence
> of these liberated spontaneities *to the margins* of consciousness.[52]

Sartre, like Henri Michaux later, adopted a curious attitude toward his hal-
lucinations, forcing them to the outside of his perception in order to create an objective space from which to view them. Like the doctors who wished to study madness by inducing it in themselves by using psychedelic drugs, Sartre appears to have believed that imaginal space could be scrutinized by rational, scientific consciousness, the way one watches television or looks at events through a window. It does not seem to have occurred to him that the phenomenological space of inquiry, far from being objective, is an imaginal realm much like any other mental realm, and subject to the same kinds of behavior as the "irrational" world of the imagination he wished to study. Sartre's inability to integrate his hallucinations may have been responsible for the unpleas-
antness of his experience. Again, according to Beauvoir, "the objects he looked at changed their appearance in the most horrifying manner: umbrellas had become vultures, shoes turned into skeletons, and faces acquired monstrous characteristics, while behind him, just past the corner of his eye, swarmed crabs and polyps and grimacing Things."[53]

Sartre's meditations were taken up after World War II by Maurice Merleau-

Ponty, who discussed mescaline hallucinations in his *Phénoménologie de la perception* (1945)—and no doubt for similar reasons (though, as far as we know, Merleau-Ponty did not actually take the drug): the hallucination is a problem for any materialist theory of consciousness.[54] In the hallucination, the one thing that is not supposed to happen to materialist consciousness happens: one sees that for which there is no sensory data. The imagination materializes. Psychoactive substances, as material agents of the imaginary, straddle the gulf between these realms that was believed to exist since the time of Descartes or Hegel.[55]

Because the psychedelics pose such an interesting phenomenological problem, a number of philosophers wrote about them or used them. After World War II, Martin Heidegger is rumored to have taken LSD with Ernst Jünger,[56] and postwar essays like "The Question Concerning Technology" (1953), with its emphasis on *aletheia* ("revealing"), hint at a mystical revelation that is psychedelic to the core, whether triggered by drugs or by art. Although it is doubtful whether they had actually taken psychedelics before doing so,[57] Michel Foucault and Gilles Deleuze both wrote essays in the 1960s that use the problem of the hallucination as a way of critiquing more orthodox notions of sense and representation.[58] "Drugs," scowled Foucault, "have nothing to do with truth or falsity: only to fortunetellers do they reveal a world 'more truthful than the real.'"[59] Instead, Foucault and others proposed a nomadic thought, constantly moving between imaginal realms, measuring their value according to the kinds of relationships they allowed, rather than a preexisting order of true and false, real and unreal.

As I have shown in the hashish chapter, Walter Benjamin had proposed something very similar in his writings on that nineteenth-century psychedelic, hashish, thirty years before, when he explored the potential revolutionary value of states of intoxication. Like Sartre, Benjamin took mescaline in a research setting with Fritz Fränkel on May 22, 1934; several pages of notes from this session written by both Benjamin and Fränkel were published in the 1970s along with the hashish material. Although Benjamin sounds as if he had a less than pleasant experience (Fränkel noted Benjamin's "sulkiness" and "inconsolable sorrow"),[60] his comments on patterning and fringes anticipate Aldous Huxley's exploration of the same subject by twenty years. Like many of the modernist writers, Benjamin dwelled on the visual excess that mescaline triggered:

The secret of Struwwelpeter: These children are all impertinent
only because no one gives them any gifts, and that is why the child
who reads him is well behaved, because it receives so many gifts already on the first page. A little shower of gifts falls there from the
dark night sky. Thus does it rain incessantly in the world of childhood. In veils, like the veils of rain, gifts fall down to the child,
which veil the world from him. A child must get gifts, or else it will
die like the children in Struwwelpeter or go kaputt or fly away. That
is the secret of Struwwelpeter.[61]

Mescaline's visual pyrotechnics are gifts that pour out of the gnostic modernist darkness, to save the psychonaut from the heaviness of the world. But
this is a temporary phenomenon, just as childhood is, a regression that cannot
hold back forever the storms of history.

Another writer who used peyote at this time was the Polish modernist
Stanislaw Ignacy Witkiewicz. Witkacy, as he was known, was a versatile man
who made important contributions as a playwright, painter, and photogra-
pher, in addition to writing both fiction and nonfiction; he had also traveled to
Australia with the anthropologist Bronislaw Malinowski in 1915. He wrote
two novels, *Farewell to Autumn* (1927) and *Insatiability* (1930), both of which
feature drug use quite prominently. In the latter book, an imaginary drug,
the "fiendish narcotic" Davamesque B2, becomes widely used in Witkacy's
dystopian society.[62] The drug is purveyed by a mysterious Malay known as
Murti Bing, who preaches a doctrine of universal contentment. The drug,
which makes users feel "as though a beam were speeding along through an unfathomable void toward some sort of crystalline creature glowing with a myriad of colors, which turned out to be the eternally elusive Maximal Dualistic
Unity,"[63] has properties similar to those of mescaline and peyote—which
Witkiewicz was experimenting with in 1929 while writing *Insatiability*. But
Bing's soma-like drug also induces mindless happiness and a state of egoless-
ness (loss of individuality) that prepare the citizens for the advanced forms of
social control they are about to experience. Similar themes emerge in Huxley's
Brave New World (1932), where soma is the drug.

Witkiewicz took a more direct nonfictional approach to the subject in his
Narcotics: Nicotine, Alcohol, Cocaine, Peyote, Morphine, and Ether (1932). Witkiewicz
began exploring drug use in the 1920s, and made notes on his paintings, and

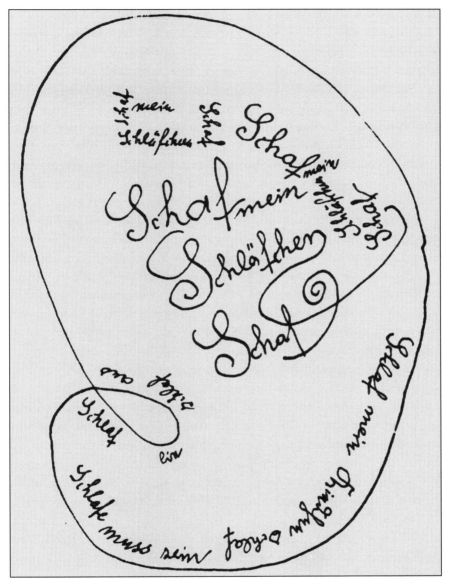

Figure 10. Embryo text: "sheep . . . little sleep . . . sheep . . ." (a play on a German nursery rhyme: "sleep, little children, sleep / your father is looking after the sheep / your mother shakes the tree / from which a little dream falls down.") Text/drawing by made by Walter Benjamin when he was under the influence of mescaline, May, 22, 1934.

in his books, as to what substances he had been using during their production. The introduction to *Narcotics* was written "'in S,' which means a state of smoking."[64]

Witkiewicz's view of drugs was profoundly modernist. He saw narcotic use as a symptom of spiritual and aesthetic decadence and weakness, but one which, to his own disapproval if not disgust, he participated in: "however far back one goes in human history, one can always come across some 'narcotic phantasm.'" Mankind was driven by a metaphysical insatiability that "if it is not eradicated by excessive satiation of real-life feelings, by work, by the exercise of power, by creativity, etc., can be appeased solely with the aid of narcotics."[65]

Insatiability results from "the limitation of each individual in Time and Space, and from his opposition to the infinite totality of Existence." Narcotics served as tranquilizers, or as replacements for religion and art. They might initially give a kind of frenzied vision, but ultimately resulted in the destruction of the artists' relationship to their audiences, "by enclosing them in their impenetrable world of deranged experiences, and by deforming their perceptions of reality to an extreme point beyond which they become incomprehensible to normal people."[66]

Witkiewicz believed that alcohol and tobacco were the most pernicious drugs known to man, since they were toxic, physiologically addictive, and available everywhere. Peyote, which Witkiewicz considered "absolutely harmless when taken occasionally, and which offers, besides unbelievable visual images, such penetrating insight into the hidden recesses of the psyche and inspires such distaste for all other narcotics, especially for alcohol, that given the almost absolute impossibility of becoming addicted to it, [it] should be used in all sanatoriums where addicts of all kinds are treated" fared the best of all the "narcotics" discussed.[67]

Witkiewicz obtained peyote from a variety of sources: initially, the Warsaw Metaphysical Society; later, through a correspondence with Rouhier and Beringer.[68] He purchased mescaline from "the splendid firm Merck."[69] Witkiewicz wrote an interesting account of a peyote experience, partially transcribed by his wife, which appeared in an expurgated version in *Narcotics*, owing to the Surrealist sexual imagery: "violet sperm-jet straight in the face, from a hydrant of mountain-genitals."[70] Profane and misanthropic, Witkiewicz's prose reads somewhat like a modernist version of Hunter S. Thompson's.

Figure 11. Peyote eyes. Stanislaw Ignacy Witkiewicz, "Portrait of Nena Stachurska," pastel on paper, October 12, 1929. Note the "T. Peyotl" signature, indicating Witkiewicz was under the influence of the drug while he was painting.

Many of the writers discussed in this section use the notion of excess in understanding the experience of peyote. Ellis' "orgy of vision," Benjamin's "shower of gifts," Witkiewicz's metaphysical insatiability, Michaux's "turbulent infinity" or "knowledge through abysses" are all indicative of the senses being overwhelmed by the drug: "Peyote eyes seem about to explode from the inexpressible intensity of the feelings and thoughts packed into them," says Witkiewicz.[71] This experience of excess through psychoactive substances was the necessary product of Witkiewicz's and the other modernist experimenters' and researchers' existential orientation. In rejecting a priori the possibility of a spiritual dimension to the psychedelic experience, they imposed a limit on their experiences that turned them into self-reflexive, self-reiterating studies of mental processes. Foucault, in his essay on the philosopher of excess, Georges Bataille, says:

> By denying us the limit of the Limitless, the death of God leads to
> an experience in which nothing may again announce the exterior-
> ity of being, and consequently to an experience which is interior
> and sovereign. But such an experience, for which the death of God
> is an explosive reality, discloses as its own secret and clarification, its
> intrinsic finitude, the limitless reign of the Limit, and the empti-
> ness of those excesses in which it spends itself and where it is found
> wanting. In this sense, the inner experience is throughout an expe-
> rience of the impossible.[72]

Along with madness, eroticism, and violence, psychedelics offered this kind of "inner experience" that seeks the infinite in the finite, that reaches the limits of language only to find itself still within language, or the body, or the mind. Indeed, one of the defining qualities of "inner experience" is a belief that it is impossible to experience anything beyond language—or that the beyond itself can be defined only as "the impossible."

Antonin Artaud lived this impossible inner experience to its limit, but he also marks the place at which it was transformed and abandoned—partly through the influence of psychedelics. In 1936, Artaud traveled to Mexico, after reading, along with other French Surrealists, about the Mexican Revolution. Artaud mistakenly believed that the revolution aimed at restoring a pre-Columbian civilization in Mexico—a restoration he wished to encourage through a series of lectures on his views on the theater and culture. He was disappointed when he reached Mexico City, but persuaded the Mexican authorities to give him permission to visit the area of northern Mexico where the Tarahumara lived, in the hope of participating in one of their peyote rituals. Artaud saw Indian Mexico as containing a still existing possibility of a direct link to the most powerful elemental forces in life, beyond those of materialistic, European, written culture, and he invited Indian culture to transform him, although it is unclear whether he knew anything about it beyond projections of his own hopes.[73]

Artaud's journey to the Tarahumara was complicated by the fact that he decided to stop taking heroin, to which he was at that time addicted, so that he could experience peyote within an uncontaminated body and mind. He was hallucinating long before he took part in the peyote rite, seeing signs and messages in the configuration of the mountains around him. When Artaud arrived in a Tarahumara village, he found out that a tribe member had died and that rites would be performed for him. Artaud was given peyote, in the form of a grated muddy gruel, along with the tribe members, and told to spit into a hole in the ground. He saw the ritual as taking place for his own benefit—or rather, for his "crucifixion"—one of his obsessions. The night passed in ritual turbulence. Artaud's initial accounts seem almost bewildered—or perhaps obscured by his own suffering.

Artaud's description of his use of peyote was radically different from most of the accounts we have seen until now. Artaud did not view peyote use as an aesthetic experiment, nor did he travel to the Tarahumara as an ethnographer—instead, he went to experience in his own body what he believed the Tarahumara knew. This kind of endeavor would become popular only with the advent of the Beats in the late 1950s. In the articles he wrote at the time of his trip to Mexico, Artaud actually said relatively little about peyote itself. He was more interested in the ritual surrounding the substance, which might provide an example of the true theater he had given up looking for the previous year, with the failure of his drama *The Cenci* in Paris.

In "The Tarahumara Peyote Rite," written when he was in an asylum in Rodez in southern France in 1943 and 1944, Artaud gave a gnostic account of peyote as a drug that annihilates nature and culture to reveal the void. Although this account is highly revisionist (Artaud was at the time struggling with acute psychiatric problems and undergoing electroshock therapy, as well as attempts to reconvert him to Catholicism), Artaud was pioneering the kind of flight into inner space, the fantastic, or the imaginary that would become common in the 1960s:

To take these dreams for realities—this is what Peyote never let you fall into—or to confound false perceptions which flee into the shallows, ragged, no longer ripe, no longer risen out of the hallucinatory unconscious, with true images and emotions. For there is in the consciousness of the Marvelous, something with which one can go beyond things. And Peyote tells us where it is, behind what strange concretions of an atavistically obscured and driven-back breath, the Fantastic is able to renew its phosphorescences, its dust hazes in consciousness. And this Fantastic has a noble quality, its disorder is only superficial, in reality it adheres to an order which develops in mystery and according to a program which ordinary consciousness has no access to, but which Ciguri allows us to reach and which is the mystery of poetry itself. But in the human being, there is another program, an obscure, unformed one . . . which also exudes adventurous sensations, perceptions. These are the shameless phantasms which affect the sick consciousness, which will be completely abandoned and vanish, if it cannot find anything to hold them back. And Peyote is the only obstacle which evil finds in this terrible place. I also had false sensations and perceptions, and I was afraid.[74]

The problem that man faces is that of distinguishing the false imaginary from the true one. Ordinary perceptions, as well as the delusions that the mentally ill are subject to, belong to the category of the false. The imaginary or fantastic that peyote gave Artaud access to was not a peripheral or pathological phenomenon, nor was it defined relative to an objective, material reality. Peyote allowed Artaud to reach the mystery at the source of all poetry, a mystery that only appears disordered (which is to say, excessive), but that constituted the order of the Real beyond the phantasms of sick consciousness. This inversion confirmed Artaud in his belief that poetry was not something that should be looked for in literature, but something that should be lived. Many of the writers who used psychedelic drugs struggled to find forms that could express the ineffable qualities of the experience. Artaud also developed a glossolalic language that would be the direct speech of the soul, material and yet beyond the phantasms of representation.

The modernist exploration of psychedelics culminated in the postwar writings of the French poet Henri Michaux.[75] Although he had described experiences with hashish and opium in his first book, *Les rêves et la jambe* (1923), Michaux first took mescaline at the end of 1954, after receiving the drug from a Spanish neurologist named Julián de Ajuriaguerra.[76] Beginning with *Misérable miracle* (1957), he wrote a series of explorations of the effects of psychoactive drugs ending around 1970.

Michaux had been interested in exploring the relationship between language (and image) and the unconscious since the 1920s. While the Surrealists experimented with automatic writing (retaining a "real" vocabulary), Michaux, in a series of drawings done in the 1920s, produced abstract, "imaginary" alphabets that developed and mutated on the page. In his texts on the psychedelics, he found new ways of achieving these effects.

Michaux used post-Mallarméan poetics, free of pre-set literary form, to record the altered states of consciousness induced by these substances. Like Artaud and Benjamin, he was interested in a hieroglyphic writing that would directly represent mental states. In *Misérable miracle,* the main text is echoed by margins that show the doubling, recursive movements of consciousness. Pages of Michaux's session notes are reproduced in the book, to show the distortion of the written word and its mutation into abstract hieroglyphs of expressivity.

> While I am still occupied looking at these extraordinary mountains, the intense urgency that possesses me, having settled on the letters "m" of the word "immense" which I was mentally pronouncing, the double down strokes of these miserable "m's" begin stretching out into the fingers of gloves, into the nooses of lassos, and these in turn, becoming enormous, shoot up toward the heights— arches for unthinkable, baroque cathedrals, arches ridiculously elongated resting on their unchanged little bases. It is utterly grotesque.[77]

In much of Michaux's writing there is a high degree of tension between the writer and the experience that he is trying to record. As Malcom Bowie notes, Michaux's apparent interest in drugs is at times puzzling.[78] He resented the machine-like dissolution of the ego that he experienced and claimed that he was not impressed by mescaline's "tawdry spectacle," which he found unpleasant, emasculating in its penetration of his cells. "Mescaline wanted my full consent. To enjoy a drug one must enjoy being a subject."[79]

In many ways, Michaux's work on mescaline was an anachronism, belonging to the prewar period. His defensive, cantankerous tone contains a strong element of nostalgia for the period of high modernism, which was already in decline at the time he was writing. Michaux sought to show that the psychedelics were vulgar products of materialist science, and wanted to preserve the avant-garde's status and perspective as a bulwark of humanism in the face of new forces (the dominance of technoscience, mass culture, and third world perspectives). His hieroglyphic literature was an attempt to adapt literature to a world in which linear, narrative, segmented structures have been replaced by immersive, electronic, acoustic space.

Despite this defensive tone, Michaux has provided us with the most detailed record of the specific way in which psychedelics perturb language; a phenomenological record of the language function, its profound connection to the ego and the sense of self, but also the revelation of its essential autonomy when studied under the influence of a drug like mescaline. We are back to Rimbaud's "I is an other," with which the avant-garde's program was initiated. But that which was a provocative poetic statement at the end of the nineteenth century had now become a clinical research program.

Michaux's work documented a slow painful adjustment to the real meaning of Rimbaud's dictum: not the absurdity of the struggle to be, but the knowledge that literature could survive the dissolution of the existential (male) ego that more or less structured Romantic aesthetics from Rousseau on. Michaux originally believed that mescaline would be existential angst in a pill, complete with a "vulgar" scientific past that would make the nobility of the writer's struggle against the materialist void stand out that much more clearly. But in 1968, in an addendum to *Misérable miracle,* he gave up this position and admitted the transcendental forces that had been nagging at his consciousness. He quoted a verse from the *Upanishads,* and concluded that the true means of uniting language and the altered state induced by mescaline was to be found in the hymn—"Vastness had found Verb."[80]

"Plato distinctly looms in from the shadows; endogenic images are the last chance at happiness left for us to experience."[81] This last sentence from Gottfried Benn's essay "Induced Life," written in 1943 (but not published until

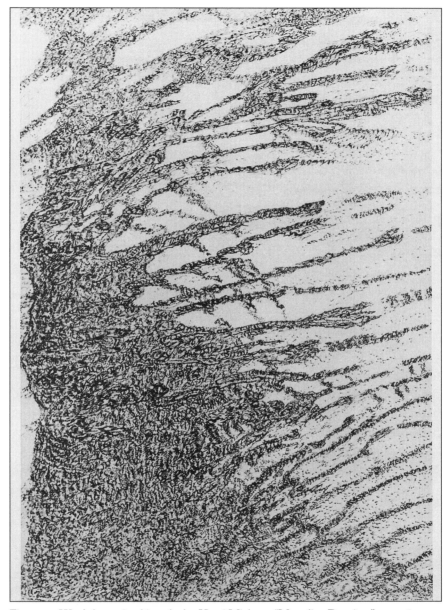

Figure 12. Words becoming hieroglyphs. Henri Michaux, "Mescaline Drawing," ca. 1956.

1949), spells out the beginning of the retreat from the domination of the physical world through nationalist ambition, political ideology, and physics into
virtual space, outer space, and the microscopic and technological worlds that,
even in the midst of the Cold War, would characterize post—World War II
culture. A few years later Ernst Jünger coined the word "Psychonaut" to describe the explorers of those worlds.[82] In that new environment, the somewhat
directionless, experimental work conducted with mescaline in the 1920s, and
the isolated, occasional experiments with drugs by writers and philosophers,
would assume a new importance, as methods of technologically manipulating,
enhancing, or controlling the mind were focused on by writers, scientists, and
states alike. As Benn observed:

> The brain is the mutative, that is, revolutionary organ par excel-
> lence. Not content but form was always its essence; its instrument
> was consciousness expansion; its desire was for stimuli. From the
> beginning, this shelter of rudiments and catacombs brought along
> its own equipment, it didn't depend on impressions and it produced
> itself when it was called. It did not by preference turn to "life," but
> also to lethal factors, hunger, fasting, walking on nails, singing to
> snakes, magic, bionegativity, death.[83]

While Benn was writing these words, Nazi researchers at Dachau were performing experiments on prisoners using mescaline, to see if they could control
their minds under the influence of the drug. A year earlier in 1942, General
William Donovan, the director of the Office of Strategic Services (OSS—the
wartime precursor of the Civilian Intelligence Agency) had begun a secret research program to discover chemicals that could be used to make people speak
under interrogation. Dr. Hubertus Strughold, whose subordinates ran the
Dachau experimentation program, was one of the German scientists invited
to join America's space program after the war.[84]

Just as physicists like Erwin Schrödinger were eager to apply the mathematical precision of physics to biology, transforming it into one of the "exact"
sciences, so a consensus developed at the end of World War II that the mind
could be manipulated according to mechanistic or at least scientific principles.
In 1953 the CIA's director, Allen Dulles, spoke of the mind being a "malleable
tool" that could be manipulated until it "becomes a phonograph playing a disc
put on its spindle by an outside genius over which it has no control."[85]

Although the first truth serum (sodium amytal) was developed in the 1930s, many people in a variety of fields believed after World War II that the contents of people's minds could be extracted like teeth, or programmed like a machine. Truth, it was believed, was an actual thing that was located somewhere in people's minds, obscured only by the will to deceive. Disrupt the functioning of the ego, and truth would appear naked out of the ruins, like a shivering civilian. In 1947, the U.S. Navy initiated a program named Project CHATTER to find a drug that would do this. Psychedelics became a part of Western culture at the moment when the manipulation and control of the imaginal realms, no longer something to be left up to God or Romantic poets, was perceived as something useful.

That moment was brief. The navy abandoned its program in 1953. Although there was some consistency to the fantasy of finding a drug that would allow access to the contents of people's minds, the actual properties of the drugs under examination, not to mention the human mind itself, were much more ambiguous, and required the various agencies interested in using them to reconfigure their goals repeatedly. When it became clear that LSD and mescaline were not reliable truth drugs, they became "psychotomimetic" drugs again, although the aim was no longer to find an experimental model for madness, but to incapacitate populations during wartime, without killing them or seriously disrupting their capacity to work. Or they could be secretly administered to enemy statesmen like Fidel Castro or Gamal Abdel Nasser in the hope of causing them to act in embarrassing or foolish ways. During the 1950s and 1960s, LSD-like mind-bending substances became a stock device in spy novels such as Ian Fleming's *From Russia With Love* (1957) and Richard Condon's *Manchurian Candidate* (1960), as well as science fiction novels like Brian Aldiss' *Barefoot in the Head* (1969), a novel that takes place after the Acid Head War, in which Kuwait has bombed Britain with "PCAs"—"the Psycho-Chemical Aerosols that propagated psychotomimetic states."[86]

Aldous Huxley's *Doors of Perception* (1954), a seventy-page essay on his experience with mescaline, is also a product of this environment. Like the CIA operatives, Huxley believed that psychedelics give access to truth hidden in people's minds. But Huxley boldly reconfigured the notion of truth into a new, cosmic one in which Hollywood Boulevard, the Dharma body of the Buddha, and the chemical basis of human consciousness came together.

Huxley came from a background in which literary and scientific pursuits had long coexisted. His grandfather, the biologist Thomas H. Huxley, had debated Darwin in the nineteenth century. Huxley had a long-standing interest in drugs. He had read Lewin's *Phantastica* before completing his dystopian satire *Brave New World* (1932), in which a futuristic society uses a drug called soma to achieve fascist states of union. Huxley also wrote some essays on the subject around the same time,[87] in which he speculated that while "all existing drugs are treacherous and harmful," the antidote for the modern world would be the discovery of a beneficial drug, capable of providing genuine ecstasy—"the man who invents such a substance will be counted among the greatest benefactors of suffering humanity."[88]

It was in the 1950s, after he had settled in Los Angeles, that Huxley became interested in mescaline. In the early 1950s, both *Time* (1951) and *Newsweek* (1953) published articles on the use of mescaline in psychiatry, and the drug was in no sense a secret.[89] Huxley contacted Humphry Osmond, at that time the clinical director of a mental hospital in Saskatchewan and an advocate of the psychotomimetic theory of the drugs he would later name "psychedelic." Huxley invited Osmond to stay with him during a visit to Los Angeles. "I was on the spot and willing, indeed eager, to be a guinea pig. Thus it came about that, one bright May morning, I swallowed four-tenths of a gram of mescaline dissolved in half a glass of water and sat down to wait for the results."[90] These results were published in *Doors of Perception* (1954) (the title being taken from William Blake's *Marriage of Heaven and Hell*) and a longer, somewhat less successful follow-up, *Heaven and Hell* (1956).

Doors of Perception blends psychological, mystical, and aesthetic speculation in a way that is both highly specific to the subject of psychedelic drugs and also the direct development of Huxley's studies of mysticism in books such as *The Perennial Philosophy* (1946), with its emphasis on the direct experience of divinity. Huxley was very much immersed in the post–World War II tribal, nonvisual space (he had poor eyesight, as it happens), and yet he attempted to validate the mescaline experience by claiming that it gave access to the world as it was seen and heard by the great European painters and composers. But Huxley did not claim that mescaline would allow the user to paint or write well. It would provide an experience of the artist's world. Art itself was of minor importance: "art, I suppose, is only for beginners, or else for those resolute dead-enders, who have made up their minds to be content with the ersatz of Suchness, with symbols rather than with what they signify, with the elegantly composed recipe in lieu of the actual dinner."[91] The radical nature of this shift cannot be overemphasized. Huxley was proposing an experiential model of the imagination and the imaginal realms that ran counter to the symbolic, representational structures that had governed Western thought for centuries. This shift was to have profound implications for art, politics, and religion that would begin to be realized in the 1960s. It would be naive to attribute this shift solely to mescaline, or indeed to Huxley. John Cage's music and Jackson Pollock's painting were heading in the same direction at the exact same time. But the new value and interest accorded to the psychedelics had everything to do with this broad shift away from an aesthetic of the symbol toward one of experience.

Much of the revulsion heaped upon Huxley at the time can be connected to this shift in paradigms. The ethnologist Weston La Barre, author of the seminal anthropological study of peyote use in native cultures and a staunch defender of Native American use of peyote, found Huxley's book with its "literary hyperbole" and its claims for "a sort of instant zen" "rather absurd." He believed that Huxley and his ilk "looked upon the plant with the Romanticism-ensorcelled eyes of Europeans," and that the Native American and Western imaginal realms must remain separate. In defense of this viewpoint, La Barre claimed that mescaline potentially caused a degeneration of consciousness and a loss of "civilization"—these presumably being acceptable when found in "primitive" cultures.[92] Similar arguments were employed by R. C. Zaehner, Professor of Eastern Religions and Ethics at Oxford, who critiqued Huxley in his *Mysticism, Sacred and Profane* (1957).[93] Zaehner, a Roman Catholic, objected to Huxley's equating his chemically induced ecstasy with those described in the great mystical traditions. Zaehner contrasted the experience of ecstasy, a debased form of spirituality that he termed "nature mysticism," with "actual communion with God." Drugs could offer only the former. When Zaehner himself tried to repeat Huxley's experiment with mescaline among the spires of Oxford, he concluded that through mescaline "'self-transcendence' of a sort did take place, but transcendence into a world of farcical meaninglessness."[94]

The shift from symbol to experience can also be seen in Huxley's heightened sensitivity to patterning and nonrepresentational aspects of form. The chair and the foldings of drapery in Huxley's room radiated auratic meaning reminiscent of that described by hashish users: "For the artist as for the mescalin taker draperies are living hieroglyphs that stand in some peculiarly expressive way for the unfathomable mystery of pure being. More even than the chair, though less than those wholly supernatural flowers, the folds of my gray flannel trousers were charged with 'is-ness.' To what they owed this privileged status I cannot say."[95]

Huxley also revived Henri Bergson's model of the brain as a reducing valve and connected it to Blake's dictum regarding "the doors of perception" to form a theory of consciousness that was at once materialist and cosmic. But what is it that the normal brain eliminates and the mescalinized brain accepts? Although Huxley uses words like "perception" and "language," he is in fact offering a theory of information—similar to the cybernetic theories being developed by Gregory Bateson, Norbert Wiener, and others around the same time. Again, the crucial shift was from a dualist model of psychedelic experience, such as Benjamin's shower of gifts pouring out of gnostic darkness into this world, to a systems model where mescaline reveals a universe that is infinitely open and interconnected, and which the human mind is a participating part of.

More than any of the other pre-1960s writers, Huxley was interested in the role psychedelics could play in society. Huxley regarded mescaline as "almost completely innocuous" for most people, although "there is a minority that finds in the drug only hell or purgatory."[96] He believed that, even if it did not provide ultimate enlightenment, mescaline could generate a profoundly educational experience (he came from a family of educational reformers).

In an essay written for the *Saturday Evening Post* in 1958, Huxley compared different styles of drug cultures, such as the alcohol- and tranquilizer-dominated United States in the 1950s, with prospective future cultures that use substances to enhance productivity. He noted dryly that if the Soviet Union were to succeed in its quest to find chemicals capable of raising intelligence and energy, the first result would be the overthrow of the Soviet government. He contrasted the political use of tranquilizers and stimulants with the religious uses of psychedelics, and predicted a future society in which chemically induced transcendental experiences would lead to a mysticism focused not on symbolic structures but on the transformation of everyday life. Huxley's final novel, *Island* (1962), takes up this theme, with its description of a chemical (but also educational) utopia, facilitated by a mushroom called moksha (the Sanskrit word for liberation).

For all of his interest in the societal uses of drugs, Huxley never managed to find a bridge between the individual experience of moksha and the psychedelic utopias he envisaged, which all too easily become rather sinister machines for mass control and hypnosis—all of course in the name of "truth" or "liberation." What separates the drugged utopia of *Island* from the drugged dystopia of *Brave New World* is more a change of sentiment than anything else. The old goal of social control, which Huxley denounced in the 1930s, was reconfigured as the new goal of "health." Huxley's speculations in *Doors of Perception* about the use of "recorders, clock-controlled switches, public address systems and pillow speakers" in psychiatric institutions, to "constantly remind" patients of the "primordial fact" of cosmic consciousness, are hardly reassuring in this regard.[97]

As psychedelic therapy became popular in the late 1950s among Hollywood figures such as Cary Grant, a number of Huxley-inspired accounts of LSD and mescaline therapy appeared, including several written by women.[98] Women had not previously written much about drug use, except in the context of narcotic addiction, and, with the exception of Anais Nin (who kept her thoughts about her LSD experiences to her diary), these writings were published as the case histories of patients, rather than the work of "experimenters." The forward to Constance Newland's pseudonymously published *My Self and I,* written by Harold Greenwald, notes that the author "seems to be the very model of the frozen, ruthlessly efficient American career woman." With "rare bravery," she faces "her rage, her fear, and her LSD-induced psychotic-like fantasies" until her "impregnable resistance" and "frigidity" are overcome, with the aid of the drug and her therapist.[99] Many women were involved in the exploration of the psychedelics: Witkiewicz and Huxley dictated to their wives; Valentina Wasson accompanied her husband on his mushroom-collecting trips; and the pioneering psychedelic researchers Jean Houston and Joan Halifax began their careers working with their husbands, Robert Masters and Stanislav Grof. Until the 1960s, with rare exceptions these women either worked in the shadows of their husbands or published their ideas pseudonymously, or in the passive context of descriptions of themselves as patients.[100]

The other great psychedelic pioneer of the 1950s was a J. P. Morgan vice president and amateur mycologist named R. Gordon Wasson. Wasson and his wife had already written a voluminous work on the history of mushroom lore,

Russia, Mushrooms, and History (1957) when, apparently through a conversation with the English poet Robert Graves, he found out about the continuing existence of a cult in Oaxaca, in southern Mexico, that used teonanacatl, the vision-inducing mushrooms that Spanish writers had talked of after the conquest of Mexico. This mushroom cult had been discovered by an Austrian-born physician, Blas Pablo Reko, and picked up on by the Harvard botanist Richard Evans Schultes, who had traveled to Oaxaca in 1938 with Reko to witness the ceremonial use of the mushrooms. Schultes' interest in the cult was botanical (he claimed that he experienced none of the visionary dimensions of the plants he "discovered"), but Wasson saw the cultural and religious significance of the story and traveled to Oaxaca, where, on August, 15, 1953, he took the mushrooms (which were of three species, the best known being *Stropharia cubensis*) with the Mazatec shaman Maria Sabina. Wasson published a widely read account of his trip in *LIFE* magazine in 1957, but was apparently appalled when others who read his account began traveling to Oaxaca. Wasson argued that psychedelic mushrooms provided the key to many of the world's religious mysteries, including the soma of the Vedas, the Eleusinian rites of Ancient Greece, certain visions related in the *Zend Avesta*, the holy scripture of Zoroastrianism, and the tree of good and evil in the Bible, but made no comment on contemporary use of the drugs. Forgetting his own *LIFE* article, he later criticized the vulgarization of contemporary discourse about the drugs, calling the term "psychedelics" "a barbarous formation,"[101] and with a group of colleagues proposed a new term, "entheogen," to describe the drugs—a term that conveniently obscures the nontheogenic nature of most twentieth-century use of the drugs.

Robert Graves also believed that the psychedelics provided a source for much of the world of classical and preclassical mythology. In a review of Wasson's work published in the *Atlantic Monthly* in 1956, he already speculated that the cult of Dionysus held mushroom orgies.[102] On January 31, 1960, when he was sixty-four, Graves took mushrooms with Wasson in New York, and wrote an essay about it called "The Poet's Paradise" (1961), which he read to Oxford students in the early 1960s. Graves described his experience in highly mythical terms, feeling that the mushrooms were taking him back to the world of Gilgamesh and the Babylonian paradise. He experienced worlds of jewels, demons, and erotic fantasy, while Wasson played a tape recording of Mazatec shaman Maria Sabina chanting. Graves was impressed, although he noted caustically, that "what was for thousands of years a sacred and secret element, entrusted only to persons chosen for their good conduct and integrity, will soon be snatched at by jaded sensation-seekers."[103] Such people would be disappointed, however, because instead of drunken oblivion they would experience heightened insight into themselves—which they might find less than recreational. Yet Graves believed that the experience of the mushroom was passive when compared to that of poetic trance: "It seems established that Tlalocan [Aztec word for paradise], for all its sensory marvels, contains no palace of words presided over by the Living Muse, and no small white-washed cell . . . to which a poet may retire and actively write poems in her honour, rather than bask sensuously under her spell."[104] A little later, Graves had an experience of synthetic psilocybin with Wasson, which disappointed everyone involved. Graves wrote that it had been "all wrong, a common vulgar *drug*, no magic, and followed by a nasty hang-over."[105] In the late 1960s he dismissed marijuana in print as being a low-class type of drug.

Graves began his literary career with a book on World War I. So, interestingly, did the German writer Ernst Jünger—although where Graves denounced warfare, Jünger characteristically celebrated it. Jünger's father was a chemist who pursued a successful career in the pharmaceutical industry, and Jünger himself studied biology in the 1920s after a stint in the army, which provided the material for *Storm of Steel*, his infamous account of the joys of fighting in World War I. In the 1920s and 1930s, Jünger was a frequent contributor to right-wing journals, though his enthusiasm for fascism waned when Hitler came to power. Nevertheless, Jünger was a German officer during World War II, and lived for several years in occupied Paris, where he wrote a disturbing but curious journal, celebrating the joys of occupied Paris.

Jünger was sent a birthday piece of fan mail by Albert Hofmann in 1947, and through the resulting correspondence he came to know about Hofmann's discovery of LSD.[106] Jünger revealed that he had been exploring the world of psychoactive drugs since World War I, but had destroyed a manuscript that he had written on the subject. Still interested in drugs, Jünger first took LSD with Hofmann in February 1951. Hofmann has left us an interesting description of a psilocybin trip he took with Jünger and the orientalist Rudolf Gelpke in 1962 in a castle in Wilflingen, Germany.[107] Jünger, Hofmann wrote, "wore a long, broad, dark blue striped kaftan-like garment that he had brought from Egypt; Heribert Konzett was resplendent in a brightly embroidered mandarin gown; Rudolf Gelpke and I had put on housecoats. The everyday reality should be laid aside, along with everyday clothing."[108] While Hofmann struggled with the void, he had flashes of Jünger as a "great magician, lecturing uninterruptedly with a clear, loud voice, about Schopenhauer, Kant, Hegel, and speaking about the old Gäa, the beloved little mother."[109]

Besides his diary notes, Jünger's two key works on drugs are his novella *Besuch auf Godenholm* (*Visit to Godenholm*, 1952), in which he transmuted an LSD experience into a mystical one, and *Annäherungen: Drogen und Rausch* (*Approaches: Drugs and Intoxication*, 1970), a philosophical review of drug experiences dating back to World War I. At 450 pages, and with sections on most known psychoactive substances, *Approaches* is the most ambitious attempt to develop a philosophical approach to drugs and intoxication. The book's title suggests Jünger's themes. Language can offer only an approximation of the limit states produced by psychedelics, and these limit states are themselves only an approximation of something more fundamental—death or dying. It is unclear what approach to take to such states—autobiography, philosophy, cultural history, psychiatry, or fiction. Literature explores terrain similar to that in which the drug user finds himself or herself. Thus Jünger begins his book with Ariosto—and the allegorical world of Renaissance epic: "To read Ariosto is dangerous. In general, literary reading introduces criteria which can never be fulfilled in reality—the field of play becomes too broad."[110] The danger of drugs, according to Jünger, is that one will get lost in the interior spaces they open up, and be unable to find a way back to reality.

Jünger's motivation for taking drugs remains unclear. He was not a formal aesthete like Michaux, did not seek enlightenment like Huxley, Wasson, or Ginsberg, and had little or no interest in the therapeutic properties of drugs. Speaking of the psychedelics, he commented that they offered neither pleasure nor relief from pain, but simply allowed something "strange" to enter the psyche—an act of "conjuration" comparable to Faust's magical experiments, offering *ekstasis* without bliss. Jünger was continually fascinated by moments of struggle and danger, which he affirmed as desirable in themselves. As Klaus Theweleit has shown, for right-wing male German writers of the Nazi period, excitement is always at its greatest when a dangerous or endangered part of the psyche is projected externally and confronted as an enemy that threatens to flood or destroy the author.[111] Through correct measurement of dosage, a topic that Jünger saw as all important, a certain immersion in danger through drugs became possible that would allow the boundaries of the psyche to be breached and then reinstated.

Jünger was interested in "inner experience": in the 1920s he had published a book entitled *Der Kampf als inneres Erlebnis (War as Inner Experience),* and it is hard not to see his interest in drugs as an extension of what fascinated him about modern warfare. He speaks of Dionysus in martial terms, comparing the longevity of his "domination" of the West with the brevity of Alexander's march into Asia: "Alexander was forced to retreat from India, while Dionysus even today reigns as a nameless host."[112] For Jünger, Dionysus represents fundamental forces that are beyond history.

Marcus Bullock and others see Jünger's interest in drugs and intoxication as symptomatic of his extreme right-wing worldview.[113] Psychedelic substances offer an escape from the limits of everyday life and the social bonds that form everyday experience, into a world beyond words, which is the experience of an elite, the few who believe they have been privileged to go beyond the laws of everyday life. Although Jünger's interest in drugs and his right-wing views are undoubtedly connected, I am skeptical of the left-wing critique of drug use employed by Bullock and similar critics, in which any deviation from revolutionary sobriety, whether drugs, esotericism, even eroticism, is deemed suspect, and the pleasures of altered consciousness are to be deferred until society is transformed.[114] Intoxication is immanent in all social acts and practices. The question is: what does one do with this knowledge?

One possibility is Jünger's search for states of intoxication that will go beyond the social. Although this could become part of a right-wing ideology, working-class intoxication, as Baudelaire (and later, the Czech satirist Jaroslav Hasek) observed, and the "spiritual" practices of traditional cultures aim at precisely this form of escape. The inverse of this practice would be Benjamin's attempt to redefine the concept of *Rausch* as a specifically social phenomenon, or Mikhail Bakhtin's celebration of the intoxicated marketplaces of Rabelais's France. But these remain theories; history shows us that the left, as much as the right, has feared the intoxicated masses, and has sought to control and obstruct them whenever possible.

Once again, we come up against the question of our relationship to the imaginary, to the transcendental in everyday life. Both Jünger's and Bullock's positions are based on the notion that the social is either real or unreal, that the imagination is either true or false. But what if the social itself is fractal?

What if rather than being the fundamental building block of reality, the solid "bricks" of the social too are part of the imaginal realms. There are in fact myriad forms of the social, all partial, all with "asocial" spaces connected to them. Benjamin attempted to envision this form of the social with his notion of profane illumination, but was blocked by his commitment to a dialectical thinking that makes the actual synthesis of transcendental and social experience impossible—or at any rate, deferred until a future moment of total revolution.

Aristocrats, bankers, German right-wing ex-military men, not to mention the CIA and the Nazis: From the 1930s to the 1960s, it is a little acknowledged fact that one of the principal sources of interest in psychedelics, aside from the interest of researchers working on specific therapeutic uses, was people of conservative or right-wing orientation. According to Schultes, Blas Pablo Reko "boasted of racial purity and spoke confidently of the imminent takeover of the world by the Germans" when Schultes traveled with him in the late 1930s.[115] His cousin Dr. Victor Reko, another Austrian living in Mexico in the 1930s, wrote *Magische Gifte* (1936–1938), the first book to catalog the full extent of New World psychedelic flora. The book celebrates the fact that Germany has overcome the ruinous effects of cocaine and morphine "thanks to the new regime," and warns of the unknown, dangerous drugs lurking in dirty bamboo huts that could at any time become the latest exotic craze in Paris.[116]

Psychedelic drugs evoked several themes that were dear to the hearts of intellectuals on the right. They were associated with the primitive, the irrational, and the mythological, and put the intrepid latter-day gentleman explorer back in touch with his "origins." Jünger cofounded the journal *Antaios* with the Romanian mythologist Mircea Eliade, and Huxley and Graves both wrote extensively about mythology. A certain nostalgia for the colonies also persists in the works of Burroughs, Jünger, and Wasson, and the historical power of the psychedelics, as Michael Taussig has shown, is very much connected to the dynamic of colonization that projects mythical or magical power onto the "Indian" at the very moment that native civilization is brought under the dominion of the colonizers.[117] Literature functioned as a part of "high culture," dignifying the experimentation of many of these figures, and allowing them to feel themselves separated from the vulgar intoxication of the masses. The "sacramental" aspect of many of the accounts of psychedelic use by this group

in the 1950s often devolves down to a fetishization of exotic or expensive lo-
cales, and the privilege of being invited into them: Wasson's New York City
apartment, Jünger's forester's cottage on the property of the castle of the
Stauffenbergs, and, later on, Timothy Leary's use of William Mellon Hitchcock's estate in Millbrook, New York, for his experiments. With the exception
of Huxley, psychedelics offered a key, for these intellectuals, to an emphatically
private imaginal realm.

The first postwar writers to use psychedelics were all over the age of forty at
the time of their first experiences. All were well connected with various levels
of society, through literary fame, or wealth, or family relationships. As such,
they were able to gain the attention of researchers and get access to drugs. All
to some degree enjoyed the sense of exclusivity that experimenting with these
drugs afforded them. There is enormous pathos in the tale of Wasson, who
believed he could write about his trip to Mexico for *LIFE* magazine, retaining
the prestige of the Indiana Jones–style gentleman explorer, without his discoveries quickly becoming a part of global popular culture. It is significant that
when research sources of the drugs began to die out in the late 1960s, owing to
new legal restrictions on their use, and a mass drug culture exploded worldwide, their interest dwindled. As Jünger says, "an audience that is not cut out
to hear" about them, had discovered them.[118]

In 1960, J. Edgar Hoover declared that, along with communists and eggheads,
the Beats were one of the three most dangerous groups in America. From the
point of view of Cold War culture, this was probably true. The Beats were the
first writers, aside from Artaud, who actually left the cities of the first world
that they lived in to search for the experience of the primitive—and then
brought this experience back home with them in one form or another.
William Burroughs was a transitional figure in this story, combining elements
of the gentleman explorers who had traveled the world in earlier times with a
fascination for the underworld culture of the twentieth century. In his first,
pseudonymously published novel *Junkie* (1953), Burroughs described taking
peyote in Mexico. In addition to intense nausea and the feeling that everything looked like a peyote plant, Burroughs reported nightmares that occurred

at the end of the trip: "In another dream, I had a chlorophyll habit. Me and about five other chlorophyll addicts are waiting to score on the landing of a cheap Mexican hotel. We turn green and no one can kick a chlorophyll habit. One shot and you're hung for life. We are turning into plants."[119] At the end of the book, the narrator says that he has kicked junk and is leaving for Colombia in search of yage. He has heard about yage's telepathic powers, which the Russians are said to be using "to induce states of automatic obedience and literal thought control" in workers—"the deal is certain to backfire because telepathy is not in itself a one-way setup, or a setup of sender and receiver at all"—unlike literature. He hopes yage will be "the uncut kick that opens out instead of narrowing down like junk . . . the final fix."[120]

Burroughs did in fact make that trip to Colombia the very same year. At the botany department of the university in Bogota, he ran into Richard Evans Schultes. When Burroughs asked Schultes (whose work he apparently knew nothing of) about yage, Schultes produced a specimen, which Burroughs handled in such a way that Schultes could see that he was no botanist. He advised Burroughs that the remote Putumayo region of southwest Colombia was the best place for him to sample the drug itself. Burroughs made two trips to the Putumayo, described in *The Yage Letters* (1963), the second with Schultes, and had an unpleasant yage trip with a local brujo (shaman). Moving on to Peru, he sampled the drug again and produced one of his most beautiful passages, which later became part of the "Interzone" section of *Naked Lunch*:

> Yage is space time travel. The room seems to shake and vibrate with motion. The blood and substance of many races, Negro, Polynesian, Mountain Mongol, Desert Nomad, Polyglot Near East, Indian—new races as yet unconceived and unborn, combinations not yet realized pass through your body. Migrations, incredible journeys through deserts and jungles and mountains (stasis and death in closed mountain valleys where plants sprout out of the Rock and vast crustaceans hatch inside and break the shell of the body), across the Pacific in an outrigger canoe to Easter Island. The Composite City where all human potentials are spread out in a vast silent market.[121]

This is not just another colonialist, exotic fantasy. Burroughs is talking about the breaking down of the symbolically ordered, overcoded Western imagination into a corporeal hyperspace in which many imaginal spaces coexist, like different operating systems on a single computer. Every imaginal space, every way of moving in, through, and out of the world, which is to say, every "human potential," is available. For Burroughs, these spaces would be connected by the Cut-Up, suggested to him by Brion Gysin in 1960, in the form of a montage, in which separate imaginal spaces (different texts for example) are brought into resonance with each other.

Peyote was part of the Beats' repertoire of drugs: Allen Ginsberg wrote the second part of "Howl" (1956) while high on the drug in San Francisco.[122] In 1960, he followed in Burroughs' footsteps by going to Peru, where he took yage in a variety of settings, including one where "the whole fucking Cosmos broke loose around me, I think the strongest and worst I've ever had it nearly."[123] Ginsberg's yage experiences were often difficult, and resulted in a terrifying confrontation with his own mortality, described in two poems, "Magic Psalm" and "The Reply." He obtained an official license from the Peruvian government to bring a gallon of yage back to New York, which he shared with Kerouac and his lover, the poet Peter Orlovsky.

Ginsberg's first experience with LSD took place in 1959 at the invitation of the anthropologist Gregory Bateson at the Mental Research Institute at Stanford University. Although Ginsberg wrote a poem about the experience, "Lysergic Acid," he noted that the attempt to write a poem while on LSD had itself had major effects on the LSD experience (probably producing the kind of feedback loops that Michaux had experienced) and distracted him from the experience that he was having. Ginsberg's interest in drugs was evolving from an interest in enhancing his own creativity through allowing him access to the realm of Blakean visions, which he had in the early 1950s, to a broader position, where he saw the drugs as political agents capable of altering mass consciousness. As Martin Lee and Bruce Shlain have shown, except for the crucial factor of choice, this fantasy was not so different from the CIA's.

Because of his advocacy of marijuana, Ginsberg was contacted by the Group for the Advancement of Psychiatry and asked to speak at its 1960 convention. He read from various works, including "Laughing Gas," and "Mescaline," "Lysergic Acid," and met Humphry Osmond, the researcher who had given mescaline to Huxley. Osmond suggested that Ginsberg get in touch with a clinical psychologist working at Harvard called Timothy Leary.[124]

Leary already had a significant track record as a clinical psychologist when he first took mushrooms in Cuernavaca, Mexico, in the summer of 1960. As a result of the experience, he ordered a batch of psilocybin from Sandoz and started a research program at Harvard. Aldous Huxley was a visiting professor at MIT at the time, and became an advisor to Leary.

Leary met Ginsberg in New York in 1960 and invited him to visit the Harvard research program. Ginsberg found Leary to be naive about the chances of psychedelic drugs being integrated into the research curriculum, and, like Huxley, advised him to give the drug to artists and poets, the "opinion formers" of society, who could express and articulate the experience of taking psychedelics. This idea may also have been somewhat naive, since the various institutional bodies that needed to be persuaded of the value of these substances did not regard writers particularly favorably. On his first mushroom trip, Ginsberg was seized with a messianic frenzy and had to be dissuaded from running naked into the streets of Boston "to tell the people about peace and love."[125] He had decided to "take on the responsibility of being the creative God and seize power over the universe."[126] The intoxicated bard, whether through Blakean visions or psilocybin, is the incarnation of the imagination, not as an other, symbolic dimension, but as the creator of all possible worlds.

Ginsberg began an increasingly energetic exploration of whatever drugs he could lay his hands on. Poems poured forth and notebooks were filled, but Ginsberg was disappointed with the results. *Kaddish and Other Poems* (1961) contains a number of psychedelic poems, along with the title poem, a long elegy to his mother. A note is added at the beginning of the book: "Magic Psalm, The Reply, & The End *record visions experienced after drinking Ayahuasca, an Amazon spiritual potion. The message is: Widen the area of consciousness.*" It is as if Ginsberg himself could not decide what the value of his psychedelic experiments was, and had to come up with a (banal) slogan to cover himself.

Ginsberg also opened his celebrity-filled address book to Leary, who continued with his program of experiments, both formal and informal. Among those who took psychedelics with Leary were Kerouac, who said "walking on water wasn't done in a day"; Neal Cassady; Dizzy Gillespie; Thelonius Monk; Franz Kline; Willem de Kooning; Robert Lowell; Arthur Koestler; Charles Olson; and Paul Bowles.[127]

Not everyone was impressed with Leary's project. Burroughs, who had taken mushrooms and DMT through the auspices of Leary,[128] while he was living in Tangier, was invited to speak at an American Psychological Association conference on his knowledge of psychedelic drugs. He also visited Leary's research project in Cambridge, but was dismayed at the lack of any real research there, and left quickly. In essence, Burroughs did not like psychedelics. At the beginning of *Nova Express* (1964), he made his position clear: "*Listen: Their Garden of Delights is a terminal sewer—I have been at some pains to map this area of terminal sewage in the so-called pornographic section of Naked Lunch and Soft Machine—Their Immortality Cosmic Consciousness and Love is second-run grade B-shit. Their drugs are poison designed to beam in Orgasm Death and Nova Ovens. Stay out of the Garden of Delights ... learn to make it without any chemical corn.*"[129]

With the austerity (if not the discipline) of a Zen monk, Burroughs was in retreat from his celebration of "infinite human potential" and its attending pantheons of deities and seekers. As an alternative to the multiplicity of imaginal realms he now proposed: silence.

Meanwhile, Leary drew on literature for a variety of purposes in his LSD work: first of all, to legitimize it through the patronage of what Huxley called the opinion formers of society; second, to provide a supportive imaginal framework for the experiences that people were having. Two of Leary's tripping manuals from the early 1960s were rewrites of Asian religious texts: the *Tao Te Ching* and the *Tibetan Book of the Dead,* modernized for the 1960s.[130] One of the organizations that Leary set up to continue his work after being thrown out of Harvard was called The Castalia Foundation, after a fictional spiritual research group in Herman Hesse's *Journey to the East.*

Aside from a few words in *Steppenwolf,* Leary's favorite writer, Hermann Hesse, did not actually talk about drugs. But as the psychedelic experience itself took center stage as a cultural form, literary testimony as to the value of the experience was increasingly sidelined. While Leary and others staked ever broader claims to transforming "reality itself" through the use of drugs, younger users turned to those writers who had already created mystical, fantastic, or imaginary worlds as blueprints for mental voyaging. Fantasy and science fiction, which staked out explicitly imaginal spaces, became the new points of reference: Lewis Carroll's *Alice* books, C. S. Lewis' *Narnia Chronicles,* Robert Heinlein's *Stranger in a Strange Land* (1961), Kurt Vonnegut's oeuvre, and, a little later, Frank Herbert's *Dune* books. The medieval scholar J. R. R. Tolkien was horrified to find that his fantasy trilogy *The Lord of the*

Rings (1954–55) was taken up by the hippies. Tolkien belonged to the World War II generation who were fascinated by mythology as a way of fleeing from the vulgarity of twentieth-century industrial mass culture. Even when, like Jünger, Graves, or Huxley, they experimented with psychedelics, this generation did not expect to see their utopian fantasies, or their private dreams of escape into the recesses of the mythical past, acted out on a mass scale. The last chapters of Leary's *High Priest* (1968), with their montage of *Gilgamesh*, Milton, *The Wizard of Oz*, the *Bhagavad Gita*, St. Augustine, the *I Ching*, and "non-fictional" accounts of various trips conducted by Leary and his friends, blur lines between fiction and nonfiction, high and low culture, the sacred and the profane in a way that was guaranteed to offend the sensibilities of the older generation, for whom, as I have shown, boundaries remained important.

Leary repeatedly manipulated the imaginal space constructed around psychedelics. While he was a clinical psychologist at Harvard, LSD was an amazing therapeutic tool; for artists, it enhanced creativity; in his interview with *Playboy* in 1965, it was the ultimate sex drug; for divinity students, it became the gateway to mystical experience; for radical students, it was revolution. On the one hand, this profusion of perspectives reflects the difficulty (or flexibility) in constructing a cultural context for the psychedelic experience and the accompanying tantric insight that all contexts are "constructed" anyway. On the other hand, it suggests again the danger of what Baudelaire called theomania: the belief that "realities" can be reimagined and reconstructed at will through drugs, without such acts of "creation" entailing any responsibilities. The idea that reality is nothing but a set of recordings or imprints waiting to be tweaked lends itself to instant self-aggrandizement, particularly when authors such as Leary, and later Carlos Castaneda, appeared to revise their stories about drugs according to the prevailing mood of the marketplace. The ego is a most potent configurer of imaginal spaces and, if not confronted directly, will turn even the most potent psychedelic experience into a self-serving and deceiving charade.

As McLuhan had prophesied, the literary culture that surrounded psychedelics in the 1950s evolved into various nonliterary forms in the 1960s. Psychedelics were associated with the return to the primacy of the oral tradition in poetry, to the figure of the intoxicated bard, Ginsberg, in Indian gear, chanting om at The First Human Be In, but also to the silent affirmation of gnosis:

direct knowledge of the divine that is beyond language. Words became music: Carroll's Alice was transformed into Jefferson Airplane's "White Rabbit." As Leary said in the introduction to *High Priest:* "the work of the psychedelic scholar-politicians (described in this history) is over, with love and confidence we turn our work and our planet over to the young and their prophets: The Beatles, The Byrds."[131] Or words became images, as in the hieroglyphic forms of the San Francisco–based underground comic book *Zap Comix* and Rick Griffin's psychedelic posters for the hippie rock and roll mecca, the Fillmore.

Ken Kesey's story is emblematic of this evolution from literature to other modes of being and expression. Kesey had answered an ad for volunteers to participate in a psychotomimetic drug research program at the Menlo Park Veterans Hospital, where he was paid twenty dollars a session to try psilocybin, LSD, mescaline, and a synthetic belladonna derivative called Ditran that was apparently rather unpleasant. Kesey was so interested in this work that he became a psychiatric aide at the same hospital, and while working on the night shift, he had full access to the medicine cabinet where the drugs were stored. Kesey worked on his first novel, *One Flew over the Cuckoo's Nest* (1962) at the hospital, developing the story of a young man called Randle P. McMurphy who enters a mental institution to avoid a prison sentence, but whose non-conformist tendencies are finally destroyed under a barrage of medication, electroshock, and finally lobotomy.

Although Kesey followed this novel up with a second one, his energies gradually were diverted toward full-scale exploration of the psychedelic world on his ranch in La Honda, California. Out of this experience evolved the Merry Pranksters' multimedia spectacle and the West Coast Acid Tests, gatherings fueled by LSD and rock music that provided the blueprint for the rave scene. Kesey did not write about this experience, and, aside from some film footage that has only recently come to light, the only major source of information about this period of Kesey's life is *The Electric Kool-Aid Acid Test* (1968), by the founder of "New Journalism," Tom Wolfe. Although the book was nominally a nonfictional record of the Pranksters, Wolfe consciously mythologized the tale, partially in the name of the fusion of real and imaginal spaces that Kesey was aiming at with the Pranksters, and partly in the name of the "New Journalism," an inventory of literary effects designed to create the effect of sensory bombardment that characterizes modern life.

This mythologization came full circle in Hunter S. Thompson's *Fear and*

Loathing in Las Vegas (1971), which takes the Horatio Alger vision of the American Dream as the mythological basis for a psychedelic rampage through Las Vegas. Thompson's point was a fundamental one, but had not been made in the context of drugs before. The neon-saturated night of Las Vegas is just as much a hallucination, a myth, a product of the imagination, as any vision triggered by LSD, and drug users themselves swiftly became mythical figures in the American imagination, as intensely fabricated an imaginal realm as any other.

> This madness goes on and on, but nobody seems to notice. The gambling action runs twenty-four hours a day on the main floor, and the circus never ends. Meanwhile, on all the balconies, the customers are being hustled by every conceivable kind of bizarre shuck. All kinds of funhouse-type booths. Shoot the pasties off the nipples of a ten-foot bull-dyke and win a cotton-candy goat. Stand in front of this fantastic machine, my friend, and for just 99¢ your likeness will appear, two hundred feet tall, on a screen above downtown Las Vegas. Ninety-nine cents more for a voice message . . .
>
> We will close the drapes tonight. A thing like that could send a drug person careening around the room like a ping-pong ball. Hallucinations are bad enough. But after a while you learn to cope with things like seeing your dead grandmother crawling up your leg with a knife in her teeth. Most acid fanciers can handle this sort of thing.
>
> But nobody can handle that other trip—the possibility that any freak with $1.98 can walk into the Circus-Circus and suddenly appear in the sky over downtown Las Vegas twelve times the size of God, howling anything that comes into his head. No, this is not a good town for psychedelic drugs. Reality itself is too twisted.[132]

In 1968, a student in the anthropology department at the University of California at Los Angeles published a book based on his doctoral work studying with a Yaqui sorceror in the Southwest. The book, *The Teachings of Don Juan: A Yaqui Way of Knowledge,* quickly became a bestseller and its author, Carlos Castaneda, an elusive but much talked about celebrity. In this book and the next, *A Separate Reality* (1971), Don Juan initiates the young anthropologist into the world of power plants—peyote, datura, and mushrooms—and the different ways they affect perception.

Shamanism had slowly developed a presence in post–World War II culture following the publication of Mircea Eliade's broad survey *Shamanism: Archaic Techniques of Ecstasy* (1951). Although Eliade himself considered psychedelic shamanism a degenerated, impure form of shamanism,[133] the rediscovery of psilocybe mushroom–based shamanism in Oaxaca by Schultes and Wasson, and the ever expanding knowledge of New World psychedelic flora, combined with increasing actual use of New World psychedelic substances, created the context for Castaneda's popularity.

Castaneda's work was taken quite seriously by readers, the academics who gave Castaneda a Ph.D., and reviewers whose pieces appeared in organs such as the *New York Times.* Many reviewers, especially those who were anthropologists and experts on Yaqui culture, did not believe that Castaneda was "authentically" describing Yaqui culture. But they praised the literary qualities of the books and Castaneda's gift in describing the "personal experience" of taking various mind-altering drugs and studying with an old Indian man. Edmund Leach observed that "Castaneda's book is certainly not a complete spoof . . . but if it had been spoof, it might not have been very different."[134] Although writers like Joyce Carol Oates went to some length to question the literal truth of Castaneda's work, it is clear that most readers were quite comfortable with the ambiguous territory, somewhere between truth and fiction, that these books described.[135] It had been the function of the exotic and the other to act as a mouthpiece for truths since at least the time of Diderot, and, for many people, these books functioned as modern myths, which could be used to provide an imaginal grid through which to negotiate psychedelic and "real" space. Since the drugs themselves tended to open the mind to mythical or archetypal formulations, it was easy to accept a work that operated on a similar set of principles.

Indigenous shamanic practitioners of course "use" the psychedelic properties of the plants too. Shamanic cultures tend not to be literary or text oriented, but the encounter between indigenous shamanic practice and the Western culture of the book has clearly left its mark on native practitioners. The Mazatec shaman Maria Sabina, whose autobiography was transcribed from oral sources in the 1970s, claimed that her healing powers came to her when, under the influence of the "saint children" one night, she had a vision of the Principal Ones, ancestral powers, who produced a book, "an open book that went on growing until it was the size of a person . . . the Sacred Book of Language."[136] Although she cannot read, the book itself "gave me wisdom, the perfect word: the Language of God. Language makes the dying return to life. The sick recover their health when they hear the words taught by the saint children. There is no mortal who can teach this Language."[137]

Michael Taussig, an Australian anthropologist who spent several years in the Putumayo living with an Indian shaman, Santiago Mutumbajoy, makes a similar observation regarding Putumayo shamanism. He connects the healing power of the shaman to his or her ability to provoke a kind of montage effect, which disrupts the narrative of everyday colonial life, allowing reconfigurations and reintegrations of consciousness to take place.[138] While Jonathan Ott observes that in Aztec shamanism, images of speech scrolls contain the synaesthetic vocal scripts (or songs) that the shaman, by singing, uses to produce certain visual imagery, and certain kinds of healing work, in a healing session, Taussig suggests that the function of the shaman's vocalizations is actually to disrupt rather than to construct a particular kind of consciousness or thought pattern. Transcripts of Maria Sabina's singing show that while she is under the influence of The Little One Who Springs Forth, even the structure of authorship is altered. Sabina says that "language belongs to the saint children. They speak and I have the power to translate."[139]

> I am a woman who shouts, says
> I am a woman who whistles, says
> I am a woman who thunders, says
> I am a woman who plays music, says
> I am a spirit woman, says.[140]

In *Food of the Gods* (1992), the ethnobotanist and philosopher of the psychedelic state Terence McKenna speculates that the acquisition of consciousness and language, which separates man from beast, occurred when African hunter-gatherers began to eat the mushrooms that grew in the dung of the cattle they followed. Consciousness itself, according to McKenna, is a psychedelic state—which is to say an imaginal state that can be modulated by chemicals.

In *True Hallucinations* (1993), his account of a 1970s trip to the Putumayo in search of a Witoto preparation called oo-koo-hé that contained DMT, McKenna speaks of the strange language-engendering beings he has encountered during DMT experiences:

> During my own experiences smoking synthesized DMT in Berkeley, I had had the impression of bursting into a space inhabited by merry elfin, self-transforming, machine creatures. Dozens of these friendly fractal entities, looking like self-dribbling Fabergé eggs on the rebound, had surrounded me and tried to teach me the lost language of true poetry. They seemed to be babbling in a visible and five-dimensional form of Ecstatic Nostratic, to judge from the emotional impact of this gnomish prattle. Mirror-surfaced tumbling rivers of melted meaning flowed gurgling around me. . . . Under the influence of DMT, language was transmuted from a thing heard to a thing seen.[141]

He compares this effect to that of the hookah-smoking caterpillar in *Alice in Wonderland* floating questions made out of smoke at Alice. When McKenna says, later in the book, that "reality is made of language," he means something very different from what social constructionists mean.[142] Most such critics believe that nothing can be perceived or expressed outside of mimetic language and representation, but for McKenna (and it must be said, for many mystics) conventional reality, fabricated by mimetic language, obscures a dynamic world that is also a product of language, in its energetic, magical, or poetic guise. This is a restatement of shamanic doctrine: the shaman is taught a secret language by the spirits, which allows him or her some control over what happens in a healing session. Language, in this sense, gives imaginal realms their shape: it is a poetic shaping of the world that occurs at every moment.

McKenna's brother and co-author, Dennis McKenna, hypothesizes the existence of a translinguistic matter, somewhat similar to that experienced in synaesthesia, in which "it is a language, but not made of words—a language which becomes and which is the things it describes."[143] This matter takes the form of a mirrory liquid, which some Amazonian users of ayahuasca claim to see and use for divination and other magical practices.

Curiously, McKenna's view of the psychedic imagination is more gnostic than Huxley's. Rather than seeing an open totality of imaginal realms, he makes an almost Platonic argument for the *otherness* of the other realms that psychedelics give access to. Psychedelics, at their most potent, offers not a transfigured version of this realm, such as that offered by hashish (or for that matter lower doses of LSD), but a radically dualist vision of other worlds that exist separately from, but are accessible from, this one.

> The other plays with us and approaches us through the imagination and then a critical juncture is reached. To go beyond this juncture requires abandonment of old and ingrained habits of thinking and seeing. At that moment the world turns lazily inside out and what was hidden is revealed: a magical modality, a different mental landscape than one has ever known, and the landscape becomes real. This is the realm of the cosmic giggle. UFOs, elves, and the teeming pantheons of all religions are the denizens of this previously invisible landscape.[144]

The shamanic epistemology proposed by McKenna is nevertheless different from native shamanic traditions, which did not rely on a substratum of biochemistry to buttress their arguments. McKenna, who has an obvious fondness for literature and the pleasures of story-telling, is always aware of the ironies of presenting the claims that he makes for the psychedelics in contemporary society. Other authors such as Ott, who have made similar claims, are too eager to resolve the ambiguities of the psychedelic experience through recourse to rhetoric, whether in the form of psychedelic evangelism or of semantics. Indeed, Ott, who has even written a dictionary of terms related to the psychedelics, appears to believe that many of the questions surrounding the use or meaning of the psychedelic experience can be solved through the "correct" use of Greek neologisms such as "entheogen" and the redefinition of "recreational" drug use as "ludibund." Ott's admirable botanical, biochemical, and ethnographic erudition does, however, suggest a curious hybrid future in which experiences of the ineffable will be linked with increasing precision to specific plants and molecules.

The Lewis and Clark of the psychopharmacological frontier are Alexander Shulgin and Ann Shulgin, who have documented their work in *PIHKAL: A Chemical Love Story* (1991) and *TIHKAL* (1997). Alexander Shulgin is a chemist who has conducted an independent exploration of the two major classes of known psychedelic substance, the tryptamines and the phenethylamines (hence the first book's title, "Phenethylamines I Have Known and

Loved"), over a period of thirty years. Best known for his part in the rediscovery of MDMA (Ecstasy), Shulgin has discovered dozens of novel psychotropic substances, and in *PIHKAL* and *TIHKAL,* he gives detailed descriptions, recipes, and dosages, and a review of the effects of nearly four hundred such substances. The first half of each of these books, however, is devoted to a fictional retelling of the author's lives, meeting, and subsequent adventures. At the beginning of *TIHKAL,* the authors describe a visit from the Drug Enforcement Agency (DEA), apparently as a result of the publication of *PIHKAL,* which resulted in Shulgin's license to do chemical analysis of restricted substances being taken away.

> Fosca [the DEA agent] looked up at me and replied, in absolute seriousness, "Yes. You're famous," he said, "And your fame has saved you."
>
> "What?" I was dumbfounded. What did he mean, our fame had saved us? From what?
>
> "Did you ever give scheduled drugs to the people in your research group?" asked Fosca, changing the subject.
>
> My stomach twisted. What an idiotic question, I thought.
>
> "No, Mr. Fosca," I said, "Please keep in mind that the book is fiction. The story part of it, I mean. Fiction."
>
> "Yes, well," said Fosca, "A lot of people don't think it's fiction."[145]

Literature serves as a strange kind of refuge, protected by the First Amendment (Alexander Shulgin has also written a large book on U.S. drug laws), for the experiments and information contained within these books. Each chemical that Shulgin develops produces a diaspora of mental states, according to dosage, set, and setting. In the Shulgins' books, these chemicals evoke states that it was previously the domain of literature to describe. Regarding DMT, the authors say,

> (with 20mg, intramuscularly) "I began to see patterns on the wall that were continuously moving. They were transparent, and were not colored. After a short period these patterns became the heads of animals, a fox, a snake, a dragon . . ."
>
> (with 50 mg intramuscularly) "I feel strange, everything is blurry. I want my mother. I am afraid of fainting, I can't breathe."

(with 6omg, intramuscularly) "I don't like this feeling—I am not myself, I saw such strange dreams a while ago. Strange creatures, dwarfs or something; they were black and moved about. Now I feel as if I am not alive. My left hand is numb. As if my heart would not beat, as if I had no body, no nothing. All I feel are my left hand and stomach. I don't like to be without thoughts." . . .

(with 100 mg, smoked) "As I exhaled I became terribly afraid, my heart very rapid and strong, palms sweating. A terrible sense of dread and doom filled me—I knew what was happening, I knew I couldn't stop it, but it was so devastating; I was being destroyed—all that was familiar, all reference points, all identity—all viciously shattered in a few seconds. I couldn't even mourn the loss—there was no one left to do the mourning. Up, up, out, out, eyes closed, I am at the speed of light, expanding, expanding, expanding, faster and faster until I have become so large that I no longer exist—my speed is so great that everything has come to a stop—here I gaze upon the entire universe."[146]

But the Shulgins' work does not perform the same function that literature does. Where literature produces imaginal structures through the interaction of mind and written page that are more or less complete in themselves, the description of dwarves and emotional states in *PIHKAL* and *TIHKAL* are hazily drawn sketches in a catalog that offers merely a textual introduction to the production of the "real" chemical and the experience of the altered mental states that it triggers.[147]

The psychedelic experience is not necessarily an aesthetic experience, let alone a literary one. Nor does the recently coined term "entheogen" cover the subject, since for many people, both now and in traditional cultures, psychedelic substances do not contain "the god within." Is there then a single unifying explanation for the psychedelics that takes into account the many ways that these drugs have been interpreted by different cultures? At first, I wanted to claim that all descriptions of psychedelic experience could be defined in terms of what Bataille calls cosmic excess, because they involve boundary breaking, cascades of visual imagery, sensory overload, and so on. But the concept of excess is as culturally specific as any notion used by the Huichol, the theosophists, Jünger, Hunter S. Thompson, or neurochemists today. Michaux and those who held firm to an aesthetic interpretation of the psychedelic experience used terms like "infinite" or "excess" because they provided a way of describing in philosophical or literary terms what would otherwise have been described through religious or scientific language. I do not mean to say that they are wrong and that those like Leary, Huxley, or Castaneda who chose a variety of religious paradigms to describe their experiences were right—their own reconfigurations of traditional religious practices were themselves highly revisionist. But the concepts of excess, "turbulent infinity," and "autonomous power," and Huxley's adaptation of Bergson's model of consciousness are no more definitive as explanations of the effects of psychedelics than any other models. And this kind of literary experimentation with psychedelics, as embodied in the work of Witkiewicz or Michaux, work, basically ended in the 1960s, replaced by an ethnographic model grounded in shamanic tradition, a scientific model blending neurochemistry and cognitive psychology, and various strange hybrids of the two. Where writing persists, it is either as "content" for the new, more direct ways of addressing the nervous system, or as a slightly nostalgic rhetorical trope, lending gravitas to a field of endeavor still viewed as somewhat sleazy by the powers that be.

The thread I have followed in this chapter concerns the imagination and the way different cultures have viewed it. If we can accept that everything is connected to an imaginal space of some sort, then how are the psychedelics any different from say, water, dancing, or the triangle? What makes psychedelic literature in particular of any interest? Psychedelics are powerful, direct activators and conduits of altered states. Psychedelics point out in a very direct and dramatic way that consciousness is mutable—not just in the slow, seemingly continuous fashion of everyday life—and that radical, rapid shifts in consciousness are possible.

The area of human experience that the psychedelics are most closely associated with—that of imaginative realms quite different from those of everyday life—is not one that can be wished away. Nor has it been wished away at any point in human history. It may have been demonized, pathologized, accessed by strange symbolic, artisanal methods involving books, paintings, or music, or woven so deeply into the fabric of everyday life that it becomes almost invisible. But it has always been there.

I have contrasted the symbolic experience of literature with the direct experience of altered states through psychedelics. But because we live (or have lived) in a culture of the symbol, the psychedelic experience has also been viewed through the lens of the symbolic. In fact, psychedelics offer a perspective on the process of symbol formation, revealing the way that the creative flux of the imagination is frozen into particular forms, concepts, words. Literature, even in the hands of those masters of chance operations the Surrealists, or a poet with a head full of acid and a notepad (or a husband and wife with a notepad), is necessarily a method of capturing the flux of the mind.

The experiences that psychedelics and literature provide are part of a continuum—and their historical development and fate are connected in curious ways. European literature evolved in the Renaissance out of a need to find ways to access the imaginal realms through the symbolic means of word and book, at a time when other options were limited or prohibited. The intensity with which the Romantics threw themselves into a struggle for direct experiences of the Real through the medium of the word, extended this trajectory, born out of struggles with and in Christian ideology, into the new, atheistic territory of art and literature. This was the moment that psychoactive drugs were discovered by Western writers and scientists—a discovery in which drugs appeared as the material embodiment of all the cravings and fantasies of previous generations. Scientific materialism grew to dominate the cultural landscape of Europe and North America in the nineteenth century, but even a stern turn-of-the-century pharmacologist like Louis Lewin turned to Isaiah and Goethe for analogies for the state of the human mind under the influence of these drugs.

There is a delicious pathos in the way that the early European and American writers and researchers grappled with the question of how to represent their experiences with peyote, mescaline, and later LSD via the written word. Psychedelics amplified the crisis that modernism found itself in with regard to the question of literary form. So long as psychedelics were experienced within an atheistic worldview, they produced convoluted, fragmentary, chaotic snakes of text. When Huxley took mescaline in a sacred context, this apparent disorder subsided into a kind of lucid clarity, as it did for Michaux when he discovered the hymn. But later nontheistic explorations of the psychedelic realms, such as Burroughs' and Hunter Thompson's, returned to textual turbulence, suggesting that it too cannot be wished away so easily.

I do not mean to sound dismissive of literature. In our hunger to flee what

McLuhan called the Gutenberg galaxy of print and our fascination with the novelty of chemical modulation of consciousness, we run a risk of missing the fact that all mental states are extraordinary, not just the novel ones. The important thing to understand here is creativity, its source and its power. Literature and the psychedelic experience are both fundamentally acts of poiesis—poiesis not as representation but as creation itself. As the authors of the *Vedas* wrote, several thousand years ago, blurring the line between deity, substance, and poet, "This restless Soma—you try to grab him but he breaks away and overpowers everything. He is a sage and a seer inspired by poetry."[148]

For at least a hundred years, science fiction writers have been filling their futuristic realms with potent psychoactive substances like Huxley's soma and Witkiewicz's Davamesque B2, which exert over future societies the wondrous and horrific powers that have in fact been exercised by states and their rulers in the twentieth century. Post-Romantic drug literature was predicated on a crisis of the writing, thinking subject, which, while it has not been solved, is being more and more skillfully avoided in ways not entirely dissimilar from those predicted by the dystopian writers. Although the ever increasing emphasis on techno-scientific innovation has made drugs themselves of increasing importance in our culture, many of the ways in which drugs are used now seem designed to bypass the problem of subjectivity altogether.

Antidepressants, sleeping pills, anxiolytic drugs, and many others are dispensed by psychiatrists or other physicians without any accompanying psychotherapy. Competence is preferred to insight or expressiveness as a measure of health. This is even true with the psychedelics. Although originally used as an adjunct to psychotherapy, Ecstasy, the drug of choice of the 1990s, is now primarily used as a euphoriant, offering pleasure and a mildly altered state, without the ego-shaking qualities of the major psychedelic drugs. The new-found popularity of the anesthetic ketamine, which offers an extremely depersonalized psychedelic experience, continues this trend. Nevertheless, neo-generic fictional works such as Irvine Welsh's *Ecstasy* (1996) and Douglas Rushkoff's *Ecstasy Club* (1997) have emerged to describe the evolving subcultures that have sprung up around these substances. For the foreseeable future, all novel recreational drugs appear likely to generate books about them that can be marketed as windows onto the world of contemporary youth or underworld culture—mostly using the now well tested approaches of De Quincey, Cocteau, and Burroughs—who now find themselves in the unlikely position of being originators of literary genres. Lester Bangs's ironic suggestion that in the future identity will be determined by the type of drug used may turn out to have some truth to it. No doubt, at this very moment, somewhere in a bedroom, a young man or woman is writing a novel entitled *The K Hole*.

The situation with antidepressants is more complicated. Books like Elizabeth Wurtzel's *Prozac Nation* (1995) make the claim that drugs allow people to function normally—and being able to write a book about your experiences is presumably one of the correlates of normality, though not one that Wurtzel dwells on. In *Prozac Nation*, depression is the chemically altered state in question. Prozac itself, which is believed to correct a chemical imbalance, is almost transparent in the book. This is also the case with William Styron's depression memoir, *Darkness Visible* (1990), even when it appears likely that the author's depression was either caused or exacerbated by use of the tranquilizer Halcion. The notion of chemically altered (or specific) states, which played an important role in the fascination that drugs held for writers from the Romantics onward, has now become generalized to all aspects of biology, so that any psychological state may now be compared to the pathological states induced by psychoactive substances, while psychoactive substances, rather than producing experimental or extraordinary states of consciousness, can now produce *normative* states, and a normative literature.

It is likely that the biochemical mapping of all aspects of our lives will continue. We have gone from a premodern period of seeing drugs as mythical, allegorical powers of nature that make their appearance in literature as symbols, to the modern period, in which drugs are "artificial" agents of the transformation of the psyche, secretly invested with the continuing power of our transcendental aspirations. We are entering a period in which many people view the self itself as a biochemical construct and literature testifies to its perturbations while drugs either exacerbate chemical imbalances or restore harmony. In the future, there may well be a genetic literature, in which the presence or absence of certain genes forms the basis of new literary genres. There is no end to this particular history. But as long as we consider ourselves, in the words of Maria Sabina, beings of water and tortilla, there will be psychoactive drugs in some form or other, to indicate the mutability of the mind, our vulnerability to and interdependence on nature at every stage of our development, our need for material manifestations and potentiators of transcendental knowledge, and there will probably be texts too, to mark out our desire to trace, in language, the fiery shapes the imaginal casts us in.

BIBLIOGRAPHY

Abel, Ernest L. 1980. *Marihuana: The First Twelve Thousand Years.* New York: Plenum.

Ackerknecht, Erwin. 1973. *Therapeutics from the Primitives to the Twentieth Century.* New York: Hafner.

Adamou, Robert, ed. 1960. "La Drogue." *Les Cahiers de la Tour Saint Jacques,* 1.

Ageyev, M. 1938. *Roman s kokainom.* Paris: Dom Knigi. Trans. by Michael Heim as *Novel with Cocaine.* New York: Harper & Row, 1984. A 1999 English-language edition with an introduction by Will Self was published in London by Penguin.

Album Mariani. 1894–1926. 14 vols. Paris: Librairie Henry Floy.

Aldiss, Brian. 1969. *Barefoot in the Head.* New York: Ace.

Allen, Stewart Lee. 1999. *The Devil's Cup: Coffee, the Driving Force in History.* New York: Soho.

Andford, Jeremy. 1973. *In Search of the Magic Mushroom.* New York: Clarkson.

Andrews, George, and David Solomon, ed. 1975. *The Coca Leaf and Cocaine Papers.*

Andrews, George, and Simon Vinkenoog, ed. 1967. *The Book of Grass.* New York: Grove.

Anslinger, Harry, and Will Oursler. 1961. *The Murderers: The Story of the Narcotics Gangs.* New York: Farrar, Straus & Cudahy.

Arber, Agnes. 1986. *Herbals: Their Origin and Evolution.* Cambridge: Cambridge University Press.

Artaud, Antonin. 1940. *Lettres à Genica Athanassiou.* Paris: Gallimard.

———1956. *Oeuvres Complètes.* 26 vols. Paris: Gallimard.

———1971. *Les Tarahumaras.* Paris: Gallimard.

———1976. *Selected Writings.* Ed. Susan Sontag. Trans. Helen Weaver. New York: Farrar, Straus & Giroux.

Ashley, Richard. 1975. *Cocaine: Its History, Uses, and Effects.* New York: St. Martin's.

Bachmann, Christian, and Anne Coppel. 1989. *La drogue dans le monde.* Paris: Albin Michel.

Bailey, George. 1968. *Sex, Pot, and Acid.* Canoga Park, Calif.: Viceroy.

Bakhtin, Mikhail. 1984 [1965]. *Rabelais and His World.* Trans. Helene Iswolsky. Bloomington: Indiana University Press.

Balakian, Anna. 1974. "Breton and Drugs." *Yale French Studies,* 50: 96–107.

Balzac, Honoré de. 1900. *Letters to Mme. Hanska.* Trans. K. P. Wormeley. Boston: Little, Brown.

———1992. *Traité des excitants modernes.* Pantin, France: Castor Astral.

Bangs, Lester. 1987. *Psychotic Reactions and Carburetor Dung.* Ed. Greil Marcus. New York: Knopf.

Bataille, Georges. 1988. *The Accursed Share.* Trans. Robert Hurley. New York: Zone.

Baudelaire, Charles. 1964. *Les paradis artificiels.* Paris: Gallimard.

———1975. *Oeuvres complètes.* 2 vols. Paris: Gallimard.

Beauvoir, Simone de. 1992. *The Prime of Life.* Trans. Peter Green. New York: Paragon.

Behr, Hans-Georg. 1982. *Von Hanf ist die Rede: Kultur und Politik einer Droge.* Basel: Sphinx.

Benjamin, Walter. 1972. *Über Haschisch.* Frankfurt: Suhrkamp. Trans. Scott Thompson as "Protocols to the Experiments on Hashish, Opium and Mescaline, 1927–1934" at <http://www.wbenjamin.org/translations.html.>

———1978. *Reflections.* Ed. Peter Demetz. Trans. Edmund Jephcott. New York: Schocken.

———1994. *The Correspondence of Walter Benjamin, 1910–1940.* Ed. Gershom Scholem and Theodor W. Adorno. Trans. Manfred R. Jacobson and Evelyn M. Jacobson. Chicago: University of Chicago Press.

———1999. *The Arcades Project.* Trans. Howard Eiland and Kevin McLaughlin. Cambridge: Harvard University Press.

Benn, Gottfried. 1986. *Sämtliche Werke.* Vol. 1. Stuttgart: Klett-Cotta.

———1987 [1949]. "Induced Life." Trans. Joel Agee, in *Gottfried Benn: Prose, Essays, Poems,* 144–153. New York: Continuum.

Berridge, Virginia. 1988. "The Origins of the English Drug Scene, 1890–1930." *Medical History,* 51–64.

——— 1990. "Special Issue: The Society for the Study of Addiction, 1884–1988." *British Journal of Addiction,* 85 (no. 8).

Berridge, Virginia, and Griffith Edwards. 1981. *Opium and the People: Opiate Use in Nineteenth-Century England.* New York: St. Martin's.

Besterman, Theodore. 1969. *Voltaire.* New York: Harcourt, Brace and World.

Bieker, Sibylle. 1992. *Die künstlichen Paradiese in der französischen Literatur des 19. Jahrhunderts.* Bonn: Romanistischer Verlag.

Blackwood, Algernon. 1909. *John Silence: Physician Extraordinary.* Boston: Luce.

Blair, William. 1842. "An Opium Eater in America." *The Knickerbocker,* July 1842.

Blood, Benjamin. 1874. *The Anaesthetic Revelation and the Gist of Philosophy*. Amsterdam, N.Y.: privately published.

————1920. *Pluriverse*. Boston: Marshall Jones.

Boissière, Jules. 1896. *Fumeurs d'opium*. Paris: E. Flammarion.

Bonnetain, Paul. 1886. *L'opium*. Paris: G. Charpentier.

Booth, Martin. 1996. *Opium: A History*. London: Simon and Schuster.

Boren, Lynda. 1983. "William James, Theodore Dreiser, and the 'anaesthetic revelation.'" *American Studies*, 24: 5–18.

Boswell, James. 1957. *Boswell's Life of Johnson*. Oxford: Oxford University Press.

Bowie, Malcolm. 1973. *Henri Michaux: A Study of His Literary Works*. Oxford: Clarendon Press.

Bowles, Paul. 1962. *A Hundred Camels in the Courtyard*. San Francisco: City Lights.

————1967. "Kif—Prologue and Compendium of Terms." Reprinted in George Andrews, ed., *The Book of Grass*, 108–114. New York: Grove.

————1993. *Conversations with Paul Bowles*. Ed. Gena Dagel Caponi. Jackson: University Press of Mississippi.

Bowles, Paul, ed. 1979. *Five Stories*. Santa Barbara: Black Sparrow.

Braden, William. 1967. *The Private Sea: LSD and the Search for God*. Chicago: Quadrangle.

Brandes, Georges. 1930. *Voltaire*. New York: Tudor.

Brandon, Ruth. 1999. *Surreal Lives*. New York: Grove.

Brau, Jean-Louis. 1968. *Histoire de la drogue*. Paris: Tchou.

Breton, André. 1972. *Manifestoes of Surrealism*. Trans. Richard Seaver and Helen R. Lane. Ann Arbor: University of Michigan Press.

Brierre de Boismont, Alexandre. 1845. *Des hallucinations, ou histoire raisonnée des apparitions, des visions, des songes, de l'extase, du magnétisme et du somnambulisme*. Paris: Baillère.

Briggs, J. R. 1887. "Muscale Buttons—Psychological Action—Personal Experiences." *Medical Register*, 1: 276–277.

Brillat-Savarin, Jean-Anthelme. 1986. *The Physiology of Taste: Or, Meditations on Transcendental Gastronomy*. Trans. M. F. K. Fisher. San Francisco: North Point.

Brouardel, Paul. 1906. "Mesures à rendre pour diminuer la morphinomanie." In Brouardel, *Opium, morphine, cocaïne, cours de médecine légale*. Paris: Baillère et Fils.

Brown, John. 1793 [1788]. *The Elements of Medicine*. 2 vols. Philadelphia: T. Dobson.

Brown, Tom. 1730. *Works of Mr. Thomas Brown*. 4 vols. London: Edward Midwinter.

Bullock, Marcus Paul. 1992. *The Violent Eye: Ernst Jünger's Visions and Revisions on the European Right*. Detroit: Wayne State University Press.

Burchill, Julie, and Tony Parsons. 1978. *The Boy Looked at Johnny*. London: Pluto.

Burke, Edmund. 1987 [1757]. *A Philosophical Enquiry into the Origin of our Ideas of the Sublime and Beautiful*. Oxford: Blackwell.

Burroughs, William. 1964. *Nova Express.* New York: Grove.

———1970. *The Job.* London: Jonathan Cape.

———1977 [1953]. *Junkie.* London: Penguin.

———1992 [1959]. *Naked Lunch.* New York: Grove.

———1993. *The Letters of William S. Burroughs, 1945–1959.* New York: Viking.

Burroughs, William, and Allen Ginsberg. 1975 [1963]. *The Yage Letters.* San Francisco: City Lights.

Burroughs, William, Jr. 1993 [1970]. *Speed/Kentucky Ham.* Woodstock, N.Y.: Overlook.

Burton, Richard, trans. 1900. *The Book of the Thousand Nights and a Night.* 16 vols. N.p.: The Burton Club.

Butel, Paul. 1995. *L'opium: histoire d'une fascination.* Paris: Perrin.

Cahagnet, Louis-Alphonse. 1850. *Sanctuaire du spiritualisme.* Paris: published by the author.

Callard, David. 1992. *The Case of Anna Kavan: A Biography.* London: P. Owen.

Cameron, Eleanor. 1956. *Stowaway to the Mushroom Planet.* New York: Scholastic.

Camporesi, Piero. 1989. *Bread of Dreams: Food and Fantasy in Early Modern Europe.* Trans. David Gentilcore. Chicago: University of Chicago Press.

Caponi, Gena Dagel. 1994. *Paul Bowles: Romantic Savage.* Carbondale: Southern Illinois University Press.

Carlyle, Thomas. 1992 [1825]. *Life of Friedrich Schiller.* Camden House: Columbia, S.C.

Caroline: Briefe aus der Frühromantik. 1913. Leipzig: Zufel.

Carroll, Lewis. 1971 [1865/1872]. *Alice's Adventures in Wonderland and Through the Looking-Glass.* New York: St. Martin's.

Castoldi, Alberto. 1994. *Il testo drogato: letteratura e droga tra Ottocento e Novecento.* Turin: Giulio Einaudi.

Chaber, M. E. 1967. *The Acid Nightmare.* New York: Holt, Rinehart, and Winston.

Chandler, Raymond. 1943. *The Lady in the Lake.* New York: Knopf.

Chardin, Sir John. 1927 [1720]. *Sir John Chardin's Travels in Persia.* Trans. unknown. London: Argonaut.

Charters, Ann. 1973. *Kerouac: A Biography.* San Francisco: Straight Arrow Books.

Chase, James Hadley. 1952 [1951]. *The Marijuana Mob.* New York: Eton Books. (Originally published as *Figure It Out for Yourself.* New York: Duell, Sloan, and Pearce.)

Chaucer, Geoffrey. 1900. *Complete Works of Geoffrey Chaucer.* Oxford: Oxford University Press.

Clark, Janet. 1961. *The Fantastic Lodge: The Autobiography of a Girl Drug Addict.* Ed. Helen MacGill Hughes. Boston: Houghton Mifflin.

Clarke, Marcus. 1976. "Cannabis Indica." In *Marcus Clarke,* ed. Michael Wilding. St. Lucia, Queensland: University of Queensland.

Clarke, William M. 1988. *The Secret Life of Wilkie Collins.* London: Allison & Busby.

Cocteau, Jean. *Opium.* 1990 [1930]. Trans. Margaret Crosland. London: Peter Owen.

Cohen, Harvey. 1972. *The Amphetamine Manifesto.* New York: Olympia.

Cohen-Solal, Annie. 1987. *Sartre: A Life.* Trans. Anna Cancogni. New York: Pantheon.

Coleridge, Samuel. 1956. *Collected Letters.* 4 vols. Oxford: Oxford University Press.

———1957. *Notebooks.* 4 vols. New York: Bollingen.

———1969. *Collected Works.* 14 vols. Princeton: Princeton University Press.

———1998. *Marginalia.* 4 vols. Princeton: Princeton University Press.

Connell, K. H. 1968. *Irish Peasant Society: Four Historical Essays.* Oxford: Clarendon Press.

Cook, James. 1821. *The Three Voyages of Captain James Cook round the World.* 7 vols. London: Longman.

Cooke, Mordecai. 1997 [1860]. *Seven Sisters of Sleep.* Rochester, Vt.: Park Street.

Cooper, Clarence. 1998 [1967]. *The Farm.* New York: Norton.

Cottle, Joseph. 1847. *Reminiscences of Samuel Taylor Coleridge and Robert Southey.* New York: Wiley and Putnam.

Corbett, John. 1967. *Invitation to a Tea Party.* New York: L.S. (Originally published as *The Secret World of Marijuana.*)

Courtwright, David. 1982. *Dark Paradise: Opiate Addiction in America before 1940.* Cambridge: Harvard University Press.

Crowley, Aleister. n.d. "The Psychology of Hashish." Available online at <www.lycaeum.org>, the website of the Fitz Hugh Ludlow memorial library.

———1909. "The Psychology of Hashish." *The Equinox* (London), 1 (2): 31–89. Available online at <http://www.theequinox.org/vol1/no2/eqi02004. html>.

———1995. *Diary of a Drug Fiend.* York Beach, Me.: Weiser.

Crumpe, Samuel. 1793. *An Inquiry into the Nature and Properties of Opium.* London: G. G. and J. Robinson.

Csáth, Géza. 1983. *Opium and Other Stories.* Trans. Jascha Kessler and Charlotte Rogers. London: Penguin.

D'Anthonay, Thibaut. 1991. *Jean Lorrain, barbare et esthète.* Paris: Plon.

Darwin, Erasmus. 1791. *The Botanic Garden.* 2 vols. Vol 1:. *The Economy of Vegetation.* Vol. 2: *The Loves of the Plants.* London: Johnson. (Facsimile edition 1978, New York: Garland.)

Dass, Ram. 1971. *Be Here Now.* New York: Crown.

Daumal, René. 1972. *Essais et notes.* 2 Vols. Paris: Gallimard.

Davis, Erik. 1998. *Techgnosis: Myth, Magic, and Mysticism in the Age of Information.* New York: Harmony.

Davis, Wade. 1996. *One River: Explorations and Discoveries in the Amazon Rain Forest.* New York: Simon and Schuster.

Davy, Sir Humphry. 1839. *Collected Works.* 9 vols. London: Smith, Elder and Co.

De Laforest, Dubut. 1891. *Morphine.* Paris: Fayard.

Delahaye, Ernest. 1925. *Souvenirs familiers à propos de Rimbaud, Verlaine, germain nouveau.* Paris: A. Messein.

Deleuze, Gilles. 1990. *The Logic of Sense.* Trans. Mark Lester. New York: Columbia University Press.

Deleuze, Gilles, and Félix Guattari. 1987. *A Thousand Plateaus.* Trans. Brian Massumi. Minneapolis: University of Minnesota Press.

Delrieu, Alain. 1988. *L'inconsistance de la toxicomanie.* Paris: Navarin.

De Mexico, N. R. 1969. *Marijuana Girl.* New York: Softcover Library.

De Quincey, Thomas. 1890. *Collected Works.* 14 vols. Edinburgh: Black.

———1971. *Confessions of an English Opium Eater.* London: Penguin.

DeRogatis, Jim. 2000. *Let It Blurt: The Life and Times of Lester Bangs.* New York: Broadway.

Derrida, Jacques. 1978. *Writing and Difference.* Trans. Alan Bass. Chicago: University of Chicago Press.

———1989. "Rhétorique de la drogue." *Autrement Revue,* 106: 197–214.

De Sacy, Sylvestre. 1809. "Mémoire sur la dynastie des Assassins et sur l'étymologie de leur nom." *Moniteur,* July 29.

Desnos, Robert. 1943. *Le vin est tiré.* Paris: Gallimard.

———1953. *Corps et Biens.* Paris: Gallimard.

Devereux, Paul. 1997. *The Long Trip: A Prehistory of Psychedelia.* New York: Penguin.

Dewey, Thomas. 1961. *The Golden Hooligan.* New York: Dell.

Dick, Philip K. 1967. *The Three Stigmata of Palmer Eldritch.* New York: Vintage.

———1991. *A Scanner Darkly.* New York: Vintage.

Dickinson, Emily. 1960. *Complete Poems.* Boston: Little, Brown.

Dieckhoff, Reiner. 1981. "Rausch und Realität: Literarische Avantgarde und Drogenkonsum von der Romantik bis zum Surrealismus." In Gisela Völger, ed., *Rausch und Realität, Drogen im Kulturvergleich,* vol. 1, 404–425. Cologne: Ethnologica.

Dimoff, Paul. 1948. "Autour d'un project de roman de Flaubert." *Revue d'Histoire Littéraire de la France,* October-December, 309–335.

Dinnick, O. P. 1996. "A Case of Repeated Anaesthesia." In A. Marshall Barr, ed., *Essays on the History of Anaesthesia,* 129–130 London: Royal Society of Medicine.

Dischner, Gisela. 1979. *Caroline und der Jenaer Kreis.* Berlin: Wagenbach.

Doctor Syntax in Paris. 1820. London: W. Wright.

Dodge, David. 1946. *It Ain't Hay.* New York: Simon and Schuster.

Dodoens, Rembert. 1595. *A New Herball or Historie of Plants.* Trans. Henrie Lyte. London: Bollifant.

Doyle, Sir Arthur Conan. 1981. *The Penguin Complete Sherlock Holmes.* London: Penguin.

Drieu la Rochelle, Pierre. 1922. *Mesure de la France.* Paris: Grasset.

———1959 [1931]. *Le feu follet.* Paris: Gallimard. Trans. as *Will o' the Wisp.* London: Marion Boyars, 1998 [1966].

Dryden, John. 1958. *The Poems of John Dryden.* 4 vols. Oxford: Oxford University Press.

Du Toit, Brian M. 1980. *Cannabis in Africa.* Rotterdam: A. A. Balkema.

Duerr, Hans Peter. 1985. *Dreamtime: Concerning the Boundaries between Wilderness and Civilization.* Trans. Felicitas Goodman. Oxford: Blackwell.

Dulchinos, Donald P. 1998. *Pioneer of Inner Space: The Life of Fitz Hugh Ludlow, Hasheesh Eater.* Brooklyn: Autonomedia.

Dumas, Alexandre. 1956. *Le comte de Monte Cristo.* Paris: Garnier.

Dunlap, Jane. 1961. *Exploring Inner Space: Personal Experiences under LSD-25.* New York: Harcourt, Brace & World.

Dunne, Michael. 1974. *Sex on Grass.* Los Angeles: Echelon.

Ebin, David, ed. 1961. *The Drug Experience.* New York: Grove.

Edgeworth, Maria. 1971 [1894]. *Life and Letters of Maria Edgeworth.* Freeport, N.Y.: Books of Libraries.

Ellis, Havelock. 1975. "A New Artificial Paradise." Reprinted in Peter Haining, ed., *The Hashish Club,* 176–190. London: Peter Owen.

Ellson, Hal. 1952. *The Golden Spike.* New York: Ballantine.

Emboden, William A. 1974. *Bizarre Plants: Magical, Monstrous, Mythical.* New York: Macmillan.

Emerson, Ralph Waldo. 1946. "The Poet." In Mark Van Doren, ed., *The Portable Emerson.* New York, Viking.

Encyclopédie, ou dictionnaire raisonné des sciences, des arts, et des métiers. 1966. Ed. Denis Diderot and Jean D'Alembert. 35 vols. Stuttgart: Frommann.

Escohotado, Antonio. 1995a. *Historia de las drogas.* 3 vols. Madrid: Alianza.

———1995b. *Histoire élémentaire des drogues: des origines à nos jours.* Trans. Abel Gerschenfeld. Paris: Editions du Lézard.

Esquiros, Alphonse. 1845. "Maladies de l'esprit: de l'hallucination et des hallucinés." *Revue des Deux Mondes,* 12: 292–325.

Euripides. 1973. *The Bacchae and Other Plays.* Trans. Philip Vellacott. London: Penguin.

F., Christiane. 1981. *Wir Kinder vom Bahnhof Zoo.* Hamburg: Gruner & Jahr. Trans. by Susanne Platauer as *Christiane F.: Autobiography of a Girl of the Streets and Heroin Addict.* New York: Bantam, 1982.

Farrère, Claude. 1908. *Fumée l'opium.* Paris: Ollendorff. Trans. by Samuel Putnam as *Black Opium.* New York: Nicholas L. Brown, 1929.

Fathman, Anthony. 1991. "Viv and Tom: The Eliots as Ether Addict and Codependant." *Yeats-Eliot Review,* 11 (2): 33–36.

Felice, Philippe de. 1936. *Poisons sacrés, ivresses divines.* Paris: Albin Michel.

Fiedler, Leslie. 1969. *Being Busted.* New York: Stein and Day.

Field, Andrew. 1987. *VN: The Life and Art of Vladimir Nabokov.* London: Macdonald.

Flaherty, Gloria. 1992. *Shamanism and the Eighteenth Century.* Princeton: Princeton University Press.

Flaubert, Gustave. 1973. *Correspondance.* 3 vols. Paris: Gallimard.

———1988. *Carnets de travail.* Paris: Balland.

Flynt, Henry. 1992. "The Psychedelic State." Available online at <http://www. henryflynt.org/depth_psy/psychostate.html>.

Foster, R. F. 1997. *W. B. Yeats: A Life.* New York: Oxford University Press.

Foucault, Michel. 1977. *Language, Counter-Memory, Practice.* Ed. Donald F. Bouchard. Trans. Donald F. Bouchard and Sherry Simon. Ithaca: Cornell University Press.

Freneau, Philip. 1907. *The Poems of Philip Freneau.* Princeton: Princeton University Press.

Freud, Sigmund. 1974. *Cocaine Papers.* Trans. S. A. Edminster et al. New York: Stonehill.

Friedman, Bruce Jay. 1974. *About Harry Towns.* New York: Knopf.

Fuller, Margaret. 1856. *At Home and Abroad.* Boston: Crosby.

Galland, Jean-Pierre. 1991. *Fumée clandestine.* Paris: Ramsay.

Gautier, Théophile. 1897. *Romans et contes.* Paris: Alphonse Lemerre.

Gelpke, Rudolf. 1966. *Vom Rausch im Orient und Okzident.* Stuttgart: Ernst Klett.

Gerould, Daniel Charles. 1981. *Witkacy: Stanislaw Ignacy Witkiewicz as an Imaginative Writer.* Seattle: University of Washington Press.

Gibson, William. 1984. *Neuromancer.* New York: Ace.

Gilbert-Lecomte, Roger. 1974. *Oeuvres complètes.* 2 vols. Paris: Gallimard.

Ginsberg, Allen. 1961. *Kaddish and Other Poems, 1958–1960.* San Francisco: City Lights.

———1966. "First Manifesto to End the Bringdown." In David Solomon, ed., *The Marihuana Papers.* New York: Signet.

———1984. *Collected Poems.* New York: HarperCollins.

———2000. *Deliberate Prose: Selected Essays, 1952–1995.* New York: HarperCollins.

Ginzburg, Carlo. 1991. *Ecstasies: Deciphering the Witches' Sabbath.* New York: Penguin.

Goines, Donald. 1971. *Dopefiend.* Los Angeles: Holloway House.

Goodman, Jordan. 1995. "Excitantia: Or, How Enlightenment Europe Took to Soft Drugs." In Jordan Goodman, Paul Lovejoy, and Andrew Sherratt, ed., *Consuming Habits: Drugs in History and Anthropology.* London: Routledge.

Graham-Mulhall, Sara. 1926. *Opium: The Demon Flower.* New York: Vinal.

Graves, Richard. 1995. *Robert Graves and the White Goddess, 1940–1985.* London: Weidenfeld and Nicolson.

Graves, Robert. 1960. *Food for Centaurs: Stories, Talks, Critical Studies, Poems.* Garden City, N.Y.: Doubleday.

———1969. *On Poetry: Collected Talks and Essays.* Garden City, N.Y.: Doubleday.

———1973. *Difficult Questions, Easy Answers.* Garden City, N.Y.: Doubleday.

Graziano, Frank, ed. 1983. *Georg Trakl: A Profile.* Durango: Logbridge-Rhodes.

Green, Michelle. 1991. *The dream at the end of the world: Paul Bowles and the literary renegades in Tangier.* New York: HarperCollins.

Grinspoon, Lester. 1971. *Marihuana Reconsidered.* Cambridge: Harvard University Press.

Grinspoon, Lester, and James B. Bakalar. 1976. *Cocaine: A Drug and Its Social Evolution.* New York: Basic Books.

Grinspoon, Lester, and Peer Hedblom. 1975. *The Speed Culture: Amphetamine Use and Abuse in America.* Cambridge: Harvard University Press.

Grosskurth, Phyllis. 1980. *Havelock Ellis: A Biography.* New York: Knopf.

Guaita, Stanislas de. 1916. "Le temple du Satan." In Guaita, *Essais de sciences maudites.* Paris: H. & H. Dulville

Guimbail, Henri. 1891. *Les morphinomanes.* Paris: Baillère.

Haining, Peter., ed. 1975. *The Hashish Club.* London: Peter Owen.

Halsted, William. 1885. "Practical Comments on the Use and Abuse of Cocaine, Suggested by Its Invariably Successful Employment in More Than a Thousand Minor Surgical Operations." *New York Medical Journal,* 42: 294-295.

Harner, Michael, ed. 1973. *Hallucinogens and Shamanism.* Oxford: Oxford University Press.

Harragan, Steve. 1952. *The Bigamy Kiss and Dope Doll.* New York: Universal.

Hartley, David. 1791. *Observations on Man, His Frame, His Duty, and His Expectations.* London. J. Johnson.

Hassler, Donald. 1973. *Erasmus Darwin.* New York: Twayne.

Hattox, Ralph. 1988. *Coffee and Coffeehouses: The Origins of a Social Beverage in the Medieval Near East.* Seattle: University of Washington Press.

Hayter, Alathea. 1968. *Opium and the Romantic Imagination.* London: Faber and Faber.

Hearn, Lafcadio. 1939. *The New Radiance, and Other Scientific Sketches.* Tokyo: Hoku-seido Press.

Heidegger, Martin. 1993. "The Question concerning Technology." Trans. William Lovitt. In Heidegger, *Basic Writings,* pp. 311-341. San Francisco: Harper-Collins.

Hell, Richard. 1997. *Go Now.* New York: Scribner.

Herodotus. 1972. *The Histories.* Trans. Aubrey de Sélincourt. New York: Penguin.

Hervier, Julien. 1995. *The Details of Time: Conversations with Ernst Jünger*. Trans. Joachim Neugroschel. New York: Marsilio.

High Times Encyclopedia of Recreational Drugs. 1978. New York: Stonehill.

Hoeniger, F. David. 1992. *Medicine and Shakespeare in the English Renaissance.* Newark: University of Delaware Press.

Hoffmann, E. T. A. 1892. *The Serapion Brethren.* 2 vols. Trans. Alex Ewing. London: George Bell.

————1963. *The Devil's Elixirs.* Trans. Ronald Taylor. London: J. Calder.

————1996. *Fantasy pieces in Callot's Manner: Conversations with Ernst Jünger.* Trans. Joachim Neugroschel. New York: Marsilio.

————2000. *The Golden Pot and Other Tales.* Trans. Ritchie Robertson. Oxford: Oxford University Press.

Hofmann, Albert. 1983. *LSD: My Problem Child.* Trans. Jonathan Ott. Boston: Houghton Mifflin.

Holmes, John Clellon. 1967. *Nothing More to Declare.* New York: Dutton.

Holmes, Oliver Wendell. 1883. *Pages from an Old Volume of Life: A Collection of Essays, 1857–1881.* Boston: Houghton Mifflin.

Homer. 1996. *The Odyssey.* Trans. Robert Fagles. New York: Penguin.

Horkheimer, Max, and Theodor Adorno. 1991. *Dialectic of Enlightenment.* Trans. John Cumming. New York: Continuum.

Huxley, Aldous. 1980. *Moksha: Writings on Psychedelics and the Visionary Experience, 1931–1963.* Ed. Michael Horowitz and Cynthia Palmer. London: Chatto and Windus.

————1990 [1954, 1956]. *The Doors of Perception and Heaven and Hell.* New York: Harper.

Iceberg Slim. 1969. *Pimp: The Story of My Life.* Los Angeles: Holloway House.

Indian Hemp Drugs Commission Report, 1893–4. 1894. Simla: Government Central Printing Office.

Inglis, Brian. 1975. *The Forbidden Game: A Social History of Drugs.* New York: Scribners.

Irish, William. 1941. *Marihuana.* New York: Dell.

Jaeckle, Erwin. 1973. *Dichter und Droge.* Zurich: Benziger.

Jahn, Ilse. 1994. "On the Origin of Romantic Biology and Its Further Development at the University of Jena between 1790 and 1850." In S. Poggi and M. Bossi, eds., *Romanticism in Science,* 75–87. Dordrecht: Kluwer.

James, William. 1917 [1896]. "On Some Hegelisms." In James, *The Will to Believe, and Other Essays in Popular Philosophy.* New York: Longmans, Green.

————1982 [1902]. *The Varieties of Religious Experience.* London: Penguin.

Jay, Mike. 2000. *Emperors of Dreams: Drugs in the Nineteenth Century.* Sawtry, Eng.: Dedalus.

————2001. "There Is Only One Valid Approach: The Forgotten History of Drugs, Science, and Self-Experimentation." Unpublished ms.

Jay, Mike, ed. 2000. *Artificial Paradises: A Drugs Reader.* New York: Penguin.

Jeanneret, Michel. 1980. "La folie est un rêve: Nerval et le docteur Moreau de Tours." *Romantisme,* 27: 59–75.

Johnson, Samuel. 1952. *Letters.* 5 vols. Oxford: Oxford University Press.

————1963. *Johnson's Dictionary: A Modern Selection.* New York: Pantheon.

Jonas, Hans. 1992 [1963]. *The Gnostic Religion: Message of the Alien God and the Beginnings of Christianity.* London: Routledge.

Jones, Jo Elwyn, and J. Francis Gladstone. 1998. *The Alice Companion: A Guide to Lewis Carroll's Alice Books.* New York: New York University Press.

Jones, John. 1701. *The Mysteries of Opium Reveal'd.* London: Richard Smith.

Jünger, Ernst. 1969. "Drugs and Ecstasy." Trans. unknown. In Joseph Kitagawa and Charles Long, ed., *Myths and Symbols: Studies in Honor of Mircea Eliade.* Chicago: University of Chicago Press.

————1990 [1970] *Annäherungen: Drogen und Rausch.* Stuttgart: Klett-Cotta. Trans. by Henri Plard as *Approches: drogues et ivresse.* Paris: Gallimard, 1973.

Kaiser, Helmut. 1962. *Mythos, Rausch und Reaktion: Der Weg Gottfried Benns und Ernst Jüngers.* Berlin: Aufbau-Verlag.

Kamstra, Jerry. 1983 [1974]. *Weed: Adventures of a Dope Smuggler.* Santa Barbara, Calif.: Ross-Erikson.

Kane, H. H. 1974 [1883]. "A Hashish House in New York." In H. Wayne Morgan, ed., *Yesterday's Addicts: American Society and Drug Abuse, 1865–1920,* 159–170. Norman: University of Oklahoma Press.

Kant, Immanuel. 1974 [1798]. *Anthropology from a Pragmatic Point of View.* Trans. Mary J. Gregor. The Hague: Nijhoff.

Karch, Steven B. 1998. *A Brief History of Cocaine.* Boca Raton, Fla.: CRC.

Kavan, Anna. 1970. *Julia and the Bazooka.* London: Peter Owen.

————1997 [1967]. *Ice.* London: Peter Owen.

Kerouac, Jack. 1976. *On the Road.* London: Penguin.

————1995. *The Portable Jack Kerouac.* Ed. Ann Charters. New York: Viking.

Kimmens, Andrew C., ed. 1977. *Tales of Hashish: A Literary Look at the Hashish Experience.* New York: Morrow.

King-Hele, Desmond. 1977. *Doctor of Revolution: The Life and Genius of Erasmus Darwin.* London: Faber and Faber.

Kingsley, Charles. 1861 [1850]. *Alton Locke.* New York: Harper & Brothers.

Klüver, Heinrich. 1966. *Mescal and Mechanisms of Hallucinations.* Chicago: University of Chicago Press.

Knight, David. 1992. *Humphry Davy: Science and Power.* Oxford: Blackwell.

Kohn, Marek. 1987. *Narcomania: On Heroin.* London: Faber and Faber.

————1992. *Dope Girls: The Birth of the British Drug Underground.* London: Lawrence and Wishart.

Kohtes, Michael, and Kai Ritzmann. 1987. *Der Rausch in Worten: Zur Welt- und Drogenerfahrung der Surrealisten und Beatniks.* Marburg: Jonas.

Krassner, Paul, ed. 1999. *Pot Stories for the Soul.* New York: High Times.

Kuhn, Reinhard. 1974. "The Hermeneutics of Silence: Michaux and Mescaline." *Yale French Studies*, 50: 130–141.

Kupfer, Alexander. 1996. *Göttliche Gifte: Kleine Kulturgeschichte des Rausches seit dem Garten Eden.* Stuttgart: J. B. Metzler.

La Barre, Weston. 1989. *The Peyote Cult.* 5th ed. Norman: University of Oklahoma Press.

Lacoue-Labarthe, Philippe, and Jean-Luc Nancy. 1978. *L'absolu littéraire.* Paris: Editions du Seuil.

Lallemand, François. 1843. *Le Hachych.* Sections are translated in Andrew C. Kimmens, ed., *Tales of Hashish: A Literary Look at the Hashish Experience,* 114–124. New York: Morrow, 1977.

Lamantia, Philip. 1959a. *Ekstasis.* San Francisco: Auerbahn.

————1959b. *Narcotics.* San Francisco: Auerbahn.

————1962. *Destroyed Works.* San Francisco: Auerbahn.

Latour, Bruno. 1993. *We Have Never Been Modern.* Trans. Catherine Porter. Cambridge: Harvard University Press.

Lawton, Frederick. 1910. *Balzac.* London: Grant Richards.

Leach, Edmund. 1976. "High School." In Daniel Noel, ed., *Seeing Castaneda: Reactions to the "Don Juan" Writings of Carlos Castaneda.* New York: Putnam's.

Leary, Timothy. 1968. *High Priest.* New York: New American Library.

Le Clézio, Jean-Marie. 1993. *The Mexican Dream, or, The Interrupted Thought of Amerindian Civilizations.* Trans. Teresa Lavender Fagan. Chicago: University of Chicago Press.

Lee, Martin A., and Bruce Shlain. 1985. *Acid Dreams: The CIA, LSD, and the Sixties Rebellion.* New York: Grove.

Lee, William (William Burroughs). 1953. *Junkie: Confessions of an Unredeemed Drug Addict.* New York: Ace.

Lefebure, Molly. 1974. *Samuel Taylor Coleridge: A Bondage of Opium.* New York: Stein and Day.

Lefebure, Molly, and Richard Gravil, ed. 1990. *The Coleridge Connection: Essays for Thomas McFarland.* New York: St. Martin's.

Leibbrand, Werner. 1956. *Die spekulative Medizin der Romantik.* Hamburg: Claasen.

Lélut, François. 1836. *Du démon de Socrate: recherches des analogies de la folie et de la raison.* Paris: Triquart.

Lenson, David. 1995. *On Drugs.* Minneapolis: University of Minnesota Press.

Lethève, Jacques. 1959. *Symbolistes et impressionistes devant la presse.* Paris: Colin.

Levinas, Emmanuel. 1996. *Transcendance et intelligibilité: suivi d'un entretien.* Geneva: Labor et Fides.

Lewin, Louis. 1998 [1931]. *Phantastica.* Trans. P. H. A. Wirth. Rochester, Vt.: Park Street.

Lewis, Barbara. 1970. *The Sexual Power of Marijuana.* New York: P. H. Wyden.

Lewis, Bernard. 1968. *The Assassins: A Radical Sect in Islam.* New York: Basic Books.

Liedekerke, Arnould de. 1984. *La belle époque de l'opium.* Paris: Editions de la Différence.

Lilly, John. 1968. *Programming and Metaprogramming in the Human Biocomputer.* New York: Julian.

———1973. *The Center of the Cyclone: An Autobiography of Inner Space.* New York: Bantam.

———1978. *The Scientist: A Novel Autobiography.* Philadelphia: Lippincott.

Lindop, Grevel. 1981. *The Opium Eater: A Life of Thomas De Quincey.* London: J. M. Dent.

Lloyd, John Uri. 1978 [1895]. *Etidorhpa, Or the End of Earth.* New York: Pocket Books.

Loessing, Gary. 1969. *Trip Out!* Las Vegas: C.

Logan, James. 1936. *The Poetry and Aesthetics of Erasmus Darwin.* Princeton: Princeton University Press.

Lonsdale, Roger, ed. 1984. *The New Oxford Book of Eighteenth Century Verse.* Oxford: Oxford University Press.

Lorrain, Jean. 1975. *Contes d'un buveur d'éther.* Verviers, Belgium: Marabout.

Ludlow, Fitz Hugh. 1975 [1857]. *The Hasheesh Eater.* Ed. Michael Horowitz. San Francisco: Level Press. 1979 edition, published in San Francisco by City Lights.

Luhan, Mabel Dodge. 1936. *Movers and Shakers.* New York: Harcourt, Brace.

Lumholtz, Carl. 1902. *Unknown Mexico.* 2 vols. New York: Scribners.

Mabin, Dominique. 1992. *La sommeil de Marcel Proust.* Paris: Presses Universitaires de France.

Mackey, Kevin. 1970. *The Cure: Recollections of an Addict.* Sydney: Angus & Robertson.

Maier, Hans. W. 1926. *Der Kokainismus.* Leipzig: Georg Thieme. Trans. by Oriana Josseau Kalant as *Cocaine Addiction.* Toronto: Addiction Research Foundation, 1987.

Maingon, Charles. 1994. *La médecine dans l'œuvre de J. K. Huysmans.* Paris: A. G. Nizet.

Malcolm X. 1992. *The Autobiography of Malcolm X.* With the assistance of Alex Haley. New York: Ballantine.

Mallat de Bassilan, Marcel. 1885. *La comtesse morphine.* Paris: Frinzine, Klein.

Mann, Ronald D. 1984. *Modern Drug Use: An Enquiry on Historical Principles.* Lancaster, Eng.: MTP.

Mantegazza, Paolo. 1859. *Sulle virtu igieniche e medicinale della coca.* Milan. Trans. by Lara Forti and Gina Alhadeff as "Coca Experiences" in George Andrews and David. Solomon, ed., *The Coca Leaf and Cocaine Papers,* 38–42. New York: Harcourt Brace Jovanovich, 1975.

Marks, Jeanette. 1968 [1925]. *Genius and Disaster: Studies in Drugs and Genius.* Port Washington, N.Y.: Kennikat.

Marks, Robert W. 1953. "The Philosophy of Benjamin Paul Blood." Ph.D. diss., New School of Social Research.

Marinetti, Filipo. 1921. "The Manifesto of Tactilism." Available online at <http://www.futurism.org.uk/futurism.htm>.

Marlowe, Ann. 1999. *How to Stop Time.* New York: Basic Books.

Marlowe, Steven. 1967. *Drum Beat Erica.* Greenwich, Conn.: Fawcett.

Masters, R. E. L., and Jean Houston. 1966. *The Varieties of Psychedelic Experience.* New York: Holt.

Matthee, Rudi. 1995. "Exotic Substances: The Introduction and Global Spread of Tobacco, Coffee, Cocoa, Tea, and Distilled Liquor, Sixteenth to Eighteenth Centuries." In Roy Porter and Mikulas Teich, ed., *Drugs and Narcotics in History.* Cambridge: Cambridge University Press.

Maupassant, Guy de. 1988. *Sur l'eau.* Paris: Marpon and Flammarion. Trans. by Marlo Johnston as *Afloat.* London: Peter Owen, 1995.

Mayor La Guardia's Committee on Marihuana. 1944. *The Marihuana Problem in the City of New York.* Reprinted in David Solomon, *The Marihuana Papers,* 277–410. New York: New American Library, 1966.

McClure, Michael. 1958. *Peyote Poem.* San Francisco: Berman.

McDonagh, Josephine. 1994. *De Quincey's Disciplines.* Oxford: Oxford University Press.

McInerney, Jay. 1987. *Bright Lights, Big City.* New York: Vintage.

McKenna, Terence. 1991. *The Archaic Revival.* New York: Harper.

———1993. *True Hallucinations.* New York: HarperCollins.

McNeil, Legs, and Gillian McCain. 1996. *Please Kill Me.* New York: Grove.

McWilliams, John C. 1990. *The Protectors: Harry J. Anslinger and the Federal Bureau of Narcotics, 1930–1962.* Newark: University of Delaware Press.

Melechi, Antonio, ed. 1998. *Mindscapes: An Anthology of Drug Writings.* Baildon, Eng.: Mono.

Merleau-Ponty, Maurice. 1945. *Phénoménologie de la perception.* Paris: Gallimard.

Meyers, Claude, 1985. *Brève histoire des drogues et médicaments de l'esprit.* N.p.: Erès.

Michaux, Henri. 1957. *L'infini turbulent.* Paris: Mercure de France.

————1959. *Paix dans les brisements.* Paris: Flinker.

————1961. *Connaissance par les gouffres.* Paris: Gallimard.

————1966. *Les grandes épreuves de l'esprit.* Paris: Gallimard.

————1972 [1956]. *Misérable miracle.* Paris: Gallimard. Trans. by Louise Varese as *Miserable Miracle.* New York: City Lights, 1963.

————1998. *Michaux: Meskalin.* Ed. Peter Weibel. Cologne: W. König.

Michelet, Jules. 1877. *Histoire de France.* 19 vols. Paris: Lacroix.

Mickel, Emanuel J., Jr. 1969. *The Artificial Paradises in French Literature.* Chapel Hill: University of North Carolina Press.

Miller, James. 1993. *The Passion of Michel Foucault.* New York: Simon and Schuster.

Miller, John, and Randall Koral, ed. 1995. *White Rabbit: A Psychedelic Reader.* San Francisco: Chronicle.

Milligan, Barry. 1995. *Pleasures and Pains: Opium and the Orient in Nineteenth-Century British Culture.* Charlottesville: University Press of Virginia.

Milosz, O. V. de L. 1944. *Oeuvres complètes.* Fribourg: Egloff.

Milton, John. 1980. *The Complete Poems.* London: J. M. Dent.

Mitchell, S. Weir. 1896. "The Effects of Anhalonium Lewinii (the Mescal Button)." *British Medical Journal,* 2: 1625–1628.

Momaday, N. Scott. 1968. *House Made of Dawn.* New York: Harper & Row.

Monfreid, Henry de. 1994 [1935]. *Hashish: A Smuggler's Tale.* Trans. Helen Buchanan Bell. London: Pimlico.

Montesquieu, Baron Charles de. 1929 [1721]. *Lettres persans.* Paris: F. Roches.

Mooney, James. 1896. "The Mescal Plant and Ceremony." *Therapeutic Gazette,* 12: 7–11. Reprinted in Strausbaugh and Blaise, ed., *The Drug User: Documents, 1840–1960,* 173–177. New York: Blast First.

Moore, Marcia, and Howard Altounian. 1978. *Journeys into the Bright World.* Rockport, Mass.: Para Research.

Moreau de Tours, Jean. 1980 [1845]. *Du Hachisch et de l'aliénation mentale.* Geneva: Slatkine.

Morgan, H. Wayne. 1981. *Drugs in America: A Social History, 1800–1980.* Syracuse, N.Y.: Syracuse University Press.

Morgan, H. Wayne, ed. 1974. *Yesterday's Addicts: American Society and Drug Abuse, 1865–1920.* Norman: University of Oklahoma Press.

Morgan, Ted. 1990. *Literary Outlaw: The Life and Times of William S. Burroughs.* New York: Avon.

Mortimer, W. Golden. 1974. *History of Coca: "The Divine Plant of the Incas."* San Francisco: And/Or.

Murger, Henri. 1854. *Scènes de la vie bohême.* Paris: Michel Lévy.

Nerval, Gerard de. 1999. "The Tale of the Caliph Hakim." Trans. by Richard Sieburth in Nerval, *Selected Writings.* New York: Penguin.

Neubauer, John. 1971. *Bifocal Vision: Novalis' Philosophy of Nature and Disease.* Chapel Hill: University of North Carolina Press.

Newland, Constance A. 1962. *My Self and I.* New York: Coward-McCann.

Nordau, Max. 1900. *Degeneration.* Trans. unknown. New York: Appleton.

Novalis. 1968. *Schriften.* 6 vols. Darmstadt: Wissenschaftliche Buchgesellschaft.

————1984. *Hymns to the Night.* Trans. Richard Higgins. New Paltz, McPherson.

Nowak, Sandra. 2001. "Viel Rausch um Nichts." Available online at <http://freenet.meome.de/app/fn/artcont_portal_news_article.jsp/60529.html>.

Noyes, Alfred. 1936. *Voltaire.* New York: Sheed & Ward.

O'Brien-Moore, Ainsworth. 1924. *Madness in Ancient Literature.* Weimar: R. Wagner.

Olson, Charles. 1978. *Mythologos: The Collected Lectures and Interviews.* Salinas, Calif.: Four Seasons Foundation.

Onians, Richard Broxton. 1954. *The Origins of European Thought.* Cambridge: Cambridge University Press.

Orieux, Jean. 1979. *Voltaire.* Trans. Barbara Bray and Helen R. Lane. Garden City, N.Y.: Doubleday.

O'Shaughnessy, William. 1842. "On the Preparation of the Indian Hemp or Gunjah (Cannabis Indica)." *Transactions of the Medical and Physical Society of Bombay,* 8: 421–461.

Ott, Jonathan. 1993. *Pharmacotheon: Entheogenic Drugs, Their Plant Sources and History.* Kennewick, Wash.: Natural Products.

Otten, Charlotte. 1970. "Homer's Moly and Milton's Rue." *Huntington Library Quarterly,* August 1970, 361–372.

Ouspensky, Peter. 1949. *In Search of the Miraculous.* New York: Harcourt Brace Jovanovich.

———— 1969 [1931]. *A New Model of the Universe.* Trans. by the author. New Haven: Yale University Press.

O. W. (Marjorie Smith). 1930. *No Bed of Roses: The Diary of a Lost Soul.* New York: Macaulay.

Palmer, Cynthia, and Michael Horowitz. 1982. *Shaman Woman, Mainline Lady: Women's Writings on the Drug Experience.* New York: Quill. Expanded edition published as *Sisters of the Extreme: Women Writing on the Drug Experience.* Rochester, Vt.: Park Street, 2000.

Papper, E. M. 1995. *Romance, Poetry, and Surgical Sleep: Literature Influences Medicine.* Westport, Conn.: Greenwood.

Parker, John. 1966. *Light Up.* New York: Wee Hours.

Parssinen, Terry. 1983. *Secret Passions, Secret Remedies: Narcotic Drugs in British Society, 1820–1930.* Philadelphia: Institute for the Study of Human Issues.

Pearson, Hesketh. 1964. *Doctor Darwin.* New York: Walker.

Peebles, Niles. 1968. *See the Blood Run.* New York: Pyramid.

Pepper, Art. 1994. *Straight Life*. New York: Da Capo.

Pernick, Martin S. 1985. *A Calculus of Suffering: Pain, Professionalism, and Anesthesia in Nineteenth-Century America*. New York: Columbia University Press.

Peschel, Enid Rhodes. 1974. "Arthur Rimbaud: The Aesthetics of Intoxication." *Yale French Studies*, 50: 65–80.

Peters, Catherine. 1991. *The King of Inventors: A Life of Wilkie Collins*. London: Secker & Warburg.

Pichois, Claude, Robert Kopp, and René Huyghe. 1955. "L'Hôtel Lauzun, Baudelaire, et le Club du Haschisch *Les Annales*, December, 45–58.

Pierrot, Jean. 1972. *Le rêve, de Milton aux surréalistes*. Paris: Bordas.

———1975. 1974. "Merveilleux et fantastique: une histoire de l'imaginaire dans la prose française du romantisme à la décadence (1830–1900)." Unpublished thesis, University of Paris.

———1977. *L'imaginaire décadent (1880–1900)*. Paris: Presses Universitaires de France.

Pitigrilli. 1982. *Cocaine*. Trans. Eric Mosbacher. London: Hamlyn.

Plant, Sadie. 1999. *Writing on Drugs*. London: Faber & Faber.

Poe, Edgar Allan. 1992. *The Collected Tales and Poems of Edgar Allan Poe*. New York: The Modern Library.

Pomeau, René. 1994. *Voltaire en son temps*. 5 vols. Oxford: Voltaire Foundation.

Pope, Alexander. 1963. *The Poems of Alexander Pope*. New Haven: Yale University Press.

Porter, Roy, and Mikulas Teich, ed. 1995. *Drugs and Narcotics in History*. Cambridge: Cambridge University Press.

Potlatch, 1954–1957. 1996. Paris: Editions Allia.

Pouvoirville, Albert de (Matgioi). 1899. *Le maître des sentences*. Paris: Ollendorff.

———1908. *L'opium*. Paris: Comité des Congrès Coloniaux Français.

Prevel, Jacques. 1994. *En compagnie d'Antonin Artaud*. Paris: Flammarion.

Pritchett, V. S. 1973. *Balzac*. New York: Knopf.

Proust, Marcel. 1987–88. *À la recherche du temps perdu*. 4 vols. Paris: Gallimard.

Random, Michel. 1970. *Le grand jeu*. 2 vols. Paris: Denoël.

Raynal, Abbé. 1776. *Histoire philosophique et politique*. La Haye.

Reko, Victor A. 1938. *Magische Gifte: Rausch- und Betäubungsmittel der Neuen Welt*. 2nd ed. Stuttgart: Enke.

Révolution surréaliste: collection complète, La. 1975. Paris: Jean-Michel Place.

Rig Veda: An Anthology—One Hundred and Eight Hymns, The. 1981. Trans. Wendy Doniger O'Flaherty. New York: Penguin.

Rimbaud, Arthur. 1954. *Oeuvres complètes*. Paris: Gallimard.

Ripa, Yannick. 1988. *Histoire du rêve*. Paris: Pluriel.

Ripley, George, ed. 1857. *New American Cyclopedia*. New York: Appleton.

Risse, Guenter B. 1988. "Brunonian Therapeutics: New Wine in Old Bottles?" In
    W. F. Bynum and Roy Porter, ed., *Brunonianism in Britain and Europe*,
    46–62. London: Wellcome Institute for the History of Medicine.

Robb, Graham. 1994. *Balzac: A Biography*. New York: Norton.

Roberts, Gareth. 1996. "The Descendants of Circe: Witches and Renaissance
    Fictions." In Jonathan Barry, Marianne Hester, and Gareth Roberts, ed.,
    Witchcraft in Early Modern Europe, 183–206. Cambridge: Cambridge
    University Press.

Robinson, Victor. 1925 [1912]. *An Essay on Hasheesh*. New York: E. H. Ringer.

Rodet, Paul. 1897. *Morphinomanie et morphinisme*. Paris: Alcan.

Rohmer, Sax. 1983 [1919]. "Dope." In Rohmer, *Fu Manchu: Four Classic Novels*. Secau-
    cus, N.J.: Citadel.

Ronell, Avital. 1992. *Crack Wars: Literature, Addiction, Mania*. Lincoln: University of
    Nebraska Press.

Rosenthal, Franz. 1971. *The Herb: Hashish versus Medieval Islam*. Leiden: E. J. Brill.

Rousseau, Jean-Jacques. 1925. *La nouvelle Heloise*. Paris: Hachette.

Roy, Louis. 2001. *Transcendent Experiences: Phenomenology and Critique*. Toronto:
    University of Toronto Press.

Rubin, Vera, ed. 1976. *Cannabis and Culture*. The Hague: Mouton.

Ruck, Carl. 1986. "Poets, Philosophers, Priests: Entheogens in the Formation of the
    Classical Tradition." In R. Gordon Wasson, Stella Kramrisch, Jonathan Ott,
    and Carl Ruck, ed., *Persephone's Quest: Entheogens and the Origins of Religion*,
    151–256. New Haven: Yale University Press.

Rudenko, Sergei I. 1970. *Frozen Tombs of Siberia: The Pazyryk Burials of Iron Age
    Horsemen*. Berkeley: University of California Press.

Rudgley, Richard. 1995. *Essential Substances: A Cultural History of Intoxicants in
    Society*. New York: Kodansha.

Rusham, G. B., N. J. H. Davies, and R. S. Atkinson. 1996. *A Short History of
    Anaesthesia: The First Hundred and Fifty Years*. Oxford: Butterworth-
    Heinemann.

Russell, Alexander. 1794. *The Natural History of Aleppo*. London: G. G. and J. Robin-
    son.

Russell, Sanders. 1947 *The Chemical Image*. San Francisco: Ark.

Sabbag, Robert. 1990. *Snowblind: A Brief Life in the Cocaine Trade*. New York: Vin-
    tage.

Sabina, Maria. 1981. *Her Life and Chants*. Trans. Henry Munn. Santa Barbara: Ross-
    Erikson.

Sacy, Sylvestre de. 1818. "Mémoire sur la dynastie des Assassins et sur l'origine de leur
    nom." *Mémoires de l'Académie des Inscriptions et Belles-Lettres*, 4: 81–85.

Sagan, Françoise. 1964. *Toxique*. Paris: Julliard.

Sahagún, Bernadino de. 1950–. *Florentine Codes: General History of the Things of New Spain.* Trans. Arthur Anderson and Charles Dibble. 13 vols. Santa Fe, N.M.: School of American Research.

Sampson, George. 1948. *The Concise Cambridge History of English Literature.* Cambridge: Cambridge University Press.

Santini, Rosemary. 1973. *The Happy Hookah.* New York: Berkley.

Sartre, Jean-Paul. 1940. *L'imaginaire: psychologie—phénoménologique de l'imagination.* Paris: Gallimard.

———1978. *Critique of Dialectical Reason, Theory of Practical Ensembles.* Trans. Alan Sheridan-Smith. London: NLB.

Sawyer-Laucanno, Christopher. 1989. *An Invisible Spectator: A Biography of Paul Bowles.* New York: Weidenfeld and Nicolson.

Scarborough, John. 1995. "The Opium Poppy in Helenistic and Roman Medicine." In Roy Porter and Mikulas Teich, ed., *Drugs and Narcotics in History.* Cambridge: Cambridge University Press, 1995.

Schivelbusch, Wolfgang. 1992. *Tastes of Paradise: A Social History of Spices, Stimulants, and Intoxicants.* Trans. David Jacobson. New York: Pantheon.

Schneider, Elizabeth. 1953. *Coleridge, Opium, and Kubla Khan.* New York: Octagon.

Schoenbein, Christian. 1842. *Mitteilungen aus dem Reisetagebuche eines Deutschen Naturforschers.* Basel: Schweighaufer'schen.

Schumacher, Michael. 1992. *Dharma Lion: A Critical Biography of Allen Ginsberg.* New York: St. Martin's

Scott, Thurston. 1952 [1951]. *I'll Get Mine.* New York: Popular Library. (Originally published as *Cure It with Honey).*

Secret Talks with Mr. G. 1978. N.p.: IDHHB.

Sedgwick, Eve Kosofsky. 1992. "Epidemics of the Will." In Jonathan Crary and Sanford Kwinter, ed., *Zone, 6: Incorporations,* 582–595. New York: Zone.

Seefelder, Matthias. 1987. *Opium: Eine Kulturgeschichte.* Frankfurt am Main: Athenäum.

Seibt, Johann Wolfgang Constantin. 1994. "Jenes vielgerühmte Kraut." *Die Zeit* (Vienna), January 21, 59.

Senaha, Eijun. 1996. *Sex, Drugs, and Madness in Poetry from William Blake to Christina Rossetti.* Lewiston: Mellon University Press.

Shadwell, Thomas. 1927. *Complete Works of Thomas Shadwell.* 4 vols. London: Blom.

Shakespeare, William. 1957. *Othello.* Cambridge: Cambridge University Press.

Shallit, Joseph. 1952. *Kiss the Killer.* New York: Avon.

Shaw, Floyd. 1954. *Devil's Daughter.* New York: Avon.

Shulgin, Ann, and Alexander Shulgin. 1991. *PIHKAL: A Chemical Love Story.* Berkeley: Transform.

———1997. *TIHKAL: The Continuation.* Berkeley, Transform.

Sieburth, Richard. 1999. Introduction to *Selected Writings,* by Gérard de Nerval. New York: Penguin.

Simpson, James. 1972. *Pot and Pleasure.* New York: Venus.

Sloman, Larry. 1979. *Reefer Madness: The History of Marijuana in America.* Indianapolis: Bobbs-Merrill.

Smart, Richard. 1985. *The Snow Papers: A Memoir of Illusion, Power-Lust, and Cocaine.* Boston: Atlantic Monthly Press.

Smith, Philip B. 1972. *Chemical Glimpses of Paradise.* Springfield, Ill.: Charles C. Thomas.

Smith, W. D. A. 1982. *Under the Influence: A History of Nitrous Oxide and Oxygen Anaesthesia.* London: MacMillan.

Snelders, H. A. M. 1970. "Romanticism and Naturphilosophie and the Inorganic Natural Sciences 1797–1840: An Introductory Survey" *History of Science,* 9: 193–215.

Solomon, David, ed. 1966. *The Marihuana Papers.* New York: New American Library.

Soucy, Robert. 1979. *Fascist Intellectual, Drieu La Rochelle.* Berkeley: University of California Press.

Southern, Terry. 1967. *Red Dirt Marijuana and Other Tastes.* New York: New American Library.

Southey, Robert. 1850. *Life and Correspondence.* London: Longman.

Spackman, Barbara. 1989. *Decadent Genealogies: The Rhetoric of Sickness from Baudelaire to D'Annunzio.* Ithaca: Cornell University Press.

Spenser, Edmund. 1912. *Poetical Works.* Oxford: Oxford University Press.

Spruce, Richard. 1873. "On Some Remarkable Narcotics of the Amazon Valley and Orinoco." *Geographical Magazine,* 1:184–193.

———1908. *Notes of a Botanist on the Amazon and Andes.* 2 vols. London: Macmillan.

Stafford, Peter. 1992. *Psychedelics Encyclopedia.* Berkeley: Ronin.

Steegmuller, Francis. 1970. *Cocteau: A Biography.* Boston: Little, Brown.

Stephenson, Neal. 1993. *Snow Crash.* New York: Bantam.

Stevens, Jay. 1987. *Storming Heaven: LSD and the American Dream.* New York: Atlantic Monthly Press.

Stewart, Omer C. 1987. *Peyote Religion: A History.* Norman: University of Oklahoma Press.

Stone, Robert. 1974. *Dog Soldiers.* Boston: Houghton Mifflin.

Strausbaugh, John, and Donald Blaise, ed. 1991. *The Drug User: Documents, 1840–1960.* New York: Blast First.

Stringer, Lee. 1998. *Grand Central Winter: Stories from the Street.* New York: Seven Stories.

Sutherland, John. 1982. *Offensive Literature: Decensorship in Britain, 1960–1982.* London: Junction.

Sutin, Lawrence. 2000. *Do What Thou Wilt: A Life of Aleister Crowley*. New York: St. Martin's Press.

Szasz, Thomas. 1974. *Ceremonial Chemistry: The Ritual Persecution of Drugs, Addicts, and Pushers*. New York: Anchor.

Tailhade, Laurent. 1905. *Omar Khayyam et les poisons de l'intelligence*. Paris: Carrington.

——1907. *La "Noire Idole."* Paris: Vanier.

——1914. *Les "Commérages" de Tybalt*. Paris: Georges Crès.

Taussig, Michael. 1987. *Shamanism, Colonialism, and the Wild Man: A Study in Terror and Healing*. Chicago: University of Chicago Press.

Taylor, Bayard. 1855. *The Lands of the Saracen*. New York: Putnam.

Terry, Charles, and Mildred Pellens. 1928. *The Opium Problem*. Montclair, N.J.: Patterson Smith.

Theweleit, Klaus. 1987. *Male Fantasies*. 2 vols. Trans. Stephen Conway. Minneapolis: University of Minnesota Press.

Thomas, Keith. 1971. *Religion and the Decline of Magic*. New York: Scribners.

Thomas, Moses. 1814. *A cursory glimpse of the state of the nation, on the twenty-second of February, 1814, being the eighty-first anniversary of the birth of Washington; or, A physico-politico-theologico lucubration upon the wonderful properties of nitrous oxide, or the newly discovered exhilarating gas, in its effects upon the human mind, and body; as they were exhibited, by actual experiment, on the evening of the twenty-third instant*. Philadelphia: Maxwell.

Thomas, Piri. 1973 [1967]. *Down These Mean Streets*. New York: Knopf.

Thompson, Hunter S. 1967. *Hell's Angels: A Strange and Terrible Saga*. New York: Ballantine.

——1989 [1971]. *Fear and Loathing in Las Vegas: A Savage Journey into the Heart of the American Dream*. New York: Vintage.

Thompson, Scott. n.d. "From 'Rausch' to Rebellion: Walter Benjamin's Uncompleted Book on Hashish." <http://www.wbenjamin.org/rausch.html>.

Thoreau, Henry David. 1906. *Writings of H. D. Thoreau*. 20 vols. Boston: Houghton Mifflin.

Thorp, Raymond. 1956. *Viper: Confessions of a Drug Addict*. London: Robert Hale.

Tonnac, Jean-Philippe de. 1998. *René Daumal, l'archange*. Paris: Grasset.

Tott, Baron de. 1973 [1785]. *Memoirs of Baron de Tott*. Trans. unknown. London: Arno Press.

Tschudi, Johann Jacob von. 1846. *Peru Reiseskizzen aus den Jahren 1838–1842*. St. Gallen: Scheitlin und Zollikofer.

Tsouyopoulos, Nelly. 1988. "The Influence of John Brown's Ideas in Germany." In W. F. Bynum and Roy Porter, ed., *Brunonianism in Britain and Europe*, 63–74. London: Wellcome Institute for the History of Medicine, 1988.

Turnbull, Laurence. 1878. *The advantages and accidents of artificial anæsthesia. Being a manual of anæsthetic agents, and their modes of administration, etc.* Philadelphia: Lindsay and Blakiston.

Ukers, William Harrison. 1936. *The Romance of Tea: An Outline of Tea and Tea-drinking through Sixteen Hundred Years.* New York: Knopf.

———1948. *The Romance of Coffee: An Outline History of Coffee and Coffee-Drinking through a Thousand Years.* New York: Tea and Coffee Trade Journal Co.

Van Vechten, Carl. 1922. *Peter Whiffle: His Life and Works.* New York: Knopf.

Varela, Francisco. 1999. *Ethical Know-How: Action, Wisdom, and Cognition.* Stanford: Stanford University Press.

Viazzi, Glauco, ed. 1978. *I Poeti del futurismo, 1909–1944.* Milan: Longanesi.

Villavicencio, Manuel. 1858. *Geografía de la república del Ecuador.* New York: R. Craighead.

Virilio, Paul, with Sylvère Lotringer. 1983. *Pure War.* Trans. Mark Polizzotti. New York: Semiotext(e).

———1986. *Speed and Politics.* Trans. Mark Polizzotti. New York: Semiotext(e).

Volger, Gisela, ed. 1981. *Rausch und Realität: Drogen im Kulturvergleich.* 2 vols. Cologne: Ethnologica.

Voltaire. 1962 [1756]. *Zadig: ou, La destinée.* Paris: J. Fabre.

Vom Scheidt, Jürgen. 1973. *Freud und das Kokain.* Munich: Kindler.

Von Hammer, Joseph. 1818. *Geschichte des Assassinen.* Stuttgart: J. G. Gotta. Trans. by Oswald Wood as *History of the Assassins.* London: Smith and Elder, 1835.

Ward, R. H. 1957. *A Drug-Taker's Notes.* London: Victor Gollancz.

Warhol, Andy. 1968. *A: A Novel.* New York: Grove.

Warner, Nicholas O. 1997. *Spirits of America: Intoxication in Nineteenth Century American Literature.* Norman: University of Oklahoma Press.

Warton, Thomas. 1802. *Poetical Works.* 4 vols. Oxford: Oxford University Press.

Wasson, R. Gordon. 1968. *Soma: The Divine Mushroom.* New York: Harcourt Brace Jovanovitch.

Wasson, R. Gordon, Albert Hofmann, and Carl Ruck. 1978. *The Road to Eleusis: Unveiling the Secret of the Mysteries.* New York: Harcourt Brace Jovanovitch.

Wasson, R. Gordon, Stella Kramrisch, Jonathan Ott, and Carl Ruck. 1986. *Persephone's Quest: Entheogens and the Origins of Religion.* New Haven: Yale University Press.

Wasson, Valentina Pavlovna, and R. Gordon. 1957. *Mushrooms, Russia, and History.* 2 vols. New York: Pantheon.

Watts, Alan. 1962. *The Joyous Cosmology.* New York: Pantheon.

Webb, James. 1980. *The Harmonious Circle: The Lives and Work of G. I. Gurdjieff, P. D. Ouspensky, and Their Followers.* New York: Putnam.

Weil, Andrew, and Winifred Rosen. 1993. *From Chocolate to Morphine.* Boston: Houghton Miflin.

Weiskel, Thomas. 1976. *The Romantic Sublime: Studies in the Structure and Psychology of Transcendence.* Baltimore: The Johns Hopkins University Press.

Welsh, Irvine. 1994 [1993]. *Trainspotting.* London: Minerva.

White, Charles. 1874. *Laughing Gas: A Negro Burlesque Sketch.* New York: De Witt.

Wilde, Oscar. 2000 [1891]. *The Picture of Dorian Gray.* London: Penguin.

Wilding, Michael. 1986. "Weird Melancholy: Inner and Outer Landscapes in Marcus Clarke's Stories." In P. R. Eaden and F. H. Mares, ed., *Mapped But Not Known,* 128–145. Netley, South Australia: Wakefield Press.

Williams, Gertrude. 1946. *Priestess of the Occult: Madame Blavatsky.* New York: Knopf.

Wilson, Peter Lamborn. 1988. *Scandal: Essays in Islamic Heresy.* Brooklyn: Autonomedia.

———1999. *Ploughing the Clouds: The Search for Irish Soma.* San Francisco: City Lights.

Wiltshire, John. 1991. *Samuel Johnson and the Medical World.* Cambridge: Cambridge University Press.

Witkiewicz, Stanislaw Ignacy. 1985. *Insatiability.* Trans. Louis Iribarne. London: Quartet.

———1992 [1932]. *Narcotics.* In *The Witkiewicz Reader,* trans. Daniel Gerould. Evanston, Ill.: Northwestern University Press.

———1996. *Witkacy: Stanislaw Ignacy Witkiewicz in the Museum of Central Pomerania in Slupsk.* Warsaw: Wydawnictwa Artystyczne I Filmowe.

Wöbkemeier, Rita. 1990. *Erzählte Krankheit: Medizinische und Literarische Phantasien um 1800.* Stuttgart: Metzlersche.

Wolfe, Bernard. 1962. *The Magic of Their Singing.* New York: Macfadden.

Wolfe, Tom. 1968. *The Electric Kool-Aid Acid Test.* New York: Farrar, Straus & Giroux.

Woodley, Richard. 1971. *Dealer: Portrait of a Cocaine Merchant.* New York: Holt, Rinehart, and Winston.

Woolf, Virginia. 1967. "On Being Ill." In Woolf, *Collected Essays,* vol. 4, 199–203. London: Hogarth.

Wright, A. J. 1992. "Diffusion of an Innovation: The First Public Demonstrations of General Anesthesia." *Anesthesia History Association Newsletter,* 10 (1): 3–16.

———1993. "Benjamin Paul Blood, Anesthesia's Philosopher-Mystic." In B. R. Fink, L. E. Morris, and C. R. Stephen, ed., *The History of Anaesthesia: Proceedings of the Third International Symposium,* 447–456. Park Ridge, Ill.: Wood Library, Museum of Anesthesiology.

———1995. "Davy Comes to America: Woodhouse, Barton, and the Nitrous Oxide Crossing." *Journal of Clinical Anesthesia,* 7: 347–355.

———1997a. "Humphry Davy's Small Circle of Bristol Friends," Part 1. *Bulletin of Anesthesia History,* 15 (2): 22–24.

————1997b. "Humphry Davy's Small Circle of Bristol Friends," Part 2. *Bulletin of Anesthesia History*, 15 (3): 16–20.

———— 1997c. "Humphry Davy's Small Circle of Bristol Friends," Part 3. *Bulletin of Anesthesia History*, 15 (4): 16–21.

Yarnall, Judith. 1994. *Transformations of Circe*. Urbana: University of Illinois.

Yeats, W. B. 1938. *The Autobiography of William Butler Yeats, Consisting of Reveries over Childhood and Youth, the Trembling of the Veil, and Dramatis Personae*. New York: Macmillan.

Young, George. 1753. *A Treatise on Opium, Founded upon Practical Observations*. London.

Young, James. 1993. *Nico: The End*. New York: Overlook.

Yvorel, Jean-Jacques. 1992. *Les poisons de l'esprit: drogues et drogués au XIXe siècle*. Paris: Quai Voltaire.

Zaehner, R. C. 1957. *Mysticism, Sacred and Profane*. Oxford: Oxford University Press.

Zeltner, Herman. 1954. *Schelling*. Stuttgart: Frommanns.

NOTES

Full citations of works cited in shortened form in the notes appear in the Bibliography. All translations from foreign-language texts listed in the Bibliography are my own unless otherwise indicated.

Prologue

1. De Quincey, 1971, 29.
2. Jünger, 1990, 9.
3. Ronell, 1992.
4. This approach is also taken by Mickel (1969) and Castoldi (1994).
5. I use the word "substance" frequently in this book to define or name drugs. By "substance," I do not intend any particular scientific meaning, nor do I even insist on the absolute materiality of the things named this way. I would, however, like the word to suggest the existence of things autonomous from human construction, things that are believed to be manifest to human beings or materially existent. In other words I would like the word to suggest a nature-culture hybrid, with an emphasis on the natural qualities of the thing. Spinoza used the word "substance" in this way.
6. Berridge and Edwards (1981, 49–61), Yvorel (1992, 31–32), and Morgan (1981, 44–63) all suggest that literary accounts of nineteenth-century drug use are not typical and cannot be regarded as describing the totality of uses of opium in England, France, and the United States at that time.
7. This is also true of Inglis (1975) and the excellent *High Times Encyclopedia of Recreational Drugs* (1978).
8. For example, Lenson (1995) and Plant (1999).
9. For excellent discussion of what a drug is, see Andrew Weil and Winifred Rosen's *From Chocolate to Morphine* (1993).
10. Lewin, 1998, 30.
11. The term "psychedelic" was coined by the LSD researcher Humphrey Osmond in 1956 in a letter to Aldous Huxley. The term "entheogenic" was coined by Jonathan Ott and his colleagues (see Ott, 1993, 15, for a history of the term).

12. See John Strausbaugh and Donald Blaise's *The Drug User* (1991), John Miller and Randall Koral's *White Rabbit* (1995), and Mike Jay's *Artificial Paradises: A Drugs Reader* (2000).

13. Varela, 1999, 7.

14. Gilbert-Lecomte, 1974, vol. 1, 126.

15. Deleuze and Guattari, 1987, 284–286, make a similar point when they say that although drugs are able to liberate the user from certain types of boundaries (by triggering visions, ego loss, and so on), they also simultaneously create new boundaries (through dependence, the possibility of imprisonment, and so on).

16. Szasz, 1974.

17. See Arber, 1986.

18. Hans Peter Duerr's *Dreamtime* (1985) is the most interesting such account. Carlo Ginzburg considers the topic only briefly at the very end of *Ecstasies* (1991), saying that "no form of privation, no substance, no ecstatic technique can, by itself, cause the recurrence of such complex experiences. Against all biological determinism one must emphasize that the key to this codified repetition can only be cultural. Nevertheless, the deliberate use of psychotropic or hallucinogenic substances, while not explaining the followers of the nocturnal goddess, the werewolf and so on, would place them in a not exclusively mythical dimension" (303).

19. Almost all the well-known accounts of drugs and literature focus on the nineteenth and twentieth centuries, such as those by Hayter (1968), Liedekerke (1984), and Mickel (1969). The richest scholarship on broad social relations has also been on the nineteenth and twentieth centuries, notably books by Berridge (1981), Yvorel (1992), Parssinen (1983), and Morgan (1981). Schivelbusch (1992) introduces "the artificial paradises" as a specifically nineteenth-century phenomenon.

1. Addicted to Nothingness

1. Orieux, 1979, 483–485; see also Pomeau (1994), Brandes (1930), and Noyes (1936).

2. Pomeau, 1994, vol. 5, 320.

3. Orieux, 1979, 486.

4. Pomeau, 1994, vol. 5, 321.

5. *Encyclopaedia Britannica*, 15th ed., vol. 29, 526. Noyes (1936, 609) notes, "Many of the tales [of Voltaire's death] are hopelessly conflicting. . . . Not a few of them are unspeakably vile and as false as they are filthy." Besterman (1969) avoids all mention of the opium incident.

6. Chaucer, 1900, vol. 4, 42.

7. Shakespeare, 1957, 65.

8. Shadwell, 1927, ccxxxiii.

9. Dryden, 1958, vol. 1, 284.

10. Tom Brown, "In Obitum Th. Shadwell, pinguis memoriae, 1693," 1730, vol. 4, 93.

11. Johnson, 1963, 273.

12. Cited by Wiltshire, 1991, 67.

13. Johnson, 1952, vol. 3, 131.

14. Boswell, 1957, 1341.

15. See Alexander Pope's *The Dunciad* (1744; 1963, 732–733); William Harrison's "In Praise of Laudanum" (1735); the anonymous "Laudanum" (1735); and Orestes' "A Sonnet to Opium" (1796), in Lonsdale, ed., 1984, 113, 283, 818; and Philip Freneau's "The Blessings of the Poppy," 1907, vol. 3, 114–115.

16. Warton, 1802, vol. 1, 73–74.

17. For example, Montesquieu's *Lettres Persans* (1929, 166–168) and Voltaire's *Zadig: ou, La Destinée* (1962, 78).

18. Chardin, 1927, 244.

19. Tott, 1973, vol. 1, 142–143.

20. Tott, 1973, vol. 1, 143.

21. Raynal, 1776, vol. 1, 184, 279.

22. Cook, 1821, vol. 2, 327.

23. *Encyclopédie,* vol. 11, 509.

24. Sedgwick, 1992, 589.

25. For biographical information on Darwin see King-Hele, 1977; Pearson, 1964; and Hassler, 1973. On Darwin's poetry, see Logan, 1936.

26. Darwin, 1791, vol. 2, 79.

27. Darwin, 1791, vol. 2, 77.

28. Darwin, 1791, vol. 2, 101.

29. See Hassler, 1973, 95–114.

30. Coleridge, 1956, vol. 1, 305.

31. Coleridge, 1956, vol. 1, 216.

32. See Risse, 1988.

33. Brown, 1793, vol. 1, 167.

34. Brown, 1793, vol. 1, 241.

35. Ackerknecht notes that "in the Austrian army, of 600 wounded, 400 died within 21 days, inebriated, that in the Prussian army after Jena the officers died intoxicated by Rhine wine, the ordinary soldiers intoxicated by ordinary spirits" (1973, 81).

36. See Neubauer, 1971, 26; Seefelder, 1987, 142; and Leibbrand, 1956.

37. See Risse, 1988, 60.

38. Jahn, 1994, 75–87. On Romanticism and Naturphilosophie, see Snelders, 1970.

39. Neubauer, 1971, 26. See also Tsouyopoulos, 1988. For further discussion of the Romantics and medicine, see Leibbrand, 1956.

40. Cited by Tsouyopoulos, 1988, 68.

41. Wöbkemeier, 1990, 90–91.

42. See Dischner, 1979, 154, and Zeltner, 1954, 36. Others mention no details of the incident. There is little record of Schelling's medical experimentation.
43. See *Caroline: Briefe aus der Frühromantik,* 1913, 753, and Wöbkemeier, 1990, 91.
44. See Neubauer, 1971, 28–29.
45. Neubauer, 1971, 104.
46. Novalis, 1968, vol. 3, 359.
47. Novalis, 1968, vol. 3, 245.
48. Novalis, 1968, vol. 3, 657.
49. Novalis, 1968, vol. 3, 662.
50. Novalis, 1984, 51.
51. Novalis, 1984, 51.
52. Novalis, 1984, 51.
53. My thanks to Terence McKenna and Erik Davis for introducing me to the concept of gnosticism. For an introduction to gnosticism, see Jonas, 1992, and Davis, 1998, 77–101.
54. Wöbkemeier, 1990, 4.
55. Berridge and Edwards, 1981, 49–61.
56. Palmer and Horowitz, 1982, 47.
57. See Palmer and Horowitz, 1982, 45–93, and Senaha, 1996. Female poets not mentioned in the text who wrote about opium include Coleridge's daughter, Sara Coleridge (1802–1850), "Poppies"; Henrietta O'Neill (1758–1793), "Ode to the Poppy"; Maria Logan, "To Opium" (dates unknown); Charlotte Smith (1749–1806), "Ode to the Poppy"; Lady Caroline Lamb (1785–1828), "Invocation to Sleep"; and Anna Seward (1747–1809), "To the Poppy."
58. Berridge and Edwards, 1981, 21–74.
59. Hayter, 1968, 191.
60. Coleridge, 1956, vol. 3, 476–477.
61. Lefebure, 1974, 65.
62. Booth, 1996, 43.
63. Coleridge, 1956, vol. 1, 394.
64. Coleridge, 1956, vol. 1, 349–350.
65. Coleridge, 1957, vol. 1, 556.
66. Lefebure, 1974, 122–129.
67. Many of Coleridge's philosophical mentors, including Erasmus Darwin, Joseph Priestley, and David Hartley commented in passing on opium. Hartley noted that "a Person who has taken Opium, sees either gay scenes, or ghastly ones, according as the Opium excites pleasant or painful Vibrations in the Stomach" (Hartley, 1791, 383–389).
68. For a review of Coleridge's writings on pain, see Smith, 1972.
69. Coleridge, 1956, vol. 1, 648–649.

70. See Papper, 1995.
71. Coleridge, 1956, vol. 3, 490.
72. Coleridge, 1957, vol. 1, entry 1421.
73. Coleridge, 1957, vol. 1, entry 1426.
74. De Quincey, 1971, 87.
75. De Quincey, 1971, 70.
76. De Quincey, 1971, 71.
77. De Quincey, 1971, 81.
78. De Quincey, 1971, 71.
79. Burroughs, 1992, xi.
80. On De Quincey's ideas about economy, see McDonagh, 1994, 42–65.
81. De Quincey, 1971, 33. The Latin reads: "he deems nothing that is human foreign to him."
82. De Quincey, 1890, vol. 13, 335.
83. De Quincey, 1971, 103.
84. De Quincey, 1890, vol. 13, 345.
85. De Quincey, 1890, vol. 13, 348.
86. Lindop, 1981, 248.
87. Kingsley, 1861, 319–335.
88. The French Romantic poet Alphonse Rabbe, who was known as a long-term opium user, committed suicide via an overdose of the drug in 1829 (Yvorel, 1992, 32–33.) The German poet Heinrich Heine used opiates in his last years for pain relief, and Kupfer suggests that several of his late poems (including, not surprisingly, "Morphine") can be connected to this usage (1996, 151–152).
89. Hayter, 1968, 255.
90. Clarke, 1988, 164. See also Peters, 1991, 303–319.
91. Hoffmann's "Kreisleriana" (1813; trans. 1996) contains his most extended meditation on intoxicant-assisted creativity. But many of Hoffmann's stories, including "The Golden Pot" (1814; trans. 2000), "The Devil's Elixirs" (1816, trans. 1963), and "The Serapion Brotherhood" (1819–1821, trans. 1892), rely on intoxicants as conduits into the worlds of fantasy. The French Romantic writer Etienne Senancour mentions opium as a cure for mysterious sufferings in *Oberman* (1804).
92. See Hayter, 1968, 136–150, for a review of Poe's fictional writings; the important stories are the original version of "Berenice," "Ligeia," "The Fall of the House of Usher," and "A Tale of the Ragged Mountains."
93. Poe, 1992, 681.
94. Gautier, 1897, 453–466.
95. Murger, 1854, 276–277.
96. Cited in Lethève, 1959, 153–154.
97. For changes that Baudelaire made to De Quincey's *Confessions,* see Bieker, 1992.

98. Liedekerke, 1984, 53–54, gives a complete run-down of mentions of drugs and a chronology of Baudelaire's opium addiction. See also Pichois' notes in Baudelaire, 1995, vol. 1, 1360-1361, and Bieker, 1992, 80-144. Pierrot, 1975, 243, lists a number of poems in which he sees opium motifs, including "Le poison," "Le voyage," "Alchemie de la douleur," "Horreur sympathique," "Rêve parisien," "Un hémisphere dans une chevelure," "Les projets," "L'invitation au voyage," "La chambre double."

99. "La chambre double" in Baudelaire, 1975, vol. 1, 280–281.

100. "Les paradis artificiels" in Baudelaire, 1975, vol. 1, 402.

101. Meyers, 1985, 75.

102. Guimbail, 1891, 15.

103. See Liedekerke, 1992. Bachmann and Coppel, 1989, and Yvorel, 1992, also contain much valuable information.

104. Cited by Bachmann and Coppel, 1989, 123.

105. Tailhade, 1907, 21–22.

106. Levinstein, *La morphinomanie,* cited by Liedekerke, 1984, 91.

107. L. de Robert, *L'envers d'une courtisane,* cited by Liedekerke, 1984, 95.

108. De Laforest, 1891, 17.

109. De Laforest, 1891, 14.

110. De Laforest, 1891, 19.

111. De Laforest, 1891, 180–182.

112. De Laforest, 1891, 73.

113. De Laforest, 1891, 128.

114. De Laforest, 1891, 209.

115. De Laforest, 1891, 217.

116. De Laforest, 1891, 257.

117. De Laforest, 1891, 112.

118. De Laforest, 1891, 260.

119. De Laforest, 1891, i.

120. On Lombroso and Nordau, see Spackman, 1989, 1–32.

121. Nordau, 1900, 15.

122. Guimbail, 1891, 38.

123. Rodet, 1897, 19–20.

124. Tailhade, 1914, 268.

125. Liedekerke, 1984, 125.

126. Tailhade, 1907, 15.

127. Spackman, 1989, 5.

128. Parssinen, 1983, 58, nn. 54–55.

129. Wilde, 2000, 176.

130. Courtwright, 1982, 68.

131. See Courtwright, 1982, 62–86, for a review of opium smoking in America.

132. Kipling, "The Gate of the Hundred Sorrows" in *Plain Tales from the Hills* (1888, 297–307); Loti, *Les derniers jours de Pékin* (1901); Segalen, *Lettres de Chine;* Weale, *The Forbidden Boundary* (1908); Hearn, "Opium and Morphia," and "Opium Dens" (1876–1877; reprinted in Hearn, 1939).

133. Liedekerke, 1984, 169.

134. Pierre Custot's *Midship* (1901) is an exposé of the ravages of opium in the French navy, and tells the story of a young sailor who finally throws himself overboard because he is suffering from withdrawal. See also Daniel Borys' *Le royaume de l'oubli* (1902).

135. *L'art indochinois* (1894), *L'Annam sanglant* (1898), *Le maître des sentences* (1899), and *Le cinquième Bonheur* (1911) (*Indochinese Art, Bloody Annam, The Sentence Master,* and *The Fifth Happiness*).

136. Pouvoirville, 1899, 55.

137. Pouvoirville, 1908, 22.

138. Pouvoirville, 1908, 23.

139. Pouvoirville, 1908, 3.

140. Pouvoirville, 1908, 3.

141. Farrère, 1929, 201.

142. Farrère, 1929, 145–146.

143. Greene also describes his opium experiences in his autobiography, *Ways of Escape.*

144. Farrère, 1929, 188.

145. Farrère, 1929, 173.

146. Farrère, 1929, 189.

147. Liedekerke, 1984, 145–176, is the best source on this period.

148. Csáth, 1983, 104.

149. Terry and Pellens, 1928, 62.

150. Terry and Pellens, 1928, 68.

151. Marks, 1968, 20.

152. Marks, 1968, 22.

153. Lewin, 1998, 49.

154. Lewin, 1998, 49.

155. Sutin, 2000, 294–297.

156. Kohn, 1992, 111.

157. See Kohn, 1992, for a full account.

158. Rohmer, 1983, 342.

159. Rohmer, 1983, 358.

160. Rohmer, 1983, 370.

161. Brau, 1968, 294, and Balakian, 1974.

162. Breton, 1972, 35–36.

163. Breton, *La Révolution Surréaliste,* 1 (December 1924): 1.

164. Brandon, 1999, 207.

165. Artaud, 1976, 100–101.

166. Artaud, 1976, 102.

167. Artaud, 1976, 339.

168. Artaud, 1976, 339.

169. See Derrida's essays on Artaud in *Writing and Difference* (1978) on this point.

170. Artaud, 1940, 309.

171. For a first-hand account of what it was like to score narcotics for Artaud, see Jacques Prevel's *En compagnie d'Antonin Artaud* (1994).

172. Gilbert-Lecomte, 1974, vol. 1, 120.

173. Gilbert-Lecomte, 1974, vol. 1, 126.

174. Steegmuller, 1970, 324.

175. Ebin, 1961, 143.

176. See Margaret Crosland's introduction to *Opium*.

177. Cocteau, 1990, 22.

178. Cocteau, 1990, 36.

179. Cocteau, 1990, 18.

180. Drieu la Rochelle, 1922, 113–114.

181. Drieu la Rochelle, 1959, 69.

182. See also Hal Ellison's *The Golden Spike* (1952) and Clarence Cooper's *The Scene* (1960).

183. Courtwright, 1982, 133–136.

184. Ginsberg, 1984, 126.

185. The most prolific poetic proponent of the Beat junkie ethos was the San Francisco–based Philip Lamantia, who wrote a series of books, *Ekstasis* (1959), *Narcotica* (1959), and *Destroyed Works* (1962), filled with Artaud- and drug-inspired world-denouncing poems. *Cain's Book* (1963), by the Scottish writer Alexander Trocchi, is equal to *Junkie* in its description of New York Beat narcotic addiction.

186. See Berridge, 1990, 1042–1044, for further information concerning Dent.

187. James Grauerholz, personal communication.

188. Burroughs, 1977, 59.

189. See Pepper, 1994, 84–85.

190. Ted Morgan, 1990, 261–262.

191. Burroughs, 1977, 58.

192. Burroughs, 1964, 12.

193. See Palmer and Horowitz, 1982.

194. Callard, 1992, 31.

195. Callard, 1992, 149.

196. Cited in Callard, 1992, 47.

197. Kavan, 1970, 101.

198. Kavan, 1970, 153.

199. Kavan, 1970, 101.

200. Examples include: in Australia, Kevin Mackey's *The Cure: Recollections of an Addict* (1970); in Scotland, Irvine Welsh's *Trainspotting* (1993); in Berlin, Christiane F.'s *Wir Kinder vom Bahnhof Zoo* (1981); in Detroit, Donald Goines's *Dopefiend* (1971); and in New York, Alexander Trocchi's *Cain's Book* (1963), Piri Thomas' *Down These Mean Streets* (1967), Jim Carroll's *The Basketball Diaries* (1978), Stewart Meyer's *The Lotus Crew* (1984), Linda Yablonsky's *The Story of Junk* (1997), and Ann Marlowe's *How to Stop Time* (1999).

201. Burroughs, 1992, xvi.

202. Marlowe, 1999, 141–142.

203. Cooper, 1998, 22.

204. Burroughs, 1970, 136.

2. The Voice of the Blood

1. Davy, 1839, vol. 3, 289–290.

2. In my discussion of the transcendental, I have drawn on Roy, 2001, as well as Weiskel, 1976, and Levinas, 1996.

3. My thanks to A. J. Wright for pointing out to me these connections. See Wright, 1995, 1997a–c.

4. Cited by Wright, 1995, 348.

5. Davy, 1839, vol. 3, 270.

6. Southey, 1850, vol. 2, 21–22.

7. Southey in Davy, 1839, vol. 3, 300–301.

8. Cottle, 1847, 201.

9. Cottle, 1847, 203.

10. Coleridge, 1969, vol. 14, part I, 269.

11. Coleridge, 1969, vol. 14, part I, 337.

12. Coleridge, 1956, vol. 2, 378.

13. Coleridge, 1956, vol. 2, 727.

14. Coleridge, 1956, vol. 2, 727.

15. Kant, in his *Anthropology, from a Pragmatic Point of View* (1798), comments regarding intoxicants that "some of these are poisons that weaken the vital force (certain fungi, Porsch, wild hogweed, the Chica of the Peruvians, the Ava of the South Sea Indians, opium), while others strengthen it or at least intensify our feeling of it (fermented beverages, wines, and beer, or at least the spirits extracted from them); but all of them are contrary to nature and artificial. A man is said to be drunk or intoxicated if he takes these to such excess that he is temporarily incapable of ordering his sense representations by laws of experience" (1974, 46). Schelling's interest in opium was discussed in Chapter 1.

16. Lefebure and Gravil, 1990, 96.
17. *Doctor Syntax in Paris,* 1820, 314.
18. Schoenbein, 1842, 387–388, translated in Smith, 1982, 35.
19. Reprinted in Melechi, 1998, 16.
20. Thomas, 1814.
21. White, 1874.
22. Cited and translated in Smith, 1982, 35.
23. See Wright, 1995.
24. Barton in Melechi, 1998, 17.
25. Horace Wells developed the idea of dental anesthesia after witnessing a druggist's assistant damaging his shin without being aware of the pain; Crawford Long, who experimented with ether on himself, noticed that even when his body was covered with bruises, he felt no pain (see Rusham, 1996, 12–13).
26. Warren, cited by Wright, 1992, 7.
27. Holmes, 1883, 265.
28. Thoreau, 1906, vol. 8, 194.
29. Fuller, 1856, 202–203.
30. Ripley, 1857, vol. 1, 507.
31. Emerson, 1946, 255–257.
32. See Warner, 1997, 32–49, for a review of Emerson on intoxication.
33. Ludlow, 1979, 270–271.
34. Cited by Yvorel, 1992, 22.
35. Cited by Yvorel, 1992, 22.
36. Lewin, 1998, 200. T. S. Eliot's wife, Vivienne, was apparently an ether user for a period of time. Virginia Woolf and others reported that the Eliots' house smelled like a hospital ward. See Fathman, 1991.
37. Cited by Yvorel, 1992, 23.
38. Pernick, 1985, 45–48.
39. Turnbull, 1878, 201.
40. Dinnick, 1996, 129.
41. Connell, 1968, 90.
42. Connell, 1968, 88.
43. Mabin, 1992, 69–77.
44. Proust, 1987, vol. 2, 385–386. See also Proust, 1988, vol. 3, 691–692, in which Bergotte speaks rhapsodically about the delights of exploring new kinds of sleep medication—before he dies from an overdose of one such medicine. The topic of sedatives, sleep, and literature requires much fuller discussion than I can give here, but it would certainly include Friedrich Nietzsche's use of chloral hydrate and Virginia Woolf's essay "On Being Ill," which includes lines in praise of chloral hydrate's sleep-inducing powers.

45. Maupassant, 1995, 73.

46. Jünger, 1990, 168.

47. Lorrain, 1975, 106.

48. Lorrain, 1975, 106.

49. Wright, 1993, 448; Marks, 1953, 3.

50. Blood, 1874, 33–34.

51. Blood, 1874, 35.

52. Blood, 1920, 211.

53. Blood, 1920, 206–207.

54. Cited in Blood, 1920, 219.

55. Blood, 1920, 224.

56. Marks, 1953, 1.

57. James, 1982, 397.

58. James, 1982, 388.

59. James, 1917, 294.

60. James, 1917, 295.

61. James, 1917, 296.

62. Holmes, 1883, 283–284.

63. James, 1917, 298.

64. James, 1917, 297.

65. Boren, 1983, 5–18.

66. In *The Varieties of Religious Experience,* James gives a description of the experiences of the English poet J. A. Symonds (1982, 390–393). See also Smith, 1972, 22–78.

67. Smith, 1972, 38, has the text of the letter and commentary.

68. Yvorel, 1992, 152.

69. Yvorel, 1992, 152.

70. For a reconstruction of Gurdjieff's talks about drugs, see *Secret Talks with Mr. G.,* 1978, 9–15.

71. Ouspensky, 1949, 8–9.

72. Webb, 1980, 112.

73. Ouspensky, 1969, 274–304.

74. Daumal, 1972, vol. 1, 53.

75. Milosz, in his "Letter to Storge" (1944, vol. 7), related a mystic experience that he had in 1914, without use of pharmaceuticals, in which he had a vision of infinity. Much of Daumal's language in his essays on the carbon tetrachloride experiments is identical to Milosz's.

76. Daumal, 1972, vol. 2, 114.

77. Daumal, 1972, vol. 2, 117.

78. Daumal, 1972, vol. 2, 115–116.

79. Daumal, 1972, vol. 1, 54.

80. Jünger, 1990, 169–179.

81. Brau, 1968, 244.

82. Moore and Altounian, 1978, 54.

83. Lilly, 1978, 163.

84. Lilly, 1978, 171.

85. Lilly, 1978, 173.

86. Lilly, 1978, 182.

87. Henri Bergson, in his essay on laughter (1900), also suggested that the perception of mechanical qualities in human actions is the source of laughter.

3. The Time of the Assassins

1. Anslinger's testimony is cited by Grinspoon, 1971, 21–22.

2. Grinspoon, 1971, 227–228.

3. Lenson, 1995, 103.

4. The paper "Mémoire sur la dynastie des Assassins et sur l'origine de leur nom" was read at a meeting of the Académie des Inscriptions et Belles-Lettres on July 7, 1809. A summary of the paper was published in the *Moniteur,* July 29, 1809. The full text was published in the *Mémoires de l'Académie des Inscriptions et Belles-Lettres* in 1818 (see Yvorel, 1992, 256, and Pichois in Baudelaire, 1975, vol. 1, 1374–1375). Sacy's work was popularized by the German Orientalist Joseph von Hammer, whose book *Geschichte des Assassins* (1818) was translated into French (1833) and English (1835). Von Hammer himself says absolutely nothing about hashish, though he does publish Sacy's memoir on the Assassins as a note.

5. For a full history see von Hammer (1818), Lewis (1968), and others.

6. Sacy, quoted in von Hammer, 1835, 233.

7. Mickel, 1969, 49–56.

8. Rosenthal, 1971, 21–22; Wilson, 1988, 209.

9. Louis Lewin cites the Abbott of Lubeck from the thirteenth century as using the word "hemp" when discussing Sabbah's magic potion, but the Latin original makes no mention of "hemp": "et tunc poculos eos quodam, quo in ecstasin vel amentiam rapiantur, inebriat, et eis magicis suis quaedam somnia phantastica, gaudiis et deliciis, imo nugis plena, ostendit" ("And then he gets them drunk with a certain beverage [poculo quodam] by which they are seized with ecstasy or mindlessness and shows them, through his magic, fantastic dreams, full of joys and delights, however worthless"). Lewin, 1998, 278.

10. See the *Indian Hemp Drugs Commission Report* (1894), vol. 1, 159–166, vol. 3, 246–254.

11. Herodotus, 1972, 295.

12. See Franz Rosenthal's prudish but erudite study *The Herb: Hashish versus Me-*

dieval Islam (1971) and Peter Lamborn Wilson's more sympathetic account in *Scandal* (1988).

13. Wilson, 1988, 200.

14. "Attributed to the thirteenth-century Spaniard Ibn Khamis or the twelfth century Syro-Egyptian Ibn al-A'ma" by Wilson, 1988, 201.

15. Thanks to Peter Lamborn Wilson for pointing me in the direction of the cultic use of cannabis.

16. According to Rosenthal (1971, 94), neither of the stories mentioned here belongs to the mainstream tradition of the *Arabian Nights:* the tale of the fisherman is found only in late manuscript versions.

17. Burton, 1900, vol. 3, 93.

18. I have quoted from a translation from the Arabic into French by J. C. V. Mardrus, reprinted in Kimmens, 1977, 32–36. It should be noted that this version is quite different, both in plot and in language, from Burton's translation of the story "The Tale of the Kazi and the Bhang-Eater" in Burton, 1900, vol. 15, 189–202.

19. *High Times Encyclopedia of Recreational Drugs,* 1978, 126.

20. See, for example, Andrews and Vinkenoog, 1967, 26–34; Grinspoon, 1971, 397–398; and Galland, 1991, 20.

21. Bakhtin, 1984, 186.

22. See Camporesi, 1989, on psychoactive substances in everyday Renaissance life. See also Chardin, 1927, 245–247, on Persian use of hemp in the seventeenth century.

23. The manuscript was first published in the *Zürcher Wochenzeitung,* and then reprinted in *Die Zeit,* no. 4, January 21, 1994, 59, signed "Johann Wolfgang Constantin Seibt." The manuscript was apparently found among some antiques that Alexander Schalck-Golodkowski had bought in Switzerland in 1993.

24. Schiller was believed to keep a box of apples under his writing desk so that the smell of them would stimulate him while he worked. Thomas Carlyle, in his *Life of Schiller,* describes Schiller's work habits in Jena, and speaks of "the pernicious expedient of stimulants" that Schiller had recourse to at night (1992, 111).

25. Just before this book was completed, an article by Sandra Nowak (2001) entitled "Much Rausch about Nothing" appeared on a German website, and there Constantin Seibt, a former editor of the *Wochenzeitung,* which first published the article, claimed responsibility for the article. Seibt commented, "Germans still stand to attention in front of education—even if they're as bored by it as the Swiss. Every theory that comes along automatically draws forth its own set of proofs as to its truth—the way an autobahn draws cars in."

26. Coleridge, 1956, vol. 1, 933.

27. Banks was not alone in believing that hashish was nepenthes. Mordecai Cooke (1997, 160) and E. W. Lane, editor of the *Thousand and One Nights,* among others

made similar speculations later in the nineteenth century, though there is little evidence to back them up. See Abel, 1980, 30. Julien-Joseph Virey, the first French author to talk about hashish (1803) also proposed this theory.

28. Coleridge, 1956, vol. 2, 934.

29. Coleridge, 1998, vol. 4, 84–85.

30. Abel, 1980, 163.

31. Pierrot, 1975, 83.

32. Pierrot, 1975, 88.

33. Moreau de Tours, 1980, 29, 37.

34. Moreau de Tours, 1980, 200.

35. See Jay, 2000, 103–104.

36. Esquiros, 1845, 324.

37. Brierre de Boismont, 1845, 205–206.

38. Baudelaire, 1975, vol. 1, 397.

39. Although medical research on opium predates Moreau's work by centuries, none of it was specifically psychological or psychiatric in its orientation.

40. Balzac apparently took dawamesk at the club, telling Mme. Hanska in a letter dated Dec. 23, 1845: "I resisted the hashish, that is, I did not experience any of the phenomena they talk of. My brain is so solid that it needed perhaps a stronger dose. Nevertheless I did hear celestial voices and saw divine pictures; after which I descended Lauzun's staircase, during twenty years. I saw gildings and paintings in a salon of fairy-like splendor. But this morning, since waking, I am half asleep, and without strength or will" (Balzac, 1900, 609).

41. See Pichois, Kopp, and Huyghe, 1955.

42. Quoted in Baudelaire, 1964, 10.

43. For a full review of all of Gautier's references to drugs see Mickel, 1969, 95–114.

44. Gautier, 1897, 467–468.

45. Gautier, 1897, 478.

46. Dumas, 1956, 335.

47. See Sieburth, 1999, 4–5; Bieker, 1992, 54–59.

48. See Jeanneret, 1980.

49. Nerval, 1999, 42.

50. Lallemand, 1977, 118.

51. Lallemand, 1977, 120.

52. First published in *Le Messager de l'Assemblée*, March 7–12, 1851.

53. Baudelaire, 1975, vol. 1, 397.

54. Baudelaire, 1975, vol. 1, 396.

55. An essay version, "De l'idéal artificiel—le haschisch" ("On the Artificial Ideal—Hashish"), also known as "Le poëme du haschisch," was first published in the *Revue Contemporaine et Atheneum Français*, September 30, 1858.

56. Benjamin, 1994, 598.
57. Jünger, 1973, 368.
58. Benjamin, 1999, 276.
59. Flaubert, 1973, vol. 3, 93–94.
60. On *La spirale,* see Dimoff, 1948; Bieker, 1992, 182–225; and Flaubert, 1988.
61. Cited in Schivelbusch, 1992, 204.
62. See Peschel, 1974.
63. Rimbaud, 1954, 270.
64. Rimbaud, 1954, 184–185.
65. Delahaye, 1925, 150.
66. Rudenko, 1970.
67. Williams, 1946, 36.
68. Kimmens, 1977, 247.
69. Guaita, 1916, 371.
70. Yeats, 1938, 295–296.
71. See Berridge, 1988, for further details.
72. Blackwood, 1909, 23.
73. Quoted in Melechi, 1998, 58.
74. Crowley, 1909, 56.
75. Quoted in Sutin, 2000, 174.
76. Quoted in Sutin, 2000, 177.
77. Crowley, 1909, 42–43.
78. Michaux, 1961, 93.
79. Benjamin, 1972, 69–70 (protocol 2).
80. Benjamin appears to have developed the idea of aura in the 1930s, after his experiments with hashish. The term is absent, for example, from his essay on Proust of 1929, but appears in his discussion of Proust in his 1939 essay on Baudelaire.
81. For information on Benjamin and drugs, I am indebted to Scott Thompson's research and writings on the subject, which can be found on his website: <http://www.wbenjamin.org/walterbenjamin.html>.
82. Kupfer, 1996, 180. For example, in protocol 7, Benjamin takes a Eukodol capsule (a form of morphine) after taking the hashish, while in protocol 5, he watches while his colleagues shoot morphine, refusing to join them, saying that he has a fear of syringes.
83. Benjamin, 1994, 323.
84. Benjamin, 1994, 396.
85. Benjamin's translators usually translate "Rausch" as "trance," but it would be better translated as "intoxication," or "high," even though it has specific qualities not captured by these words—"rush," "blasted," and similar words also being relevant. See Gelpke, 1966, for a discussion of the word.

86. Benjamin, 1978, 142.

87. Benjamin, 1978, 144–145.

88. Benjamin, 1978, 177–192.

89. Benjamin, 1978, 179.

90. Benjamin, 1978, 190.

91. Thompson, n.d.

92. See the letters to Scholem in Benjamin, 1994, 321 and 396.

93. Taylor, 1855, 141–142.

94. Ludlow, 1979, 17.

95. *Putnam's,* September 1856.

96. Grinspoon, 1971, 101–102.

97. See Ronell, 1992, 29.

98. Dulchinos, 1998, 87.

99. "Perilous Play" (1869), reprinted in Kimmens, 1977, 217–232. See also H. H. Kane, "A Hashish-House in New York" (1883).

100. Equally interesting is the Poe-like tale of the Australian outback "Holiday Peak" (1873), with its dreamlike shifting scenes and opium-smoking Chinaman. See Wilding, 1986, for further details.

101. Abel, 1980, 222–223.

102. See Morgan, 1981; Sloman, 1979; and McWilliams, 1990.

103. Anslinger and Oursler, 1961, 37.

104. Anslinger and Oursler, 1961, 37–38.

105. See Sloman, 1979, 110.

106. See Sloman, 1979. 166–7.

107. Pulp fiction books involving marijuana published in America in mid-century in-clude: William Irish's *Marihuana* (1941), David Dodge's *It Ain't Hay* (1946), Thurston Scott's *I'll Get Mine* (1951), Steve Harragan's *Dope Doll* (1952), Joseph Shallit's *Kiss the Killer* (1952), James Hadley Chase's *The Marijuana Mob* (1952), and Floyd Shaw's *Devil's Daughter* (1954).

108. Scott, 1952, 59.

109. Chase, 1952, 6–9.

110. Chase, 1952, 100.

111. Reprinted in Ebin, 1961, 96.

112. Grinspoon, 1971, 15.

113. Sloman, 1979, 178–179.

114. Sloman, 1979, 172.

115. Sloman, 1979, 177.

116. Ginsberg, 1966, 231.

117. Pamphlet cited in Stafford, 1992, 207.

118. Fiedler, 1969; *New York Times,* May 1, 1970.

119. On pot smoking in bohemia, see Bernard Wolfe's *Magic of Their Singing* (1962) and Jon Parker's *Light Up* (1966). For pot-smoking "erotica" and "studies of sexual behavior under the influence of pot," see George Bailey's *Sex, Pot, and Acid* (1968), Barbara Lewis' *Sexual Power of Marijuana* (1970), James Simpson's *Pot and Pleasure* (1972), Rosemary Santini's *Happy Hookah* (1973), and Michael Dunne's *Sex on Grass* (1974).

120. See Henry de Monfried's *Hashish: A Smuggler's Tale* (1935), Edwin Corley's *Acapulco Gold* (1972), Jerry Kamstra's *Weed: Adventures of a Dope Smuggler* (1974), Jack Curtis' *Eagles over Big Sur* (1981), T. C. Boyle's *Budding Prospects: A Pastoral* (1984), Steve Chapple's *Outlaws in Babylon* (1984), Ray Reed's *Mendocino Sinsemilla* (1989), Howard Marks's *Mr. Nice* (1997), and Kim Wozencraft's *The Catch* (1998).

121. See also Mel Frank's *Marijuana Grower's Insider's Guide* (1988) and Ed Rosenthal's *Marijuana Question? Ask Ed* (1989).

122. See Krassner, ed., 1999.

123. See Bowles, 1993, 63, for the recipe.

124. Caponi, 1994, 135.

125. Green, 1991, 102.

126. Burroughs quoted in Andrews and Vinkenoog, 1967, 207.

127. "Kif," according to Bowles, meant both the marijuana plant and the small leaves of the plant, ground up into a powder for smoking (1967, 112).

128. Sawyer-Laucanno, 1989, 360.

129. Green, 1991, 153.

130. Benjamin, 1972, 67 (protocol 1).

131. According to Grinspoon (1971, 42) Wood himself lost consciousness after taking cannabinol while preparing zinc ethyl and nearly died.

132. Abel, 1980, 203.

133. "In the nineteenth century their interest [that of 'the peoples of Europe'!] was raised to a high pitch because of the fictional reports of the smoking of hashish given by the romanticists of that period. These individuals, who had the power of the pen, experimentally indulged in the smoking of hashish, and described in an expansive, subjective manner the effects the drug had upon them. A review of the fanciful literature reveals that in most instances these writings referred to the authors' experiences with toxic doses. Summed up, the conclusions were that hashish could cause psychotic episodes and even death and that prolonged use would result in physical and mental deterioration. The exalted position held by these romanticists tended to influence the Europeans to accept their conclusions as scientific monographs on the subject of hashish, so that the smoking of hashish did not become popular with them." *The La Guardia Commission*, in Solomon, ed., 1966, 285.

134. The two most famous cases, Baudelaire's *Fleurs du mal* in Paris and Burroughs'

Naked Lunch in Massachusetts (1965), turned on complicated definitions of obscenity in which sex, drugs, and violence are all involved, as did the banning in London in 1967 of *Last Exit to Brooklyn*, by Hubert Selby, Jr. The banning of Alexander Trocchi's *Cain's Book* in London (1964) appears to have been exclusively due to its descriptions of drug use; in his decision, Lord Chief Justice Parker commented: "the book, highlighting as it were the favorable effects of drug taking, so far from condemning it, advocates it and . . . there is a real danger that those into whose hands the book comes might be tempted, at any rate, to experiment with drugs and get the favorable sensations highlighted by the book" (Sutherland, 1982, 46).

4. Induced Life

1. Weil and Rosen, 1993, 36.
2. De Quincey, 1971, 77.
3. Heidegger, 1993, 312.
4. Deleuze and Guattari, 1987, 282.
5. Ukers, 1948, 15–16.
6. Ukers, 1948, 22–23.
7. Ukers, 1948, 19.
8. Hattox, 1988.
9. Smith in Goodman, ed., 1995, 151–156.
10. Steele in *The Tatler* (1709), vol. 1, no. 1.
11. Ukers, 1948, 71–73.
12. Schivelbusch, 1992, 57–59.
13. Allen, 1999, 174.
14. See Ukers, 1948, 232–253.
15. Pope, 1963, 230.
16. Michelet, 1877, vol. 17, 171–173.
17. Brillat-Savarin, 1986, 107.
18. Balzac, 1992, 23.
19. Balzac, 1992, 39.
20. Balzac, 1992, 44.
21. The sexual resonance contained in the image was hardly accidental. Balzac believed that the energy of the body was finite and that a whole economics of the body was involved in any expenditure of energy: "Sperm for him was an emission of pure cerebral substance, a sort of filtering out and loss, through the penis, of a work of art. And after some misdemeanour or other, when he had neglected to apply his theory, he turned up at the home of Latouche, crying 'I lost a book this morning!'" (cited by Robb 1994, 179).
22. Virilio, 1983, 31.

23. Pritchett, 1973, iii; Lawton, 1910, 75.

24. Robb, 1994, 401.

25. Quoted in Mortimer, 1974, 26.

26. Reprinted in Andrews and Solomon, 1975, 41.

27. Reprinted in Andrews and Solomon, 1975, 39.

28. Cited in Bachmann and Coppel, 1989, 116.

29. In "Provoziertes Leben," Benn claims that the Tibetans also measure time by cups of tea and their effects (1987, 144).

30. Bachmann and Coppel, 1989, 102.

31. Doyle, 1981, 89–90.

32. Ashley, 1975, 40, citing Dr. Myron Schultz, "The 'Strange Case' of Robert Louis Stevenson," *Journal of the American Medical Association,* 216 (1971): 90–94.

33. Freud, 1974, 164.

34. Cited in Liedekerke, 1984, 250.

35. Cited in Liedekerke, 1984, 31.

36. Freud, 1974, 10–11.

37. Vom Scheidt, 1973, 51–63.

38. Freud, 1974, 165.

39. Freud, 1974, 161.

40. Freud, 1974, 205.

41. Halsted, 1885, 294.

42. Graziano, 1983, 12.

43. See especially Kupfer, 1996, 163–166, on mescaline and colors in Trakl's poetry.

44. Graziano, 1983, 15.

45. Crowley, 1995, 47–49.

46. Maier, 1987, 49.

47. Maier, 1926, 138.

48. On Nabokov and *Novel with Cocaine,* see Field, 1987, 135–136. In his introduction to a 1999 edition of the English translation of the book, Will Self suggests the book may be a hoax, written in the second half of the twentieth century in the West (xvi). He points to a series of possible anachronisms in Ageyev's descriptions of cocaine use, but a Russian edition of the text published in Paris in the 1930s certainly exists (Michael Heim, personal communication).

49. Marinetti, 1921, no page number.

50. Reprinted in Viazzi, 1978, 461.

51. Jünger, 1973, 288–289.

52. For Crevel, see *La mort difficile* (1926) and *Etes-vous fous?* (1929); for Desnos, see the poem "L'ode a Coco" (1919/1953) and a gloomy novel, *Le vin est tiré* (1943).

53. Brau, 1968, 293.

54. Reviewed in Kupfer, 1996, 159–161.

55. Benn, 1986, 45.

56. Benn, 1987, 151.

57. Benn, 1987, 145.

58. Benn, 1987, 145.

59. Benn, 1987, 151.

60. *Current Literature*, 1910, 633.

61. Pitigrilli, 1982, 46.

62. Pitigrilli, 1982, 95.

63. Pitigrilli, 1982, 169.

64. Pitigrilli, 1982, 143.

65. Virilio, 1986, 75–95.

66. Pitigrilli, 1982, 173.

67. Virilio, 1983, 33.

68. See, for example, René Schwaeblé's *La coco à Montmartre* (1920), John Rhode's *A.S.F.: The Story of a Great Conspiracy* (1924), and Dorothy Sayers' *Murder Must Advertise* (1934).

69. Desnos, 1953, 29–30.

70. Grinspoon, 1975, 18.

71. Grinspoon, 1975, 19.

72. Jünger, 1973, 267.

73. Charters, 1973, 59–63.

74. Holmes, 1967, 78–79.

75. Charters, 1973, 194.

76. Kerouac, 1976, 6.

77. Kerouac, 1976, 205.

78. Kerouac, 1976, 206.

79. Kerouac, 1976, 208.

80. Kerouac, 1976, 208.

81. All the quotes in this paragraph are from "Essentials of Spontaneous Prose," in Kerouac, 1995, 484–486.

82. "Ginsberg Talks about Speed" in Ginsberg, 2000, 107–108.

83. Portables appeared in 1909 and electric typewriters in 1920.

84. Cohen-Solal, 1987, 372–373.

85. Sontag in Palmer and Horowitz, 1982, 283.

86. Terry Southern's short story "Blood of a Wig" (in Southern, 1967) has an excellent description of an amphetamine-triggered transition from productive work to psychosis.

87. Burroughs Jr., 1993, 146.

88. McNeil and McCain, 1946, 13–14. See also Taylor Mead's *On Amphetamine and in Europe* (1968) and Harvey Cohen's *Amphetamine Manifesto* (1972).

89. Other "oral histories" and "as told to" books in which amphetamine plays a role include Victor Bockris and Gerard Malanga's *Uptight: The Velvet Underground Story* (1983) and Legs McNeil and Gillian McCain's *Please Kill Me* (1996).

90. Burchill and Parsons, 1978, 78.

91. DeRogatis, 2000, 37-38, 235-236.

92. Bangs, 1987, 154-155.

93. Bangs, 1987, 199.

94. Poly-drug use is a feature of speed and to a lesser extent cocaine use, most famously with the speedball—a mixture of heroin and cocaine.

95. Dick, 1991, 234.

96. Gibson, 1984, 7-8.

97. Derrida, 1989, 205.

98. Gibson, 1984, 6.

99. Stephenson, 1993, 200.

100. Malcom X, 1992, 156.

101. Iceberg Slim, 1969, 11.

102. Iceberg Slim, 1969, 219.

103. Iceberg Slim, 1969, 132.

104. For further accounts of smuggling cocaine between Colombia and the United States, see Charles Nicholl's *The Fruit Palace* (1985) and Bruce Porter's *Blow* (1993).

105. Sabbag, 1990, xiii.

106. Smart, 1985, 105-106.

107. Stringer, 1998, 14-15.

108. Burroughs Jr., 1993, 168.

5. The Imaginal Realms

1. Milton, 1980, 54.

2. Milton, 1980, 55.

3. Milton, 1980, 71.

4. Milton, 1980, 67.

5. Milton, 1980, 71.

6. Milton, 1980, 320.

7. Milton, 1980, 322.

8. Milton, 1980, 323.

9. Milton, 1980, 364.

10. Dodoens, 1595, 587.

11. Otten, 1970, 361-372. This is the same tree that Richard Rudgley hypothesizes to be the source of the sacred beverages the haoma of the Zend-Avesta and the soma of the Vedas, owing to the fact that the tree contains the alkaloid harmaline—also

found in ayahuasca—and to its geographical distribution on the Iranian plateau and the Central Asian steppes (1995, 70).

12. The Elizabethan herbals that Otten reviews say little of psychoactivity, and Otten interprets the literal references to eye-cleansing properties in the herbals as being allegorized by a series of authors from Heraclitus through the neo-Platonists (1970, 368) to a new meaning of "insight." We know that "rue" is spoken of often in Shakespeare, as a medicinal herb (see Hoeniger, 1992, 250). According to Otten, the mythological impact of Michael's other drug, euphrasy, "is nonexistent, its medicinal use quite specific"—it was made into a tonic for the eyes (1970, 368).

13. Studies have been made of the identity of some of these substances. For nectar and ambrosia, see Onians, 1954, 292–299. O'Brien-Moore discusses the use of hellebore to treat madness in Greece and Rome (1924, 30–47).

14. See Davis, 1998, for a key discussion of the imaginal as it relates to technologies.

15. See Wasson, Hofmann, and Ruck, 1978.

16. Spenser, 1912, 139.

17. Sahagún, 1963, vol. 12 (book 11), 129.

18. Sahagún, 1961, vol. 11 (book 10), 173.

19. Cited and translated by Ott, 1993, 84.

20. See Stewart, 1987, 17–45, and Ott, 1993, 82–85, for reviews of Spanish, Mexican, and American accounts of Meso-American peyote use prior to the twentieth century.

21. Flaherty, 1992, 59–66.

22. Quoted in Flaherty, 1992, 54.

23. See Jones and Gladstone, 1998, 76.

24. Cooke, 1997, 257.

25. Carroll, 1971, 17.

26. See, for example, Eleanor Cameron's *Stowaway to the Mushroom Planet* (1956) and Steven Cerio's *ABC Book: A Drug Primer* (1998).

27. McKenna, 1991, discusses further examples of psychedelic fantasy, including H. G. Wells's story "The Purple Pileus" and a curious anonymously published 1915 story called "Monsieur Meets the Mushrooms."

28. Lloyd, 1978, 253.

29. Lloyd, 1978, 212.

30. Lloyd, 1978, 276.

31. Villavicencio, 1858, and Spruce, 1873 and 1908.

32. See Stewart, 1987, for a full account of the history of the peyote religion. An influential Native American literary account of peyote use in an apparently fictional storefront peyote church in Los Angeles can be found in Momaday, 1968, 109–114.

33. Mooney, 1896.

34. Lumholtz, 1902, vol. 1, 358.

35. Lumholtz, 1902, vol. 1, 375.

36. See Briggs, 1887, and Mitchell, 1896.

37. Grosskurth, 1980, 166.

38. Ellis, 1975, 178–179.

39. Ellis, 1975, 180, 184–185.

40. Foster, 1997, 178.

41. Ellis, 1975, 182.

42. Ellis went on to discuss his research on peyote in *The World of Dreams* (1911, 27–28).

43. Ellis, 1975, 187.

44. Luhan, 1936, 265–279. See also Van Vechten, 1922, 210–212.

45. Luhan, 1936, 275.

46. Cited by Stewart, 1987, 237.

47. See Ott, 1993, 106, on the various names and spellings given to peyote and mescaline over the years.

48. *La plante qui fait les yeux émerveilles—le peyotl (The Plant Which Fills the Eyes with Wonder*, 1927), and *Les plantes divinatoires (Divinatory Plants*, 1927).

49. Lewin, 1998, 77.

50. Klüver, 1966, 16.

51. Klüver, 1966, 18.

52. Sartre, 1940, 201–202.

53. Beauvoir, 1992, 169.

54. Merleau-Ponty, 1945, 385–397.

55. For a recent phenomenological study of psychedelics (and critique of phenomenology), see Flynt, 1992.

56. Ronell, 1992, 33.

57. According to Foucault's biographer James Miller (1993, 245–251), Foucault took LSD for the first time in 1975 in Death Valley, California.

58. See Deleuze's "Porcelain and the Volcano," in Deleuze, 1990, 154–161, and Foucault's "Theatrum Philosophicum," in Foucault, 1977, 165–196.

59. Foucault, 1977, 191.

60. Benjamin, 1972, 134 (protocol 11).

61. Benjamin, 1972, 140–141 (protocol 11).

62. Witkiewicz, 1985, 325.

63. Witkiewicz, 1985, 355.

64. Witkiewicz, 1992, 245.

65. Witkiewicz, 1992, 250.

66. Witkiewicz, 1992, 252.

67. Witkiewicz, 1992, 252.

68. Gerould, 1981, 17.

69. Witkiewicz, 1992, 247.

70. Witkiewicz, 1992, 264.

71. Witkiewicz, 1992, 260.

72. Foucault, 1977, 32.

73. Jean-Marie Le Clézio has recently called into question whether Artaud ever actually visited the Tarahumara (1993, 161–172). He claims that no documentation of Artaud's trip to Tarahumara country exists, and that beyond the train ride into northern Mexico, it remains unclear how Artaud, who spoke no local language, could have found the Tarahumara, let alone participated in their rituals.

74. Artaud, 1956, vol. 9, 27–28.

75. In *Ecuador* (1929) and *La nuit remue* (1935) Michaux discussed the effects of ether. Michaux's books on mescaline and other psychoactive substances include: *L'infini turbulent* (1957), *Paix dans les brisements* (1959), *Connaissance par les gouffres* (1961), and *Les grandes épreuves de l'esprit* (1966).

76. Michaux, 1963, 28.

77. Michaux, 1963, 10.

78. Bowie, 1973, 151–170.

79. Michaux, 1972, 6.

80. Michaux, 1972, 181.

81. Benn, 1987, 153.

82. Jünger, 1990, 354–362.

83. Benn, 1987, 152.

84. See Lee and Shlain, 1985, 3–43.

85. Lee and Shlain, 1985, 27.

86. Aldiss, 1969, 16.

87. "A Treatise on Drugs" (1931) and "Wanted, a New Pleasure" (1931), reprinted in Huxley, 1980, 3–10.

88. Huxley, 1980, 5.

89. "Button, Button," *Time,* June 18, 1951, 82–83; "Mescal Madness," *Newsweek,* February 23, 1953, 92–94.

90. Huxley, 1990, 12.

91. Huxley, 1990, 29–30.

92. La Barre, 1989, 227–230.

93. Zaehner launched further attacks on Huxley in *Drugs, Mysticism, and Make-Believe* (1972) and *Zen, Drugs, and Mysticism* (1972).

94. Zaehner, 1957, 199, 200, 226. Incidentally, such feelings are often said to be a sign of what is called a "threshhold experience," in which the dose of the drug given is not enough to cause a decisive break in ego functioning.

95. Huxley, 1990, 33.

96. Huxley, 1990, 66.
97. Huxley, 1990, 58.
98. For example, *Exploring Inner Space* by Jane Dunlap (1961) and *My Self and I* by Constance A. Newland (1963). See also Ward, 1957 (apparently, the first personal account of LSD therapy), and Braden, 1967.
99. Newland, 1962, 7.
100. See Palmer and Horowitz, 1982, 177–210.
101. Wasson et al., 1986, 30.
102. "Centaur's Food," reprinted in *Food for Centaurs* (1960). A review of Wasson's "Soma, Mushrooms, and Religion" was published in *Difficult Questions, Easy Answers* (1973)—in which Graves notes that Wasson does not credit him for developing the idea of Greek soma. The book also contains another essay on the mushroom experience, "The Universal Paradise."
103. Graves, 1969, 380.
104. Graves, 1969, 382.
105. Richard Graves, 1995, 306.
106. Hofmann rather discreetly stresses that it was Jünger's poetic, rather than political, work that he admired.
107. Gelpke wrote an excellent book on intoxication, *Vom Rausch in Orient und Okzident* (1966), and an account of his own LSD experience, published in Jünger and Mircea Eliade's magazine, *Antaios* (1962).
108. Hofmann, 1983, 162.
109. Strausbaugh and Blaise, 1991, 80.
110. Jünger, 1990, 9.
111. Theweleit, 1987, vol. 1, 229–435.
112. Jünger, 1969, 328.
113. Bullock, 1992, 177–225. See also Helmet Kaiser's *Mythos, Rausch und Reaktion* (1962).
114. This is a critique that stretches from Marx's dictum that religion is the opium of the people to the smug dismissal of Michaux and his ilk in Guy Debord's journal *Potlatch:* "Madness and drugs remain the eternal means of diversion of a rearguard that patently lacks anything better to do with itself, and that contributes in its own little ways—along with the gossip in *Elle,* the most recent discoveries of Hitchcock, and the Young Turks of the radical parties—to the great job of stupefying the crowds" (1996, 127–128).
115. Davis, 1996, 99.
116. Reko, 1938, 25–31.
117. Taussig, 1987.
118. Hervier, 1995, 43.
119. Burroughs, 1977, 147.

120. Burroughs, 1977, 152.

121. Burroughs, 1992, 96.

122. See also Sanders Russell's *The Chemical Image* (1947), Michael McClure's *Peyote Poem* (1958), and Lenore Kandel's "Peyote Walk" (in *Word Alchemy*, 1967).

123. Burroughs and Ginsberg, 1975, 51.

124. Schumacher, 1992, 342–343.

125. Schumacher, 1992, 345.

126. Schumacher, 1992, 345.

127. See Olson, 1978, vol. 1, 20–62, and Morgan, 1990, 369.

128. Burroughs tried many substances over the years. He sampled DMT (under the name of Prestonin) in 1961 in Tangier with Paul Bowles. The same year, he took mushrooms with Timothy Leary, Ginsberg, Gregory Corso, and various members of the Beat coterie.

129. Burroughs, 1964, 10.

130. See also Alan Watts's *Joyous Cosmology* (1962) and Ram Dass's *Be Here Now* (1971).

131. Leary, 1968, acknowledgments page.

132. Thompson, 1989, 46–47.

133. According to Devereux, however, at the end of Eliade's life the "ancient American dates for hallucinogenic usage forced him to change his mind on this issue, and . . . he had come to accept that there was no essential difference between ecstasy achieved by plant hallucinogens and that obtained by other archaic techniques" (1997, 108).

134. Leach, 1976, 37.

135. F. Bruce Lamb's *Wizard of the Upper Amazon* (1971), purportedly the tale of a Peruvian ayahuasca shaman's coming of age, raises similar issues.

136. Sabina, 1981, 47.

137. Sabina, 1981, 50.

138. Taussig, 1987.

139. Sabina, 1981, 97.

140. Sabina, 1981, 105.

141. McKenna, 1993, 7.

142. McKenna, 1993, 49.

143. McKenna, 1993, 74.

144. McKenna, 1993, 112.

145. Shulgin, 1991, 29.

146. Shulgin, 1997, 416–417.

147. A key figure in this form of science/literature is John Lilly, whose work I discussed in the anesthetics chapter. See Lilly's books on his LSD research: *Programming and Metaprogramming the Human Biocomputer* (1968) and *The Center of the Cyclone: An Autobiography of Inner Space* (1972).

148. *Rig Veda*, 1981, 121.

ACKNOWLEDGMENTS

This book developed out of my doctoral thesis in the Department of Comparative Literature at New York University. I thank my thesis advisor, Richard Sieburth, who has supported and guided this project ever since I first opened a copy of *Les paradis artificiels* in one of his Romanticism seminars, and Jennifer Wicke, for understanding what I was trying to do better than I did, and then helping me to make it happen. Thanks also to the rest of my committee, Mikhail Iampolski, George Makari, and Avital Ronell for their valuable comments, and to Margaret Cohen, Andrew Ross, and Michael Taussig, who all gave me important advice at various times. I am also indebted to John Sutherland and Eric Mottram, who first showed me that writing and thinking about books could be an honorable profession, and to my editor, Lindsay Waters, and to Nancy Clemente and Tom Wheatland at Harvard University Press, who made the preparation of this book for publication a pleasurable process.

Thanks to James Grauerholz, Virginia Berridge, and A. J. Wright for sharing their research with me, and to Jennifer Vinopal at the NYU library, and to the librarians at the New York Academy of Medicine Rare Book Collection for their generous assistance with my research. For help with images, I thank Michael Horowitz and the Fitz Hugh Ludlow Memorial Library, Steve Bloom at *High Times* magazine, Peter Hale at the Allen Ginsberg Archive, Hanna Edwards at Corbis, Madame Micheline Phan Kim, Claude Pichois, and Bob at Spectra Photographic Services.

Special respect to several old friends: to Nick Noyes and Dave Wondrich, my collaborators on that hitherto unpublished masterwork of drug literature, "Gonzaga," and many other projects; to Erik Davis, whom I have been lucky enough to encounter at the crossroads on many occasions over the last decade, and whose sage advice has often shown me the way forward; to Nick Triggs, who shared a vision of this project with me back when we were nineteen-year-olds, and in whose hands I will be delighted to place this book; and to Richard

Grant, for keeping everything real down through the years and always picking up the phone.

Thanks to the many other friends and colleagues who encouraged me and offered their insights; in particular, thanks to Nick Noyes, Mark Green, Ben Ratliff, Yuval Taylor, David Wondrich, Jon Ende, Joseph Sonnabend, Peter Lamborn Wilson, Jamie Byng, Kristin Leigh, Dalia Kandiyoti, Ilsa Gilbert, Ingrid Kemperman, Mike Dulchin, Richard Ledes, Jessica Chalmers, Megan Walch, Julian Dibbell, Sparrow, Hilary Harp, Clay Thurmond, Kenneth Goldsmith, Charles Parrack, and Gwen Brown. Thanks also to Gelek Rinpoche, David Life, Sharon Gannon, Eddie Stern, and Joan Suval for their instruction, which I hope shines through occasionally in this book.

Thanks to the Boon and Hunter families, who have supported me throughout this project, in particular, Annette Boon, for her estimable translation services; Tim Hunter for countless discussions and access to his complete set of Holloway House first editions; and Kate Hunter, for inspiration, proofreading, and more than I can say here.

Thanks to all my students at New York University, the New School University, and Eugene Lang College for enthusiastically participating in my "Drugs and Culture" seminar over the years.

The quote from Mark E. Smith at the front of the book is taken from the introduction to "Lost in Music" from *The Infotainment Scam* (Matador, 1993).

I gratefully acknowledge permission from Klett-Cotta Verlag to quote Gottfried Benn's "Kokain" in his *Sämtliche Werke*, volume 1; from Editions Gallimard to quote from Robert Desnos' "Ode à Coco" in his book *Corps et Biens* (© Editions Gallimard, 1953); from McPherson & Company, Kingston, N.Y., to quote from Novalis' "Hymns to the Night," translated by Dick Higgins (copyright © 1978, 1984, 1988 by The Estate of Richard C. Higgins; all rights reserved); and from HarperCollins Publishers, Inc., to quote from Allen Ginsberg's "Howl" from *Collected Poems, 1947–1980*, p. 126 (copyright © 1955 by Allen Ginsberg).

My research was supported by a Mellon Research Grant for European Studies, by a New York University Dean's Dissertation Fellowship, and by the Faculty of Arts at York University, Canada; I thank them all.

I am eager to learn about any drug-related texts or any authors that I have not mentioned in this book. I welcome correspondence on this subject at <marcus@hungryghost.net>.

ILLUSTRATION CREDITS

1. Courtesy of the Wellcome Library, London.
2. Reproduced by permission of Peter Owen Ltd., London.
3. Courtesy of the Henry W. and Albert A. Berg Collection of English and American Literature, the New York Public Library, Astor, Lenox, and Tilden Foundations.
4. Courtesy of the Henry W. and Albert A. Berg Collection of English and American Literature, the New York Public Library, Astor, Lenox, and Tilden Foundations.
5. Courtesy of the Wellcome Library, London.
6. From Random, 1970, 96. Photo by René Maublanc.
7. Private collection.
8. *The Hasheesh Eater* from Ludlow, 1975, 212, and *Assassin of Youth! Marihuana*, published by Northland, 1943, both courtesy of the Fitz Hugh Ludlow Memorial Library; *A Hundred Camels in the Courtyard*, photo by Paul Bowles, copyright 1962, 1986, by City Lights Books, reprinted by permission of City Lights Books; *Pot and Pleasure*, published by Venus Books, 1972, courtesy of David Watson.
9. *Cocaina*, 1923, courtesy of the General Research Division, the New York Public Library, Astor, Lenox and Tilden Foundations; *Dealer: Portrait of a Cocaine Merchant*, published by Holt, Rinehart & Winston, 1970; *A Scanner Darkly*, published by DAW, 1977 (copyright © 1984 by Bob Pepper; reprinted with the permission of DAW Books, Inc.; all rights reserved); *Speed*, published in Great Britain by Sphere, 1971.
10. From Benjamin, 1972, 138; © Suhrkamp Verlag, 1972.
11. From Witkiewicz, 1996, image 88. Collection of the Museum of Central Pomerania, Slupsk, Poland.
12. From Michaux, 1998, 88; © 2002 Artists Rights Society (ARS), New York/ADAGP, Paris.

INDEX

Addiction: discovery of, 36–37, 47–48; changing definition of, 74, 83–84

Adorno, Theodor, 150

Ageyev, M., 187–189, 193

Alcott, Louisa May, 154

Aldiss, Brian, 249

Algren, Nelson, 74

Allen, Stewart, 173

Anslinger, Harry, 123–124, 152, 156–157, 159, 168, 169

Anstie, Francis, 226

Artaud, Antonin: and opium, 17, 28, 39, 66–68, 149; and peyote, 230–231, 242–244, 245, 326n73

Aubert-Roche, Louis, 132–133, 134

Bakhtin, Mikhail, 129, 257

Ballard, J. G., 194

Balzac, Honoré de: *L'opium,* 41; views on anesthesia, 101–102; and the Club des Hashishins, 134, 316n40; coffee use of, 174–175, 189–190, 215, 320n21

Bangs, Lester, 170, 204, 205–206, 276–277

Banks, Sir Joseph, 131

Barton, William, 95–96, 97

Bataille, Georges, 13, 73, 149, 242, 272

Bateson, Gregory, 261

Baudelaire, Charles: and opium, 41, 44–46, 51, 308n98; theories of intoxication, 57,

257, 264; and cannabis, 134, 139–142, 144, 147, 152, 167, 169

Beauvoir, Simone de, 236

Beddoes, Thomas, 34–35, 87, 89

Benjamin, Walter: and hashish, 140–142, 147–151, 167, 317nn80–82,85; and stimulants, 195; and mescaline, 237–238, 239, 242, 245

Benn, Gottfried, 190–192, 217, 246, 248

Bergson, Henri, 252

Beringer, Kurt, 234, 240

Berridge, Virginia, 4

Bible, 219–220, 234

Blackwood, Algernon, 145–146

Blair, William, 41, 61

Blake, William, 12–13, 250, 261

Blavatsky, Helena, 145

Bloch, Ernst, 148

Blood, Benjamin Paul, 106–109, 111, 120, 122

Boccaccio, 125

Bodhidharma, 172, 175

Boismont, Alexandre Brierre de, 132, 134

Boissard, Fernand, 134–135

Boissière, Jules, 55–56

Bonnetain, Paul, 55

Boswell, James, 20

Bowles, Jane, 163, 164

Bowles, Paul, 80–81, 155, 163–166, 167

Brau, Jean-Louis, 4

Breton, André, 64–66

Brillat-Savarin, Jean-Anthelme, 174

Brown, John, 23, 25–28, 89

Brown, Tom, 19–20

Browning, Elizabeth Barrett, 47

Bruce, Lenny, 214

Bullock, Marcus, 257

Burchill, Julie, 204–205

Burke, Edmund, 38

Burroughs, William: *Naked Lunch,* 1, 35, 58, 75, 78–81, 84, 163, 164–165; *Junkie,* 1, 74–75, 76–77, 78; and solutions to the "drug problem," 13, 84; and the "great health," 28; and opium, 39; *Nova Express,* 81; and cannabis, 160, 164–165; and psychedelics, 258, 259–261, 262–263, 274

Burroughs, William, Jr., 197, 202–203, 210, 215, 216, 217

Burton, Sir Richard, 128

Cahagnet, Louis-Alphonse, 145

Camporesi, Piero, 14

Capote, Truman, 199

Carlyle, Thomas, 41

Carroll, Jim, 84

Carroll, Lewis, 226–228, 263, 269

Cassady, Neal, 160, 197

Castaneda, Carlos, 264, 266–267, 273

Chardin, Chevalier de, 21

Chase, James Hadley, 158

Chaucer, Geoffrey, 19

Clarétie, Jules, 48

Clarke, Marcus, 154

Club des Hashishins, 134–137, 166

Cocteau, Jean, 39, 40, 58, 70–71, 80, 84, 276

Coleridge, Samuel Taylor: and opium, 18, 21, 25, 28, 31, 32–36, 39–40, 42, 46, 61, 62, 85, 306n67; and nitrous oxide, 87–88, 89, 91–92; and cannabis, 131–132, 136

Colette, 8, 179

Collins, Wilkie, 42

Cook, Captain James, 22

Cooke, Mordecai, 226–227

Cooper, Clarence, 81, 85

Cottle, Joseph, 90–91

Cowley, Abraham, 177–178

Crevel, René, 65, 190

Crothers, Thomas, 48

Crowley, Aleister: *Diary of a Drug Fiend,* 63, 186–187, 188, 193; on the drug laws, 66; and ether, 112; "The Psychology of Hashish," 146–147, 167; and peyote, 233

Crumb, Robert, 163

Csáth, Géza, 59–60

Cyberpunk, 208–211

D'Alembert, Jean, 22. See also *Encyclopédie*

Dante, 125

Darwin, Erasmus, 23–25, 91

Daudet, Leon, 69–70

Daumal, René, 68, 69, 113–116, 120, 121, 122, 149

Davy, Sir Humphry, 34–35, 87–88, 90–92, 133

Debord, Guy, 327n114

Decadence, 50–53, 182–183

Deleuze, Gilles, 10, 171, 237, 304n15

Dent, John, 78, 79

De Quincey, Thomas: *Confessions of an English Opium Eater,* 1, 13, 36–40, 43; and the origin of "drug literature," 13, 14, 18; opium use of, 31, 32, 34, 46, 57, 80, 136, 170, 232; *Suspiria de Profundis,* 40–41; influence of, 41–42, 45, 133, 153, 276; and narcotic laws, 60–62; and cannabis, 132

Derrida, Jacques, 209

Desnos, Robert, 65, 190, 195–196

Devine, Robert James, 155, 157

Dick, Philip K., 119, 189, 203, 206–208, 210, 216, 217

Dickens, Charles, 53

Diderot, Denis, 22, 174. See also *Encyclopédie*

Dodoens, Rembert, 221

Doyle, Sir Arthur Conan, 8, 53–54, 180–182

Dreiser, Theodore, 105, 121

Drieu la Rochelle, Pierre, 71–73

Dr. Syntax in Paris, 93–94
Dryden, John, 19–20, 173
Dubus, Edouard, 52
Dumas, Alexandre, 137

Edgeworth, Maria, 87
Eliade, Mircea, 258, 267
Ellis, Havelock, 231–232, 242
Emerson, Ralph Waldo, 99–101
Encyclopédie, 22–23, 226
Escohotado, Antonio, 4
Esquirol, Jean Etienne, 132
Esquiros, Alphonse, 134

Fabulous Furry Freak Brothers, The, 163
Fang Tribe, 8
Fantastic tales, 42–44, 137, 226
Farrère, Claude, 56–58, 66, 179
Fiedler, Leslie, 162
Fielding, Henry, 173
Fisher, Carrie, 214
Fitz Hugh Ludlow Memorial Library, 163
Fitzgerald, F. Scott, 176
Flaubert, Gustave, 142–143
Fleming, Ian, 249
Forster, Georg, 226
Foucault, Michel, 29, 237, 242
Fränkel, Fritz, 148, 237
Freud, Sigmund, 8, 40, 181, 182, 183–184, 195, 217
Friedman, Bruce J., 212–213
Fuller, Margaret, 98–99
Futurists, 189

Gaboriau, F. K., 145
Gautier, Théophile, 41, 43–44, 133, 134–137, 144, 167, 232
Gelpke, Rudolf, 255
Gibson, William, 208–209
Gilbert-Lecomte, Roger, 12, 68–69, 85
Ginsberg, Allen: and the junkie-saint, 75; and William Burroughs' narcotic use, 80, 81; and cannabis, 160–162, 164, 165,

169; views on stimulants, 199; and psychedelics, 261, 262, 264
Ginzburg, Carlo, 304n18
Girard, Jules, 145
Gnosticism: defined, 30–31; and Baudelaire, 46; and Artaud, 67–68, 243–244; dangers of, 86; and science fiction, 208–209
Goethe, Johann Wolfgang von, 24, 26, 27, 29, 130–131, 226, 234–235, 274
Goldoni, Carlo, 173
Goldsmith, Oliver, 173
Graham-Mulhall, Sara, 61
Grand Jeu, Le, 68, 113
Graves, Robert, 254–255, 258
Greene, Graham, 57
Grinspoon, Lester, 153
Grof, Stanislav, 253
Guaita, Stanislas de, 51–52, 145
Guattari, Félix, 171, 304n15
Guimbail, Henri, 51
Gurdjieff, Georges, 69, 112, 113
Gysin, Brion, 81

Halifax, Joan, 253
Hallucination: discovery of, 132–134, 136–137; problems of defining, 236–237
Halsted, William, 184–185
Harrington, Raymond, 233
Hasek, Jaroslav, 257
Hayter, Alathea, 4
Hegel, Georg Wilhelm Friedrich, 109–111, 117, 120, 201
Heidegger, Martin, 8, 171, 237
Heine, Heinrich, 307n88
Heinlein, Robert, 263
Helbrant, Maurice, 74, 77
Hemingway, Ernest, 199
Herbert, Frank, 263
Herodotus, 126, 144, 225
Hesse, Hermann, 234, 263
High Times, 163
Himes, Chester, 158

Hoffmann, E. T. A., 37, 42–43, 137, 138, 149, 226, 307n91
Hofmann, Albert, 255
Holmes, John Clellon, 197
Holmes, Oliver Wendell, 98, 110
Homer, 19, 38, 123–124, 131, 221
Hoover, J. Edgar, 259
Horowitz, Michael, 163
Houston, Jean, 253
Huxley, Aldous, 231–232, 237, 238, 249–253, 259, 262, 263, 269, 273, 274, 276

Iceberg Slim, 8, 212, 217
Indian Hemp Drugs Commission, 156
Isherwood, Christopher, 164

James, William, 108, 109–111, 113, 120, 122, 147, 231
Joël, Ernst, 148
Johnson, Samuel, 20
Journalists: and coffee, 173; and cocaine, 192–195; and amphetamines, 204–206
Jünger, Ernst: and dangers of literature, 1; and anesthetics, 105, 117; and drive to take drugs, 142; and cocaine, 189, 196–197; and questions of dosage, 216, 227; and psychedelics, 248, 255–258, 259, 273

Kaempfer, Engelbert, 22
Kane, H. H., 61
Kant, Immanuel, 26, 27, 34, 39, 44, 87–89, 91–92, 101, 105, 111, 136–137, 311n15
Kavan, Anna, 82–83
Kerouac, Jack: as typist for Burroughs, 81; and cannabis, 160–161, 164, 184; and amphetamines, 197–199, 201, 202, 215, 216, 217; and psychedelics, 261, 262
Kerr, Norman, 103
Kesey, Ken, 204, 265
Kingsley, Charles, 41
Klüver, Heinrich, 234, 235
Koran, 126

Krascheninnikow, Stephan, 225
Krassner, Paul, 163
Kupfer, Alexander, 4

La Barre, Weston, 233, 251
Lafitau, Joseph-François, 225
Laforest, Dubut de, 49–50
Lagache, Daniel, 235
La Guardia Commission on Marijuana, 158, 169, 319n133
Lallemand, François, 139
Laloy, Louis, 71
Lamantia, Philip, 310n185
Lamarck, Jean de, 167–168
Latour, Bruno, 10–11, 40
Law: Harrison Laws, 60; Taxation of Marihuana Act, 123–124, 156–157; and the *Thousand and One Nights*, 128–129; legal trials of drug books, 319n134
Leary, Timothy, 162, 187, 259, 261–265, 273
Lee, William. *See* William Burroughs
Leidekerke, Arnould de, 4
Lenson, David, 4, 124–125
Leon, Pedro Cieza de, 177
Levinstein, Edouard, 48–49
Lewin, Louis, 7, 62, 102, 170–171, 231, 233, 234–235, 250, 274
Lewis, C. S., 263
Lilly, John, 118–119
Linnaeus, 167
Lloyd, John Uri, 228–229
Lombroso, Cesare, 48, 50, 74
Lorrain, Jean, 106
Lovecraft, H. P., 146
Ludlow, Fitz Hugh, 101, 146, 152–154, 155
Luhan, Mabel Dodge, 233
Lumholtz, Carl, 230–231

Magendie, François, 102
Maier, Hans, 187
Mailer, Norman, 162
Malcolm X, 2, 111
Mallat, Marcel, 48

Malraux, André, 57
Mantegazza, Paolo, 178
Mariani, Angelo, 178–179
Marinetti, Fillipo, 189
Marks, Jeanette, 61
Marlowe, Ann, 39, 57, 79, 80, 84–85
Masters, Robert, 253
Matgioi. *See* Pouvoirville, Albert de
Maupassant, Guy de, 104–105
McInerney, Jay, 213
McKenna, Terence, 268–270
McLuhan, Marshall, 9, 79, 117, 171, 179, 187,
    195, 232, 235, 264, 275
Merleau-Ponty, Maurice, 236–237
Mezzrow, Milton "Mezz," 159–160
Michaux, Henri, 147, 154, 236, 242, 244–246,
    247, 261, 273, 274
Michelet, Jules, 174
Milton, John, 218–223
Mitchell, S. Weir, 231
Mitchill, Samuel, 90
Montagu, Ashley, 162
Mooney, James, 230
Moore, Marcia, 118, 121
Moreau de Tours, Jean-Jacques, 132–134,
    135, 144, 234
Mortimer, W. Golden, 176
Mrabet, Mohamed, 166
Musset, Alfred de, 41

Nabokov, Vladimir, 187
Native American Church, 230, 233
Nerval, Gérard de, 134, 137–139, 140, 152
Newland, Constance, 253
Nietzsche, Friedrich: and the "great
    health," 28, 29; narcotics and nihilism,
    73; and signs, 181; drugs and the Super-
    man, 212, 216–217; and chloral hydrate,
    312n44
Nin, Anais, 253
Nordau, Max, 50–51
Normandy, George, 182–183
Novalis, 26, 28–31, 43, 53, 83, 85

Osmond, Humphry, 250, 261, 303n11
Ott, Jonathan, 268, 270, 303n11
Ouspensky, Peter, 112–113
O.W., 82

Parsons, Tony, 204–205
Partnership for a Drug-Free America,
    11, 85
Pellens, Mildred, 60
Pepper, Art, 80, 81
Pitigrilli, 188, 193–195, 210
Plant, Sadie, 4
Plato, 246, 269–270
Pliny, 221
Pneumatic Institution, 87–88, 90–93
Pocarini, Sofronio, 189
Poe, Edgar Allan, 39, 43, 61
Poinsot, Charles, 182–183
Polo, Marco, 123–124, 125
Pope, Alexander, 173
Pouvoirville, Albert de, 56
Pravaz, Charles-Gabriel, 47
Priestley, Joseph, 89, 96–97
Proust, Marcel, 103–104, 176, 312n44

Rabbe, Alphonse, 307n88
Rabelais, François, 129–130, 163, 166, 169
Ramsay, Sir William, 108–109
Raynal, Abbé, 22
Reko, Blas Pablo, 254, 258
Reko, Dr. Victor, 258
Retté, Alphonse, 52
Rheiner, Walter, 190
Rigaut, Jacques, 65, 71
Rimbaud, Arthur, 143–144, 147, 246
Ripley, George, 99
Robinson, Mary "Perdita," 31
Robinson, Victor, 156
Rodet, Paul, 51
Rohmer, Sax, 63–64
Ronell, Avital, 4
Roschlaub, Andreas, 26
Rouhier, Alexandre, 234, 240

Rousseau, Jean-Jacques, 174
Rowell, Earl Albert, 157
Rushkoff, Douglas, 276

Sabbag, Robert, 213
Sabbah, Hasan-i, 81, 135, 137, 144, 164, 165
Sabina, Maria, 232, 254, 267–268, 277
Sacy, Sylvestre de, 125–126, 138, 314n4
Sagan, Françoise, 82
Sahagún, Bernardino de, 224–225
Sartre, Jean-Paul: on Drieu la Rochelle,
    71; and coffee, 176; and amphetamines,
    199–201, 215, 216; and mescaline, 235–236
Scheidt, Jürgen vom, 183
Schelling, Friedrich von, 26, 27, 29
Schiller, Johann, 130, 315n24
Schivelbusch, Wolfgang, 173
Schlegel, Caroline, 27
Schoenbein, Christian, 94–96
Schultes, Richard Evans, 254, 258, 260
Scott, Thurston, 158
Scott, Sir Walter, 35
Sedgwick, Edie, 203
Sedgwick, Eve, 23
Shadwell, Thomas, 19–20
Shakespeare, William, 19
Shelley, Percy, 35
Shulgin, Alexander, 270–272
Shulgin, Ann, 270–272
Simpson, Sir James, 102
Sloman, Larry, 157
Smart, Richard, 213–214
Sontag, Susan, 200
Southey, Robert, 33, 87, 90, 92, 94
Spenser, Edmund, 224
Spinoza, Baruch, 34, 303n5
Spruce, Richard, 229–230
Steele, Sir Richard, 173
Stephenson, Neil, 209, 211
Stevenson, Robert Louis, 49–50, 54, 182
Stringer, Lee, 214
Styron, William, 277
Sufis, 126–127, 144, 166, 172

Surrealism, 64–66, 190, 242
Swift, Jonathan, 173
Symons, Arthur, 232
Szasz, Thomas, 13

Tailhade, Laurent, 51, 52
Tao Te Ching, 263
Tarahumara, 230–231, 243
Tasso, Torquato, 224
Tatler, The, 173
Taussig, Michael, 258, 268
Taylor, Bayard, 151–152, 153
Teletubbies, 228
Tennyson, Alfred, Lord, 108
Terry, Charles, 60
Theweleit, Klaus, 256
Thompson, Hunter S., 198, 204, 213, 240,
    265–266, 273, 274
Thoreau, Henry David, 98, 99
Thorp, Raymond, 74
Thousand and One Nights, 127–129, 167
Tibetan Book of the Dead, 263
Tolkien, J. R. R., 263–264
Tott, Baron de, 21
Trakl, Georg, 59, 185
Trocchi, Alexander, 39, 310n185
Tschudi, Johann Jakob von, 178
Turnbull, Lawrence, 102–103

Upanishads, 246

Vailland, Roger, 68, 69
Varela, Francisco, 10
Vedas, 275
Verlaine, Paul, 144
Vico, Giovanni, 226
Villavicencio, Manuel, 229
Virilio, Paul, 171, 175, 194–195, 215
Voltaire, 17–18, 85, 173, 174

Warhol, Andy, 203
Warren, John Collins, 97
Warton, Thomas, Jr., 20–21

Wasson, R. Gordon, 253–255, 258, 259

Wasson, Valentina, 253

Welsh, Irvine, 84, 85, 276

Wilde, Oscar, 53, 111

Witkiewicz, Stanislaw Ignacy, 8, 218, 238, 240–242, 273, 276

Wolfe, Tom, 265

Wood, Alexander, 47

Woodley, Richard, 210, 212

Woodward, Bob, 214

Woolf, Virginia, 312n44

Wordsworth, William, 91

Wurtzel, Elizabeth, 277

Yeats, William Butler, 145, 232

Yvorel, Jean-Jacques, 4

Zaehner, R. C., 251

Zap Comix, 265

DATE DUE

HIGHSMITH #45115